# Controlling Crime, Controlling Society

## Thinking About Crime in Europe and America

Dario Melossi

polity

First published in 2008 by Polity Press

Polity Press
65 Bridge Street
Cambridge CB2 1UR, UK.

Polity Press
350 Main Street
Malden, MA 02148, USA

ISBN-13: 978-0-7456-3428-9
ISBN-13: 978-0-7456-3429-6(pb)

A catalogue record for this book is available from the British Library.

Typeset in 10.5 on 12 pt Palatino
by SNP Best-set Typesetter Ltd., Hong Kong
Printed and bound in Great Britain by Biddles Ltd, Kings Lynn, Norfolk

The publisher has used its best endeavours to ensure that the URLs for external websites referred to in this book are correct and active at the time of going to press. However, the publisher has no responsibility for the websites and can make no guarantee that a site will remain live or that the content is or will remain appropriate.

Every effort has been made to trace all copyright holders, but if any have been inadvertently overlooked the publishers will be pleased to include any necessary credits in any subsequent reprint or edition.

**For further information on Polity, visit our website: www.polity.co.uk**

# Contents

*Detailed Contents*                                                    vii
*Preface*                                                                x

Introduction                                                             1

**Part I   State, Social Order, and "the Criminal Question"**
**in Modern Europe**                                                    13
1   Leviathan's Subjects: From the Social Contract to
    Cesare Beccaria                                                     15
2   The "Positive School," Urban Crowds, and the
    Social Question                                                     39
3   Emile Durkheim's Sociology of Deviance                             65

**Part II   Democracy, Social Control, and Deviance**
**in America**                                                         83
4   Social Control and Deviance in the New Republic                    85
5   Social Control and Deviance in Chicago                             99
6   The 1930s: Between Differential Association
    and Anomie                                                        128
7   From the "Neo-Chicagoans" to Labeling Theory                      150
8   From "Labeling" to a "Critical" Kind
    of Criminology                                                    176

**Part III   The "Crisis Decades": "State," Social Control, and Deviance Today**                                                    197
9        The End of "the Short Century" between Inequality
             and Fear                                                          199
10      The Cycle of the Canaille                                      229


*Notes*                                                                         253
*References*                                                                 266
*Index*                                                                        294

# Detailed Contents

Preface     x

**Introduction**     1
*The Penal System between "Exclusion" and "Inclusion"*     4
*Transformations in Concepts of Social Order and Representations*
*of Crime*     7

**Part I   State, Social Order, and "the Criminal Question"**
**in Modern Europe**     13
  **1**     **Leviathan's Subjects: From the Social Contract to**
       **Cesare Beccaria**     15
       *From the Constitution of Subjects to the Contract to*
          *the "Penitentiary Invention"*     17
       *Freedom, Self-Control, Discipline*     23
       *Cesare Beccaria's Version of Enlightenment*     28
       *On Crimes and Punishments*     30
       *The Realism of Beccaria's Concept of "Free Will"*     32
       *The Dialectic of Enlightenment*     35

  **2**     **The "Positive School," Urban Crowds, and the**
       **Social Question**     39
       *The City Crowd*     40
       *The Emergence of Positivism*     44
       *Quételet and Guerry's Sociological Positivism*     45
       *The Italian Positive School*     47
       *"Scientific" Criticism of the Positive School*     49

*"Contextual" Criticism of the Positive School: The*
   *"Southern Question"*                                           52
*The Positive School and the Crisis at the Turn of*
   *the Century*                                                   55
*Freud's Psychoanalysis and Crime*                                62

**3    Emile Durkheim's Sociology of Deviance**          65
*The Division of Labor in Society*                                65
*Anomie*                                                          67
*Suicide*                                                         68
*The Sociology of Deviance*                                       71
*Durkheim's Concept of State and Democracy*                       78
*Two Laws of Penal Evolution*                                     80

**Part II  Democracy, Social Control, and Deviance
in America**                                                      83
**4    Social Control and Deviance in the New Republic**  85
*A Prologue: "America"*                                           85
*Protestantism, Republic, Social Control*                         88

**5    Social Control and Deviance in Chicago**          99
*State and Social Control*                                        100
*Chicago: An Attitude of "Appreciation"*                          103
*Robert Park: "The Public" and Social Control*                    105
*Chicago Sociology of Deviance between "Ecological"*
   *Theory and "Social Disorganization"*                       110
*Democracy and Social Control*                                    116
*Language and Social Control*                                     119
*Sister Carrie's Less Eligibility*                                124
*Louis Wirth: Urbanism as a Way of Life*                          126

**6    The 1930s: Between Differential Association
and Anomie**                                                      128
*Crime and the New Deal*                                          130
*The Theory of Differential Association*                          133
*White-Collar Crime*                                              137
*Talcott Parsons's "Problem of Order"*                            141
*Robert K. Merton's Theory of Anomie*                             144
*Crime, Democracy, and "the American Dream"*                      147

**7    From the "Neo-Chicagoans" to Labeling Theory**    150
*The Tradition of Chicago: Social Control and the*
   *"Power Elite"*                                             150
*The Dialectic of Social Control: The Mass Media*                 153
*Labeling Theory*                                                 159

*David Matza: From "the Subterraneans" to "the Ban"*       165
*The Sixties: "Sympathy for the Devil"*                    170

**8    From "Labeling" to a "Critical" Kind of
       Criminology**                                       176
*Zookeepers of Deviance*                                   178
*A "Critical" Kind of Criminology: The "Criminal
  Question"*                                               180
*The Critique of "Total Institutions" from Goffman
  to Foucault*                                             184
*Michel Foucault Cutting Off the Head of the King*         185
*Ethnomethodology*                                         188
*The Contribution of Feminism: Social Control and the
  Constitution of a Gendered Subject*                      189

**Part III    The "Crisis Decades": "State," Social Control,
and Deviance Today**                                       197
**9    The End of "the Short Century" between
       Inequality and Fear**                               199
*The Social Crisis of the 1970s and Mass Imprisonment
  in the United States*                                    199
*"Realist" Criminologies*                                  203
*Control Theory*                                           205
*Criminologies of the Self and the Other*                  208
*Criminologies of the Self*                                209
*Victimization and Self-Report Studies*                    211
*Actuarialism*                                             213
*Broken Windows and Zero Tolerance*                        214
*The Criminology of "the Other" and the "Underclass"*      216
*The Turn of the 1990s*                                    221
*Automated Control*                                        224

**10    The Cycle of the Canaille**                        229
*A Theory of Long Cycles*                                  229
*The Perennial Reproduction of the Canaille*               234
*Post-Fordist Corrections*                                 237
*What Does "Rehabilitation" Mean?*                         241
*Penality and Government of Populations*                   243
*Post-Fordism, Globalization, and Social Control*          247
*Conclusions: Crime, Punishment, and Social Structure*     249

**Notes**                                                  253
**References**                                             266
**Index**                                                  294

# *Preface*

The pages that follow are a reflection of my own personal journey between the United States (more precisely California, where I lived between 1977 and 1993) and Italy, where I lived before and after those dates. The work is devoted to reconstructing the development of theories about social control (and the State), deviance, and crime in Europe and America. In so doing, I was led to revisit some of the motifs originally developed in *The Prison and the Factory*, written with Massimo Pavarini in Italian in 1977 (1981), and then subsequently my own *The State of Social Control: A Sociological Study of Concepts of State and Social Control in the Making of Democracy* (1990). The first result of this work of reconstruction was a volume in Italian, *Stato, controllo sociale, devianza: Teorie criminologiche e società tra Europa e Stati Uniti*, published by Paravia Bruno Mondadori Editore, Milan, in 2002. This was the work that is the ancestor, so to speak, of the present volume that I have now written in English.

Since 1993, when I returned to the School of Law of the University of Bologna, I have been teaching courses in criminology (understood as sociology of deviance and social control), and it is on the basis of this experience that I have now written this volume. From the two main concepts which oriented *The State of Social Control* – the all-European idea of "the State" and the all-American idea of "social control" – I have now moved to stressing a third orienting concept, that of "crime," or "deviance." From the political and social theory I have therefore moved to a more straightforward criminological interest, while at the same time remaining true to David

Matza's intimation of never separating "the study of crime from the workings and theory of the state," the original sin, so to speak, of "criminological positivism" (Matza 1969: 143).

The present text is divided into three parts. The first, dedicated to "European" theories from the Classical to the Positive School to Emile Durkheim's pioneering sociology, is a reconstruction of the relationship between the development of concepts of the "State," the idea of deviance (or to be more philologically correct, "crime"), and the broader framework of the political organization of society and social reaction to crime in nineteenth-century Europe. The second part focuses on the analysis of the emergence of a concept of social control at the dawn of the first "mass democratic" society, i.e. the United States of America, and the reconstruction of the subsequent sociological theories of deviance between the beginning of the twentieth century and the 1970s. The third, more complex and open part retraces the events of the "current" period since the early 1970s, a period characterized by an unprecedented rise in the volume of penality in the United States and a somewhat limited "export" of American policies to Europe. This was a period when the social form of *mass* democracy was first extended from the United States to Europe, before entering a deep crisis, which was also marked by the emergence of what I have termed "automated control" (as opposed to "social control").

The object of this work is therefore the reconstruction of the ways of thinking *control*, broadly speaking, in relation to the different modes of social organization and the prevailing concepts of "deviance" and "crime" therein. In fact, social organization and concepts of deviance imply each other in a stricter way than is usually thought – as Emile Durkheim pointed out early on.

In a sense, I started thinking about this work almost 20 years ago, after the publication of *The State of Social Control*. It is therefore practically impossible to thank all those who, through exchange of ideas, collaborations, and all kinds of human and social relations, have contributed to what follows. I shall therefore limit myself to remembering those who have been my mentors, none of whom is unfortunately still with us. They are Franco Bricola and Alessandro Baratta in Italy – to whose names is forever linked the impulse toward a deep renewal of critical thinking in Italian criminology – and "Don" Cressey and "Ed" Lemert in California. I had in fact the honor of being Don's last PhD student at the University of California, Santa Barbara, from 1979 to 1986, and then colleague to Ed at the University of California, Davis, between 1986 and 1993. They were wonderful mentors, both to the young PhD student and to the subsequent junior colleague, and exceptional representatives of that high tradition of American sociological criminology to which I will be forever indebted.

My most heartfelt thanks also go to the hundreds and hundreds of students who, in courses and seminars on criminology that I have held since 1993 at the School of Law of the University of Bologna, have taught me and led me in the writing of the pages that follow, through their questions, their comments, their understandings, and oftentimes even their misunderstandings. These pages undoubtedly owe a lot to them. Special thanks go also to my friends and colleagues Malcolm M. Feeley, Rosann Greenspan, and Jonathan Simon, of the Center for the Study of Law and Society at the Boalt Hall School of Law of the University of California, Berkeley, for very generously tolerating my presence at the Center for several summers, a presence that has helped me complete several stages of this long journey (and that was often made possible thanks to the EAP Faculty Exchange Program between the University of California and the University of Bologna). A heartfelt "thank you" also goes to my Argentinean colleague and friend, Maximo Sozzo, who has painstakingly read the entire manuscript and given me invaluable help, also with an eye to the future Spanish translation. Emma Longstaff, Jonathan Skerrett, and Fiona Sewell, of Polity, have crucially helped me with preparing this volume in its final form, showing great generosity in dealing with an author for whom the English language is still, after all, a "second" language! I would also like to thank the Italian publisher Paravia Bruno Mondadori Editore for generously allowing me and Polity to freely use the Italian manuscript of *Stato, controllo sociale, devianza* as the initial building blocks for this work. And, last but not least, thank you so much, Peggy and Emilia, for your love, support, and patience!

# Introduction

When, between the 1960s and 1970s, a number of young European and American scholars from legal and social studies started looking into the apparently novel ideas of "social control" and "deviance," within such notable organizations as the European Group for the Study of Deviance and Social Control or the "School of Criminology" of the University of California at Berkeley, it was rather typical of such intellectual efforts to consider the two concepts of "the State" and "social control" as strictly linked when not almost synonymous. The State was often seen as the "author" of social control. It reminded one of that kind of anthropomorphic conception that legal theorist Hans Kelsen had dubbed the *Makroanthropos* (Kelsen 1922: 3), the State as a very large human being, who "does" this and that, "organizes," "imposes," "prohibits," and sometimes even assigns rewards and punishments of various sorts. The State was therein seen as a kind of "great father," which Freud, unsurprisingly, had made the object of some of his "metapsychological" studies (Freud 1913, 1921).

Under the impact of crucial contributions by Michel Foucault (1975, 1978), it became necessary, for those young scholars, to start questioning this authoritarian, paternalist, and essentially phantasmagoric idea of the social order. In a previous volume (Melossi 1990), I tried to reconnect to such an intellectual heritage, albeit trying to show, at the same time, that the essentials of such questioning had already developed to some degree within the very origins of the social sciences in the United States. In one of its most characteristic and original statements, for instance, Arthur Bentley, the founder of North American political science, in his pioneering *The Process of Government* (1908), had contemptuously set aside the concepts of "State" and "sovereignty" as mere survivals of a mythical past. So much was this so that a great political philosopher of the twentieth century, Alessandro Passerin d'Entrèves, in reconstructing "the notion of the State," was brought to observe that in contemporary political science, especially in its American version, a true "dissolution" of the State concept had taken place, such that "[t]he disruption of the notion of the State in modern political science is such a challenging and portentous event that it is surprising no detailed study should yet have been made to account for it and to explain it" (Passerin d'Entrèves 1967: 60).

In place of "the State" another key concept emerged. The idea of social control took shape in the intellectual laboratory that characterized the Progressive Era in the United States in the early decades of the twentieth century. The notion of social control certainly had a much lesser pedigree than that of the State. It belonged decisively to the social sciences rather than to political philosophy. It belonged, indeed, within the "social engineering" of the early decades of last century. It was a concept designed to capture the idea of an "intelligent" government of social change rather than the metaphysical "essence" of social order – an essence that had, when the occasion demanded, to be wrenched from the recalcitrant social body by force. This emergent view of social order was no longer a vision descending from the heavens of political philosophy in a still predemocratic society. It was instead a perspective according to which the social sciences were coming to terms with the ongoing processes of construction of consensus among the masses. It was in fact the cooperation and collaboration of the latter that were at stake. Even in this case, social intervention descended from on high, but instead of imposing its "sovereignty" on civil society, its function was to capture, channel, and guide the deepest currents of social change. In short, the crux of the matter was a shift from the imposition of coercion to the organization of consensus. That shift was fundamental to the emergence of "democratic" societies as they came to be understood.

At the same time, however, as we shall see in this volume, every theory of the social order incorporates a theory of deviance implicitly or explicitly (which amounts to saying that every theory of deviance can be traced back to the general theory of social order that to some degree supports it). For instance, in European contractualist theories, centered on the concepts of the State and the individual, the source of deviance was essentially rooted in some kind of individual failure – whether such failure be located in an anti-juridical rationality, as in Enlightenment-based theories, or in some kind of constitutional defect, as in positivism at the end of the nineteenth century.

Already in the emerging criminological interest of the early social sciences, however – for example in the work of Guerry, Quételet, and later of course Durkheim – the main emphasis was placed on the processes that produce a criminality understood as a *social fact*. Each sociological theory of the social order will then produce a specific theory of deviance. Indeed, as we shall see, there seem to be two distinct contenders. On the one hand, a line of thought from Durkheim to Parsons to Merton conceives of crime as a product of *structural* factors. On the other hand, instead, an alternative line of thought considers crime as a kind of behavior grounded in culture, and which can be transmitted through social learning (from the Chicago School to the various strains of interactionism).

In the former, structuralist tradition, a monistic concept of social control coincided with an essentially individualist vision of the emergence of deviance. The latter, interactionist tradition, originally inspired by Georg Simmel's theory, instead saw behaviors socially labeled as deviant as the outcome of cultural and/or normative conflict, thus linking the idea of deviance to a view of normative pluralism. This was a sociology of deviance that had already answered the objection that critics such as Colin Sumner (1994) would bring much later, according to which the relativity of a concept of deviance would inevitably bring forth the dissolution of that very concept (this is an objection that is better brought against a structural type of theory, because interactionist and relativist theories in reality started from the point made by such objections). Finally, the current period – moving from the deep crisis of sociological theories of deviance after the 1970s – witnessed a curious divarication of disciplinary orientations. There was, especially in the United States, a reawakening of nineteenth-century ideological inspirations, whether of the neo-classical or neo-positivist variety, that accompanied the resurrection, in the 1960s, of Nietzsche's "pale monster," the State. At the same time, however, a "culture of control" emerged that aspired to make deviance impossible by technological means, through an intervention in the "environment" of deviance and crime (Garland 2001a; Marx 2005). This was a novel orientation, in the sense that it seemed to break with the very twentieth-century notion of a relationship between control, consent, and democracy.

## The Penal System between "Exclusion" and "Inclusion"

It is customary today to think of the penal system as one of "social exclusion" (Steinert and Pilgram 2003; Young 1999). This may be perceived as the penal system's "real" function and outcome but certainly, especially in its very beginnings, it was not imagined as pursuing such a goal. This emphasis on "exclusion" – typical of a society permeated by a rhetoric of "democratic participation" – tends to obfuscate the extent to which penitentiary institutions especially were originally conceived as mechanisms of in-clusion, or in-corporation, I would say, into a social contract. This was particularly the case in republican or proto-democratic societies, such as the United States, in their beginnings (Dumm 1987 on de Tocqueville 1835, 1840, following Foucault 1975).

Post-structuralist and 1970s "critical" thinking pointed out that prisons and "ideological state apparatuses" in general had been "invented" within a broader societal effort of "making up subjects" (Matza 1969; Althusser 1970; Foucault 1975; Hacking 1986) or, in the more direct and transparent language of North American reformer Benjamin Rush (Dumm 1987: 88), "Republican machines": citizens, that is, who will know how to govern themselves, this being a necessary prerequisite for a system based on self-government. In the pages that follow, we will devote quite a bit of reflection to such statements. What I would like to point out, however, is that the terms of any such "incorporation" into the social contract, into the social body, clearly respond to the conditions and conflicts most characteristic of that society and to the way in which social order is therein framed and conceived of.

A number of "classic" commentators, from de Beaumont and de Tocqueville (1833) to Rusche and Kirchheimer (1939), have pointed out the affinity between the main features of the penal system in a given society in a given period and the consideration that society gives its members, and especially its *laboring* members. According to Rusche and Kirchheimer, the valorization of labor would typically be connected with an attitude of inclusion and incorporation of the lowest strata of the working class into the productive process and society more generally. This would also be the main orientation of the penal system. The *de*-valorization of labor instead – in a situation, for instance, of high unemployment – would be usually connected with a concept of the penal system as exclusion, as a system at most of "warehousing" inmates.

This way of thinking about the relationships between the social structure and the penal system carries certainly more than a grain of truth. It is, however, at the same time, still quite mechanistic, because the definition of a given situation and of the policies required therein is never something objectively "given" according to strict economic standards, but is the discursive product of hegemonic processes in which political and economic elites' "definitions of the situation" have a very important say. What is a "social crisis," for instance, depends a great deal on the perspective of the one defining it (O'Connor 1987; Hall et al. 1978; Sparks 1992: 55–77). And from the perspective of social elites, a crisis is first and foremost an assault on their power, whether political or economic.

I would therefore submit that two situations might obtain from the standpoint of penality. In the "exclusionary" penal mode, society is (successfully) described as being in a state of "crisis," where order needs to be re-established and the social fabric mended and brought back to unity after having been lacerated and torn apart. Here, it is often the metaphor of the State that appears: Leviathan as a purveyor of order and unity or, better, of unification (*reductio ad unum*) and hierarchy – as David Matza explained powerfully (1969). Because one of the main powers of the State is the power to punish (Beccaria 1764), penality is particularly apt to be used to define the powers and boundaries of sovereignty. In such a situation, the task characteristic of the system of criminal justice is one of bringing society to unity by eliminating fragmentation and anarchy.

In the situation instead where a tendency toward inclusiveness develops, this is because the social order is perceived as suffocating and unfair, and social change as necessary. The task characteristic of the system of criminal justice becomes then one of allowing for experimentation and "innovation" (in the Durkheimian sense of a type of deviance that triggers social and normative change).

How can we sociologically explore such oscillations? From a *quantitative* perspective, one could show, for instance, that the "productivity" of a penal system increases in situations of moral panic and crises (particularly when such crises are perceived by elites as threatening the dominant form of social relations, i.e. their power). We can see that incarceration rates tend to increase in situations of crisis (economic and/or political). *Qualitatively*, however, we can observe that the representations of the criminal offender change too, i.e. the representations of the criminal that society produces, and in which criminologists play a part (Melossi 2000a). By "representation" I mean the descriptive portrayal of criminals, in criminological discourse, in the public opinion, or in aesthetic discourse, as a distinctive "type" presenting identifiable moral, physical, and social characteristics according to specific locales of time and space (Leps 1992; Rafter 1997; Sparks 1992; Fritzsche 1998).

These two perspectives, quantitative and qualitative, are indeed related: the devaluation of the person who is at the center of the penal system, either as a criminal or as an inmate (usually seen by the public as synonyms), is related to a rise in the number of such persons. There is an *affinity* between those social processes that increase the number of inmates and those that change – for the worse – the representation of the criminal. Or rather: it is the same social process, in which the changed representations – in orienting social action – make it possible for the numbers to go up or down, and the numbers' seesawing in turn feeds back on the quality of the representation (because if many members of a given category of people go to prison, this is taken socially to mean that those who belong to that category are indeed very bad, or inherently dangerous).

I have therefore advanced the idea that the sphere of penality, in its quantitative and qualitative variability, constitutes a sort of "gazette of morality" (Melossi 1993) through which a varying pressure is exercised on the generality of the public (given that, as we shall see in more detail, I follow Durkheim – and, for that matter, the classical theorists – in conceiving the main function of the penal system as being one of controlling society more than the criminals, who should actually be regarded as the "useful" "bearers" of such control; Foucault 1975).

In the situation characterized by a tendency to exclusion, we may observe in fact that criminologists (*as well as* public opinion *and* "aesthetic" productions, not to mention politics) assume an attitude of distance or antipathy toward the criminal: the deviant is the producer of evil (whether he or she wants it or not), social order is represented as a *given order* that is to be established or re-established, and the representations of the criminal are under the constellation of the *monstruum*, the monstrosity, far removed from any common experience and hence from the possibility of empathy.

In the situation characterized instead by a drive to include, criminologists (as well as public opinion and fictional accounts) tend to assume an attitude of vicinity or sympathy toward the criminal: the deviant is seen as in some sense a victim of society, social order is represented as justly or at least reasonably contested, and the representations of the criminal are located under the constellation of "innovation," when not of a heroic and quasi-tragic striving against the tyranny of fate or social conditions.

## Transformations in Concepts of Social Order and Representations of Crime

Essentially, what I intend to do in this volume is to develop, for the case of criminological theories, a conception inspired by Georg Rusche and Otto Kirchheimer's views – views that, I would add, may be related to a "long cycle" or "long wave" perspective. This is an outlook according to which socio-economic development happens in long cycles where the "peak" and the "trough" are separated by about 25 years. This would be a concept more easily employed to understand what is an essentially cultural process of change, like that of penality, characterized by long-term movements instead of short "business cycles." This approach conceives of cyclical movement as acted upon by economic and political actors. Innovation would then appear to be, for instance, a crucial instrument used by entrepreneurs in order to diffuse the power of labor in conditions of prosperity and profoundly change the type of economy in which the working class has reached a high level of power. Rusche and Kirchheimer's concept of a linkage between punishment and the labor market could then be seen as one of the aspects of this broader picture. Imprisonment increases, and the situation within prisons becomes less tolerable, when economic and political elites are on the attack in order to hit the high levels of power reached by the working class. Then, after the re-establishment of their hegemony, imprisonment would again become "softer" and penality more bent on "reform." This is what, in the last chapter of this volume, I call "the cycle of the canaille."

All of this ought not to be conceived as an "understructure" "determining" a "superstructure" but, in Max Weber's way, as relations of "elective affinity," with long-cyclical movements produced by the discursive interaction of all the actors involved. Such movements are in fact strictly related to, and crucially facilitated by, changing representations. Particular representations tend to dominate within given cyclical periods. For instance, during prosperous and innovative periods of the cycle, a fragmented and rapidly changing society conceives of itself, through its production of social and criminological theory, as a plural and conflictual entity, where the concept of deviance, or indeed of crime, is relative to the standpoint of the one who is talking, and the representation of the criminal is a fundamentally controversial and contested representation. *Some* criminals at least get a "fair break" and are cast in the role of innovators and heroes rather than in that of villains. Examples of this kind of society are Europe and North America around 1900 and then again in the 1920s and in the "extended" 1960s. It is then no surprise that these periods are also characterized by declining imprisonment rates and by a public discursive rhetoric centered in social innovation, experimentation, and change.

In the opposite ideal-typical situation instead, there are long-cyclical periods when the fragmentation has reached "intolerable limits," at least from the perspective of elites, and the need for a re-establishment of unity, authority, and hierarchy (even if under a somewhat changed balance of power) is of paramount importance on the political and cultural agenda. These periods suggest theories of social order characterized by an idea of unity and cohesion (I would call them "monist" theories) where the basic normative frame is consensually shared and where the image of the criminal is one of "the public enemy," to use the FBI's telling 1930s label. The criminal is now a morally repugnant individual (as described by criminologists as well as in "the public opinion" or in fiction), the one who brings a deadly threat to society's moral order. The causes of such a threat, if at all relevant, are to be found within the criminal himself or herself, and not in social relationships (as was instead the case in the other ideal-typical situation). Examples are the periods when nation-states were first established in the nineteenth century, the world-wide Depression in the 1930s, and the period from 1973 till today, which Eric Hobsbawm has very aptly dubbed "the crisis decades" (Hobsbawm 1994: 403–32). This theoretical approach should then be particularly useful – as I will try to show in the last chapter – in order to understand the relationships between mass imprisonment after 1973 and the profound transformations of the American economy in the same period (usually described as "post-Fordist"), in particular the connections between the disciplining of the heavily racialized, deskilled manual labor force and the process of "McDonaldization" of American society (Ritzer 1993). Once again, it is no surprise that during these periods imprisonment rates tend to increase, and the public rhetoric is one re-emphasizing the value of the collectivity around concepts such as "the State," "the Nation," "the Community."

I do not claim that the chronology and the impact of events are the same in all societies and cultures, or even all societies and cultures of the same type. There are time lags and there are specific cultural traditions that should be emphasized and taken into account (Nelken 1994; Savelsberg 1994; Melossi 2001; Melossi forthcoming). For instance, there is the issue of why some of the same processes in "post-Fordist" Europe could occur without mass imprisonment as the goad (the 2006 book by Michael Cavadino and James Dignan, *Penal Systems: A Comparative Approach*, offers relevant material to that end).

Even if it was not entirely original to him, Michel Foucault was probably the most effective proponent of the idea that, after all, imprisonment is a sort of instantiation of the criminal. "The penitentiary technique and the delinquent are in a sense twin brothers," Foucault wrote (1975: 255). The "production" and "presentation" of criminals within prison is then applied to the criminal in general, to the criminal *sans phrase*, as the Italian Positive School especially made clear. Representations of crime and criminals follow the destiny of imprisonment in their uneasy relationship with economic, social, and labor conditions. Further, one has to remember Kai Erikson's insight that representations of crime and punishment in the public arena are projections of deeper social and cultural concerns (Erikson 1966). Criminologists usually refer to social control as a "response" to deviance, and particularly to legally sanctioned deviance, "crime." I believe any such connection between social control and crime to be a contingent matter, which depends on the specific nature of what is meant by "social control" and "crime" in a given socio-historical situation (Melossi 1994; Black 1984). During most of the twentieth century, the control of crime was subaltern to social practices largely based on the construction of consensus (Melossi 1990) and directed at controlling the generality of the public rather than the few who are responsible for what is officially defined as "crime." In this sense, *controlling crime* competed with, and often took back seat to, *controlling society*. Indeed, controlling crime has often been but an instrument used in order to control society. This was also the view of many "classical" social theorists, most notably as clearly expressed by Durkheim:

> [Punishment] does not serve, or serves only very incidentally, to
> correct the guilty person or to scare off any possible imitators. From
> this dual viewpoint, its effectiveness may rightly be questioned; in
> any case it is mediocre. Its real function is to maintain inviolate the
> cohesion of society by sustaining the common consciousness in all
> its vigour ... Thus, without being paradoxical, we may state that
> punishment is above all intended to have its effect upon honest
> people. Since it serves to heal the wounds inflicted upon the collec-
> tive sentiments, it can only fulfil this role where such sentiments
> exist, and in so far as they are active. (Durkheim 1893: 62–3)

Words not very different can be found in George H. Mead (1917–
18) and, of course, more recently, in Foucault (1975). "Representations" of deviance, and deviants, perform the work, in a sense, of
reconnecting "structural" change and change in penal policies in a
way that the more economistic view of Georg Rusche and Otto
Kirchheimer had left to some degree unexplored. Marie-Christine
Leps (1992) effectively showed, for instance, in her reconstruction
of the cultural climate in the nineteenth-century *fin de siècle* years,
that each cultural environment in fact produces a given "knowledge" of the criminal that spans different discursive forms, from
scientific tracts to newspapers to fictional accounts. Such representations perform a work in society, which consists, among other
things, in orienting public morality. This work of representing and
giving moral orientation can be accounted for according to a
concept of the relationship between social structure and culture,
which is one of "elective affinity." Social practices that are usually
ascribed to "structure" show affinity for social practices usually
ascribed to "culture" (Weber 1904–5; Howe 1978). If rates of punishment, for instance, seem to "respond" to change in the economy,
at least in given societies and periods (Chiricos and DeLone 1992;
Melossi 1998a), this is not because of some kind of homeostatic
"blind" mechanism – even if social theorists may end up so describing it – but because ideas expressed in a publicly available language about where "the economy" is going, what a "social crisis"
is, what causes it and who is to blame for it, and so on, appear to
change, in society, together with and in a tight cultural exchange
with publicly available ideas about crime, punishment, and responsibility. Even if the social theorist's description is simply a *reduced
form* description (that is, a description that takes into account only
exogenous and endogenous variables, without indulging in reflections about "intervening variables"; Hanushek and Jackson 1977:
227) ultimately the connection between such disparate aspects of

social life is a work performed by discourse, i.e. by that discursive interaction that makes social co-ordination and therefore social practices possible. Representations are in a sense the answer to Marx's proverbial riddle of the relationship between "structure" and "superstructure" (Marx and Engels 1845–6; Mead 1934; Smith 1976; Melossi 1985).

This kind of approach is bound to be eminently "reflexive." Whereas what is usually called a "positivistic" attitude has powerfully contributed, especially in the last 20 or 30 years, to obscuring a "reflexive" view in criminology, sociological theory has instead tried to come to terms, for instance in the work of authors such as Anthony Giddens (1984), with the concept of reflexivity – with the challenge, that is, brought to a science of society by the scientist's awareness of the necessary implication of his or her ideas, with the material that he or she strives to describe by means of those ideas. Not so in criminology. Or rather: the pronounced reflexivity of key works that appeared in the late 1960s and early 1970s, such as Matza's (1969) or Taylor, Walton, and Young's (1973), has brought the field too close to what one might call an act of euthanasia to be tolerated within the boundaries of a social science whose fate has always been intimately linked with the issue of political legitimation.

# Part I

## State, Social Order, and "the Criminal Question" in Modern Europe

# 1

## *Leviathan's Subjects: From the Social Contract to Cesare Beccaria*

The theory of the social contract was the form within which the age of Enlightenment – and still, in a sense, our age – was able to express and conceive the idea of political order. It was an idea that started taking form during the dissolution of medieval society. The fundamental poles of the contract – on the one hand the concept of a multitude of individuals, and on the other the idea of the State – both found their origins within the crisis of the medieval order and of the theocratic thought that supported it. The theoretical concepts as well as the institutions informed by those concepts originated within a process of "liberation" from social and conceptual structures that belonged in the Middle Ages. From within the dissolution of such an order, both "the State" and its "subjects" emerged.

British historian of philosophy Quentin Skinner has noted that "the surest sign that a society has entered into the secure possession of a new concept is that a new vocabulary will be developed, in terms of which the concept can then be publicly articulated and discussed" (Skinner 1978, vol. 1: xii–xiii; see also 1978, vol. 2: 352, and 1979). It is in the work of Machiavelli that we can locate the origin of the modern concept of the State, along with the early uncertain instances of a modern usage of the word. The ones who established the two directions of political and social thinking in the centuries that followed, however, were Hobbes and Locke. Between Hobbes and Locke, between the State as Leviathan and the State as civil society, a new vocabulary was originated, a vocabulary that allowed modern Western society to express the question of order.

Yet the roots of such a new vocabulary are to be found in that "moral disorganization" – we may venture to say today – that was described by the man who, in 1513, had been the all-powerful Secretary to the Florentine Republic:

> Here the question arises: is it better to be loved than feared, or vice versa? I don't doubt that every prince would like to be both; but since it is hard to accommodate these qualities, if you have to make a choice, to be feared is much safer than to be loved. For it is a good general rule about men, that they are ungrateful, fickle, liars and deceivers, fearful of danger and greedy for gain. While you serve their welfare they are all yours, offering their blood, their belongings, their lives, and their children's lives . . . – so long as the danger is remote. But when the danger is close at hand, they turn against you. Then, any prince who has relied on their words and has made no other preparations will come to grief; because friendships that are bought at a price, and not with greatness and nobility of soul, may be paid for but they are not acquired, and they cannot be used in time of need. People are less concerned with offending a man who makes himself loved than one who makes himself feared: the reason is that love is a link of obligation which men, because they are rotten, will break any time they think doing so serves their advantage; but fear involves dread of punishment, from which they can never escape.
> (Machiavelli 1513: 47–8)

This imagery suggests a crucial connection between "the political entrepreneur," the prince, and the "anarchy" of his subjects. Machiavelli's prince was to give form to human nature through the use of his skill, his craft (his *virtù*). Machiavelli's men and women were egoist, deceptive, tricky – as in his play *La mandragola*, or *The Mandrake Root* (1519). In Machiavelli's art, as had been the case in Boccaccio's *Decameron* (1348–53) or Chaucer's *Canterbury Tales* (1386–1400), a world was portrayed peopled by double-crossers and vagabonds, artisans and teachers in the newly created universities, poor peasants and soldiers, penniless artists and corrupt officials. It was also the world of the "free cities" of Central and Northern Italy and of Germany, as well as of a countryside run by mercenaries, bandits, and all kinds of political and social dissidents.

The themes of *Il principe* were certainly present in Hobbes's reflections, especially *Leviathan* (1651). Hobbes shared Machiavelli's harsh view of humankind, and his concept of a state of nature was one in which "the life of man [is] solitary, poor, nasty, brutish, and short" (1651: 100). Fear constituted therefore the foundation of the social contract. Hobbes's solution to these conditions of anarchy was, however, different from that sought by the Florentine secretary. Hobbes did not share the notion that the prince's virtue and fortune are the basis for political society. Moving from the state of the prince to the State of Leviathan meant discovering the principle of an abstraction and personification of unity and power, that is, Leviathan. Leviathan is – Hobbes wrote – "a COMMONWEALTH, or STATE, in Latin CIVITAS, which is but *an artificial man*; though of greater stature and strength than the natural, for whose protection and defence it was intended" (1651: 19). This is built "by the *art* of man," similarly to the way a watch is built. The State was now therefore an "automaton," funded by a contract of men, a contract that gave life to a *persona*. No longer a passive instrument of the will of powerful seigneurs, it was now an active agency, already quite close to Kelsen's "macro human being." It was a principle of unity and cohesion destined to counter the terrible fate of the war of all against all.

Both Machiavelli's and Hobbes's solutions should in fact be viewed against the backdrop of the social and historical situations the two authors were addressing. They saw the century-long dissolution of medieval society and the emergence of a new age. A dialectical movement was begun that other social contract theorists were later to develop. The compact that established the State was the product of members' free will. Society's members were supposed to cede their claims to individual sovereignty voluntarily. However, as Hobbes was careful to point out, their contract was a *hypothetical construct*, not an historical event. In what sense, then, was the members' contractual will truly "free"? The State, a creature of its members' free volition, was at the same time the very enforcer of the voluntary, rational character of the contract. It was the State itself therefore that, by means of "its" rules and institutions, led the "subjects" toward their "free" appreciation of its own rationality. A "rational" State – a State built according to the principles of natural philosophy – was the best evidence for the rational necessity of its existence.

## From the Constitution of Subjects to the Contract to the "Penitentiary Invention"

How were such subjects "constructed" so that they could come to appreciate the rationality of their Great Father? The conceptualization of the State could not be separated from the conceptualization of its constituents, the subjects (Tinland 1985). During the late Middle Ages and the Renaissance, a number of conditions brought about an enhanced experience and notion of the individual. The rise of capitalism, the emergence of absolutist political regimes, and the Reformation were all answers to what Machiavelli's and Hobbes's contemporaries perceived as lawlessness and anarchy. The newly emerging order of these three historical movements centered on the transformation of pre-Durkheimian "anomic" individuals into legal subjects, bearers of rights and obligations, protected and enforced by a legal order promulgated by the State (Burckhardt 1860: 81–103; Costa 1974; Orrù 1987). Together with the State, the individual too became an *a priori* starting point for social analysis (as Dewey was to observe much later, there is more than a passing relationship between the idea of the legal subject and that of the knowing ego with which Descartes had inaugurated the course of modern philosophy about a century before Hobbes's *Leviathan*; Dewey 1927: 88).

A precisely delimited, measurable property and its rational, *civil* proprietor constituted the decent Utopia about which society's members had to be enlightened. The social compact, by virtue of which a civil state was to be created, came to be a veritable myth of the modern age and an operating assumption of the political and intellectual leaderships of the eighteenth century. The cultivation of rationality in society, and the establishment of a legal order with social institutions geared to this end, were one and the same thing. Because the State rested on the willed consent of rational, proprietary individuals, a society of such persons became the objective of the State itself.

Although "private" institutions could perform the same functions as "public" institutions (Althusser 1970; see below), this happened not so much because the former were also controlled by the State as because both "public" and "private" institutions were established on the same basic rationalist premises. The invention of a whole array of social machines geared toward the rationalization of people and things – such as Bentham's Panopticon (made famous for a wider and later audience by Michel Foucault (1975)) – was not necessarily a product of the action of public authorities. The early Dutch workhouses, as well as Bentham's treasured invention, were initially conceived as private, profit-making institutions. They were devised for propertyless men and women deemed unworthy and unable to be a party to the social contract because they were lazy, self-indulgent, and criminal. As historical studies on such institutions have shown (Melossi and Pavarini 1977), they were intended to transform the members of the "dangerous classes" into fully rational subjects who would at least understand themselves as owners of their own labor, able to dispose of it in the form of a labor contract. The State was also seen as the beneficiary of such institutions, insofar as a "reformed" individual was able to enter the *civil* state and leave his or her own *private* state of nature. Public powers became involved as the agents of rationality, in other words, because rationality was the *raison d'être* of the State – a line of thinking that was later developed especially by the greatest German philosopher, Georg W. F. Hegel (1821). For those who could lift themselves up to comprehend the rational character of the State, the legal order represented the enactment of the natural laws of the state of nature that protected and developed the basic rights of life, liberty, and property.

Both in the practice and in the theory of emerging bourgeois societies, the concept of social contract therefore underwent a bizarre inversion. The "State" that supposedly was constituted by the power of a contract among its subjects – subjects who could express such power by virtue of their "rationality" – set for itself, as its fundamental task, the molding of its own subjects, i.e. furnishing them with the "rationality" that would undoubtedly help them appreciate the rationality of the State. What kind of "rationality" was here at stake, however? It meant predictable behavior based on work and ascetic virtues, the habit of a methodical life, discipline measured by the "artificial" time of the clock, regulated during everyday life experience by expectations concerning the individual's moral life – expectations famously investigated by authors as different as Max Weber (1904–5) and Michel Foucault (1975, 1976a, 1978). In other words, the human type that was supposed to be the author of the social contract and that found himself increasingly at the source of power – the adult white male European proprietor, preferably Protestant – was to be expanded and "exported" to larger and larger sections of the population. The twin processes of rationalization and democratization that took place in the following centuries were therefore also, at the same time, processes of "colonization," by this particular form of rationality, of those "lifeworlds," alternative rationalities, social areas, classes, cultures, and whole countries that were still "outside" the colonized area (Habermas 1981a: 318–73).

To speak of "imperialism" in this respect is more than a metaphor. In the same way in which capitalism has been feeding itself on a continuous expansion toward "subsistence economies" that had previously escaped it – an ongoing process under our very eyes – similarly the "ethic of capitalism" was to be expanded toward new peoples to conquer, be such new peoples "domestic" to core areas (youth, women, peasants, marginal proletarian strata) or "outsiders." These outsiders belonged to societies and cultures at first, in the nineteenth century, colonized, and then, after the twentieth-century decolonization movement, subject "only" to economic expansion (a process that coincided with the transition of global hegemony from the "old" European powers to the United States). The social contract – on its way to becoming what we now call "democracy" – was increasingly capturing and incorporating newer and newer strata of populations who were uprooted from a "natural" way of life to be magnanimously and benevolently included into a "superior" way of life – a process supported of course by the power of military penetration in case those people were unable to see the great good fortune that was offered to them. What is often today expressed through the rhetoric of "social *exclusion*" was therefore, first and foremost, "social *inclusion*," whether by choice or by force – very similar to the way in which, at the dawn of modernity, both "deserving" and "undeserving" poor would be institutionalized in basically the same "workhouses," but the former as a form of relief and reward for their willingness to be included, and the latter as a form of punishment for their unwillingness to be included.

A "family" of social institutions conceived from the sixteenth century onward played a crucial role in this overall process of "subjectivation" – an institutional genus that we could characterize as "the penitentiary invention" (Foucault 1975; Melossi and Pavarini 1977; Ignatieff 1978; Garland 1985, 1990). "Invention" is not a misnomer, because until then the prison had essentially been an instrument of confinement to other ends, not to the end of punishment itself. A place of detention was of course necessary for those waiting for trial or for a punishment already meted out and which the condemned would have certainly rather escaped, like a corporal punishment, or the pillory, or capital punishment itself. It was only under modernity that the prison became the site of a definite form of punishment: the punishment of detention for a pre-established amount of time. This was a modality of punishment that had already appeared in the Middle Ages but only for the religious personnel of European monasteries (Treiber and Steinert 1980). Here too, however, with the Reformation, the experience of the few was to become the experience of the many, and punishment was to be laicized:

> *Luther*, we grant, overcame the bondage of *piety* by replacing it by the bondage of *conviction*. He shattered faith in authority because he restored the authority of faith. He turned priests into laymen because he turned laymen into priests. He freed man from outer religiosity because he made religiosity the inner man. He freed the body from chains because he enchained the heart. (Marx 1844b: 182)

Between the second half of the sixteenth century and the first half of the seventeenth century, the ecclesiastical pattern inspired by penance, consisting in isolation in a *cell* for a pre-determined period of time, met with the more recent "invention" of the "manufacture," the proto-factory, in a world that was deeply renewed by the social transformation driven by the Reformation. Indeed, it was in the areas where a proto-capitalist development met the experience of Protestant Reformation that we find those kinds of proto-prisons or ur-prisons, the *workhouses* or *houses of correction* or, in England, *bridewells*. They went from London to Hamburg to the other cities of the Hanseatic League in Northern Germany, from Geneva to probably the most famous and paradigmatic case, that of the *Rasphuis* in Amsterdam (the most famous partly thanks to the studies by Thorsten Sellin (1944), who reconstructed that historical experience on the basis of the work of the Dutch historian A. Hallema (1936, 1958)). All such experiences were later to feed the institutions of the English colonies in North America – especially in William Penn's "holy experiment" in the new Quaker State of Pennsylvania (see below, chapter 4). Later on, they spread also to Catholic countries, such as France and Italy (the first and most interesting example in Italy being the House of Correction of Milan under the enlightened kingdom of the Austrian Maria Teresa, inaugurated in the same year when Cesare Beccaria published, in Leghorn, *On Crimes and Punishments*). From the start, this new kind of institution was reserved to those who were guilty of behavior that expressed "social insubordination," such as vagrancy, mendicancy, and the refusal to work on conditions imposed by a legislation that, in times of scarcity of labor power, was trying to compel the newcomers from the countryside to adapt to the new discipline of cities and manufactures.

The "revisionist" literature of the 1970s expressed two main orientations toward such topics. The first one followed in the tracks of the classic work by Georg Rusche and Otto Kirchheimer, *Punishment and Social Structure* (1939), focusing on the relationship between punishment and the labor market. The second orientation was the one that can be found in Foucault (1975) and in Melossi and Pavarini (1977) concerning the relationship between punishment and "discipline." In *Punishment and Social Structure*, Rusche and Kirchheimer had in fact established a relationship between the "value" of labor power – as determined by the labor market – and the function of punishment. They claimed that when the demand for labor is high and labor power is a scarce resource, the value of labor tends to increase and the function of punishment accordingly moves toward "keeping," "integrating," or "reintegrating" labor power, trying to coerce labor into offering its services on given conditions. On the contrary, when the labor market sees a surplus of labor offer, the value of labor tends to decrease, the fungibility of labor becomes even higher than usual, and therefore there is no reason to try and "spare" labor power. In this instance, the orientation of the main punitive institutions will tend to be "Malthusian" – that is, contemptuous of the value of human life and labor – and the only limit to the dissipation of labor power will be constituted by the historically given but changing threshold of "decency" in the treatment of prisoners and, more generally, of convicted persons (since Rusche and Kirchheimer's analysis applies not only to the punishment of detention but also to other forms of punishment).

So, for instance, in the late Middle Ages, when there was plenty of labor power available, a very repressive legislation developed and there was a generous use of corporal and capital punishments, whereas in the previous period, in the early medieval epoch, the scarcity of labor power had found expression in a broad use of pecuniary punishments, especially in Central Europe, so-called *Wergeld*. After the penitentiary invention the same set of principles could be applied to imprisonment. Prisons would tend to be orderly, concerned with the welfare of their guests, not crowded, and oriented toward "rehabilitation," partly through indoor work, in some periods (seventeenth century, nineteenth century in the United States, and after World War II). They would instead be overcrowded, poorly kept, and in any case oriented toward deterrence in other periods (during the industrial revolution and the nineteenth century in Europe, between the two world wars and after the mid-1970s in the twentieth century).

## Freedom, Self-Control, Discipline

Rusche and Kirchheimer's theory was geared toward explaining neither the *birth* of the prison, nor the more "qualitative" variations in the administration of penalties – even if it fitted the case of imprisonment particularly well. Attempts at tackling both issues can be found instead in the contributions by Foucault (1975) and Melossi and Pavarini (1977). The common presupposition of these contributions was the realization that the kind of society that "invented" prisons was also the society that, for the first time in history, placed the value of "freedom" at the center of its organization. The idea of freedom is in fact central to the concept of contract, which is, in turn, constitutive of modern society, both in its political meaning – through the myth of the social contract – and from the standpoint of production, through the concept of the labor contract (the sociology of the end of the nineteenth century would not miss this aspect, from Spencer (1879) to Tönnies (1887) to Durkheim (1893)). Punishment could therefore be conceived as a "deprivation of freedom" for a given period of time only in this kind of society – as Sutherland and Cressey were to observe in their theory of the "cultural consistency" of punishments (1978: 489–94). Obviously, the punishment of depriving a person of his or her freedom would not have had much meaning in a society based on slavery or in serfdom, and in fact German legal theorist Gustav Radbruch had postulated a historical causal relationship between the institution of slavery and penal servitude (Radbruch 1938; Sellin 1976). Within such a crucial historical transition, between the end of the sixteenth century and the beginning of the seventeenth, when at the same time both a capitalist mode of production and the newly reformed Protestant ethos had their origins (Weber 1904–5), we can also find the juncture between Rusche and Kirchheimer's contribution and the "disciplinary" literature. According to the former in fact, this is the period when the scarcity of labor power gave impetus to the creation of so-called "workhouses," the ancestors of the institutions that would be called "penitentiaries" in the eighteenth century. The question asked in the "disciplinary" literature is why only at this moment the scarcity of labor power gave rise to this specific solution and not, as had happened before, for instance, to a more intensive usage of pecuniary punishments. The literature's answer is that only at this moment were discovered not only the discipline of the work ethic, of the manufacture, of production, but also the strictly related discipline of life and *method* of the Protestant Reformation.

It is only when the fundamentals of capitalism have emerged that labor power becomes "free," "unattached," "outside of the law," as Marx would have called it, i.e. free from legal and political ties – at least in theory. Labor subordination is no longer now permanent subordination, a quality of the working person (a slave, a serf), but is "voluntary" subordination for a time, as in a "labor *contract*." If there is any form of coercion to work, this in principle will be outside of the legal/political realm – where "alone rule Freedom, Equality, Property, and Bentham" (Marx 1867: 176) – and belong in an economic kind of coercion, in the "dull compulsion of economic relations" (Marx 1867: 737). Economic pressure is, however, dependent on the conditions of the labor market and that is why, under given conditions, the strength of labor on the market may bring back aspects of legal-political coercion. In the ordinary course of things, however, "free" labor answers much more efficiently to the needs of economic development: labor is "free" to go where it is wanted. After all, what is the point in trying to impose ourselves on those who do not have any desire for us? Migratory processes assume therefore, under capitalism, a new quality, from the countryside to the city, even if the distance between the countryside of origin and the city of reception tends to become increasingly greater with time.

At the onset of all this, however, during what Marx called the "primitive" or "original" accumulation of capital, such dislocation took place between the rural areas immediately surrounding the cities and the cities themselves. In Northern and Central Italy, the free commons abolished the institution of serfdom (Bologna, e.g., in 1257) and this, together with the early attempts at rationalizing agriculture, produced a "surplus" of population in the rural areas that started pouring into the cities. "Stadtluft macht frei" was to be the motto of Northern German cities: city air makes you free, both because you are now free to roam around and finally end up in the city, and because when you are there nobody knows you and there are nobody's expectations to be met – or at least, so it seems. As

Georg Simmel, Robert Park, and Louis Wirth will tell us in the twentieth century (see below, chapter 5), the city (and, equally if not more important, *the journey to the city*) equates to the fraying of face-to-face social controls. The other side of such freedom was, however, also soon apparent, and was called lack of employment, vagrancy, mendicancy, rural theft, brigandage, banditry – in one word, *crime*.

It was also a freedom that had anyway to be checked in at the gates of the workplace. Working in those proto-factories, the manufactures, was very different from working under the aegis of sun and seasons. It meant working in closed spaces, dark and poorly ventilated, for a number of hours and at a pace that were not those imposed by nature but that were determined by the employer through his underlings. It was therefore within this overall project of disciplining and rationalization, embedded in the new social inventions symbolized by the workhouse, that the new subjects were to be constituted, the protagonists of the new society, an urban, industrial, and "rational" society. The new subject had to be able to read, write, and compute, he had to be on time, predictable. He (usually a man) had to be "autonomous," in the sense that he had to regulate himself without fear of an external threat. This is the process of *subjectivation*: the constitution of subjects. The main instruments of social organization and control – whether they are managed by "the State" or by "private institutions" – have as their ultimate goal the creation of subjects constituted in such a way that they should be able to see the supreme rationality of those instruments and institutions. Beyond philosophical, political, and legal mythologies, the construction of political power on the one hand and of the subjects of/to that power on the other is the outcome of complementary processes within which the function of economic, political, and intellectual elites is crucial.

In *Discipline and Punish*, Foucault expressed all of this in the metaphor of the "Panopticon." As was typical of "progressive" thinkers in general (such as, in Italy, Cesare Beccaria and Carlo Cattaneo), so also for the champion of Utilitarianism, Jeremy Bentham, rationalization meant the reform of penal institutions, starting from the prison and his project for a Panopticon. Bentham claimed to have derived from his brother, the architect Samuel Bentham, an architectural concept originally devised for the arsenals of Prince Potemkin in Russia (Bentham 1787). The structure of the Panopticon was based on a central watchtower reserved to the warden and his men, while the inmates were confined within cells disposed in stacked circles around the tower. A crucial feature was that the warden and his men could watch the inmates in their cells but the latter could not know whether they were being watched, because of a system of blinds protecting the inner side of the tower.

The conceptual essence of Bentham's concoction was not only the idea of continuous inspection – which would not have been particularly parsimonious – but also the idea of injecting into the inmates the more "useful" fear of being watched. The result was that subjectivation was to be the by-product of economy. The structure not only required fewer personnel and was therefore less costly – an aspect very important to Bentham, the Utilitarian – but was also based on the involuntary, and unpaid, recruitment of the inmates in their own surveillance, because the fear of being inspected would end up developing a sort of self-control. In Freudian terms, we could define the Panopticon as a kind of machine for the production of a superego. The "Panopticon" – Bentham wrote – is an "inspection-house: containing the idea of a new principle of construction applicable to any sort of establishment, in which persons of any description are to be kept under inspection" (1787: 40). He goes on to say that the principle is therefore applicable to, for example, "penitentiary-houses, prisons, houses of industry, work-houses, poor-houses, manufactories, mad-houses, lazarettos, hospitals and schools" (ibid.).

In *The Prison and the Factory*, I called this panoply of institutions "ancillary" to "the factory" (Melossi 1977), in the sense that they were crucial to constituting and reproducing the social discipline demanded by a capitalist mode of production. This seems to me to underlie Michel Foucault's *Discipline and Punish* also (Foucault 1975). According to Marx's reconstruction, in fact, once the laborer has entered the not-so-metaphorical gates of the sphere of production, it is within those gates that, as if by miracle, the sale of his or her labor power eventually gives more to the capitalist than the latter has anticipated for the various costs of production. This difference, which is at the basis of the capitalist's profit, can come into being, however, only if the "freedom" of the sphere of circulation turns into the kind of (temporary) servitude of the "sphere of production." In fact, the capitalist will be a full-title capitalist only if, having bought the worker's labor power, she will be able, like every good proprietor, to use and enjoy her property as she likes, and therefore to impose that *discipline* of production that alone warrants the difference that makes her profit. Because one has to note that, in a most "unfortunate" manner, the labor power, which is the merchandise the capitalist has bought, comes with a human being attached, often behaving in ways that are different from those predicted and demanded by the capitalist. This struggle between a human being, the laborer, and the laborer as mere carrier of labor power is the substance of "class struggle." Therefore it is not correct to say, as it is often said, that Marx's theory is "economistic." Rather, as the subtitle to *Capital* reads, it is a *"critique* of political economy" that locates the core of the matter in the conflict between capital and labor about exploitation. It is about a political ("class") struggle over the management of human resources. The society that is ruled by capital is therefore organized around the constitution and maintenance of "discipline," a discipline that permeates all the fundamental social institutions.

How can one therefore state that the "Marxist theses" on penality "do not depend upon specifically Marxist arguments such as the theory of surplus value" (Garland 1990: 130), and try to sharply sever Foucaultian theory from Marxian theory? The example indicated by Garland, the theory of surplus value, which is indeed the core of Marxian theory, is quite surprising, because the concept of "discipline" could not be more strictly linked to such a concept. It is in fact only if the discipline "in the sphere of production" warrants the extraction of surplus value that a capitalist system can even exist as such. Whether or not one agrees with the general validity of this view – and that is an altogether different question – there is, however, no doubt that the connection between "ancillary" institutions and the sphere of production, as institutions of reproduction of that *disciplined* labor power that is necessary to produce surplus value, is the very clear theoretical linkage between Marx, Foucault, and the neo-Marxists (Melossi and Pavarini, rather than Rusche and Kirchheimer, in this context). In "ancillary institutions" there rules an authoritarian style that is, however, geared to producing self-governing and therefore "free" subjects, subjects also able to govern themselves collectively in the trajectory from the social contract to the republic to democracy. These subjects – capable of self-government because capable of self-control – would soon become those individuals endowed with "free will" by criminal and penal theorists of the Enlightenment, the most famous among these being Cesare Beccaria.

## Cesare Beccaria's Version of Enlightenment

The theory that still today holds sway among legal theorists and criminal lawyers is based on contractualist and Utilitarian positions, in such texts as Cesare Beccaria's *On Crimes and Punishments* (1764) and Jeremy Bentham's *An Introduction to the Principles of Morals and Legislation* (1789). It is a theory that portrays the author of crime as a kind of business person, who is able to rationally calculate the costs and benefits associated with a specific criminal enterprise. The utility that he or she is going to obtain from committing the crime – in terms of goods or services or some kind of psychological satisfaction – will be balanced against the perception of risk, i.e. the likelihood and severity of punishment. If the benefits appear to be greater than the costs (a calculation that more recent authors have tried to formalize in a mathematical model; Becker 1968), he or she will opt for enacting the criminal behavior. Otherwise, the deterrent effect of punishment will prevail.

Such a peculiar concept of crime was produced during a century, the eighteenth, when a bourgeoisie of merchants, artisans, small entrepreneurs, and various kinds of intellectuals was aggressively emerging, first in the most developed countries, such as England and France, later in all other European (and American) countries. In the eyes of the members of this new class, the most characteristic features of traditional society were political centralism and authoritarianism on one side and a kind of rural conservative mentality on the other. Such features represented therefore a fundamental obstacle to the full development of those ideas of political and economic freedom that the new class championed. According to them, in fact, the caprice of the powerful, religious superstition, and the habits of life and work of a backward, rural country constituted the main barriers on the path of the destiny that the Italian poet Leopardi would have, soon after, bitterly called *le magnifiche sorti e progressive* (1845). Such "grand destinies and progressive hopes" were mainly carried by the impetuous encroachment on the vestiges of the old world by an instrumental rationality based on accounting and profit. This new kind of rationality had slowly emerged from long centuries of transition from feudalism to capitalism, from rural to industrial work, from the countryside to the city. During the second half of the eighteenth century, Enlightenment thinkers strongly affirmed the primacy of this new rationality, according to which the light of reason was to inspect all forms of associated life, every small corner of the old society, and dispel the darkness and "obscurantism" of tradition.

The field of "crimes and punishments" was soon to appear crucial in such a battle, both for its lasting symbolic function (as Durkheim would clearly show; see below, chapter 3), and also because it was a field that directly implied the centrality of the value of freedom to the project of the Enlightenment. If, on the one hand, such a project was centered on concepts of autonomy and liberty (Kant 1784), on the other hand, as we have seen, the acknowledgment of these concepts was tightly linked to the coming into being of rational and moral subjects that could be trusted to be free because able to exercise self-government. The "government of the self," therefore, was assuming a double meaning. Applied to the field of public and political liberties, it meant the faculty of a group of individuals to exercise control over their own affairs on the basis of free and rational conviction (it was linked, in this sense, to visions of the polity that were first "contractualist," later "republican" or even "democratic"). Applied instead to the single individual, it meant the faculty of each individual to behave as a "mature" and "responsible" person and citizen, i.e. to be a rational subject endowed with self-control. One was to be the condition of the other. As Marx would note soon after, there cannot be political "liberty" without inner "servitude" to the light of reason, and there cannot be individual self-control if not within a free "common good" where the principles of reason are free to affirm themselves and win the day.

Such ambivalence is at the root of the characteristic "duplicity" of the Enlightenment, which has therefore produced both convinced followers of that project (Rawls 1971; Ferrajoli 1990) and perplexed and skeptical critics (Nietzsche 1887; Horkheimer and Adorno 1944; Foucault 1975). If, in fact, on the one hand the project of the Enlightenment implied legal principles inspired by the safeguarding of civil liberties and the utility of punishments, on the other hand it is deeply rooted in historically given anthropological concepts implying projects of the transformation of the individual by means of education and penality. The most authoritative interpreters of the Enlightenment on matters of law and punishment, such as Bentham and Beccaria, in fact saw the best penal policy in a wider and wider implementation of a "penitentiary" institution.

## On Crimes and Punishments

We can find all such themes displayed within the text that is probably the most famous in the history of criminal law and criminology, Cesare Beccaria's *On Crimes and Punishments* (1764). As noted by Piers Beirne, "Beccaria's short treatise of 104 pages was an instant and dazzling success . . . By 1800 there had been no less than twenty-three Italian editions, fourteen French editions, and eleven English editions (three printed in the United States)" (Beirne 1993: 13). *On Crimes and Punishments* was the product of intellectual exchange within the Milanese circle of the journal *Il caffè* (inspired by the English *Spectator*), made up of Beccaria, the Verri brothers, and other minor figures. It was also, however, the butt of vitriolic criticism, especially by Catholic writers such as the Dominican friar Ferdinando Facchinei, "a cantankerous mouthpiece of the Inquisitorial Council of Ten in Venice" who in 1765 "published a tract that accused Beccaria of sedition, impiety and a new heresy that he termed 'socialism'; Facchinei derided Beccaria as 'the Rousseau of the Italians'"[1] (Beirne 1993: 14).

Liberal and humanist themes deriving both from the French Enlightenment and from the Utilitarian orientation of the Scottish Enlightenment are present in *On Crimes and Punishments* (Beirne 1993). Beccaria criticizes the arbitrariness and irrationality of the kind of criminal law he could witness as well as the practices of torture and capital punishment. He advocates the principles of legality and prohibition of retroactivity that were to become two mainstays of modern criminal law. Law was to be sharply separated from theology and morality. Beccaria's concept of man is that of a human being who is endowed with free will, able to make the "wrong" choices, sanctioned as such by criminal law.

The starting move of Beccaria's short treatise is the State's right to punish, which is grounded in the notion of social contract. According to Beccaria, the social compact implies that citizens yield a part of their freedom to the State in exchange for security and tranquility:

For there is no enlightened man who does not love the public, clear, and useful compacts that guarantee the common security, comparing the small portion of useless freedom that he has sacrificed with the sum of the freedoms sacrificed by others who, without the laws, could become conspirators against him. (Beccaria 1764: 105)

The sum of these freedoms becomes then a "repository" that no citizen will be allowed to withdraw from, and this is the foundation of the right of the State to punish its citizens:

But it was insufficient to create this repository; it was also necessary to protect it from the private usurpations of each individual, who is always seeking to extract from the repository not only his own due but also the portions that are owing to others. What were wanted were sufficiently tangible motives to prevent the despotic spirit of every man from resubmerging society's laws into the ancient chaos. These tangible motives are the punishments enacted against lawbreakers. (Beccaria 1764: 9)

Such punishments, and the right of the sovereign to punish, are necessary in order to prevent a falling back into that state of nature. They are, however, to be expressed as "tangible motives" in order to preserve that balance and security that is the outcome of the social contract. To this end, not only is the "right" to punish very important but also the "how" to punish. According to Piers Beirne, it is in this respect that the influence of "the Scottish school" of psychology[2] is most pronounced in Beccaria's work, articulated under the four concepts of Utilitarianism, probabilism, associationism, and sensationalism (Beirne 1993: 33–43).

*Utilitarianism* represents Beccaria's starting point. In the "Introduction" to *On Crimes and Punishments*, Beccaria notes that, generally speaking, laws ought to be "dictated by a cool observer of human nature, who has brought the actions of many men under a single gaze and has evaluated them from the point of view of whether or not they conduce to *the greatest happiness shared among the greater number*" (Beccaria 1764: 7). This Utilitarian standpoint is connected with two essential aspects. The first one is the principle of legality, central to the canons of the founder of what would be called the "Classical School." According to Beccaria, in fact, security and freedom – realized through the establishment of laws – are the fundamental grounds for happiness. The other crucial element is that the seriousness of crime should be based not on any "subjective" element having to do with the offender but on "the harm they do to society" (Beccaria 1764: 19), i.e. on a wholly "objective" notion of crime. The main feature of classical criminal law (and criminology) is in fact that "crime," and not "the criminal," ought to be at its center.

Beccaria's other works had been those of an economist,[3] so much so that in a letter by Pietro Verri of April 6, 1762, Beccaria was mentioned as "a profound mathematician . . . with a mind apt to try new roads if laziness and discouragement do not suffocate him" (Beirne 1993: 25). This is a type of judgment that makes one wonder about Pietro Verri's appreciation of his friend's moral fiber. At the time Beccaria was writing an essay about monetary circulation in Milan. Later on, almost contemporaneously with *On Crimes and Punishments*, Beccaria published an essay in *Il caffè* where he applied an algebraic treatment to understanding the costs and benefits of the crime of smuggling. In that, he asked the question: "given the proportion of the goods smuggled that will on the average be seized by the authorities, what is the total quantities that smugglers must move in order to be left without either gain or loss?" (Schumpeter 1954: 179).

A concept of *probabilism* is strictly connected to those passages where Beccaria calls for the necessity for a much greater predictability and certainty of the law. Furthermore, the idea of probabilism is articulated with the other twin concepts of *associationism* and *sensationalism* (Beirne 1993: 33–43). In order for deterrence to become really effective, in fact, the psyche of the potential, would-be criminal should be open to a strong and immediate connection between crime and punishment. Punishments are to be "speedy," i.e. there should not be an excessive gap of time allowed between the commission of the crime and the meting out of punishment, otherwise the principle of deterrence would be undermined. Furthermore, concepts are rooted in sensations: a public, sensationalist spectacle of punishment is necessary in order to emphasize the reality and probability of this consequence to a crime.

## The Realism of Beccaria's Concept of "Free Will"

Piers Beirne points out that Beccaria's psychological orientation – together with other aspects that we shall consider shortly – to some degree challenges the "absolute" character of his doctrine of "free will." The idea that human nature is behaviorally malleable, and that it is a goal of social and penal policy to forge a human type that can be reconciled with "wise" government, is in fact implicit in the Utilitarian approach, as we have seen. Otherwise, it would be difficult to understand not only Bentham's but also Beccaria's appreciation of imprisonment, as well as Beccaria's engagement in the day-to-day administration within the efficient "Austrian" bureaucracy that ruled the Milanese State at the time. Between 1771 and his death in 1794, Beccaria was in fact successfully involved in many such responsibilities. In other words, even if in the last instance his system rests on the notion of individual free choice, his concept of the nature of man, his "criminology," so to speak, is less "classical" than his criminal law, and yields to the possibility that human beings may be at least in part "determined" in their actions. Beirne intends to show that the cultural roots of the Milanese Enlightenment from which Beccaria emerged were less distant from those of the later Italian Positive School than would appear from the usual representation we have of the conflict between "classicism" and "positivism" (this was a conflict in part artfully constructed by Cesare Lombroso in order to emphasize the novelty of his "school"; see below, chapter 2).

The threat of punishment is therefore finalized as general prevention and has to be able to deeply impress the senses of potential criminals, on whom the punishment of imprisonment will constitute the most adequate sanction, helping them to become more responsible parties to the social contract. This is the psychological ground for Beccaria's conclusions in *On Crimes and Punishments*, where he states that *"[I] n order that punishment should not be an act of violence perpetrated by one or many upon a private citizen, it is essential that it should be public, speedy, necessary, the minimum possible in the given circumstances, proportionate to crime, and determined by the law"* (Beccaria 1764: 113, original emphasis). In other words, criminal law, and imprisonment within it, are to be part of the broader project of Enlightenment – indeed they represent one of Enlightenment's milestones.

An especially interesting section of *On Crimes and Punishments* are the chapters toward the end of the book dedicated to the problem of preventing crime: "It is better to prevent crimes than to punish them. This is the principal goal of all good legislation, which is the art of guiding men to their greatest happiness, or the least unhappiness possible . . . Do you want to prevent crimes? Then see to it that enlightenment and freedom go hand in hand" (Beccaria 1764:

103–5). The idea then follows that a well-educated public, appreciative of the idea of freedom, is also a public able to exercise self-control, to live therefore within that "enlightened monarchy" (later on, a "republic") that constituted the political ideal of the Milanese group. By contrast, the man who is not educated will not be able to lift himself up to a sufficient level of rationality. He will only be ready therefore to live in an autocratic regime of coercion and repression (similar ideas had been expressed by Montesquieu in *The Spirit of Laws* (1748)).

A fundamental premise of the Enlightenment's position is in fact, as we have seen, that the subjects, recognized by the legal and political system, have been to some degree "formed," and therefore deserve such recognition. Beccaria is, however, at the same time realistic enough to realize that many such subjects belong in the poorest and least educated sections of society and that therefore, in their case, the gift of "free will" that rational human beings are supposed to be endowed with is a mere potentiality rather than a reality. For instance, when he deals with the issue of "theft," he sees the "fitting punishment" for this crime in "the only sort of slavery which can be called just, namely the temporary enslavement of the labor and person of the criminal to society" (Beccaria 1764: 53), which meant, at the time, the punishment of imprisonment in the house of correction. In one of the most famous passages of the whole treatise he goes on:

> Thefts without violence should be punished with fines. Whoever seeks to enrich himself at the expense of others ought to be deprived of his own wealth. But, since this is generally the crime of poverty and desperation, the crime of that unhappy section of men to whom the perhaps "terrible" and "unnecessary" right to property has allowed nothing but a bare existence, [and since fines only increase the number of criminals above the original number of crimes, and take bread from the innocent when taking it from the villains,] the most fitting punishment shall be the only sort of slavery which can be called just, namely the temporary enslavement of the labor and person of the criminal to society, so that he may redress his unjust despotism against the social contract by a period of complete personal subjection. (Beccaria 1764: 53)

Exactly at the time when Beccaria was penning these words, Maria Theresa's Milanese State was erecting a "house of correction," one of the very few cases of "penitentiary innovation" in Italy in this period, an institution reserved for the offenders convicted of lesser crimes, to be punished through isolation and work (Melossi 1977: 73–4).

Beirne also shows how, in certain passages of *On Crimes and Punishments*, the author's emphasis shifts from the action to the author, from the "damage brought to the nation" to the observation that such damage will much more likely be brought by individuals belonging in certain social strata than in others. Beccaria pauses on images of a multitude of individuals who are in some way devoted to a life of crime, inclined toward "a desperate return to the original state of nature" (Beirne 1993: 46), and who are going to be taken by "a murky and mysterious rapture rather than by clear and calm reason" (Beirne 1993: 46). It is the initial appearance *in nuce* of that concept of the "dangerous classes" that will assume paramount importance during the first half of the nineteenth century (Beirne 1993: 46).

## The Dialectic of Enlightenment

As we have seen, Beccaria had written, "Enlightenment and freedom should go hand in hand." Why are "the lights" necessary for freedom? In 1783, a German journal asked a host of famous thinkers of the time the question, "What is Enlightenment?" to which one indeed among the most famous, Immanuel Kant, answered that, "Enlightenment is man's release from his self-incurred tutelage. Tutelage is man's inability to make use of his understanding without direction from another" (Kant 1784: 83). This state of maturity, this condition of not having to turn to any higher authority for guidance, the two German philosophers Max Horkheimer and Theodor Adorno, in their *Dialectic of Enlightenment* (1944), would later see best represented in the "libertine" *par excellence*, le divine Marquis de Sade (Horkheimer and Adorno 1944: 81–119). Sade's characters, such as Juliette (1797), would express that unbridled freedom, that hubris of subjective right, that was to be the torment of all the authors who, in the course of the nineteenth and twentieth centuries – from Hegel to Durkheim, from Freud to Parsons – saw in the horrors of the French revolution and of the subsequent civil unrest nothing else but the graphic display of Hobbes's *homo homini lupus*, of the war of all against all (see below, *passim*). Propelled by nature toward the pursuit of their pleasure, de Sade's characters are not restrained, and indeed they ought not to be restrained, according to their own ethics, by any law or morality, indeed by any "tutelage." Whereas de Sade's particularity may reside in the delight he took in describing some of the peculiar consequences of a world constructed on the grounds of Utilitarian radicalism – and whether this is the particularity of a critic or of an apologist I am certainly not qualified to tell – the arguments that are presented in order to justify his Utopian (or Dystopian?) world of unbridled pleasure are indeed quite common to the thought of the time.

A central example of this is the short tract included in de Sade's *Philosophy in the Bedroom* (1795), entitled *Yet Another Effort, Frenchmen, If You Would Become Republicans*, an atheist and quasi-anarchist pamphlet against all "higher guidance," where de Sade brings the Enlightenment style of thinking to the extreme consequence of claiming that there are no sound philosophical grounds on which to justify the punishment of *any* crime. In her introduction to the French edition of de Sade's *Complete Works*, Annie Le Brun writes of this pamphlet "as a desperate effort by de Sade to return the atheist machine to its primary function of cleaning up ideologies and to prevent it, once it has been perverted, from sewing fresh values in the still-free terrain of a world without God" (1986: 157). This is the extra effort that de Sade was asking of his countrymen. Le Brun points to the conflict within the Enlightenment between those who wanted to replace the old *idola* with the new simulacra of their acquired power – as in Robespierre's Supreme Being or even Rousseau's *religion civile* – and those instead who, like de Sade, wanted to be true to the Enlightenment's program to its extreme consequences.

What is most disturbing to those readers of de Sade who have even a passing acquaintance with "progressive" rhetoric is the fact that de Sade's arguments, as well as the arguments of some of his "monstrous" creatures, sound uncannily familiar, as in fact arguments rooted in the thought of the Enlightenment ought to.[4] The positions taken in *Yet Another Effort, Frenchmen*, sound therefore like delirious versions of Beccaria's *On Crimes and Punishments* (1764), or the *Plan de législation criminelle*, a plan for penal reform drafted by the medical doctor Jean-Paul Marat, the future leader of the French revolution (Marat 1780). It is as if the most extreme consequences derived by de Sade, such as his defense of what others define as "murder," were all in all rejected by his contemporaries for reasons of prudence and opportunity, for a sort of Freudian *Verdrängung*. What all these arguments have in common is indeed the faith in modernity, the idea of following one's own path without being led by the hand of any higher authority. And one should not think that de Sade's argument was so extreme as to be seen as a monstrosity. His pamphlet was even circulated as propaganda material during the 1848 revolution in France.

In describing a world where there is no "moral tutelage" left, except the one that is, so to speak, self-administered, and which therefore opens the door to the possibility of an extreme individualism and the attempt at overcoming and pushing aside any type of social bond, de Sade seems to point to the possibility that what is called "crime" may be but the expression of a concept of "subjective right," a right without objectivity, a right that does not acknowledge the recognition of the other. No need is left, from such an extreme position, to come to terms with the necessity of social cohabitation. It is therefore no accident that shortly afterward, one of the most acerbic critics of the French revolution, and of liberalism, the German philosopher Georg W. F. Hegel, in his *Philosophy of Right*, would characterize the essence of punishment as the moment of transition from right to morality, the moment, that is, when the individual is brought to realize that he or she is not alone, but has to meet the necessity of sharing social space with the other (Hegel 1821: 73–4). (In a not altogether different way Nietzsche, in his *Genealogy of Morals* (1887: 61–2), will define punishments as "mnemotechnics," because, through punishments, the moral commandments are inscribed in the individual's memory.)

Similarly, even if much more recently, in *Seductions of Crime*, an ethnographic type of work based on research into those who engage in predatory crime – specifically on the "righteous slaughterers," "badasses," and "street elites" – American sociologist Jack Katz (1988) comes to the conclusion that, given the very limited economic purchase of the type of predatory crime the subjects of his research engage in, their fundamental motivation has to be sought in an attempt at affirming their subjectivity faced with the other. What from the perspective of official society, and of their victims, appears as crime and violence, from the perspective of the perpetrators appears as the instantiation of their "subjective right" in the very denial of the individuality and the right of the other.

This was the basic reason why, as we have seen, the social and political thought that started with the Enlightenment always stressed that the gift of Enlightenment *may* certainly be for everybody, *potentially* – because we are all equal in the eyes of Mother Nature – but *in actuality* one has to be educated into becoming a worthy subject of Freedom and Reason. In the words of one of the most feverish, albeit pessimistic, later defenders of this kind of civilization, "Where id was, there ego shall be. It is a work of culture – not unlike the draining of the Zuider Zee" (Freud 1933: 80).

# 2

# The "Positive School," Urban Crowds, and the Social Question

First in England, later on in Continental Europe, the early decades of the nineteenth century were years of serious social turmoil and political and economic crises. Under the continuous pressure of economic transformations in the countryside, causing the marginalization and expulsion of wide strata of rural population, vagrancy, crime, and banditry spread throughout Europe (Lefebvre 1932; Foucault 1975). The "rationalism" of the Enlightenment appeared to contemporaries an "abstract" approach, unable to come to terms with the transformations in social reality. Against such an abstract attitude, a realist or, as it would be called, a "positivist" stance appeared increasingly to prevail, as a more efficacious way of dealing with such transformations.

Classic criminology's basic scenario, according to which a rational subject of rights is responsible for actions that he or she chooses freely, was now considered as a concept that did not take into consideration crucial social conditions and constraints.[1] Therefore, right after the Enlightenment period, in France, between the revolution and the restoration, commentators started drawing attention to increasing recidivism and a spreading fear of crime (Beirne 1993: 69–71). In *The Great Fear of 1789*, for instance, French historian Georges Lefebvre tells us how fear of banditry and crime were sweeping the French countryside just before the beginning of the French revolution, and establishes a link between such fear and the situation of crisis and social instability that would soon usher in the revolution (Lefebvre 1932). After the restoration in 1815, a pervasive fear would emerge again but this time connected to urban crowds and "the social question." A main motif of nineteenth-century conservative thinking was born, centered in the connection between crime and revolution.

## The City Crowd

These two fears found a common object in the fear of "the crowd." The crowd emerged as a threat, and a menace, a crowd of bour-geois city dwellers, but also of workers and lumpenproletarians, a crowd that moves as a swarm in the city streets, a crowd that reminds the onlookers of revolutionary movements and of "dangerous" classes. Indeed, such is the situation of poverty within the lowest strata of the urban working class in these years that there is almost no distinction between such strata and *la classe dangereuse*.

Actually, this overall process had already been progressing for a long time, fed by the expulsion from the countryside of rural workers who were then obliged to take refuge in the cities, a new "surplus population." This had been a constant process character-istic of capitalist development. Starting with what Marx had dubbed a "primitive accumulation" from the English countryside to the cities, each new phase of capitalist development and crisis would then be followed by an economic expansion. With each new expansion, social figures that had been up to that point "external" to development would be literally incorporated within the new way of life – urban, industrial, "methodical." These figures would be "external" either socially, because within the geographic bound-aries of capitalist domination but still finding themselves outside of the urban, industrial or "agriculturally developed" sections of it, or literally "external," in the sense of living in geographic areas not yet touched by the military and economic conquest of capital-ism. As in Thomas More's famous invective against the English sheep "that used to be so gentle and eat so little" but that had then begun to "devour the men" (1516: 9) (a result of enclosing the land that used to be for agriculture and was now more con-venient for pasture), those so expelled from the land had no other resort than turning to manufactures and factories, built on the outskirts of towns and in particular areas of the cities. From Engels's description of working-class Manchester in the 1840s (Engels 1845), all the way to Fritz Lang's 1927 expressionist film *Metropolis* – with its proletariat crowded within the guts of the

monster industrial city – going through representations by Baudelaire, Poe, Hugo, Dostoyevsky (Berman 1988), the image of the city
between the early nineteenth century and the early twentieth
century is one and the same. The city is where the crowd nests, a
crowd that is sometimes working-class, more often scum, rabble,
the canaille.

In fact, during the second half of the nineteenth century, the
faster and faster development of commerce and industrial production – together with the process of rationalization in agriculture
– was pushing an increasing flow of population from the "countryside" to "the city," a countryside and a city located at a greater
and greater distance. Many authors during this period gave
expression to this pervasive fear of the crowd. They were almost
obsessed with it, giving up any hope about the possibility of
"controlling" the crowd. The most famous among these was probably the French Gustave Le Bon (1892), the author of *Psychologie
des foules* (strictly speaking "crowd psychology," but it was translated as *The Crowd* in English, 1960).[2] Le Bon framed the problem
in a frankly reactionary perspective, starting with the stereotypical
imagery of the French revolution. He portrayed the crowd as
swarming through the streets and the squares of Paris, hunting
noblemen and women and rich bourgeois. It was almost a nightmare – or maybe a "spectre," as Marx and Engels (1848) had
memorably written a few years earlier – that snaked through
nineteenth-century French culture, and not only there. Every time
the crowd took to the streets, this fear rooted itself more deeply,
reaching its climax in the probably most famous revolutionary
event of the second half of the nineteenth century, the Parisian
Commune, to which Marx was to dedicate one of his most famous
political works (1871).

The literature of the period had developed, however, a much
keener sensitivity about the crowd. Walter Benjamin (1939), the
German maverick philosopher in love with a Paris that he saw as
"the capital of the nineteenth century," drew our attention to the
sonnet by Charles Baudelaire, "A une passante":

> La rue assourdissante autour de moi hurlait.
> Longue, mince, en grand deuil, douleur majestueuse,
> Une femme passa, d'une main fastueuse
> Soulevant, balançant le feston et l'ourlet;
>
> Agile et noble, avec sa jambe de statue.
> Moi, je buvais, crispé comme un extravagant,

Dans son œil, ciel livide où germe l'ouragan,
La douceur qui fascine et le plaisir qui tue.

Un éclair . . . puis la nuit! – Fugitive beauté
Dont le regard m'a fait soudainement renaître,
Ne te verrai-je plus que dans l'éternité?

Ailleurs, bien loin d'ici! Trop tard! Jamais peut-être!
Car j'ignore où tu fuis, tu ne sais où je vais,
O toi que j'eusse aimée, o toi qui le savais![3]

Benjamin comments:

In a widow's veil, mysteriously and mutely borne along by the
crowd, an unknown woman comes into the poet's field of vision.
What the sonnet communicates is simply this: far from experiencing
the crowd as an opposed, antagonistic element, this very crowd
brings to the city dweller the figure that fascinates. The delight of the
urban poet is love – not at first sight, but at last sight. It is a farewell
forever which coincides in the poem with the moment of enchant-
ment. Thus the sonnet supplies the figure of shock, indeed of catas-
trophe. (Benjamin 1939: 169)

He goes on to comment on the arresting description of the London
crowd, "as gloomy and fitful as the light of the gas lamps over-
head," by Edgar Allan Poe in "The Man of the Crowd" (Poe 1840;
Benjamin 1939: 171). Later on, however, Benjamin was to note
that, "Fear, revulsion, and horror were the emotions which the
big city crowd aroused in those who first observed it" (1939: 174).
Another great commenter on the city scene, German social philosopher Georg Simmel, observes in "The Metropolis and Mental
Life" that, to the intensified "nervous stimulation" of the big city,
the "metropolitan type of man . . . reacts with his head instead of
his heart" (Simmel 1903: 410). The big city is for Simmel the scenario *par excellence* of a tragic dialectic of "life" and "form." The
products of the continuous creativity of a "subjective" spirit are
at the same time crystallized in an "object" that immediately the
subject finds opposite to himself as a barrier and a limit. The more
the big city dweller tries to affirm his creativity and authenticity
– his subjectivity – an attempt that the big city satisfies probably
to a greater extent than ever before in human history – the more
he is caught in a web of forms ("spirit objectified") that he himself
has produced. Like a hero of ancient Greek tragedy, he brings his
fall upon himself. The only possible answer, according to Simmel,

is the *blasé* individual – the modern urbanite whose "nerves" are overwhelmed by the metropolitan environment. All social and human relationships in the big cities are based on monetary economy and are therefore fungible. As we have seen, the motto of the German free cities in the Middle Ages – "Stadtluft macht frei" – dominates the metropolis: the air of the big city makes one free. And yet such freedom reminds one of that uncanny freedom of the outlawed peasant described by Marx in the first volume of *Capital*, the peasant expelled from the land and "freed" therefore of every and all relations with his past life, made "proletarian," that is, owner only of the strength of his arms, a slave of his newly acquired freedom. The opposition between primary, face-to-face social control in the country or the small city, and the freedom of the big city, where the gaze of the other does not restrain one any longer from deviant action, appears here for the first time to the sociological imagination – it will later be developed at length, within the "sister city" to Berlin, by Chicago School sociologists. The big city is also, however, where secondary, formal social control "at a distance" – as Louis Wirth would later call it – has to be established, the social control of police and the criminal justice system (and especially, later, of the mass media of communication).

Whereas the "industrial revolution" – first in England, later on the Continent – had sowed the socio-economic premises of modernity, the Napoleonic period after the French revolution forged its political and bureaucratic structures (even if the political, legal, and administrative path followed "on the Continent" was quite different from the one followed in England and the English colonies). The French State under Napoleon, exported together with the Napoleonic conquest, was deeply rationalized and became much more powerful than under the *ancien régime*. As was said at the time, Napoleon's soldier brought a copy of the *Code civil* in his rucksack. Many among the European nineteenth-century States found a first configuration of their basic profile under Napoleonic domination and then slowly developed after the restoration of 1815. One has only to think of the compulsory draft (particularly hated by rural masses that, at least during prosperous periods, missed the precious arms lent to the army), the extension and rationalization of taxation (once again, the reason for many rural riots all throughout the nineteenth century), the police (a term that from the original meaning of "welfare institution" increasingly approximated its current meaning), the prison system (which we will have a chance of discussing at much greater length), and finally, more recently, the system of mass education and the political and electoral systems.

## The Emergence of Positivism

Responding to such an overall situation, the "social sciences" developed, within the first half of the nineteenth century, together with a "positivist" orientation based also on a critique of the "abstract" character of the Enlightenment. At the same time, they positioned themselves in an intermediate territory, between the individual and the State, which had been instead, up until then, the two exclusive reference points of the disciplines concerned with social reality, such as political philosophy and political economy. The social sciences tried to reclaim a terrain that was intermediate between the individual and the political, and which they saw as co-extensive with the domain of "morality," i.e. the domain of those impulses to action irreducible to either self-interest or coercion. Especially with Durkheim, as we will see in the next chapter, the specific domain of the social sciences would be found in "social structures." These are collective social facts, which "receive" single individuals when they come into the world, and yet are reproduced by the action of each individual – such as language or parenthood. It was in any case a set of social realities independent of the individual or the State, and which was claimed by social sciences as their own jurisdiction.

A correspondent "epistemological" program accompanied such an "ontological" move. A general definition of (sociological) positivism could in fact be *the attempt at applying methods and paradigms that are typical of the natural sciences to the study of society*. In both cases, the scientist bases his study on the observation of "facts." Even if this attitude has been deeply contested in the twentieth century – raising for instance the non-trivial issue of "what is a fact" – one should not forget that "positivist" scientists saw themselves as modern knights of knowledge reacting against the religion-based metaphysics of previous, *obscure* centuries. They were genuinely "progressive" in their attempts at introducing the methods of the natural sciences into the field of society and basing their results on "objective" and "neutral" observation of social phenomena (hence the use of statistics, quantitative methods, "clinical" observation).

In the following century, such a positivist orientation would become deeply contested. The fundamental objection to positivism would be that, especially in the case of the social sciences,[4] the observer participates in the same social world with the observed, partly because much of what is observed in social sciences is constituted through discursive practices, the essential media of which, language, is common to the observer and the observed. The observer therefore is hardly "external" to what is observed, as in the (normal) case of the natural sciences. The observer is deeply involved with, and not all that independent of, the material observed. The philosophy of the twentieth-century social sciences would therefore be basically skeptical on the basic claims of positivism.

## Quételet and Guerry's Sociological Positivism

Criminological positivism is not only represented by its most famous – indeed maybe notorious – version, Cesare Lombroso's theory of "the born delinquent" (see below). Early contributions by two French-speaking authors, Adolphe Quételet (1835) and André-Michel Guerry (1833), went first to shape a *sociological* type of positive analysis. Quételet and Guerry were among the first to develop the instruments of the newly born "science of the State," *la statistique*, to phenomena of "social pathology." The name of the new scientific instrument was no misnomer. The reorganization and rationalization of the modern State, which had been greatly enhanced during the Napoleonic period all throughout Europe, meant that, together with an array of new or renewed institutions, the new State would start also producing knowledge systems of the reality that the State itself administered, controlled, and sometimes had brought into being. In France, for instance, a "Compte général de l'administration de la justice criminelle" ("General account of the administration of criminal justice") started being published in 1827 (Perrot 1976; Perrot and Robert 1989; Beirne 1993: 73–5) and turned out to be a real gold-mine for sociologists and criminologists in the years to come. The new mass conscription was to become a source of copious data about new draftees also.

The Belgian Quételet was a mathematician and an astronomer. In his treatise on "social physics" (1835) he applied some of the notions derived from those sciences to the study of social and criminal questions. He was the first to identify the concept of the "average man," i.e. the possibility of representing a population through its average statistical characteristics. He was also the very first to observe the stability of certain social occurrences, in this preparing the groundwork, so to speak, for the foundation of sociology by authors such as Durkheim about half a century later (Beirne 1993: 75–97). None other than Karl Marx, in one of his reports for the *New York Daily Tribune*, writes,

> Now, if crimes observed on a great scale thus show, in their amount and their classification, the regularity of physical phenomena – if as Mr. Quételet remarks, "it would be difficult to decide in respect to which of the two" (the physical world and the social system) "the acting causes produce their effect with the utmost regularity" – is there not a necessity for deeply reflecting upon an alteration of the system that breeds these crimes, instead of glorifying the hangman who executes a lot of criminals to make room only for the supply of new ones? (Marx 1853, quoting Quételet 1835)

Quételet developed a number of other interesting observations, among them that the higher rates of certain crimes seem to be connected not with higher rates of absolute poverty but with higher inequality in income and class distribution. He therefore anticipated the concept of "relative deprivation" and its link with crime – something that Robert K. Merton would delve into at much greater length about a century later. Jock Young (2004) has recently pointed out that Quételet was also the first to warn researchers about the importance of the so-called "dark number" of crimes, the number of putative "crimes," that is, that go somehow unreported, so that the amount of crime we know is actually the product of the crimes committed multiplied by an unknown variable that represents the quality and quantity of social reaction to those crimes (see below in this chapter).

Guerry, in his *Statistique morale*, published in 1833, produced a "social cartography" of crime. He cross-referenced data on development and wealth, by the various French departments, with statistical data on crime, such as the quantity and quality of offenses. He too concluded that the crucial relationship was not between crime and poverty but between crime and unequal development. Furthermore, whereas crimes against property were prevalent in the Northern sections of France, crimes against the person were prevalent in the South. Finally, the commonplace relationship between criminality and ignorance also turned out to be unconfirmed (Beirne 1993: 111–33).

## The Italian Positive School

If Quételet and Guerry had framed a "positivist" understanding of the criminal question through *sociological* concepts, the later Italian "Positive School" of Lombroso and Ferri drew its main concepts from "criminal *anthropology*." The *positive* observation of the reality of crime and criminals shifted now to a conception steeped in the very *nature* of the criminal. Cesare Lombroso and Enrico Ferri saw themselves as scientists fighting on the side of "progress" against an "obscurantism" largely derived from religious precepts. Whereas the specificity of the Italian Positive School of criminal law and criminology cannot be understood without referring to Charles Darwin's revolutionary "discovery" of the secrets of human evolution in the mid-nineteenth century, the particular application of his theory to the question of crime, and to the question of crime *in Italy*, cannot be grasped outside of the specificity of Italian history (and more generally, of European history) in the period to which Lombroso belonged. We will consider these two aspects in turn.

Lombroso's fundamental scientific contribution is to be found in the concept of *atavism*. According to Ernst Haeckel's theory of *recapitulation* – who derived it from coupling Lamarck with Darwin (Gould 1977) – individual *ontogeny*, i.e. the development of each individual belonging to a species, would in fact "recapitulate" *phylogeny*, i.e. the development of the species. According to Lombroso, there would be individuals whose development would not progress beyond previous stages of human development. They would be throwbacks, in other words, to earlier, *atavistic* stages of human development. Their primordial nature would then push them in the direction of crime, or madness. According to Ian Taylor, Paul Walton and Jock Young (1973: 41), Darwin had atavism in mind when he suggested that, "[W]ith mankind some of the worst dispositions which occasionally without any assignable cause make their appearance in families, may perhaps be reversions to a savage state, from which we are not removed by many generations" (Darwin 1871: 137; however, the standpoint of contemporary biology is severely critical of these views (Gould 1977: 120–5); similar concepts will be found in much more sophisticated and "modern" authors than Lombroso, such as Sigmund Freud – see below). These atavistic individuals were "the born criminals." Lombroso claimed that he had discovered the secret of atavism while he was examining the skull of a "brigand" named Vilella:

> This was not merely an idea, but a flash of inspiration. At the sight of that skull, I seemed to see all of a sudden, lighted up as a vast plain under a flaming sky, the problem of the nature of the criminal – an atavistic being who reproduces in his person the ferocious instincts of primitive humanity and the inferior animals. (Lombroso 1911: xiv, cited in Taylor et al. 1973: 41)

According to Lombroso, whereas the "Classical School" of criminal law, together with theorizations of religious inspiration, had claimed that criminals would be endowed with faculties similar to those of "normal" men and that therefore they would engage in "evil" acts because of "free and conscious choice" (so that the systems of criminal law built on such premises would consider the seriousness of the criminal act as ground for the punishment), the "Positive School of criminal law" would instead claim that criminals do not commit crimes because of a conscious and freely willed act. Rather, criminals would have "evil tendencies," tendencies that find their origin in a physical and psychic organization different from that of the normal man. The Positive School would therefore consider that the basis for society's right to act against criminals is not their evil will but their *dangerousness*. Furthermore, criminal anthropology would establish that criminals, and especially their most characteristic type, the "born criminal," would be affected by a number of abnormal anatomical, biological, and psychological traits, many of which are atavistic, because they "repeat" traits typical of the pre-human ancestors of man. Lombroso also believed that such atavistic traits were associated with criminal behavior, a type of behavior both normal and frequent in animals and in "primitive" and "savage" peoples. To such criminals therefore this behavior is "natural," depending on the criminals' structural and functional inferiority of physical and psychic organization, similar to the organization of primitive and savage peoples.[5] In the second edition of his work, he would sum up the essence of his theory thus:

Whoever has read this book will have to come to the conclusion that many of the characteristics found in savages, and among the colored races, are also very often to be found in habitual criminals. These are: thinning hair, lack of strength and weight, low cranial capacity, receding foreheads, highly developed frontal sinuses, a high frequency of medio-frontal sutures . . . darker skin, thicker, curly hair, large or handle-shaped ears, a greater analogy between the two sexes, a lesser corrigibility in women, a lesser sensitivity to pain, a complete lack of moral awareness, sloth, the lack of any remorse, improvidence that appears at times as courage, and courage mixed with cowardice, a great vanity, a passion for gambling, alcohol, and their surrogates, fleeting but violent passions, a facile superstition, an exaggerated susceptibility as to one's "ego," and even a relative concept of divinity and morality. (Lombroso 1878: 375–6, my translation)

With such premises, the reader will readily understand how Lombroso's theory became the target of much criticism, sometimes even the butt of ridicule. His prose is indeed a sort of nightmare for "political correctness." It is, however, useful to consider some of this criticism in order to open up discussion also on issues, problems, and conceptualizations that are apparently much more nuanced, sophisticated, and up-to-date than Lombroso's.

## "Scientific" Criticism of the Positive School

The most obvious "scientific" critique of the Positive School – an "internal" critique, that is, that comes from the very internal logic of these positions – addresses Lombroso's hypothesis about the existence of a "criminal nature" independent of the legal (and therefore relative and variable in time and space) roots of what is socially given as "crime." However, as will appear clearly in Durkheim's theory (and then especially in so-called "labeling" theory), "crime" is by definition the result of the application of a given legal label to a behavior or anyway a social fact.

The second criticism is the so-called "causal fallacy" consisting in transforming an observable association of two variables in a causal type of relationship (Sutherland and Cressey 1978: 63–6). For instance, in the case of Lombroso, not only did he make the mistake of postulating an association between criminality and given physical anomalies – as the English penitentiary physician Charles Goring would show in *The English Convict* (1913), after trying, without success, to "replicate" Lombroso's "discoveries" – but also he came to the wrong conclusion that a given anatomic morphology was to be attributed to "atavism," and that this in turn would be the cause of the criminal behavior of a sizable number of delinquents (Beirne 1993: 187–213).

This discussion is not merely academic or "archaeological," but addresses problems still present in social and criminological research. The first aspect the researcher should pay attention to, is the necessity of a control group. In other words, one has to verify whether, given an element $y$ that we are trying to account for – the *explanandum* – and which we have found present in our target group, the element $x$ – our theorized *explanans* – is present, first of all, in the $y$-carrying group. We then have to evaluate whether, in another random (not-$y$) group, $x$ is absent. If $x$ is present also in the control group then obviously our hypothesis – of the necessary association between $y$ and $x$ – is falsified. This was in fact the way in which Charles Goring falsified Lombroso's theory: he found that the anatomical characteristics highlighted by Lombroso as linked to criminality were distributed in the student population of a college near to the penal institution where he worked to an extent not significantly different from that in the inmate population of the prison.

However, this does not imply that our hypothetical theory linking $x$ to $y$ may not be falsified in the future, because the association between $x$ and $y$ may actually be *caused* by the impact of a heretofore hidden third element, $z$, on both $x$ and $y$ making them "move" together, giving the impression to the observer that $x$ is the *cause* of $y$. What is necessary therefore is, on the one hand, offering a credible explanation of the relationship between $x$ and $y$ (a credible "story"), and, on the other hand, considering all possible alternative explanations based on other factors. One such factor may be anyway found in the future, so the "truth" of all theories lasts only until their falsification (Popper 1959).

Many examples of this fallacy could be derived from Lombroso's work. One example out of the many is his observation about sensitivity to pain, that is, the fact that, according to Lombroso, criminals would be less sensitive to pain or, put in another way, have a high pain threshold. Now, even if we grant that, on the basis of the control group methodology, this turned out to be exact, who were "the criminals" analyzed by Lombroso? Largely they were those who were convicted and imprisoned in Lombroso's Italy, such as Villella "the brigand." It is quite likely that the pool of people – in terms of gender, socio-economic conditions, types of activity, etc. – from which convicts were derived was a pool of people whose life conditions and biographies had habituated them to norms of pain toleration higher than those observed by the medical doctors who analyzed them, the lawyers who defended them, or the university professors who taught lectures about them.

A rather common contemporary criminological mistake of a kind similar to the one Lombroso made is the connection apparently established (prevalently in the United States and the United Kingdom) between what is called "race" in those countries – mostly meaning persons of African origin – and crime, and the connection apparently established instead in Continental Europe between immigration and crime. This connection is made in both cases because of the high presence of blacks, in the United States, and of (generally undocumented) migrants, in Continental Europe, within criminal justice systems and especially within prisons. This, however, means exempting from consideration the complexity of what is called the criminalization process – with the result of ultimately justifying racist and/or xenophobic positions, because such a short circuit between race and national origins on the one hand and crime on the other ends up defining the quality of being criminal as a "personal" quality of the black person or of the stranger – instead of a "quality" of complex social processes.

In order to clearly understand this point, let us go back to Lombroso. He generally examined, as instances of "criminals," people who had already been socially selected for the end result of conviction and/or imprisonment.[6] All the aspects that regulate such a long process of selection – starting with the coming into being of the "inclination" to commit certain crimes and ending with the prison gate closing behind the convict – were not explored. The one who had been convicted or who even found himself in prison was taken as a witness to a theory concerned not with the social processes of convicting and incarcerating but with the very "anthropological constitution" of the individual. A theory has to be set instead at the level of the object that intends to explain. If prisons are filled with people exhibiting a peculiar skin pigmentation or a peculiar national origin, one is not allowed to explain crime by skin pigmentation or national origin. At most, one will be able to explain imprisonment by skin pigmentation or national origin. The rate of incarceration is as much a measure of criminalization as it is a measure of criminality. On this, one should never forget Sutherland and Cressey's reference to the so-called "Sellin principle":

> The crimes that are reported to the police and recorded by the police
> are designated "crimes known to the police." These statistics have
> not been established as an index of the true crime rate. Yet the deci-
> sion to use this rate is probably the best way out of a bad situation,
> for as Professor Sellin has repeatedly pointed out, "The value of
> criminal statistics as a basis for measurement of criminality in geo-
> graphic areas decreases as the procedure takes us farther away from
> the offence itself." That is, these police records are a more reliable
> index than arrest statistics; arrest statistics are more reliable than
> court statistics; and court statistics are more reliable than prison sta-
> tistics. (Sutherland and Cressey 1978: 30, referring to Sellin 1951)

The social mechanisms that produce those data may range from the
high visibility of migrants' and blacks' crime *vis-à-vis* the extremely
low visibility of other kinds of crime ("crime in the street" vs.
"crime in the suites," as it is often put) to the discriminatory behavior of many public institutions, and from the migrants' and blacks'
being deprived of the fundamental right to have an efficient defense
to the impossibility of applying to migrants a host of pre- and after-
trial benefits that keep natives out of prison but that railroad foreigners into detention. And of course this does not even touch on
the basic issue of the social, economic, cultural, and legal conditions
of disadvantage that many migrants and blacks start from. Therefore, using statistics taken from the penitentiary in order to address
the question of "crime" is absurd. Equally absurd, however, is using
convictions or data on arrests of reported suspects to the same end,
because even if this may indeed be "the best way out of a bad situation," as Sellin reasonably stated, a huge gap remains between the
universe of crimes committed (what criminologists – as we have
seen, starting with Quételet – have called "the dark number" of
crime) and the end of the very first but crucial selection process that
takes us to the beginning of a criminal investigation, a selection that
is due to a host of social and legal processes where the "reaction"
to crime by citizens, media, and the police forces plays a paramount
role.

## "Contextual" Criticism of the Positive School:
## The "Southern Question"

Again because of extensive criticism, Lombroso started to distance
himself from his original theory, based on criminal anthropology,
and from the concept of the "born delinquent," and to write about

other types of criminal: the epileptic, the mad, or the occasionally criminal. In the direction that the Positive School took under the increasing influence of Enrico Ferri's work, furthermore, ecological and social factors also became important, until in the end the positions of the Positive School were not far distant from that "multifactorial theory" that, at the beginning of the twentieth century, became a sort of "received view" in criminology. Both the very coming into being of Cesare Lombroso's theory, however, and its future transformations cannot be separated from the broader historical context of Italian Unification after 1861 and the position of the lower classes in this period – a connection that may indeed shed light on other situations, beyond Italy. Whereas in Northern Italy the "social question" largely concerned factory and agricultural waged workers, in Southern Italy a process of annexation of large provinces had taken place after Unification. Piedmontese (now "Italian") army troops became engaged in a bloody repression of peasant "brigands" who, if on the one hand they were legitimately portrayed as instruments of the previous regime and the Church, on the other hand were also resisting the penetration of their society and culture by processes of "modernization" not particularly appreciated, such as mass army conscription, taxation, and the confiscation of common and Church land (Molfese 1964; Hobsbawm 1959, 1969; Adorni 1997).

This was the not irrelevant backdrop to Lombroso's story. Lombroso himself had been for a short period, in 1862, a medical officer in the Piedmontese army in the Southern region of Calabria. He was impressed by the different culture of its inhabitants, a difference that he tried to explain on the grounds of "race" as well as of other factors (Lombroso 1862; Baima Bollone 1992: 43; Teti 1993: 13–14, 158–65). The skull of Villella, studying which, less than ten years later, he would have the famous revelation of the theory of the born criminal, belonged to a peasant from Calabria, incarcerated till his death for being a thief and a brigand (Baima Bollone 1992: 114–25). There's a certain bitter irony in this. It seems almost as if criminological knowledge were to seal – with an additional act of scientific domination – a military and class domination that had already been established, literally, in the field.

It is hard not to see, in Lombroso's theory, a sort of somatic transfiguration of a cultural difference so deep[7] that it could not be understood on its own terms, but had to be *racialized* in the difference between North and South, between Europe and the Mediterranean, between normality and atavistic pathology (Teti 1993). It

may be interesting to consider a relatively recent article, uncon-
nected to the specificity of Lombroso but not to the subject of this
question, "Why Is Classical Theory Classical?" by R. W. Connell
(1997), who juxtaposes a "colonization" model for social theory's
origins to the usual one based on "modernization." It seems to me
that the Italian case shows that such a juxtaposition is problematic
because the two insights strongly imply each other. In other words:
the "civilizing gaze" that eventually was directed at non-"Western,"
"colonized" people, in all European countries was first experienced
by and developed toward domestic and mainly rural lower classes.
The long-lasting stereotypes attributed to colonized peoples are
very similar to those first applied to one's own rural lower classes.
They are both usually described as stupid, lazy, dirty, dark, sexually
and emotionally easily aroused, crime-prone, etc. This is still today
the inferiorizing stereotype of the poor migrant in Europe or of
the ghetto dweller in the United States, but it is not much different
from the stereotype of the Jew between the two wars in Europe, or
indeed of the peasant in early Renaissance literature in Italy or in
Elizabethan theatre in England. It is a general stereotype that the
urban dweller applies to the rural poor peasant (the reader may also
check both Lombroso's list above and, more recently, Gottfredson
and Hirschi's description of the criminal in their 1990 work (see
below, chapter 9) to add examples to this list).[8] Indeed many of the
physical characters that were identified by Lombroso in criminals
were also ascribed to Southerners. The deep historical difference
between industrial Northern masses that had already been "pro-
cessed through" the machine of modernity and were therefore ready
for self-government at the same time that they were ready to enter
the gates of factories and offices, and Southern masses who were
instead tied to a particularly "backward" type of rural life, finds its
roots in history (Putnam 1993). At the time, it was still so deep,
however, that it had to be represented in the myth of the heritage
of human evolution as this connected with races and individual
dispositions – in one word "atavism." In 1926, Gramsci would note,
in his famous essay on *la questione meridionale* ("the Southern
question"):

> It is well known what kind of ideology has been disseminated in
> myriad ways among the masses in the North, by the propagandists
> of the bourgeoisie: the South is the ball and chain which prevents the
> social development of Italy from progressing more rapidly; the
> Southerners are biologically inferior beings, semi-barbarians or total

barbarians, by natural destiny; if the South is backward, the fault does not lie with the capitalist system or with any other historical cause, but with Nature, which has made the Southerners lazy, incapable, criminal and barbaric – only tempering this harsh fate with the purely individual explosion of a few great geniuses, like isolated palm-trees in an arid and barren desert. The Socialist party was to a great extent the vehicle for this bourgeois ideology within the Northern proletariat. The Socialist party gave its blessing to all the "Southernist" literature of the clique of writers who made up the so-called positive school: the Ferri's, Sergi's, Niceforo's, Orano's and their lesser followers, who in articles, tales, short stories, novels, impressions and memoirs, in a variety of forms, reiterated one single refrain. Once again, "science" was used to crush the wretched and exploited; but this time it was dressed in socialist colors, and claimed to be the science of the proletariat. (Gramsci 1926: 444)

Actually, Gramsci's article followed by many years the lively debate about "the Southern question" or *meridionalismo* that had been raging at the turn of the century, especially between 1898 and 1906 and that saw in the initiative of the journal *Il pensiero contemporaneo* its center (see the very useful anthology of this debate by Vito Teti (1993)). Indeed, Gramsci had not been the first to note the connection between positive theories and the stereotyping of Southerners – Napoleone Colajanni's work being probably the most critical of the positivists from a sociological perspective (Colajanni 1903). Furthermore, it is usually pointed out that Enrico Ferri, a leading socialist politician and Lombroso's follower, innovated on the theory of his mentor by introducing a more sociological consideration of criminal "tendencies." I believe, however, that the shift of emphasis in the Positive School, from Lombroso's theory of the born criminal to the more sociologically oriented position of Enrico Ferri, should be traced back also to a change of protagonists or personas *in* criminal representation and correspondingly to strata and types of working-class populations expressing different "criminal" figures – an overall change that had to do with a social, geographic, and temporal change.

## The Positive School and the Crisis at the Turn of the Century

In fact, things had changed quite a bit, in Italy and Europe, since the time when Cesare Lombroso had discovered atavism in

Villella's skull. Accordingly, things changed also within the ranks, and the scientific orientation, of the School. Harsh labor and political battles had almost overcome the resistance of backward Italian political and social elites to the recognition of the socialist and trade union movements, especially in the North of the country. To the betterment of the conditions of the Northern working class, in the South there corresponded a generalized migration movement of the "surplus" population outside of the country and especially toward "the Americas," especially the United States and Argentina. Whereas in the period immediately after Unification, in 1861, the already high imprisonment and unemployment rates in the whole country were even higher in the South – and it was difficult to tell where criminal penalties ended and where the military repression of "brigandage" started – instead, between the 1880s and World War I, in Italy like in the rest of Europe, the better conditions for the working class in the North, together with the massive migration from the South, corresponded to generally declining imprisonment rates (Sutherland 1934; Rusche and Kirchheimer 1939: 138–65; Pavarini 1997; Melossi 1998b). Furthermore, industrial and economic development made for increasing commercial and financial complexity, and a whole string of financial scandals and frauds ensued.

The new elaborations in the Positive School in some way reflected all of this. Enrico Ferri, for instance, before becoming a prominent socialist leader, was a very successful lawyer and criminal law professor, at least as famous for his scientific theories as for his legal defenses, being an orator of great success (see Sir Leon Radzinowicz's recollections of his encounter and apprenticeship with Ferri (Radzinowicz 1999: 1–25)). Born in the Northern rural district of Mantua, one of the very first rural areas where in Northern Italy a working-class movement made its appearance due to the more advanced level of "capitalist" land tenure and agriculture, he defended as one of his first cases a group of peasant agitators from that area. The Mantua peasants had been engaged in a wider movement of Northern rural masses called *la boje* – a movement that demanded better wage conditions for agricultural daily workers, and the name of which came from the rallying cry used by the peasants, in their dialect, "la boje, la boje, e deboto la va de fora!" ("it boils, it boils and soon it will boil over!"; Sereni 1948: 386). In Enrico Ferri's defense in court, one gathers that the proximity of the orator to the "criminals" he was defending could not be greater, a proximity that is first geographic, then cultural and political. The mode of his defense turns on concepts of innovation, social justice, social causes of crime, if indeed one can speak of "crime" in this case. Indeed, for Ferri, these men are close to heroes:

> As a student of social pathology, I am given to the observation of criminals in prison and in free life, and following the steps of my teachers, I have noticed their moral and physical characteristics which, together with the social environment, drive them to fight the inexorable struggle for existence through the means of crime.
>
> Now, as a professor of criminal sociology, I am very happy to state that from this trial my anthropological studies did not profit a bit, because I had to come to the conclusion – a reassuring one for the lawyer – that no trace of criminality can be found in these defendants. On the contrary, I have to declare that we know from the laws of psychology that heroic souls like Siliprandi and honest people like his colleagues will never be able to become common wrongdoers. These are monstrosities, that can be imagined only by those who do not know the laws of the human heart or who are blinded by passions or personal resentments (*applause*).
>
> And I desire to state that I would always be proud to shake hands with these men whether they will come back to being free men or, by absurd hypothesis, might go back to wearing the prisoner's uniform (*burst of applause*).
>
> But if the professor has idly opened his books of criminal anthropology for this trial, the student and the lawyer together have had to gaze into another page of the great book of life, marred by other pains and other sighs; with patient and painful anatomy, he has had to dissect the poverty that hopelessly oppresses the workers of his native province. (Ferri 1886: 9)

In a display of socio-legal sensibility rather unusual among jurists not only back then but also later, in tens and tens of pages Ferri went on to reconstruct the just causes of the complaints raised by the peasants "of his native province" by analyzing the economic and social conditions of the region in great detail. The rhetoric is one of social change: those who have been unjustly charged with crime are actually the pioneers of a new world, more just and more humane. They are not criminals, they are indeed "our" heroes. How far are we from the harsh Southern mountains where the brigand Villella had been fighting his own primitive and uncivilized "struggle for existence"![9]

One might, however, object that we are talking of very different types of crime, according to a distinction similar to the one that at the time another leading positivist author, Baron Raffaele Garofalo, famously dubbed the distinction between "natural" and "artificial" crimes (1891), that is, the distinction between a supposedly "universal" type of crime, the repugnance for which would be embedded in human nature, and an "artificial" type of crime, the creation only of political convenience and opportunity. However, I believe that the choice of which type of crimes criminologists (as well as the courts, the media, etc.) focus upon is indeed part of our *explanandum*, what we need to explain, because our orientation toward specific "facts" of analysis, knowledge, entertainment, etc., is inscribed within and directed by historically variable sets of values (Weber 1904). One could even dare suggest that the criminals themselves are not immune to the prevailing social discourse on criminality, ready to confirm it with their own actions and in their own self-images. Criminals too belong in a web of social and historical relationships: the particularly cruel character of their deeds or, in other circumstances, their sophistication and innovation depend at least in part on the environment into which they find themselves thrown.[10]

In other words, we cannot really understand Lombroso's and Ferri's different emphases, on the "born delinquent" or on "social conditions," without considering the specificity of Italy's dualistic socio-economic development, which meant very different types of economic growth, rates of unemployment, types of working class, in the North and in the South. The incorporation of a more developed and combative working class in the North brought a more inclusive and sympathetic attitude toward the kind of problems – even criminal problems – that were emerging there. At the same time, a more exclusionary attitude prevailed toward the poor peasants in the South, whether such an attitude meant semi-starvation in the fields or outright expulsion through emigration. As we have already seen in chapter 1, and as will appear even more clearly when we come to discuss North America (see below, chapter 4), the main limitation of the social pact typical of the modern "democratic" form of polity is to be found in the essentially similar identity required of the subjects who are admitted to it. When extreme difference, and conflict, tend instead to obtain, then the prevailing attitude is not one of "democratic inclusion" but of radical exclusion, to the point of constructing those perceived as radically different as "others" who are, maybe, human beings, but biologically, often "racially," different, inferior, and evil.

Enrico Ferri's treatise *Criminal Sociology* (1884) went on in different editions well until the 1920s. He was also the one who tried to translate the teachings of the Positive School into legal principles, by drafting, in 1921, a project for a penal code centered on the notions of "dangerousness" and "social defense" instead of the "classic" ones of "crime" and "punishment." The "Ferri Project," as it came to be known, found admirers outside of Italy, from the United States, to the newly created Communist Soviet Union, to Latin America – wherever a "realist" jurisprudence tended to prevail. Less so, however, in Italy, where the newly formed Fascist regime was suspicious of the positivists' contempt for the law and preferred the more conservative orientations of a normativistic and statalistic kind. Enrico Ferri's late "conversion" to Fascism – a rather widespread event in 1920s Italy – helped little in overturning the fortune of the School with the new regime. Some positivistic concepts, however, within the framework of a fundamentally "classic" legal structure, entered the new Fascist Penal Code of 1930 and contributed to the making of this new code, the Rocco Code – as it came to be known from the name of Alfredo Rocco, minister of justice – a true international model of codification both for authoritarian and for democratic regimes (Marques 2007).

The social and cultural change in Italy reflected on the School because, on the one hand, it encouraged Lombroso to distance himself, as we have seen, from the concept of the "born delinquent," and to accept the existence of other types of criminal: the epileptic, the mad, or the occasionally criminal. On the other, it meant, especially among Lombroso's younger collaborators, an increasing interest in diverse forms of criminality, so much so that one could well state that, within the Italian Positive School, there was already present, in a nutshell, that impressive flowering of socio-criminological investigation that would follow in the new century in the United States. Rodolfo Laschi, for instance, after having written with Lombroso an essay on "political criminality" (Lombroso and Laschi 1890; Lombroso 1894; Ruggiero 2006), discovered "bank criminality" or, if you prefer, "financial criminality" (Laschi 1899). Obviously, for the positivists the problem was how to reconcile the anthropological root of Lombroso's theory with the reality of the financial scandals that plagued Italy at the time and whose protagonists were members of the elites. Social and cultural explanations are therefore at the center of Laschi's analysis, with a series of observations that anticipate the future acquisitions of sociological criminology. Laschi places due emphasis on the importance of individualism and the lack of respect for social and legal norms, in a way that reminds one of Durkheim, as well as the absolute lack of stigma attached to this type of criminality, in a way instead that will be much further developed by Sutherland's idea of "white-collar crime" (see below, chapter 6). A concept of "evolutive" criminality – whether of the "political" or "financial" kind – was therefore counterposed to "atavistic" criminality (Martucci 2002).

Much closer to the original teachings of the *maestro* were instead the treatment of women's criminality by Lombroso and Guglielmo Ferrero (1893) and Scipio Sighele's work on the "criminal crowd" (1891).[11] As Mary Gibson and Nicky Rafter point out in their edition of the Lombroso–Ferrero work, the book on women's crime suffers from ambiguity. This is not only because Lombroso and Ferrero have to reconcile their time-honored idea of women's inferiority with the theory of atavism, but especially because Lombroso was in contact with the most advanced sectors of the Italian political and cultural intelligentsia, and within those circles the salience of the "woman question" was increasing very rapidly. The misogynistic tone of the volume had therefore to be reconciled with "politically correct" statements that Lombroso and Ferrero obviously felt obliged to make. The first source of ambiguity and confusion was the fact that Lombroso saw women as "less evolved" than men. Because, however, as we have seen, he also saw the source of crime in the "backward" character of criminals' evolution – atavism – it was very difficult to reconcile this "theory" with the reality of what appeared to Lombroso to be a much lesser criminality among women. In part, Lombroso and Ferrero had to have recourse to the idea that the preferred form of women's "degeneracy" was not really crime but "prostitution," by which essentially they meant any form of what society at the time saw as deviance in prescribed female sexual mores. In part, Lombroso and Ferrero had to conceive of criminal women as "more masculine," so that the female offender was in a sense a misconceived woman. This field was, however, one where, more than perhaps anywhere else, Lombroso's characteristic contradictoriness, confusion, and lack of methodological rigor were particularly apparent. Furthermore, this was not helped by the fact that, while he was writing the pages of *The*

*Female Offender*, a regular invitee to his house in Turin was Anna Kuliscioff, the leading Russian feminist and the companion of the leader of Italian socialism, Filippo Turati. Anna was the vehicle of Lombroso's conversion to progressive political ideas and socialism, "slipping Lombroso's daughters a copy of J. S. Mill's *The Subjection of Women*" (Gibson and Rafter 2004: 13; Martucci 2002: 77). According to Gibson and Rafter, it was Kuliscioff who converted the family to socialism, starting with "the girls", and then Lombroso followed.

One of the brightest students of Enrico Ferri was Scipio Sighele, the author of *La folla delinquente* (*The Delinquent Crowd*). As we have seen, Sighele disputed the paternity of crowd psychology with Gustave Le Bon. According to a *leitmotiv* of nineteenth-century sociology and psychology, crowd situations were thought to cause a true debasement of human behavior, which would become that of a beast, of an animal. Both Le Bon and Sighele were eager, in their books, to offer plenty of examples to their prurient bourgeois readers, taken from events that supposedly happened during the various revolutions of the century. What was the reason for such egregious behavior? Sighele, true to his mentors, saw in crowd behavior a sudden fall into a momentary atavistic condition that would push human beings back to their primordial state. There was a concept here of the wild, savage, animalistic man lurking under the surface within each human being. Whereas in the case of the born criminal such a savage essence would be out in the open, because in this individual, evolution had found a sudden stop to its development, in the case instead of the normal, civilized man, such a savage essence would be hidden, precariously overcome by civilization but always ready to emerge if the bonds of society were suddenly removed by some external cause, such as the violent irruption of a crowd in a revolutionary event (for more "rationalist" accounts of crowd behavior in twentieth-century sociology, see McPhail 1991). There is even, in Sighele, the idea of a "stratification" of the human soul that would be fully revealed in the case of hypnotic suggestion, according to the teachings of Ribot and of many others who at the time, especially in France, studied hypnosis – a stratification that would oppose a civilized entity within the individual to his animalistic double. Both this concept of a divided soul and the Lamarckian idea of "repetition" show more than one similarity between the ideas of the Positive School and the basic concepts developed a few years later by the founder of psychoanalysis, Sigmund Freud.

## Freud's Psychoanalysis and Crime

Many are the currents of thought that relate anthropological positivism to psychoanalysis, on the one hand, and the thoughts of the founder of psychoanalysis to the broader issue of the study of deviance and social control, on the other – even if we limit ourselves, as we have been doing throughout this study, to suggestions of a sociological character. In a way similar to Lombroso's – and actually to that of many other thinkers of their age – Freud used Lamarckian recapitulation theory in order to connect his "deep" individual psychology to "group" or "mass" psychology. For instance, in *Totem and Taboo* (Freud 1913; Gould 1977: 154–64), Freud established a parallelism among the behavior of children, neurotic individuals, primordial men, and "savages" (in fact, *Totem and Taboo*'s very subtitle reads *Resemblances between the Psychic Lives of Savages and Neurotics*). And we have seen how, especially in Sighele's analysis of the individual under the influence of the crowd, this idea of a sort of "archaic unconscious" compressed under a thin veneer of civilization is quite strong. It reminds one of Freud's "dissection of the psychic personality," where he distinguished the influence of an "id" – the site of instincts – from that of the "ego" – the site of conscience – from that of the "superego" – the site of civilization's presence inside the mind, modeled on the paternal figure (Freud 1933: 71–100). Freud's central idea of the "Oedipus complex" referred to the basic conflict that according to Freud dwelled within each (male) individual, i.e. the competition with the father for the possession of the woman, the mother, and the desire therefore, if not the act, of killing the father and possessing the mother (Freud 1917). In *Totem and Taboo*, Freud connected this "individual" sort of myth to a historical-collective kind of myth, in a way not too different from that of the social contract (Carole Pateman pointed out this connection from a feminist perspective in *The Sexual Contract* (1988); see also Melossi 1990: 72–96). Contemporaneously with the very first "discoveries" of cultural anthropology, Freud tried to explain the totemic system and the exogamic culture of "primitive" civilizations – i.e. the basic taboo on incest – by reference to Darwin's and Robertson Smith's hypotheses of a "primeval horde" of "brothers" who at some point revolted against the father-king's monopoly on resources – the most crucial being the possession of the women – and sacrificed and (literally) introjected the body of the father-king by having recourse to their cannibalistic customs. By so doing, from the very sense of guilt connected to such a criminal deed, a new morality of sharing, common to the society of brothers so established, emerged and, together with it, the very instantiation of civilization (this anthropological hypothesis, quite mythical and naive, was to be seriously questioned by Alfred Kroeber (1920, 1939) and Bronislaw Malinowski (1926)). This basic drama, which is, according to Freud, at the very roots of our culture – Freud's attempts to "read" in the same manner the basic premises of Christianity in *Moses and Monotheism* (Freud 1939) are fascinating – would in fact, be *repeated* in the early phases of the life of each individual human being (even if it is only possible to note *en passant* that the whole conceptual mechanism seems to work quite well for men, less so for women).

In his later work, *Group Psychology and the Analysis of the Ego* (1921), Freud went on to discuss a number of essays that had attempted to explain "crowd" behavior, including indeed Scipio Sighele (1891) and Gustave Le Bon (1892), plus others (Gabriel Tarde 1890; W. Moede 1915; Wilfred Trotter 1916; and William McDougall 1920). After criticizing these works, which relied on explanatory mechanisms such as atavism, imitation, and suggestion, Freud presented a "group psychology" (*Massenpsychologie*) explanation that was informed by the fundamentals of his psychoanalytic theory. In a manner reminiscent of Nietzsche, Freud explained the psychic bond among members of a group by describing the libidinal relationship between individual members and the group's leader. For Freud, the leader was an image of the members' ego-ideal, which was ultimately rooted in the father's image.

These very foundations of the doctrine of psychoanalysis allowed Freud also to sketch, more than properly develop, his own contribution to a theory of criminal behavior, based on his clinical observation of cases where his patients would confess "forbidden actions" they had committed. Freud came to the conclusion that those actions had been committed precisely because they were forbidden. Committing them meant in fact the sentencing to a punishment that these patients actually cherished and desired, in order to appease an "original" sense of guilt derived from the "Oedipus complex":

[which is] a reaction to the two great criminal intentions of killing the father and having sexual relations with the mother. In comparison with these two, to be sure, the crimes committed in order to account for the sense of guilt were comparatively light ones for the sufferer to bear. We must remember in this connection that parricide and incest with the mother are the two greatest crimes man can commit, the only ones which in primitive communities are avenged and abhorred as such. And we must remember, too, that other investigations have caused us to entertain the hypothesis that the conscience of mankind, which now appears as an inherited power in the mind, was originally acquired from the Oedipus complex. (Freud 1916: 332)

The last sentence is a reference to the theory exposed in *Totem and Taboo*. A disciple of Freud, Theodor Reik, developed these intuitions in a book entitled *The Compulsion to Confess* (Reik 1925; see also Alexander and Staub 1931). Of course, a major difference that set Freud's psychoanalysis apart from Lombroso and Ferri's "positive" criminal anthropology was not only Freud's much greater intellectual sophistication but especially the fact that, if atavism was still a fading premise in Freud's conceptualizations, no automatic consequence was derived from that as to criminality or illness. Individual maladjustment was much more an issue of problematic adjustment to reality – usually, according to Freud, a reality represented by the father and the mother figures – therefore pertaining to the potential reality of each individual, rather than an almost "automatic" consequence of constitutional heritage. Certainly, this may have had something to do with the fact that Lombroso had "discovered" his theory dissecting the skull of a "fiery" and "primitive" brigand, whereas Freud would converse with the sons and daughters of the Viennese bourgeoisie. Once more, the social distance between analysts and analyzed had to reflect on the conceptualization of such a distance in theory, between the social category in which the analyst "naturally" belonged, and the social category in which the analyzed "naturally" belonged. Clearly, types like Villella did not have a chance, in life as in science.

# 3

# Emile Durkheim's Sociology
# of Deviance

To Walter Benjamin, Paris, capital of France, was also "the capital
of the nineteenth century." Indeed, during the century, France
seemed to be the society where the cultural expressions of
modernity were developing faster than anywhere else. We have
also seen that a sociological kind of criminology had first developed there. In fact, the social sciences, and more particularly the
very notion and concept of "sociology," were to have their birthplace in work by authors such as Henry de Saint-Simone, August
Comte, and Gabriel Tarde. It is only fitting therefore that the
work of the author who more than any other is considered to
be "the father" of sociology, Emile Durkheim, emerged in France,
in the last quarter of the nineteenth century. To a large extent,
his work attempted to be a reflection on many of the issues
that we have already touched on, characteristic of nineteenth-
century European society. And, even if Durkheim's contributions
are contributions to the very formation of the social sciences
generally – in the same way in which Karl Marx's or Max
Weber's were – nonetheless, within his sociology, issues of deviance and social control (albeit not under these terms) loomed
large.

## The Division of Labor in Society

In his first and probably most important contribution, *The Division of Labor in Society* (1893), Durkheim identified a fundamental

historical and social tendency toward an increasing complexity and differentiation in the division of labor. Under the influence of such a tendency, he postulated a transition from a *mechanical* kind of solidarity, "or solidarity by similarities" – that is, a solidarity among individuals who perform social tasks that are simple and very similar to one another, like cogs in a machine, or "segments" – to an *organic* type of solidarity – that is, a solidarity among individuals who perform tasks that are quite complex and different from one another, like the organs of the human body.[1] Because, however, the concepts of mechanical and organic solidarity are theoretical constructs that are not observable in reality, we need an observable "indicator" of the kind of society we are facing. According to Durkheim, an *indicator* of the type of society being observed is the type of *law* that prevails in it. In a society where solidarity is mechanical, the collective consciousness will focus on defending few, but very strongly held, general sentiments. The latter will be defended therefore by means of the most powerful instrument, criminal sanctions. In an organic solidarity society instead, sentiments emphasizing the importance of the individual and of his interests are going to be pre-eminent. The kind of law that protects such sentiments is the one based on what Durkheim calls "restitutory" sanctions, i.e. basically civil or private law.

One of the crucial problems Durkheim was trying to address at the time was the problem of "individualism."[2] However, he did not share the opinion of other, contemporary authors, such as British sociologist Herbert Spencer (1879), who, in a modern society dominated by individualism and "contractualism," saw all concepts of morality yielding to principles of self-interest and market exchange. On the contrary, Durkheim was interested in investigating the grounds for a *morality of individualism* that was to be typical of organic solidarity. So much is this so that one of the most interesting arguments by Durkheim, later received and developed by Talcott Parsons (1937: 319) and the ethnomethodologists, is that of the so-called "non-contractual elements of contracts," those normative elements, in other words, that in all legislations come to frame the "will of the parties" in order to guarantee the validity and functionality of contracts (Durkheim 1893: 154–65; cf. on this the work by Stewart Macaulay (1963)). Back of all contracts, in other words, there is a socially laid and legally enforced "morality" that is essential to the very existence of the institution and that is an expression of a social interest, not simply of self-interest.

## Anomie

According to Marco Orrù's imposing reconstruction (1987), the term *anomie* is an ancient one, going back at least to classical Greece and running through the length of the development of European culture until, at the end of the nineteenth century, it surfaced again in Durkheim's review of Jean-Marie Guyau's book *L'irréligion de l'avenir* (Durkheim 1887; Guyau 1887; Orrù 1987). It was only six years later, however, in *The Division of Labor in Society*, that Durkheim dealt extensively with the concept of anomie, to pick it up again, and in a different fashion, in his subsequent volume on *Suicide* (1897). Essentially, for Durkheim, anomie is the lack – or, better, the inadequacy – of moral norms, faced with the development of the division of social labor. Durkheim maintains that the problem lies not so much in increased social complexity and differentiation as in the difficulty of coming into being of a corresponding organic solidarity, or morality (especially for certain individuals, or sectors of society). This is another way of framing the problem of the "morality of individualism" that is central to Durkheim's research (Giddens 1971: 65–118). It is the set of problems that develop, in other words, when a type of organic solidarity becomes unable to support the kind of society in which individuals and groups happen to find themselves.

The processes of increasing division of labor, complexity, and differentiation in society have to proceed together and in accordance with a "morality" adequate to those transformations. Individuals need motivation to find themselves within such a deeply changing society. We have seen at the beginning how France was at the edge of modernity in this period. Formerly a deeply religious society, at least since the French revolution religion had been giving way, as the main ground for morality, solidarity, and social cohesion. Spencer (1879) in the United Kingdom and Tönnies (1887) in Germany had given a possible answer: self-interest, the market, contractual relationships would suffice to grant the construction and maintenance of social order. Durkheim was severely critical of such answers (Giddens 1971: 65–81). He saw his own search for the grounds of the morality of individualism as competing with both Spencer's and Tönnies's apologies for the capitalist market, on the one hand, and with a burgeoning socialist movement, on the other. To Durkheim in fact socialism was a force that, by recommending class war, would go in the direction of class division and against social cohesion, therefore increasing anomie, instead of "repairing" it.

Critics have also pointed out that by diagnosing an increasing division of labor in a period when, in France also, mass production was starting to unfold and the foundations were laid for subsequent Taylorism and Fordism, Durkheim was quite anachronistic or, at the very least, not particularly insightful (Pizzorno 1963). Such developments had not completely escaped Durkheim, however, who, in *The Division of Labor in Society* (1893: 353–88), saw "anomic" and "forced" types of division of labor – typical of the industrial division of labor – as "pathological forms," ways in which the increasing division of labor would actually produce a sort of "collective" anomie (instead of the "individual" forms of anomie that he would later explore in *Suicide*). Whereas an "anomic" division of labor refers to the anomie brought into society by class war, a "forced" division of labor is the division of labor determined from the outside by some kind of coercive power. They are both to a different degree forced on the individual. In his later "Preface" to the second edition of *The Division of Labor* (1902), Durkheim was to indicate in "professional groups" (*corporations*), uniting all those belonging in a trade or skill, whether owners or waged workers, a possible solution to this problem (this is the path that early twentieth-century authoritarian political movements, such as Italian Fascism, would take). However, it is easy to see that the further "progress" of industrial development would have increased the anomic or forced division of labor, rather than the contrary. Therefore the solution of "corporatism" could only unfold within an authoritarian political regime and therefore increase anomie rather than reduce it (Pizzorno 1963).

## Suicide

In *Suicide* (1897), Durkheim carried his thoughts about anomie further. There, he distinguished between three types of suicide: what he called "egoistic" suicide, "anomic" suicide – but they share something, both having to do with the general theme of anomie – and something completely different, "altruistic" suicide. As we have already seen, for Durkheim a condition of anomie results from the coming into being of what we could call a "gap" between the progress in the division of labor in society, on the one hand, and the development of forms of solidarity able to "keep up" with such progress, on the other. Translating such language in individual terms – since it is the expression of social phenomena at an individual level that occupies the field in *Suicide* – this means that, under conditions of anomie, the individual finds no social motivation to sustain his or her relationship with the other members of society. He or she finds no grounds for integration within the social group.

Durkheim's methodology in this study is very interesting and forms a true landmark in the development of sociological thinking and research. He analyzes the rates of suicide within the various jurisdictions of France and more generally of Europe, and relates them to a number of social variables (indicators) such as the prevailing religious confession, the state of families (such as the rate of divorce), the average level of education. For instance, suicide rates tend to be higher where the membership in Protestant denominations is higher and there is a higher rate of dissolutions of family bonds and a higher level of educational attainment. Durkheim reads these three variables as indicators of individualism and comes to the conclusion that the rate of suicide will be higher where indicators of individualism are higher. In such circumstances, social integration, and therefore solidarity, is lower and the likelihood of individual "failure" (or sense thereof), hence of a higher rate of suicide, is therefore also higher. This is the type of suicide that he defines as "egoistic."

Why, according to Durkheim, may these three variables in particular be taken as indicators of a higher level of individualism? Whereas the rate of divorce may be taken as an intuitive indicator of such a higher level, the justification is more complex for the other two. Protestant confessions, based on the concept of a direct relationship between the believer and the divinity, seem to Durkheim to promote a sense of individuality that is missing instead in the more communitarian and authoritarian Catholicism (where the structure of the Church "mediates" between the believer and the divinity). Durkheim considers a higher level of educational attainment as also an indicator of individualist development, because it allows for a more complex and richer development of the personality (the direct reading of the Holy Scriptures – contrary to the situation in the Catholic Church where it is the

priest who, in the church, reads them to the crowd of believers –
in a sense captures in one shell and unites the two indicators,
individualism and education).[3] Durkheim points, however, to an
exception, the Jewish community, characterized by a low level of
suicide (more similar in this to Catholics than to Protestants), but
by a high cultural level. Durkheim, himself of Jewish ancestry,
explains this apparent contradiction by the strong communitarian
tradition of the Jewish people, nourished and at the same time
imposed by centuries of experience of persecution and isolation
as a group.

There is then a type of suicide that Durkheim defines as
"anomic" proper. In a way similar to the distinction made in *The
Division of Labor in Society* between the two "pathological" forms
of division of labor, the "forced" and the "anomic," here too the
logic of the two types of suicide, egoistic and anomic, is the same
– the falling apart of the bond between the individual and the
community. Whereas, however, in the egoistic suicide, emphasis is
placed on the deepening individualism of the member of society,
in the anomic type of suicide the accent is on sudden social
changes, such as economic crises, that "unglue" the bond between
individual and society. It is significant in fact that Durkheim finds
that the sudden betterment of economic conditions – and not only
the sudden worsening – seems to be connected with an increase
in the number of suicides. The logic in both cases is the same:
something happens that all of a sudden makes the sustenance of
the individual member of society by the bonds of common solidarity problematic. It may be seen – as Merton would see it later on
(see below, chapter 6) – as a problem of adaptation. Unsupported
by a sense of collective belonging, the individual is unable to keep
his or her orientation and succumbs to anomie. This idea of anomie
as expression of a negative form of individualism, i.e. an individualism that is not supported by adequate moral development, is
a motif that will become very important in twentieth-century
sociology of deviance, such as in the contribution by Robert K.
Merton.

The third type of suicide is the opposite of the first two. It is the
kind of situation in which suicide is caused by excessive altruism,
instead of excessive egoism or isolation from the community. It is
the type of suicide that we would call "self-sacrifice" in a soldier,
when the identification of the individual with his or her community
is so total that it results in the literal annihilation of individual personality. The classic example would be the Japanese *kamikaze* pilots

during World War II, plowing their planes packed with high explosives into enemy warships. In recent years, it has also become a means of struggle by members of radical Islamic organizations fighting in the Middle East, not to mention, of course, the case of the September 11, 2001, attack on the Twin Towers in New York City.

## The Sociology of Deviance

Durkheim made a fundamental contribution to the foundation of sociology as a discipline in his text *The Rules of Sociological Method* (1895a). In it, almost *en passant*, one finds also Durkheim's most enlightening and probably enduring contribution to a "sociology of deviance" (even if these were not his terms, as we will see). In *The Rules*, Durkheim intends to discuss the basic concepts of sociological investigation. The first move therefore must be to show what sociology is about, what is the object of its investigations. Durkheim describes such an object as "social facts." It is important to note that, in doing this, he is also claiming a new scientific territory, a territory that at the same time legitimizes the creation of a new science, sociology, and creates a whole area of human experience as sociology's exclusive domain. In indicating the preferred object of sociological thinking in what he calls the social fact, Durkheim is at the same time taking a stand against "methodological individualism," the view, that is, that all human experience and institutions may in some way be reduced to individual action, and the political and legal institutions that give expression to such individual action. This was the view of the two main "social" sciences that occupied the scene before sociology's advent, i.e. economics and political science – or, as it was often called at the time, political economy. The domain of "social facts" draws in a sense a new map of social reality, a reality that cannot be reduced to individuals. It seems to me that this new domain of investigation accompanies the growth in the nineteenth century of what was called "civil society" and the web of organizations and associations that were in some way intermediate between the individual and the State. Against the "abstract" voluntarism and rationalism of eighteenth-century conceptualizations, *in primis* the idea of the social contract, Durkheim's sociology – in ways reminiscent of what had been Hegel's position – takes a strong position in favor of the *given* historical reality of society, a reality that is not easy to change at whim (Melossi 1990: 52–7).

What does Durkheim mean by a "social fact"? In order to answer this question, Durkheim in turn asks, how do we recognize a social fact when we see one? The two characteristics that, according to him, allow us to recognize a social fact are its "exteriority" to our consciousness and its "constraint" or coercive power (Durkheim 1895a: 50–9). By its being "external" to individuals, Durkheim means that a social fact is somehow independent of individuals; we are "thrown" into it, as existentialist philosophers might later have said. Paradigmatic examples are language and the structure of parental relationships. At the same time, it is also true, as was made clear later on, that by introducing ourselves into pre-existent social structures, we also perform the job, so to speak, of reproducing them (Giddens 1976). They would not exist without our – however small – contribution. Again, a good example is derived from language. Whereas it would take a rather arrogant attitude to say that we reproduce, by speaking it, a large living language, such as English, or Spanish, or Chinese, it is at the same time true that when, in some remote corner of the Caucasus, the hundred-year-old man who is the last speaker of a certain language or "dialect" is about to die, ethnolinguists from all over the world flock to him to record his speech and "preserve" a language that would otherwise die with him. This makes us understand that, even in the case of Chinese, or English, we, with our everyday minute action of speaking it, writing it, reading it, contribute to reproducing it and, to a very limited extent, to imperceptibly changing it.[4]

The "coercive power" of social facts means, at the same time, that these structures impose on us and, if we try to skirt their existence – as it were – we are "sanctioned" (not necessarily by a "legal" sanction, more often by a "social" sanction, such as isolation, ridicule, the impossibility of performing certain tasks together with other members of society). "The first and most basic rule," Durkheim adds, "is *to consider social facts as things*" (Durkheim 1895a: 60). It is a sort of "social realism" that he recommends, in which social facts have the same social reality as, in physical reality, Dr Johnson's proverbial stone. Dr Johnson's biographer, James Boswell (*Life of Johnson*, August 6, 1763), recounts how he and Dr Johnson "stood talking for some time together of Bishop Berkeley's ingenious sophistry to prove the non-existence of matter . . . I shall never forget," Boswell goes on, "the alacrity with which Johnson answered, striking his foot with mighty force against a large stone, till he rebounded from it – 'I refute it thus'." The pain that Dr Johnson must undoubtedly have felt in his foot may well be taken to represent the "sanction" of which Durkheim is writing, reserved to those who may try and ignore reality; the only difference being that, whereas Dr Johnson was trying to disprove George Berkeley's denial of physical reality, the sanction he is experiencing is indeed physical. The sanction instead for those trying to ignore social reality (the universe of social facts) is social.

One such social fact is deviance. In his discussion of suicide, Durkheim had moved from the observation of the rather paradoxical fact that a decision that indeed should be one of the most personal and idiosyncratic, such as the decision to take one's own life, in fact shows an exceptional statistical stability (as do many other such demographic and social kinds of data). Year after year, within a given jurisdiction, the number of suicides tends to oscillate around what we could call a mean value. It is as if a structural process of production of suicides were at work in society, churning out every year substantially the same number of people taking their own lives. We could think of it in the form of a "lottery," which selects every year more or less the same number of designated victims. Something not very different happens with the main criminal phenomena (so much so that, when sociologists see rates of crime change decisively, as in the 1990s, they look for changes in the "social structure" that produces them!). When, therefore, in Chapter III of *The Rules*, Durkheim moves on to discussing what it takes to decide whether a social fact is "normal" or "pathological," and rather provocatively chooses to discuss the social fact of "crime" in this regard, the stability of criminal statistics year after year seems to be the first observation that brings him to conclude that indeed crime seems to be "normal," at least in the sense of a "statistical normality."

This, however, is certainly not enough for Durkheim. Something else is needed, in order to decide that crime is indeed a "normal" and not a "pathological" social fact, and this something else is a sense of its "function" in society. Crime must somehow be "useful" to society. Now, in order to understand Durkheim's reasoning – which is as disconcerting to us as indeed it turned out to be to his contemporaries[5] – we should move a step back and return to that section in *The Division of Labor in Society* where Durkheim had presented his ideas about "mechanical solidarity" and had indicated in "repressive," i.e. penal, sanctions the legal indicator of a "mechanical" state of solidarity. However, given the great variability, from society to society, of the behaviors that are labeled as criminal, how can we come to some kind of general and not merely formal definition of what is a crime? We can only observe that, in each society, "an act is criminal when it offends the strong, well-defined states of the collective consciousness" (Durkheim 1893: 39); and, again, even more incisively, "crime offends very general sentiments, but ones that are strongly held" (Durkheim 1893: 39–40). Such "strongly held states of the collective consciousness" are shared by the generality of society's members and protect few and strongly held "goods." They are therefore characteristic of a society that is not much differentiated, with a "mechanical" or uniform solidarity. A higher level of development will instead be characterized, as we have seen, by "organic" solidarity, indicated by the presence of "restitutory" law. This does not mean, however, that in a developed society criminal sanctions will disappear, but simply that they will become less and less important – in the general "economy" of law – *vis-à-vis* restitutory rules. It is worthwhile paying attention now to a passage with which Durkheim brings to a conclusion this second chapter of *The Division of Labour* as well as his argument about crime and penality, a passage that will then allow us to go back to the more succinctly put argument in *The Rules*:

Although [punishment] proceeds from an entirely mechanical reaction and from an excess of passionate emotion, for the most part unthinking, it continues to play a useful role. But that role is not the one commonly perceived. It does not serve, or serves only very incidentally, to correct the guilty person or to scare off any possible imitators. From this dual viewpoint its effectiveness may rightly be questioned; in any case it is mediocre. Its real function is to maintain inviolate the cohesion of society by sustaining the common consciousness in all its vigour. If that consciousness were thwarted so categorically, it would necessarily lose some of its power, were an emotional reaction from the community not forthcoming to make good that loss. Thus there would result a relaxation in the bonds of social solidarity. The consciousness must therefore be conspicuously reinforced the moment it meets with opposition. The sole means of doing so is to give voice to the unanimous aversion that the crime continues to evoke, and this by an official act, which can only mean suffering inflicted upon the wrongdoer. Thus, although a necessary outcome of the causes that give rise to it, this suffering is not a gratuitous act of cruelty. It is a sign indicating that the sentiments of the collectivity are still unchanged, that the communion of minds sharing the same beliefs remains absolute, and in this way the injury that the

crime has inflicted upon society is made good. This is why it is right
to maintain that the criminal should suffer in proportion to his crime,
and why theories that deny to punishment any expiatory character
appear, in the minds of many, to subvert the social order. In fact such
theories could only be put into practice in a society from which
almost every trace of the common consciousness has been expunged.
Without this necessary act of satisfaction what is called the moral
consciousness could not be preserved. Thus, without being paradoxical, we may state that punishment is above all intended to have its
effect upon honest people. Since it serves to heal the wounds inflicted
upon the collective sentiments, it can only fulfil this role where such
sentiments exist, and in so far as they are active. (Durkheim 1893:
62–3)

In this passage – probably the most compelling defense of public
punishment ever written – there are many aspects that are indeed
worth emphasizing. First of all, in referring, albeit obliquely, to the
controversy that the Italian Positive School had brought to France
too – "why theories that deny to punishment any expiatory character appear, in the minds of many, to subvert the social order," theories that are therefore nothing less than "subversive" – Durkheim
takes a position not only on the debate between a "positive" and a
"classical" school, for the latter of which he clearly stands ("This is
why it is right to maintain that the criminal should suffer in proportion to his crime").[6] He takes a position, at the same time, and more
generally, that justifies punishment on the ground of its general
function of social control in society, much more than of its "preventive" effects, of which Durkheim shows himself to be clearly doubt-
ful. So much so – and this is probably his most remarkable assertion
– that "we may state that punishment is above all intended to have
its effect upon honest people."

Let us try to understand what is at stake here. In all ages, certainly at least in the modern age, there are two main ways of
thinking about the social function of and justification for that particular kind of public policy that is called "punishment." One,
which is usually offered in law schools and is commonly shared
by the public, sees punishment as directed toward the resocialization, rehabilitation, reintegration, re-education, etc., of the offender
and, at the same time, as Beccaria also maintained, toward the
deterrence of other possible wrongdoers from entertaining the idea
of doing the same. It is the point of view that we could call the
"expert's," the point of view of those working in the criminal
justice system, of concerned individuals, welfare workers, social

and political reformers, usually also of criminologists (but this is not really important). Durkheim is skeptical about the good grounding of such perspective: "From this dual viewpoint its effectiveness may rightly be questioned; in any case it is mediocre." There is, however, another perspective, and it is the perspective that we could call that of "social control," meaning by this, however, not the control of the wrongdoer – Durkheim does not care about the wrongdoer, or shares the skepticism of the hardened "cop" that much could be done with him (usually a "him") – but the control that actually matters from the "general" perspective of society, i.e. the control of "honest people," of the hard-working people upon whom, after all, the whole social order is based. The spectacle of crime and punishment – for which the criminal-offender-convict is recruited – is mainly for them; they are the intended audience of the whole show, the "honest people." The representation of the mystery play where the judge and the criminal, good and evil, face each other is really what matters, to the point that, after all, we could even simply hire actors to play the role of suffering convicts, and the end result would be reached nonetheless. Certainly, it would be difficult to guard the secret of their being actors, and real criminals are more spontaneous and believable. They also come cheaper. After all, in our society, much more than in Durkheim's, such fictional representation already happens, given that we are subjected daily to a barrage of stories about crime and punishment, some described as "news," but much more often offered as "fiction," in TV, newspapers, films, books. However, the fact that we know that actually somewhere this whole representation is not a fiction, that somewhere it is *really* happening, is what gives substance to the show, and to our identification – an identification that, as psychologists have explained to us, is both with the "criminal" and with the "executioner" (the criminological literature inspired by Freud's teaching often makes such a point; Alexander and Staub 1931).

It is this overall position that, once more, Durkheim expresses in his discussion about the "normality" of crime in the third chapter of *The Rules* (1895a: 85–107). He takes his paradox further. Let us suppose, he says, that a given society may be successful in banning all kinds of criminal behavior: will crime then disappear from the public discourse and policy of that society? After all, if the end of the existence of something we define as "crime" in society were only that of stamping out socially undesirable behavior, once that end has been reached, we could do without a criminal law and a definition of "crime." However, this is not what would happen – Durkheim maintains – because new penal norms would be created, having as their object forms of behavior that were not previously criminalized or that were only infractions of moral rules or of rules of etiquette. The "normality" of "crime" is to be found therefore in society's need of always having at its disposal an "area" of legally sanctioned evil that allows the rest of society, the "honest people," to experience group identification and social cohesion *a contrario*, because, if nothing else, they will at least share "the unanimous aversion that crime continues to evoke." The very existence of a category of "crime," in other words, is much more essential to society than the filling of that category with specific objects (and people).

In the 1960s, sociologist Kai Erikson (1966) would derive a sociology of deviance from Durkheim's position (mixed with contributions from the so-called "labeling approach"; see chapter 7 below). According to Erikson, public debate about notorious deviant or criminal cases is a way by which society questions itself and its own "moral boundaries" in periods of deep crisis or change. In his work *Wayward Puritans*, he referred to famous historical events in seventeenth-century Massachusetts, such as the Antinomians' trial, the Puritans' fight against the Quakers, and, most famous of all, the case of Salem witches. However, Erikson's intuition could be easily transposed to more recent material such as the very example he gives in his "Introduction," namely the period of McCarthyism in the early 1950s, understood as a way to make clear to the American public that World War II alliances had changed, and that the Communist Soviet Union had gone from being a former ally to an enemy in the so-called "Cold War."

Such a work of repositioning boundaries is not simply a way to make deviant what, up to a point, had been a licit form of behavior. The same happens also in the opposite direction, when a social process of "normalization" unfolds in a society *vis-à-vis* events or behaviors that were formerly deemed socially or legally deviant. This is a case in which deviance becomes a sort of conduit for innovation, an anticipation of a morality of the future (Guyau 1887). The most obvious example is probably in the realm of political change. It happens quite often that personalities persecuted for their political or religious beliefs, once the political situation has changed, may become leaders in the very societies where they were previously condemned. A president of the Italian Republic from 1978 to 1985, Sandro Pertini, had spent many years in prison under the Fascist regime between the two wars. And Nelson Mandela, when, on May 10, 1994, he became president of the Republic of South Africa, stated, "We, who until a short time ago, were considered outlaws, have today the rare privilege of welcoming the world's nations to our land."[7] Durkheim believed that deviance is something variable in time and space, according to processes of social change and innovation that concern the very social structures, and by so doing he anticipated much that would become central to so-called "labeling theory" almost a century later.

## Durkheim's Concept of State and Democracy

In a less known book, reporting his 1898–1900 lectures at the University of Bordeaux on professional ethics and civic morals – a sort of sociology of the law and the State – Durkheim applied his theory of increasing social differentiation, complexity, and rationalization to the themes of politics and the State (Durkheim 1898–1900). In a very "French" way, in this essay Durkheim considers the State as the great "rationalizer" of collective consciousness. In a democratic regime, an aspect of the more general process of shifting from a mechanical to an organic type of solidarity unfolds, a process where the communication between rulers and the ruled increases and the State has therefore the chance of making such a connection more "rational." Durkheim counters the commonplace according to which an absolutist State would be a stronger State. The opposite is true, because while absolutism may be strong against the single individual, who can be crushed by the State, an absolutist State is, however, quite powerless to direct social organization. Paradoxically, therefore, a democratic State is stronger and better able to produce social control than is an autocratic government.

Durkheim implicitly seems to go back to aspects of what his countryman Alexis de Tocqueville had written a few decades earlier in *Democracy in America* (1835, 1840; see below, chapter 4). De Tocqueville was critical of American democracy for what he called the "tyranny of the majority," i.e. those dangers of totalitarianism present within the very functioning of a democratic society. If the so-called principle of "free speech" had, on the one hand, been an indispensable tool in the struggle against the ancient regime, on the other it had become a very powerful instrument of social control. Freedom of speech means in fact only the freedom of those who have the effective power of expressing themselves and reaching the greatest number of citizens.

Durkheim is against an idea of democracy as simply the expression of the will of the majority. Neither is his theory of the State akin to Hegel's "ethical" one. We could call it rather a "rationalist" theory:

> The State, we said, is the organ of social thought. That does not mean that all social thought springs from the State. But there are two kinds. One comes from the collective mass of society and is diffused throughout that mass; it is made up of those sentiments, ideals, beliefs that the society has worked out collectively and with time, and that are strewn in the consciousness of each one. The other is worked out in the special organ called the State or government . . . Deliberation and reflection . . . are features of all that goes on in the organ of government . . . Within every one of us, then, there is at all times a host of ideas, tendencies and habits that act upon us without our knowing exactly how or wherefore. To us they are hardly perceptible and we are unable to make out their differences properly. They lie in the subconscious. They do however affect our conduct and there are even individuals who are moved solely by these motives. But in the part of us that is reflective there is something more. The ego that it is, the conscious personality that it represents, does not allow itself to follow in the wake of all the obscure currents that may form in the depth of our being . . . [B]y the gradual flow of ideas the State has little by little lost this kind of transcendence that isolated it within itself. It drew nearer to men and men came to meet it. Communication became closer . . . By these signs we recognize one of the distinctive features of what is usually called democracy.

We must therefore not say that democracy is the political form of a society governing itself, in which the government is spread throughout the *milieu* of the nation. Such a definition is a contradiction in terms. It would be almost as if we said that democracy is a political society without a State.[8] In fact, the State is nothing if it is not an organ distinct from the rest of society. If the State is everywhere, it is nowhere. The State comes into existence by a process of concentration that detaches a certain group of individuals from the collective mass. In that group the social thought is subjected to elaboration of a special kind and reaches a very high degree of clarity . . . This is what gives democracy a moral superiority. Because it is a system based on reflection, it allows the citizen to accept the laws of the country with more intelligence and thus less passively. Because there

is a constant flow of communication between themselves and the
State, the State is for individuals no longer like an exterior force that
imparts a wholly mechanical impetus to them . . . The role of the
State, in fact, is not to express and sum up the unreflective thought
of the mass of the people but to superimpose on this unreflective
thought a more considered thought, which therefore cannot be other
than different. (Durkheim 1898–1900: 79–92)

In other words, Durkheim seems to acknowledge democracy's
primacy not so much in the sense of its greater capability for people's "representation" as insofar as it confers on the State a much
broader possibility of effective government, because it allows an
intensification of communication between the elites and the masses.
It therefore favors the exchange of ideas and an increase in rationalization – in a way not dissimilar from what Max Weber would
also claim. Furthermore, those conflicts that in the past had been
tackled through coercive and military means will now be governed
through a conflict that takes place in the sphere of public opinion,
and that can be solved peacefully by steering the public through
the use of rational means – where "rational means" does not mean
mere "philosophical" tools but the concrete, technical tools of a free
press, and later on the audiovisual apparatuses. Political elites have
of course to cede something in exchange, that is, they have to yield
to citizens' demand for the right to associate and express themselves
freely. So if the classical theory of democracy considers these freedoms as part of the inevitable progress of the human spirit,
Durkheim instead emphasizes their importance to the end of a
much greater potential for political and economic mobilization in a
democratic social formation.

## Two Laws of Penal Evolution

Almost at the same time as he wrote about democracy and the State,
Durkheim (1900) published an article about "penal evolution,"
where he tried to clarify the connection between his theory of punishment and his more general view of the division of labor in
society. In this article, Durkheim distinguished between a "law of
*quantitative* [penal] variation" and a "law of *qualitative* [penal] variation." The latter consists in the fact that punishments depriving the
offender of his freedom (the prison) had historically become the
"normal" type of penal repression – a trend that, at the time,

Durkheim could judge as one toward an increasing civilization in punishment. He saw such a law of qualitative variation as nothing but a specification of the former law, that of quantitative variation, according to which a historical nexus would exist between a greater intensity of punishment and a lesser level of social evolution (which we have seen was a position already advanced in *The Division of Labor in Society*).

In fact, Durkheim finds an explanation for such a nexus in his more general theory of social evolution, according to which, moving from a "mechanical" type of social solidarity toward the more evolved and sophisticated "organic" social solidarity, a "repressive" type of law would increasingly yield to a "restitutory" type of law, because the sensitivity of collective consciousness moves at the same time from protecting a few strongly held, almost sacral goods toward the protection of individual rights. To such an overall movement, in the criminal law there corresponds a "softening" transformation that implies the general adoption of detentive punishment[9] and that Norbert Elias (1939) would have similarly seen as belonging in a more general progress toward "civilization." There is, however, an exception to this process, according to Durkheim: the absolutist political regimes of the seventeenth and eighteenth centuries, which represented a fall back toward an almost "sacral" concept of criminal law, with the proliferation of "lese majesty" cases and the accompanying increase in severe and atrocious punishments.[10] According to Durkheim, the absolutist regimes' repressive harshness may be considered efficacious against the single individual, who can be, literally, crushed. It is not, however, a very sophisticated tool of government. On the contrary, the "leniency" of punishments – as Beccaria had memorably said[11] – and the much greater communicating capability of the democratic State are able to put in place a much greater level of "social control," because they *direct* individuals instead of *stopping* them.[12]

Taking together Durkheim's writings of 1898–1900 – a true sociology of the State, law, and punishment – we come to the conclusion that, according to Durkheim, within the backdrop of an increasingly differentiated, rational, and civilized society, penality knows two "progressive" modifications. On the one hand, the area of penality contracts *vis-à-vis* the amplification instead of "restitutory" law; on the other hand, penality is transformed in the direction of norms of rationality, humanity, and civility. According to Durkheim, the generalization of a detentive kind of punishment – the prison – with its emphasis on a "spiritual," instead of a "corporal," type of punishment, belongs in full to such an overall transformation. And, indeed, that was the general picture that an observer would have drawn at the time of what was happening in the field of punishments. Together with the general betterment of labor's conditions of life and work, the living conditions within the institutions that had become the central punitive institutions, prisons, also showed some indication of improvement, while the ranks of those who saw them as their "natural" destination would slowly diminish, between the last two decades of the nineteenth century and the first of the twentieth (Rusche and Kirchheimer 1939: 138–65; Sutherland 1934; Christie 1968).

# Part II

## *Democracy, Social Control, and Deviance in America*

# 4

# *Social Control and Deviance in the New Republic*

## A Prologue: "America"

The "cultural object" called "America," America-as-a-state-of-mind, was born as a sort of Utopia of Europe. What often goes unnoticed when one reads expressions such as "the new world" or "New England" is that they refer not only to the "discovery" – from the Europeans' standpoint – of "new" lands. They also refer to, and wish to emphasize, the fact that, in the new land, the pilgrims, pioneers, or colonists wished to build a *renewed* version of the societies they had just left. Like all migrants, they lived in a love-hate relationship with those societies. In spite of the "natural" attraction one is bound to have for the land where he or she was born and grew up, those were also societies migrants often escaped from, persecuted for political or religious motives (often the same thing in those times). Even those who would not qualify today as tried and true "political refugees," however, would often leave behind what they saw as the usurpation of their rights, intolerance, rebellion against suffocating constraints (which at times had led them to crime), and poverty. The society they were going toward, that they wished to build, was a society where all of this would no longer happen, where "life, liberty, and the pursuit of happiness"[1] would be granted to everyone, just for being a human creature.

Sigmund Freud's student and follower Paul Federn had an inspired intuition in the revolutionary period after World War I. He in fact condemned the Communist revolutions that were being attempted in Europe at the time, because they were giving birth to *Vaterlose Gesellschaften*, "fatherless societies," societies that denied the authority principle embodied in the father figure, a principle strongly revered by Freudians. Federn's intuition was to compare those societies to what was being built in the "new world," a world of sons who were deserting their fathers, unable therefore to build a real civilization. In 1930, Freud[2] would write that,

> [T]he danger [lies in] a state of things which might be termed "the psychological poverty of groups." This danger is most threatening where the bonds of society are chiefly constituted by the identification of its members with one another, while individuals of the leader type do not acquire the importance that should fall to them in the formation of a group. The present cultural state of America would give us a good opportunity for studying the damage to civilization which is thus to be feared. (Freud 1930: 115–16)

In other words, the situation of a land of immigrants who had left their "fathers" behind and who hoped to find a "brotherhood" in the New World, in the same way in which they were trying to find it in post-revolutionary societies (Federn 1919: 598), was a situation of "psychological poverty" that posed a threat to "civilization." Undoubtedly, for Freud this situation constituted a danger threatening the father–son "social bond," running through the whole hierarchy of social "groups," from the family to the State. In the introductory pages of his "The Freudian Thing," Jacques Lacan would retell an interesting episode of Freud's relation to the United States:

> Thus Freud's words to Jung – I have it from Jung's own mouth – when, on an invitation from Clark University, they arrived in New York harbor and caught their first glimpse of the famous statue illuminating the universe, "They don't realize we're bringing them the plague," are attributed to him as confirmation of a hubris whose antiphrasis and gloom do not extinguish their troubled brightness. To catch their author in its trap, Nemesis had only to take him at his word. We would be justified in fearing that Nemesis had added a first-class return ticket. (Lacan 1956: 116)

This would be a lasting European view of America (Gerbi 1955), a view that was received, paradoxically, by much later American sociology and criminology. I believe that this view can be contrasted with the opposite one by European authors such as Kelsen, appreciative instead of an idea of democracy as a "fatherless society," and Gramsci (Melossi 1990: 86–91). Indeed, that comparison between the building of Communism and the building of a "new world" may have more than a literary value (except of course for the ultra-authoritarian fate, unknown to Federn, of those post-Bolshevik societies). Emigration was often the outcome of the revolutionary agitations that were intermittently shaking the "old continent." The very persecution of radical Protestantism was often mingled with persecution for social and political reasons, given that some of the Protestant sects often followed principles of radical egalitarianism. The radicalism of the positions that had surfaced during the peasants' revolt in sixteenth-century Germany – as in the teachings of Thomas Müntzer (Engels 1850) – would again reappear in milder form in the most radical North American sects (like the Quakers) as well as in Europe, within that completely laicized Protestant radical movement, Communism. In the course of the seventeenth, eighteenth, nineteenth, and even twentieth centuries, at every new convulsion or agitation, sectors of European society tried to free themselves of what Italian Marxist Antonio Gramsci[3] called "the thousand parasitical remnants of Europe's civilization" – a freedom that could often be reached only by leaving Europe.

Therefore, something bizarre would follow from all this: that this new society built in North America – a genuine workers' society, built by craftspeople, peasants, daily workers, a society that, for the first time in world history, claimed to be run by people who earned their living – this society gave birth to the biggest capitalist concentration ever seen by the human eye. On the one hand this, after all, should not be so surprising, because capital is nothing else than the other face of labor. The overall result, however, was the creation of an extremely dynamic social model, able to expand to ever new markets, and exercise hegemony over wider and wider expanses of land, so that the descendants of those who had been expelled from the lands of Europe as miserable *cafoni* were later able to go back as masters of the world and to have Gramsci's "parasites" – the descendants of their parents' masters – toe the line. Indeed they represented a true incarnation of that

> [c]onstant revolutionizing of production, uninterrupted disturbance of all social conditions, everlasting uncertainty and agitation [that

distinguishes] the bourgeois epoch from all earlier ones. All fixed,
fast-frozen relations, with their train of ancient and venerable preju-
dices and opinions, are swept away, all new-formed ones become
antiquated before they can ossify. All that is solid melts into air,[4] all
that is holy is profaned, and man is at last compelled to face with
sober senses, his real conditions of life, and his relations with his
kind. (Marx and Engels 1848: 83)

It has been in fact the chilly wind of a working-class attitude – meant
as an orientation toward a fully instrumental kind of rationality –
which would literally raze to their foundations and reconstruct
those countries, cities, and rural landscapes that those migrants, no
longer peasants and not yet factory workers, had once sadly left
behind.[5]

## Protestantism, Republic, Social Control

One of the fundamental elements that is useful in order to comprehend American society even today is the central role played by
radical Protestantism, as this was brought to the American shores
by the early colonists in the seventeenth century. New England
Protestants saw themselves as heirs to English common law and
held a vision of natural law deeply rooted in history. The conception
that natural rights are the rights of the British subject and that they
had been developing historically, by accretion and from below, as
it were, was an alternative to the idea of natural law on the European Continent, which saw it as a rational construction from above,
destined to shed light on the obscurity and confusion of historical
development (Ullmann 1961).

Another important aspect of Protestant tradition as this was
brought to America was the emphasis laid by Protestant sects
(Weber 1906) on the idea of community, without much distinction
– a distinction that had been and would be crucial to Catholicism
and also, to a certain extent, to the Church of England – between a
separate priesthood and the community of believers (with some
sects, like the Quakers, denying any role to a separate concept of
priesthood).[6] The social basis of such a cultural orientation (Moore
1966) was what de Tocqueville had called "the general equality of
condition among the people" (de Tocqueville 1835: 3), given the
wide expanse of land available (i.e. taken from the natives), the lack,
at least at the beginning, of a rural gentry, and the extension of small

peasant property (with the exception of course of two of the "three races that inhabit the United States" (de Tocqueville 1835: 331–434), namely those who already inhabited North America before the arrival of the colonists, and those who were deported there by force, the slaves from Africa).

We may find a sort of litmus test of the above in the discussion of penality. Soon after the Declaration of Independence of the United States, in 1787 the "Philadelphia Society for Alleviating the Miseries of Public Prisons" was created in that city, so that "such degrees and modes of punishment may be discovered and suggested, as may, instead of continuing habits of vice, become the means of restoring our fellow creatures to virtue and happiness" (Barnes 1930: 127). It was under the leadership of the Society that, in the garden of the old Walnut Street Jail, a cellular prison was created, the main organizing principle of which was to be solitary confinement (Takagi 1975; Sellin 1953). The new institution reflected not only Beccaria's new doctrine, well known to the former colonists (Beirne 1993: 13), but also other famous European institutions and projects belonging in the new atmosphere of the Enlightenment, like Ghent's Maison de Force, in Belgium, completely rebuilt in 1775, and Jeremy Bentham's Panopticon (1787; see above, chapter 1).

At the same time, it also reflected endogenous roots, which had been developed in the colony, nourished by the new religious doctrines, among which the Quaker doctrine had played a crucial role. Pennsylvania, the Quaker colony and, after Independence, a Quaker state, had been created in 1681 through a grant of the British Crown to the Quaker leader William Penn, who decided to try, in the new, vast territory under his rule, what he called the "holy experiment," an enlightened State *ante litteram* where "friendly persuasion" had to prevail over instruments of coercion and repression (Dumm 1987: 65–86). This was to be particularly important in the criminal and penal realms, because Penn's reform preceded by almost a century some of the most important among Beccaria's formulations, such as the calls for abolition of torture and of the death penalty. A particularly important role was to be played by imprisonment, inspired by correctional and reintegrative ends, once again a century earlier than the Enlightenment and American independence. Penn established that, "all Prisons shall be workhouses for felons, Thiefs, vagrants, and Loose, abusive, and Idle persons, whereof one shall be in every county" (Dumm 1987: 79) – making reference to the relatively recent experience of English and especially Dutch workhouses (see above, chapter 1). Penn's "holy experiment" did not survive him. After his death in 1718, the British Crown imposed its law again, a law that Quakers judged barbaric and old-fashioned. It was only natural therefore that as soon as independence was achieved, Pennsylvania would go back to Penn's doctrine, a doctrine that constituted therefore the nexus between the new "penitentiary" institution created after independence and the old form of seventeenth-century *workhouses, bridewells*, and *rasphuis* (see above, chapter 1), tried and true ancestors of the modern penitentiary, especially in the idea of centering correction on the value and practice of work (McKelvey 1977: 1–5; Barnes 1930: 104–11).

How was it, however, that Quakers were so sensitive to a view of punishment that, within Protestantism, distanced them, for instance, from the harshness of Calvinism? According to David Cayley, we can find an answer to this question in the reconstruction by English theologian Timothy Gorringe, according to whom "the Christian doctrine of atonement" would have had a "formative influence on Western thinking about punishment" (Cayley 1998: 295). However, according to Gorringe, this would have inspired two different traditions. In one, God himself would have required the sacrifice/punishment of his son for the sins/crimes of the world, so that Christ would have been executed, as a man, through the Roman crucifixion (a common instrument of capital punishment at the time) for the crime of heresy and, as the Son of God, for the sins of the world. According to the other tradition, instead, first put forward by Abelard in a polemic against Anselm of Canterbury, "redemption is not achieved by a token traded against God's wrath but by the inspiring power of Christ's example" (Cayley 1998: 295). Gorringe traces this "exemplarist view of the atonement" from Abelard down to

> the Renaissance humanism of Erasmus and Soncinus, and . . . Anabaptists like Thomas Müntzer, who argue that "the remission of sins occurs without any punishment being exacted." It carries on in the seventeenth century in the inner light tradition of the Ranters, Diggers, and Quakers, and is powerfully present in the late eighteenth and early nineteenth centuries in the poetry and prophecy of William Blake. (Cayley 1998: 296)

Such a tradition would have fought against Luther's and Calvin's Protestant "orthodoxy" no less than against Catholicism, as the sixteenth-century "peasant wars" in Germany showed quite clearly. Herbert Marcuse, for instance, in an essay in which, in 1936, he had introduced the Frankfurt School's study on the authority and the family (Marcuse 1936), emphasized the authoritarianism of Luther's political theory:

> The condition of absolute isolation and atomization into which the individual is thrown after the dissolution of the medieval universe appears here, at the inception of the new bourgeois order, in the terribly truthful image of the isolation of the prisoner in his cell: "For God has fully ordained that the under-person shall be alone unto himself and has taken the sword from him and put him into prison. If he rebels against this and combines with others and breaks out and takes the sword, then before God he deserves condemnation and death."[7] (Marcuse 1936: 65)

As a matter of fact, the newly created institutions after American independence seemed to take more from Luther's words than from the Quaker theory of reconciliation, in spite of the fact that the Quakers had been their main proponents. The basic principle around which penitentiaries were organized was horizontal separation, the isolation of the criminal/sinner from his companions, and the establishment instead of vertical communication with the representatives of religious and temporal authority. The underlying idea was one shaped after monastic life, as the latter had developed in the medieval monasteries of Europe for a specialized caste of sinners (Treiber and Steinert 1980). According to the principles of the Protestant Reformation, however, the method had to be extended to all creatures. In the same way in which the Protestant believer could not find *indulgence* in a complacent Church (Weber 1904–5), so the North American inmate could not escape the rigors of punishment in the new institutions. Indeed the main penitentiary institutions contrived in the United States soon after independence, inspired by radical Protestant sectarianism (Weber 1906), seemed to be an attempt to realize the program exposed by Marx where he had written that Lutheranism had generalized priesthood to the whole of humanity (Marx 1844b: 182). The principle that inspired the "penitentiaries" was separation, i.e. the isolation of the sinner from his fellow creatures and his being allowed relations only with the representatives of divine and secular authority. The model was that of penance, now secularized and extended to all the members of God's flock. The main point was that the believer could not find solace in the intermediation of the Church, an intermediation that, for the rich, consisted in "buying" their way to salvation. Such a commerce had of course been one of the very bases for the accusations directed against the corrupt, power-hungry, and fundamentally skeptical Church of Rome, whose "indulgences" were more a means of securing temporal power than true compassion for the weakness of the flesh. The Philadelphia inmate had no resort other than gazing at the depth of his fall in the solitary confinement of his cell. No "pagan" delusion could save him from staring at the terrible spectacle of God's rage. No wonder that the new system soon appeared to be connected to an impressive rise in suicides – in an uncanny forewarning of a theory that the French sociologist Emile Durkheim would spell out, as we have seen, only at the end of the century (see above, chapter 3).

To the eye of the keen observer, however, it might seem incongruous that the American republic, praised then and later as the most direct vessel to ferry peoples and intellects from the Land of the Social Contract to that of Democracy, would at the same time be the place to harbor an institution – the prison – that, however enlightened its conception, is usually identified with pain, suffering, and oppression. This was probably a not irrelevant aspect of what Horkheimer and Adorno would later dub the "dialectic of enlightenment":

> Since de Tocqueville, the bourgeois republics have attacked man's soul, whereas the monarchies attacked his body; similarly the penalties inflicted in these republics also attack man's soul. The new martyrs do not die a slow death in the torture chamber but instead waste away spiritually as invisible victims in the great prison buildings which differ in little but name from madhouses. (Horkheimer and Adorno 1944: 228)[8]

In the few pages of "A Theory of Crime" in *Dialectic of Enlightenment*, from which this quote is taken, one can see *in nuce* the thesis that will fully unfold 30 years later in *Discipline and Punish* (Foucault 1975). In fact, it was quite a coincidence that Alexis de Tocqueville, the French aristocrat who had arrived in America in 1831 to write about penitentiaries with his colleague and friend Gustave de Beaumont, found himself not only deserting his original topic (Sellin 1964), but producing instead the book *Democracy in America* (de Tocqueville 1835, 1840), which is one of the most important and lasting contributions to the theory of democracy. Could it be that the two topics had so much in common? According to American political theorist Thomas Dumm, following in Foucault's footsteps, they did, because

> [T]he emergence of the penitentiary in the United States was a project constitutive of liberal democracy. That is, the penitentiary system formed the epistemological project of liberal democracy, creating conditions of knowledge of self and other that were to shape the political subject required for liberal and democratic values to be realized in practice. The American project, a system of self-rule, involved not only the establishment of representative government with an extensive suffrage, but also the establishment of institutions which would encourage the internalization of liberal democratic values, the creation of individuals who would learn how to rule their selves. (Dumm 1987: 6)

The crucial term here is – following Foucault – self-government, or the government of the self. On the one hand, de Tocqueville was fascinated by American democracy and yet at the same time he understood that the most terrible danger for liberty was to be found in the very functioning of democracy, what he called the "tyranny of the majority," the fact, that is, that exactly because a democratic society is a society based on the consent of the governed, the construction and homogenization of consent in one and only direction are much more important than in an authoritarian society. As Foucault would have shown in depth – and as Horkheimer and Adorno had sensed – an authoritarian regime is interested in the body of its subjects whereas a democratic one shows an interest in their "souls" (the Quakers' "friendly persuasion").

According to de Tocqueville, therefore, American society might have been characterized by a "weak state" (Hamilton and Sutton 1989) but the society itself, its degree of social cohesion, was much stronger than any authoritarian society because it was able to mobilize its citizens to a much higher degree. This happened, however, not through the traditional tools of government, such as coercion and fear, but through the construction of consent and friendly persuasion,[9] not so much through the negative springs of repression and censorship as through the positive suggestion of motives for action. De Tocqueville's pages on free speech are surprisingly modern in this respect, because they suggest how the principle of *free speech*, embodied in the freedom of the press, is much more crucial to social control than is censorship. According to de

Tocqueville, "democratic republics have applied despotism to the minds of men" (de Tocqueville 1835: 263–5). Through the formulation of speech, in fact, one may offer motives for action that are much more efficacious than the merely negative drive of censorship.

The making of the penitentiaries was part and parcel of this overall project. Indeed, as Foucault would have shown, it symbolized it very well. Benjamin Rush, the Quaker philanthropist and reformer, one of the leading intellectuals of the period, described the task of penitentiaries, as we have seen, as that of producing "Republican machines," human beings who, not yet civilized or having strayed from the path of civilization, should become good citizens and good workers, able to enter a conversation with their neighbors (the basic prerequisite of democracy). In a sense, we could state that the American penitentiary was erected by the Founding Fathers of the Nation as an imposing and monumental Gateway to the Republic. In his sharp essay reflecting on the origins of the United States and Mexico, and comparing them, Mexican writer Octavio Paz observed:

> If the different attitudes of Hispanic Catholicism and English Protestantism could be summed up in two words, I would say that the Spanish attitude is inclusive and the English exclusive. In the former, the notions of conquest and domination are bound up with ideas of conversion and assimilation; in the latter, conquest and domination imply not the conversion of the conquered but their segregation. An inclusive society, founded on the double principle of domination and conversion, is bound to be hierarchical, centralist, and respectful of the individual characteristics of each group. It believes in the strict division of classes and groups, each one governed by special laws and statutes, but all embracing the same faith and obeying the same lord. An exclusive society is bound to cut itself off from the natives, either by physical exclusion or by extermination; at the same time, since each community of pure-minded men is isolated from other communities, it tends to treat its members as equals and to assure the autonomy and freedom of each group of believers. The origins of American democracy are religious, and in the early communities of New England that dual, contradictory tension between freedom and equality that has been the leitmotiv of the history of the United States was already present. (Paz 1979: 363–4)

In other words, a major prerequisite of the republican social contract is the identity of the parties to the contract, their basic commonality of civilization. They were in fact to be part of a rational discourse. They could not simply be *peones* at the bottom of the social pyramid, as could happen in the Catholic, authoritarian structure of the Spanish Conquest. The colonists of North America were too ambitious about the greatness and the goodness of the institutions they were building – a *new* England! – to allow uncivilized men and women to become part of it simply as labor power. Their *souls* had to be conquered. That is, they had to enter into a conversation with the other members of the American covenant. After all, had not Cesare Beccaria himself proclaimed that, to the end of preventing crime, the best policy would have been, as we have seen, to "see to it that enlightenment and freedom go hand in hand" (Beccaria 1764: 103–5)?

The natural consequence of such lofty ambitions therefore – as Paz observes with chilling logic – was the extermination of those whose souls (if indeed they had been endowed with one) could not be reached, such as the native inhabitants of North America; those who, in other words, were perceived as unable, or unwilling, to enter into an enlightened, republican, democratic dialogue (Fitzpatrick 1995). Paradoxically, therefore, the "democratic" – or better, to use the language of that period, republican – element implicit in the American compact became a reason for the isolation, marginalization, and eventual destruction of those populations that could not become part to the compact. In contrast, the authoritarianism of the Spanish conquest – an authoritarianism that was not only religious but also political – made sure that the natives were "integrated," in a semi-servile state, at the bottom of the social pyramid.[10]

For those lucky ones who, in spite of their being uncivilized or having lost their civilization (as in the case of the criminal colonists), were still similar enough to the members of the religious covenant to be accepted at least as potential members, then it was necessary to arrange those instruments that would lead them to become part of the republic. Of the two "races which inhabit the territory of the United States," whose destiny deeply moved de Tocqueville in *Democracy in America* (1835: 393–456), one, the Native American, was too *different* to be conducted through such narrow passage. The second, "the colored," once free, would have been instead generously exposed to the philanthropy of the new penitentiary institutions. For a long time, the "two races" were treated in an exclusionary mode, for Native Americans to the extent of genocide. "Indians," considered as foreign nationals (Fitzpatrick

1995), were continuously pushed West, until their land was almost completely taken over by white colonists (Takaki 1979: 80–107). As Ronald Takaki notices, citing de Tocqueville, what particularly amazed the French nobleman was "the ability of white society to deprive the Indians of their rights and exterminate them 'with singular felicity, tranquilly, legally, philanthropically . . . It is impossible to destroy men with more respect for the laws of humanity'" (Takaki 1979: 81 citing de Tocqueville 1835: 352–3, 364). There was no place, at the time, for Native Americans in the white men's penitentiaries, exactly because, as argued above, the penitentiary was deeply connected to an *inclusionist* ideology. It was intended to be the entrance into a social contract that one had voluntarily or involuntarily ignored but for which one was deemed to be at least potentially fit.

Often, an original policy of exclusion turned eventually into a policy of inclusion (through the gates of the prison). At the dawn of the Republic, however, the same exclusionist policies applied generally to all the "black or tawny" races, a label that Benjamin Franklin (1751), for instance, applied to practically all non-English settlers (in fact the occasion of this essay by Franklin was his preoccupation with the increasing numbers of Germans in Pennsylvania; Takaki 1979: 14; Cohn-Bendit and Schmid 1992: 96). In 1850, though, blacks were still largely concentrated in the South as slaves. Their special status meant that they could not be admitted to the honors of the penitentiary, their discipline "of choice" being domestic (Sellin 1976: 133–44). In fact black incarceration rates in the South in 1850 were less than half those of whites. The opposite was true in the North, where, despite the small number of black men and women, their "free" condition had already opened them the gates of penitentiaries (Sabol 1989: 408–9), starting that situation of a very high disproportion between African American minority and white majority that would remain a constant in North American prisons. De Beaumont and de Tocqueville had already noticed in their report on the penitentiary system that:

> A young society, exempt from political embarrassments, rich both by its soil and its industry, should be supposed to furnish fewer criminals than a country where the ground is disputed foot by foot, and where the cries produced by political divisions tend to increase the number of offenses, because they increase misery by disturbing industry.

Yet if the statistical documents, which we possess of Pennsylvania, should be applied to the rest of the Union, there are in this country more crimes committed than in France, in proportion to the population. Various causes of another nature explain this result: on the one hand, the colored population, which forms the sixth part of the inhabitants of the United States, and which composes half of the inmates of the prisons; and on the other hand, the foreigners pouring in every year from Europe, and who form the fifth and sometimes even the fourth part of the number of convicts. (De Beaumont and de Tocqueville 1833: 99)

In the North, therefore, the freed colored population and the immigrants had to go through the gateway to the republic – prisons. This would start happening also in the South, after the civil war, when many of the "freed" blacks would again be reduced to servitude, this time penal servitude, through the convict lease system that flourished in the Southern states after the civil war, the clients of which were largely blacks (Sellin 1976: 409). By 1870 in the South, the black incarceration rate was triple that of whites and almost 15 times what it had been 20 years before, before the civil war and the blacks' "liberation" (Sabol 1989: 408). However, the disproportionality rate in the South remained lower than in the North (Sabol 1989: 409) because in the North it accompanied the process of the migration of blacks from the rural South to Northern cities such as Chicago.

In the Protestant New England mold of American culture – a mold that still has a firm grip on the essentials of American culture – there is no place for the fuzzy, authoritarian, and deeply conservative indulgence of Catholicism. Right or wrong, white or black, whoever is (or is perceived to be) on the wrong side of the law shall be punished. But, alas, like with everything else in society, whoever breaks the law and is powerful (economically, politically, ethnically, racially, culturally, by virtue of sex, and so on and so forth) can afford a full use of the "safeguards" that a developed legal system provides. For the others, tough luck. All in all, this policy, however weak on the side of social justice, is "useful," because an economic system based on competition cannot work without punishments and rewards. Whoever is at the bottom of the social pyramid is perceived as being tempted to break the law more often: less to lose and more to gain. Isn't it therefore only fair that the law pay more attention to their behavior? As, once again, de Beaumont and de Tocqueville went on,

> If we should deduct from the total number of crimes, those commit-
> ted by Negroes and foreigners, we should undoubtedly find that
> the white American population commits less crimes than ours. But
> proceeding thus, we should fall into another error; in fact, to separate
> the Negroes from the whole population of the United States, would
> be equal to deducting the poorer classes of the community with us
> [in France], that is to say, *those who commit the crimes*. (de Beaumont
> and de Tocqueville 1833: 99, my emphasis)

# 5

## Social Control and Deviance in Chicago

The question of social control – so defined – emerged for the first time within North American society at the beginning of the twentieth century. It was an idea that carried a great affinity for the concept of "democracy," because it had to do with a vision of social order based on the participation of a great number of people, and the construction of a "consensus" among those (Melossi 1990).

The fundamental outline of the social and political organization of North American society emerged after the civil war and especially between the 1880s and World War I. This was the period when the United States started a process of transition from an eminently rural country to becoming the most powerful industrial society in the world. Industrialization went together with urbanization and immigration, first from Northern European countries, such as Germany and Ireland, later on from Eastern and Southern Europe, and from Asia. After World War I and the stop to immigration in the 1920s, a massive flow of internal migration, from the Southern states toward the Midwest and the West, followed. This multifarious and complex process of social change placed a very heavy strain on a society that had grown during the nineteenth century as a rural society, based on small peasant property and without serious social problems (with the exception of the major Eastern seaboard cities).

In particular, the period between the beginning of the twentieth century and 1915 was dubbed "the Progressive Age" because it was characterized by a massive effort by the major social and political institutions to adapt to the new phenomena of industrialization, urbanization, and migration. In this period, labor and union conflicts became paramount because, in a situation in which the main political and legal institutions clung desperately to the old representation of American society as purely *laissez-faire*, class conflict was often bound to express itself through open confrontation, and often violent clashes.

## State and Social Control

Faced with a sometimes literally explosive reality, a strong temptation emerged – especially among the most conservative circles – to adopt a "European" solution to the ills of American society, by strengthening "the State," a concept, however, that was essentially foreign to American consciousness:

> American political science was, since its inception under the aegis of Francis Lieber at the University of Carolina and later at Columbia college, and until World War I, dominated by the German idea of the state – the state whose origin is in history, whose nature is organic, whose essence is unity, whose function is the exercise of its sovereign will in law, and whose ultimate end is the moral perfection of mankind. (Fries 1973: 391)

Outside the classrooms of the Departments of Political Science, however, German *Staatswissenschaft* never became very popular. It was too alien to an American tradition rooted in Lockean philosophy, common law, and democracy. It was wholly unable, furthermore, to give a conceptual answer to the American crises of the time. New conceptual paths had instead to be explored (Fries 1973; Wolin 1981: 51–2). Eventually, a young scholar, the political scientist and philosopher Arthur F. Bentley, offered a new vision, inspired by Pragmatism. In his first and very influential work, he emphatically rejected the concept of the State and the related concept of sovereignty, and adopted instead that of "government":

> The "state" itself is, to the best of my knowledge and belief, no factor in our investigation. It is like the "social whole": we are not interested in it as such, but exclusively in the processes within it. The "idea of the state" has been very prominent, no doubt, among the intellectual amusements of the past, and at particular places and times it has served to help give coherent and pretentious expression to some

particular group's activity. But in either case it is too minute a factor to deserve space in a work covering as broad a range as this. Nor need the state, as "the tyranny of the minority over the majority," concern us. We are not conducting a propaganda. . . . I may add here that "sovereignty" is of no more interest to us than the state. Sovereignty has its very important place in arguments in defense of an existing government, or in verbal assaults on a government in the name of the populace or of some other pretender, or in fine-spun legal expositions of what is about to be done. But as soon as it gets out of the pages of the lawbook or the political pamphlet, it is a piteous, threadbare joke. So long as there is plenty of firm earth under foot there is no advantage in trying to sail the clouds in a cartoonist's airship. (Bentley 1908: 263–4)

Political philosopher Alessandro Passerin d'Entrèves noted, about statements such as this one by Bentley, that "[t]he disruption of the notion of the State in modern political science is such a challenging and portentous event that it is surprising no detailed study should yet have been made to account for it and to explain it" (1967: 60). However, the movement away from European ideas became more and more obvious, as Americans began to develop a distaste for the role of the law and the State in social control, and to appreciate instead the importance of public opinion and social relationships in general. Certainly, legal reform was at the core of the Progressivists' "program." The use of the law was accompanied, however, by a keen awareness of the powerless character of a legal system not sustained by the life of the community – the sin that had characterized formalism. A sociological position within jurisprudence, from Oliver Wendell Holmes to Roscoe Pound, from John R. Commons to Luis Brandeis, pleaded for a rejection of formalism, or what Pound called "mechanical jurisprudence" (Pound 1908). These thinkers advocated instead the adoption of a living, processual concept of law, grounded in the actual social interests at stake. Therefore, a double and paradoxical movement took place. The legal tool no doubt acquired increased importance during the Progressive years. But this happened together with the disappearance of the traditional aura of legal form, no longer an expression either of the will of a State-God, as in Europe, or of the cumulative wisdom of common law, as in previous Anglo-American tradition. The law was now conceived as an instrument of social engineering (Pound 1922: 99, quoted in Geis 1964: 283), to be used in order to reach given policy goals. In order to realize this transformation, a sharp awareness of the *limits* of legal tools was necessary. The law could be efficacious only if it were an expression of a cohesive public whose opinion was solidly formed around the issues to be decided, and *acted upon*. Thus the "European" problem of decision was taken out of the realm of coercion and considered instead as the problem of shaping consensus.

Within the emerging discipline of sociology, Edward A. Ross was the first, in 1901, to introduce the term "social control" as a major organizing theme. Framed in the dominant social Darwinian scheme of the time, the term itself was derived from a rather casual usage in Herbert Spencer's *Principles of Sociology* within the treatment of what the British philosopher called "ceremonial institutions" (1879: 3–35). However, already in Ross's work, one can find some of the main themes that relate the birth of sociology in Europe in the nineteenth century to its future development in North America in the next century. Ross connects a critique of capitalism (McMahon 1999: 9), and of the traditional reliance on "the State" by ruling elites on both sides of the Atlantic, to a critique of economics and political science, the two prestigious and time-honored disciplines with which the new-born discipline of sociology had to contend. As Engels had argued some time earlier, when he referred to a "State" that ought to have been on its way out "into the museum of antiquities, next to the spinning wheel and the bronze axe" (1884: 232), so for Ross the antics of "Government" are "archaic" and belong in "the museum of history" (1901: 80; see also McMahon 1999: 37, 47, 51). At the same time, Ross established a connection between the basic nature of the social system (which he thought was constituted through either heterogeneity or homogeneity), and its shifting reliance on either "political" means, "operating through prejudice of fear," or "ethical" means, "mild, enlightening and suasive" (1901: 124–5). He held that the greater the degree of heterogeneity, the greater would be the reliance on "political" means (a line of reasoning that, as we have seen, can also be traced from de Tocqueville to Durkheim to Gramsci; Melossi 1990: 100–3).

Ross's idea of democracy typified a Midwestern, agrarian, nativist democracy (McMahon 1999: 107–35), as C. Wright Mills was famously to point out in one of his early essays (1943). Accordingly, the problem of the assimilation of new immigrants was paramount in Ross's interests, from the standpoint of a superior morality typical of the American, white, and Protestant Commonwealth and contemptuous of the poor manners of the newcomers, often non-Protestant, non-urbanized, and of "suspicious" "race"

(Southern Europeans, Jews, etc.). Ross's position represented therefore the American counterpart to an elitist position that had already been developing for a few decades in European social sciences, expressing fear and resentment of the unwelcome entrance of "the crowd" or "the masses" into the social and political life of European societies. As we have seen, this attitude had found voice in works such as Gustave Le Bon's *The Crowd* (1892) or Scipio Sighele's *La folla delinquente* (1891). The migrant "surplus" masses that crowded the European countryside and that moved to European cities, either to embark on the adventure of migration or to stay on as an "army reserve of labor" for domestic capitalism, were then doubly labeled as "uncivilized" and "dangerous," first by their own elites, then by the elites of the host countries, were these Argentina or the United States (Teti 1993; Salvatore and Aguirre 1996).

However, such a backward-looking attitude, if it was perhaps appropriate to the old-fashioned socio-economic class structures of Continental Europe (rapidly evolving toward their disastrous Fascist outcomes), became quickly unacceptable within the context of the fast-paced development of the United States in the Progressive Age. The elitist attitude certainly did not disappear, but its intentions and goals were to be transformed into a project of the inclusion and incorporation of emerging crowds within the main social covenant. The concept of "social control," the "great social secret" Ross had discovered (McMahon 1999: 31–56), became central to this still elitist but enlightened new project, at that crucial juncture in the development of American social science between the Chicago School of Sociology and Pragmatism – the only philosophical orientation genuinely "American." It was a concept of social control that was all-pervasive because it responded to the need of the new society to incorporate large masses of newcomers in its midst, on grounds of factual cooperation rather than through the traditional authoritarian instruments of politics and the law.

## Chicago: An Attitude of "Appreciation"

Outcasts from all over Europe, tired of being harassed by landowners, army and police officers, local bosses and their thugs, started heading en masse toward those ports of embarkation that would take them to the New World in search of good fortune. In Southern Italy, for instance, the descendants of Villella the brigand

and many others like him, after having dealt for many years with the arrogance of Northern army officers and local *massari* – the rural middle strata that would be connected with the emergence of *Mafia* – moved toward the ports of Naples and Palermo. Both the Southern rural masses and their enemies, the Southern gentry and the Northern elites, in a sense considered emigration as a "substitute" for brigandage and crime, a gesture of revolt against a situation that was perceived as not changeable (Teti 1993: 24–5; in fact, mass migration in 1890–1913 might have been a cause of decreasing imprisonment rates in Italy in the same period). The emigrants, the "Americans," as they were called, were seen as deviant, non-integrated, traitors to their customs and their land. "Escaping to America" was equivalent to "taking to the mountains" (the choice of becoming brigands). This imagery fuelled at the same time the contemporary panic about immigrant crime that was developing in those years on American shores, from the streets and alleys of New York to those of Buenos Aires (Salvatore and Aguirre 1996).

Southern Italians were of course not the only ones. With them, driven by similar circumstances, were Russian Jews and various Eastern European peoples, replacing the Irish and the Germans who had crowded Ellis Island's barracks earlier on. Chicago, even more than New York, was a big draw for these men and women, with its factories, its stockyard, its rail- and river-ways in a privileged position in the Midwest of America. Migrants were flocking by the tens of thousands to Chicago, the fastest-growing city in America in those years. And in Chicago it was therefore natural for the newly founded Department of Sociology, in the university newly founded in 1890 by oil magnate John D. Rockefeller, to find the central metaphor of the social process in the issue of migration, in the same way in which many Chicagoans found reasons for their own militancy and advocacy in migrants' causes (many of the sociologists and criminologists heretofore mentioned were themselves, in different ways, also outsiders, if not migrants or descendants of migrants). Jane Addams's Hull House – the leading experiment of the settlement movement in the United States – was a vital center of these interests, where the likes of John Dewey, George Herbert Mead, and William I. Thomas would congregate, discuss the events of the day, converse with the migrants, and generally understand "the social process" as this was taking place in Chicago (Addams 1910; Bulmer 1984; Deegan 1988; Lindner 1990; Knight 2005; Glowacki and Hendry 2004).[1]

Many volumes have been written about the experience of the Chicago School. The point that I would like to emphasize, however, is what David Matza would later call an attitude of *appreciation* by the Chicagoans toward the "deviant" worlds they were describing: the immigrants, the hoboes, the taxi-dancers, the prostitutes, the juvenile delinquents. Such an appreciation had its roots in a proximity of the sociologist to his object that in some cases simply came from a feeling of political and moral solidarity, in other circumstances from the researcher's having shared at least part of his subjects' experiences. This had been the case for the second-generation Thorsten Sellin, the criminologist, or Nels Anderson, the author of the landmark study *The Hobo* (1923), who had been a hobo himself, or William Isaac Thomas, the author of *The Polish Peasant* (Thomas and Znaniecki 1918–20) and *The Unadjusted Girl* (1923), who, in spite of his almost 20 years of teaching at Chicago, was thrown out of the university when surprised in adulterous relation with a much younger woman in a "Loop Hotel."[2] The connection between such a proximity and the particular methodology used by the Chicagoans, an ethnographic approach that involved the need for talking to, living with ("participant observation"), and getting to know the people they were writing about, seems self-evident enough.

The concepts of social order and social control that emerged from Chicago could only reflect such attitudes: social control was a matter of interaction in a world sharply divided along lines of language, culture, religion, class, ethnicity, an eminently *relative* and *plural* concept, where the official definitions of social control and therefore of deviance were in the worst case due to the brutal suppression of opposition and in the best case to that democratic process that "the Chicagoans" valued so highly. Never was social order, however, conceived as given or crystallized. On the contrary, Pragmatist thought, the overarching philosophical expression of the Chicago *Zeitgeist*, stressed the fluid becoming of social life, and ideas such as those of "the social experiment" and "the social laboratory," applied particularly to the Settlement movement and Hull House (Dewey 1931; Addams 1910).

## Robert Park: "The Public" and Social Control

Once the European tradition of social integration based on concepts of State and sovereignty was abruptly brushed aside, as we have seen, what was to be the foundation of social order? In the first page of their very influential *Introduction to the Science of Sociology*, a compendium of the new sociology of the University of Chicago, Robert E. Park and Ernest W. Burgess noted that sociology had emerged from the failure of political and legal controls. Without knowledge of regularities in human behavior, they stated, governments are completely powerless, unable to cope with an age of social movements and organizations (1921: 1). It was therefore up to social scientists, and especially sociologists, to frame the conceptual fabric of American society. Many of the themes that had been announced in Ross's pioneering contributions were to be developed in that budding school of sociology, at Chicago, particularly by Park, the man who would personify, intellectually and administratively, Chicago sociology.

As was common at the time, Park had done his doctoral studies in Germany, and more specifically in that sort of twin sister of Chicago, Berlin, where he had studied with the German philosophers Georg Simmel and Wilhelm Windelband (Georg Simmel's thought was particularly interesting to Chicago authors; according to Simmel's sociology, in fact, each individual belongs at the same time in many "social circles"; she finds herself at the intersection of these social circles, a situation that may give rise to many conflicts, inside the individual and between the individual and her environment; each of the social circles in which she belongs manages in fact to exercise a kind of social control on her that she has to contend with, finding herself often at the center of contrasting imperatives (Simmel 1908)). In his German dissertation, *Masse und Publikum* (*The Crowd and the Public*, 1904), Park tried to give an answer to the fervent debate that had been central to European social sciences about "mass psychology" (see previous chapters). Park had formerly been a journalist, and he was not afraid of the crowd. On the contrary, he conceived of the crowd not as a dangerous, dark, subversive force, but as something that could be domesticated, tamed, enlightened, by turning it into "public opinion." This had already been Durkheim's position in *Professional Ethics and Civic Morals* (1898–1900), as we have seen, but Durkheim had seen this project as the task of the State, "the organ of the social thought" (1898–1900: 49–51). For Park, it was instead the free intellectual enterprise of the elites that could fulfill that civilizing function.

It is no surprise then that Robert E. Park and Ernest W. Burgess proclaimed social control to be "the central problem of society"

(1921: 42). It is interesting that, at about the same time, Park was studying the issue of "the immigrant press" and "its control" (1922). This was a very charged political issue in those years, following the famous "free speech fights" of the Industrial Workers of the World (IWW), World War I and the debate about the loyalty of enemy immigrants, and especially the "red scare" – Attorney General Palmer's "raids" after the traumatic Bolshevik revolution. The pressure of revolutionary labor and political organizations such as the IWW (otherwise known as the "Wobblies"), a pressure that had been mounting since the beginning of the century, peaked in the wave of strikes that took place in 1919 and in episodes such as the Seattle general strike (Brecher 1972: 101–43). Attorney General Palmer responded with his notorious "red raids," jailing organizers and deporting immigrants. It became increasingly clear, however, that social order could not be maintained with the courts and the "Pinkertons."[3] Part of this general picture was the "problem" of the "immigrant press," which was in fact much politicized at the time under the influence of the socialist and anarchist leanings of European immigrant organizations. In his essay, characteristically, Park concluded that the only way to break down ethnic or political barriers was to favor the development of immigrant discourse toward a shared, more universalistic conceptual and linguistic horizon. The solution to the problem of exercising social control, in other words, should not be censorship but "competition" in the arena of free speech, a position that was not much different from that being advanced at the time in the dissenting opinions on matters of free speech crafted by the most enlightened and innovative members of the Supreme Court, such as Justices Louis Brandeis and Oliver Wendell Holmes (Kairys 1982b).

Other fundamental works from Chicago, such as William I. Thomas and Florian Znaniecki's analysis of immigrant Polish peasantry (1918–20), shared the same inspiration. In an important "methodological note" that constituted an introduction to their book (1918–20: 1–86), Thomas and Znaniecki observed that Chicago sociologists denied the possibility of social control by means of the "magic" of the law, or government "by decree." In a sharp criticism of legalistic delusions, they wrote:

> The oldest but most persistent form of social technique is that of "ordering-and-forbidding" – that is, meeting a crisis by an arbitrary act of will decreeing the disappearance of the undesirable or the

appearance of the desirable phenomena, and using arbitrary physical action to enforce the decree. This method corresponds exactly to the magical phase of natural technique. In both, the essential means of bringing a determined effect is more or less consciously thought to reside in the act of will itself by which the effect is decreed as desirable and of which the action is merely an indispensable vehicle or instrument; in both, the process by which the cause (act of will and physical action) is supposed to bring its effect to realization remains out of reach of investigation; in both, finally, if the result is not attained, some new act of will with new material accessories is introduced, instead of trying to find and remove the perturbing causes. A good instance of this in the social field is the typical legislative procedure of today. (Thomas and Znaniecki 1918–20: 3)

On the contrary, according to Thomas and Znaniecki, "rational" control could only be based on the knowledge of the various aspects of the social processes involved, a knowledge that would clarify other possible courses of action. Not an authoritarian act of will, but a democratic act of reason, would therefore bring about the solution to social problems. Thomas and Znaniecki identified "social disorganization" as the central issue of modern society, and saw in this disorganization the results of the dislocations that characterized society itself (1918–20: 1127–32, 1303–6).

Given the fundamental optimism typical of the Progressive Era, and the associated plastic concept of human nature, education, socialization, and integration became natural alternatives to coercion (Wiebe 1967: 154; Lasch 1965: 141–80; Diggins 1981: 23–5). Society's members could discover the most rational way of solving conflicts by broadening the arena of discourse. Park's book on *The Immigrant Press and Its Control* (1922), Nels Anderson's *The Hobo* (1923), and Park and Burgess's *Introduction to the Science of Sociology* (1921: 425–31) all stressed that the way to deal with ethnic or political dissent was to break down linguistic and cultural barriers and create a common universe of discourse. This was the proper terrain of *social control*. Competition among different vocabularies would be the social scientist's central interest. The many native languages of the immigrants, as well as the vernacular of the "Wobbly," would be analyzed and treated as instances of limited worlds. These could only be overcome by promoting practical integration and linguistic entrance into the larger universe of American society.

It is no surprise therefore that the crucial social issue of free speech and the struggles that punctuated its affirmation in

American society became an exemplary test bed for this new approach to the problem of order. As already mentioned, in the period between 1909 and 1915, the all-American revolutionaries of the IWW engaged in a nationwide campaign to obtain enforcement of what they saw as their Constitutional ("First Amendment") right to speak in public (Kairys 1982b: 150–3). The Wobblies' "free speech fights" represented probably the most salient instances of a long struggle by the American labor movement to see recognized its right to organize. Labor organizers, and in particular the Wobblies, realized that the substance of speech is not the mere expression of an opinion, the description of a standpoint, as it were, about some disembodied aspect of social reality. Working-class activists were particularly able to appreciate the fact that speech is the main form of social action thanks to which society's members organize their social experiences. The central slogan of the IWW, "Organize!" was the essence of their "free speech fights."

The American progressive intelligentsia accepted the challenge. After World War I, Justices Louis Brandeis and Oliver Wendell Holmes had articulated the bases of the future free speech doctrine in a series of dissenting opinions, according to which expression of opinion should be regulated in a manner consistent with free-market rules, instead of authoritarian monopoly rules (Kairys 1982b: 150–3; Ginsberg 1986: 36–40). Kairys quotes from Brandeis:

> Those who won our independence ... believed that freedom to think as you will and to speak as you think are means indispensable to the discovery and spread of political truth; that without free speech and assembly discussion would be futile; that with them, discussion affords ordinarily adequate protection against the dissemination of noxious doctrine; that the greatest menace to freedom is an inert people; that public discussion is a political duty; and that this should be a fundamental principle of the American government. They recognized the risks to which all human institutions are subject. But they knew that order cannot be secured merely through fear of punishment for its infraction; that it is hazardous to discourage thought, hope and imagination; that fear breeds repression; that repression breeds hate; that hate menaces stable government; that the path of safety lies in the opportunity to discuss freely supposed grievances and proposed remedies; and that the fitting remedy for evil counsels is good ones. Believing in the power of reason as applied through public discussion, they eschewed silence coerced

by law – the argument of force in its worst form. Recognizing the occasional tyrannies of governing majorities, they amended the Constitution so that free speech and assembly should be guaranteed. (*Whitney v. California*, 274 U.S. 357, 375–6 (1927), quoted in Kairys 1982b: 155)

Progressive legal theorists like Brandeis were certainly no friends of the Wobblies. They believed, however, that by adhering to the principles of democratic government, *and taking the chance of the risks involved*, radical positions, like those of the Wobblies, could be tamed, and order could be secured in a much firmer and stronger manner than by using billy clubs and guns. This kind of legal and political outlook also furnished social, economic, and political leaders with the technical skills necessary in order to win the competition for the masses' trust (Ginsberg 1986: 87, 224–5). This momentous social transformation, however, cannot be reduced to a conspiratorial substitution of the public relation manager for the censor, as Benjamin Ginsberg and others seem to suggest (Ginsberg 1986: 225; Graebner 1987: 36–57). It is only by firmly believing in democracy – that is, in the free flow of communication and in the best outcome of the competition – that the battle for the people's hearts and minds can be won. The shift from a control centered in censorship to one centered in the production of social meanings was also a shift from governmental social control by means of the law to social control produced by informal social interaction. I suggest that this overall transformation can be summarized in two models: a censorship model of political order, in which the messages directed toward controlling the players' behavior may be eliminated through centralized coercion; and a social interaction model of political order, in which behavior is controlled through the offering (at least *de jure* open to all) of affirmative messages.

## Chicago Sociology of Deviance between "Ecological" Theory and "Social Disorganization"

The central inspiration of the Chicago School came from so-called *ecological* theory, the idea, that is, that the socio-cultural environment within which a group finds itself largely determines the type of behavior prevailing within it. The socio-cultural environment is in turn strictly linked to economic and historical factors.

Clifford Shaw and Henry D. McKay in particular established a relationship between the spatial structure of the city of Chicago, the immigrant population settlements therein, and indicators of the various "social pathologies," such as the crime rate (Shaw and McKay 1942) and the rate of mental illness (Farris and Dunham 1934). They advanced the idea of *social disorganization*, the notion, that is, that, according to such an ecological hypothesis, the various types of social pathology did not derive from qualities pertaining to single individuals, but were rather qualities of the socio-cultural areas where individuals resided. For instance, the dwellers in the core area of Chicago, near "the Loop," the business district, showed a higher degree of social pathology because they resided in an area where social mobility, heterogeneity, and "anonymous" relationships were much higher. To the Chicagoans, this was the cause of the coming apart of social controls, and particularly of *primary* social controls – i.e. those that depend on direct, intimate relationships among individuals – because the social mobility, heterogeneity, and anonymity of "transitional" areas, such as the Loop, meant that lasting ties among individuals could not be built. They did not know each other and they did not care for each other. They did not care about what other people thought of them and expected from them. The gaze of their neighbors, or of passers-by, did not control them because they did not know them, often they did not have ways to communicate with them, and they did not consider them anyway as part of their "reference groups" – as this view would be formulated later on (Shibutani 1962).

Such a view was strictly linked with observation of what was happening within one of the central phenomena in Chicago, that of immigrant settlements and their various cultures. The first generation of immigrants, in fact, especially if they were young single males, as often happened, seemed to conform to such behavior, and rather than being "controlled" by the broad interaction with American society (and its cultural expectations) they seemed to be controlled by the types of orientations they carried within themselves, so to speak, from their original culture, reinforced by the creation of ethnic enclaves. As soon as they, however, and especially their offspring, to some degree "integrated" within a more established area of Chicago, they started adjusting to the type of cultural influence that was specific to that area, and that even different immigrant groups would "consign" one another. So for example the area of the "Cabrini project" in Chicago always had a very high murder rate when it was inhabited by Sicilians first and by blacks later.

The Chicago School helps us formulate a number of hypotheses about a possible relationship between migration and crime – hypotheses that, at the time, the School verified in the context of the city of Chicago. According to such hypotheses, first-generation migrants tend to reproduce the quantity and quality of crime in their original culture, even if, because of the mechanism of spatial localization and real-estate value in the receiving society, they may find themselves at first residing within high crime rate areas – defined by low primary social control – into which therefore they would tend to integrate. Immigration policies are always very important in defining the characteristics of such areas. In a country like the United States in the Chicago School days, by and large open to immigration, the disadvantage of migrants was essentially of a socio-economic and cultural nature, introducing them at the bottom of the social stratification. In situations instead in which migration policies are oriented toward closure – like in Europe today – such a socio-economic disadvantage would be amplified by the substantial illegality of migrants, pushed toward the black labor market and illegality by the very working of migration laws that, in such cases, have a definite criminogenic character (Calavita 2005; Melossi 2003b). Later on, migrants tend to leave transitional areas and move toward "ethnic enclaves," characterized by crime rates into which they tend to integrate. It could not be more incorrect, therefore, to hypothesize that integration and crime are at opposite poles. On the contrary, integration may mean integration within specific criminal traditions and activities, and may result in a higher crime rate than the one characterizing the migrant group in its culture of origin. So, for instance, Robert Sampson showed that in the 1990s Mexican immigration to the United States was one of the factors contributing to declining crime rates in that period (Sampson 2006).

Back to Chicago School days: Shaw and McKay went on, in fact, to formulate what they called a "theory of the gradient," according to which, as one moves further away from the center of the city, the socio-economic status of the dwellers increases and the crime rate characterizing the area diminishes. Shaw and McKay rejected, however, a merely economic explanation but pointed to the fact that, in richer areas, those elements that characterize high crime rate areas – such as heterogeneity, mobility, and anonymity – tend to decrease. In this respect also, therefore, they found

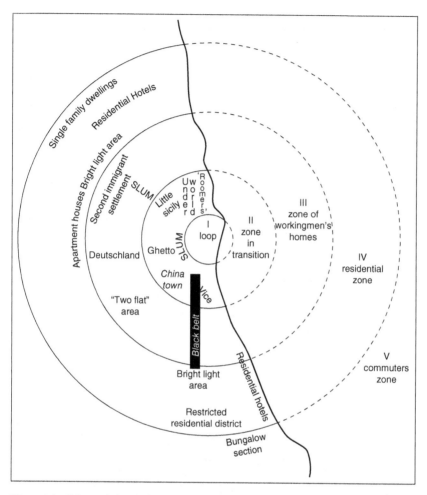

Figure 1   Map of the urban areas according to the Chicago School (Park et al. 1925: 55)

reasons to reaffirm their overall point of view emphasizing the importance of the twin concepts of social disorganization and social control.

The map reproduced in figure 1 is probably the most famous in the history of sociology. It represents Chicago as a series of concentric *semi*circles corresponding to the main transition from one socio-economic status to the next (the black line from top to bottom corresponds to the Lake Michigan shore, with Chicago itself to the left). The center is the Loop, the business district, around which, at the end of the nineteenth century, stood middle-class residencies inhabited by business people and their families. Factories and working-class residences were located further out – a layout that is still today rather typical in Europe (even if fast changing). However, starting at the beginning of the twentieth century, the business district tended to expand at the same time as the introduction of mass transport – from horse-powered tramways to electric tramways to the subway to urban freeways later on – made it increasingly easier for the middle class to chase after the dream of "the garden city" and move toward a much greener but much more distant suburban area (Yago 1984).[4] Residences around the business district lost quickly their real-estate value and became the "favorite" (because most inexpensive) residences for the late-comers in the urbanization game, the most recent immigrants, whether from abroad, the South, or the countryside. Immigrants and the shadiest activities – types of work that natives did not want to do anymore – were then both increasingly located in such an area, the one the Chicago sociologists called the area of transition. Here one could find specific "ethnically" specialized services, such as "Chinese" laundries, as well as the skid-row and red-light districts. Saloons, brothels, flophouses, the first fast food joints,[5] temporary employment agencies, all crowded in this area. Later on, during Prohibition, this was the area of the speakeasies, with the "gangsters" holed up inside.

Of course, the entry point for the various waves of first-generation migrants was such an area of transition. They then tried to move on to circles farther out, usually in areas where they could find people like themselves (see in figure 1 "Little Sicily," "Deutschland," "the Ghetto" (by which was meant the Eastern European Jewish settlement), and the "Black Belt"). Moving from one circle to the next, they tended to leave the cultural characteristics of the circle they were coming from and assume instead those of the circle in which they were settling – including crime rates. The most important conclusion reached by the Chicago School insofar as the sociology of crime is concerned was therefore that *deviant characteristics are a property of the environment and not of given groups or individuals.*

The idea of "social disorganization" was also at the basis of the program of social prevention of crime that Shaw and McKay devised, giving birth to the very first, most famous, and most lasting among such programs, the "Chicago Area Project." Shaw and McKay's reasoning was simple. If the fundamental problem was one of "social disorganization," then what was necessary was to "restore," "repair," or indeed "reorganize" social relationships in a given area to the end of preventing crime. We have also seen, however, how the cause of social disorganization was, for these theorists, the coming apart of primary social controls. The repairing intervention could not consist therefore in an intervention coming "from the outside," as it were. It had to be an "internal" effort at reorganizing, aiming at restoring primary, face-to-face social controls (on the distinction between "primary" and "secondary" social controls see the section below on Louis Wirth). The promoters of the Chicago Area Project tried therefore to entrust resources and responsibilities to "natural leaders" in the neighborhood, relying at the same time on already existing "seeds" of organization, such as religious, sporting, or recreational associations. Of course, this last aspect points to a fundamental difficulty common to all such programs (Hope 1995): the fact that they seem to work best where there is already present an organizational structure, whereas they are more difficult to implement where there is no such organization – that is, where they would be most useful.

The exploration of urban ecology was, however, but an aspect of the sociological wealth produced by the Chicago School, even in the mere ambit of deviance. The highest accomplishment of the School was perhaps the exploration of a whole universe of action, behavior, and social categories that, up to that time, had been excluded from any kind of "scientific" investigation and had been of interest instead only to literature. One of the distinctive characteristics of the Chicago School, in a sense its trademark, was a type of ethnographic work carried out not among "primitive peoples" – as cultural anthropologists had already begun to do – but within contemporary, urban areas. One has only to mention, for instance, Nels Anderson's *The Hobo* (1923), about a human type that was central to the urban social composition of America in those years. Somewhere in the middle between the vagabond, the bum, and the seasonal migrant worker, hoboes had mobilized, at the end of the nineteenth century, in the Washington marches to ask for bread and work, and were thereafter among the rank and file of the Wobblies, who were, as we have seen, the most original and distinctive American working-class organization. Mostly, they commuted between Chicago, where they sort of hibernated during the winter, and the Southern and Western regions of the United States, where they were traveling during the rest of the year, to harvest, mine, and do all kinds of daily, seasonal work (from fruit harvests in California to the ice harvest in Alaska). They moved usually by "train-hopping," giving birth to the kind of legends and ballads and that specific Western lore sung about, for instance, by Woody Guthrie, Bob Dylan's inspiration and mentor. Besides the hoboes, however, and besides the central concerns of the School with the city, communication, and migration (Park et al. 1925; Thomas and Znaniecki 1918–120; Stonequist 1937), the Chicago sociologists were curious about all kinds of "marginal" human behavior, from Frederic Thrasher's work on young "gangsters" (1927) to Paul Cressey's "taxi-dancers" (1932), from "hotel life" (Hayner 1923) to prostitution (Reckless 1933), from the opposite worlds of "high society" and the "slum" (Zorbaugh 1929) to more classic objects of sociological investigations such as suicide (Cavan 1928) or juvenile delinquency (Shaw 1930).

## Democracy and Social Control

George Herbert Mead, a Chicagoan philosopher and social psychologist in strict contact with the tradition of American Pragmatism and especially with John Dewey (Thayer 1982), focused on the relationship between democracy and social control.[6] The point of view of Pragmatism was deeply connected with the construction of a mass democracy in "Progressive" America. Democratic political life – as well as a dynamic industrial "capitalist" society – required a convinced, consensual acceptance by society's members. The problem of the construction of consensus – the way in which the members of a common enterprise come to see eye to eye on matters of common concern – set the stage for Mead's theory of "social control." The fundamental question, according to him, was one of exploring the ways through which those who participate in a common endeavor come to share the same perspective. For Mead, in a move that was intentionally antagonistic to a Cartesian type of philosophy, the constitution of "society" and "self" are one and the same thing. The process that links these two aspects is indeed social interaction, because the development of a self – and, eventually, of a strong "I" – as well as of social control, is predicated on the specifically human ability to assume the attitude of the other, an other that, in its most developed form, is a "generalized other" (Mead 1925, 1934). According to Mead, therefore, the self "dwells" within wider and wider spheres of social reality, orienting itself toward "reference groups" (Shibutani 1962) the horizons of which become increasingly larger. The development of the self is possible only insofar as the self is subjected to social control. That is, the process through which our very tendency toward developing our personality and individuality pushes us toward assuming the standpoint of others. Only in so doing will we eventually become able to assume the position of the "I" and strive therefore for freedom, "authenticity," and "individuality." The process of social control can therefore be defined as the process by which we are able to establish the *shared* meaning of the object of our interactions (this is why Herbert Blumer (1969) would later speak of "symbolic interactionism," an essential position in order to understand some of the 1960s sociological currents, such as "labeling theory"; see below, chapter 7[7]).

It is therefore through an interactive exchange, first with her parents, then within the sundry social situations in which she enters, that the child learns the meaning of given words. This is true, however, of every learning process. We can therefore extend the experience we all have in childhood to other learning experiences, and this was particularly important in the situation of Chicago because of migration. In the same way in which a child has the problem of inserting herself within a new and foreign world, so it is for the immigrant – with the additional difficulty of already "having" a world, a world that is now, to a certain extent, to be deserted (Schutz 1944).

However, by placing at the center of the social process the issue of interaction, we place there the question of communication, and therefore also that of the mass *media* of communication. Especially for the "generalized other," in fact, communication becomes paramount, and face-to-face interaction gives way to more generalized, universalistic, and standardized forms of communication. This is the juncture at which the more specifically political struggles in the arena of social control open up, and the tensions and conflicts between democracy and social control become sharpest. It follows in fact from Mead's ideas that those agencies that have the highest power to construe a universe of shared meanings in society are those that are also able to exercise the deepest form of social control (C. Wright Mills would follow this line of thought, from his discussion of Mead's thought in his PhD dissertation, *Sociology and Pragmatism* (1942), to his mature masterwork, *The Power Elite* (1956); see below, chapter 7).

It also follows from all of this (not only from Mead's ideas, but from the complex of the contributions of the Chicago School) that the whole superimposition of legal and political structures basically rests on social control, and the only chance of such structures being somehow effective lies in trying to influence the general constitution of meaning, entering into competition, so to speak, with other agencies and other conceptual structures. The distribution of the chances of influencing the constitution of meanings is not at all reflective, however, of the distribution of political rights, which are of course individualized. On the contrary, such a distribution has become more and more concentrated in society, following and accompanying the concentration of economic and political power – an overall line of thought that would be expressed, in terms of political philosophy, from the John Dewey of *The Public and Its Problems* (1927) to the later C. Wright Mills of *The Power Elite* (1956).

Therefore, insofar as social control is concerned, it is quite clear that these reflections move our attention from the legal-coercive level to the level of communication. For Mead, democracy was grounded in a process of cultural homogenization, which made possible a conversation among individuals and the groups in which individuals belong. In 1915, he wrote an article on "natural rights," in which he defined democracy as "revolution incorporated in the institution of government itself," an "institutionalising of revolution" (Mead 1915: 150–1). He added, in typical Chicagoan fashion, that "human rights are never in such danger as when their only defenders are political institutions and their officers" (1915: 169). Legal protection, in fact, is but a "weak" and limited form of social control, which is destined "to cease with the completion of the socialization of those" who are participants in the legal order (ibid.). In other words, if social control is a process that does not unfold at the level of consent, persuasion, culture, but is confined to law and politics, then it will not be effective, will not be real "social control." This seems to me to be a crucial point in order to understand the ethic of the period and of democracy more generally. Mead's polemic objective was the idea of a social transformation governed "from the top," as it were, unable to produce social change in the desired direction. On the contrary, social change "from the bottom" would be able to change social conditions and then look for legal and political sanction. The Chicago School, in its highest theoretical expressions, teaches us not to consider social control as an outcome of legal and political decision but, on the contrary, to see the State and the law as an expression of social control – a process of social control that takes place within communicative exchange and that rewards therefore those forces and standpoints that are able to exercise the highest level of efficacy within that exchange (for an elaboration on this general point see Melossi 1990).

## Language and Social Control

In his teaching at the University of Chicago,[8] Mead had situated himself within a philosophical concept that shifted the locus of discourse from the traditional introspective mode of Western, Cartesian thought to an interactive mode. In other words, neither Mead, nor Dewey, nor other Pragmatists saw discourse as their European ancestors had seen it – as a product of the reflection of the "I" in its relation to the "world." Rather, to them it was a product of the conversation that takes place between the "I" and "the other" (Mead 1934; Joas 1980, 1983: 9). A fundamental presupposition for all this was a concept of language not as a simple expression of a state of consciousness – the old manner in which we tend to think of language, going back to Descartes's classic philosophy and his *cogito* (*cogito ergo sum*, "I think therefore I am," with its corresponding postulation of a *dualism* of "mind" and "matter") – but as a vehicle for consciousness. Consciousness is not something that we "find" "inside" ourselves and that we then "express" through the medium of language (once again, C. Wright Mills, in his early work, especially moved from, and developed sociologically, these concepts by Mead, when he wrote, "[T]he major reorientation of recent theory in sociology of language emerged with the overthrow of the Wundtian notion that language has as its function the 'expression' of prior elements within the individual" (Mills 1940: 439)). Rather, we "learn" our consciousness – or at least its contents – from the outside, we learn to think – and we learn some of the main organizing concepts for thought, such as "I," "me," etc. – through linguistic exchange. At the same time, such linguistic exchange belongs in an eminently *practical* type of activity, grounded as it is in conversation. Conversation, words, therefore our thinking, are never far removed from social organization and the practicalities of social life. Words are never mere "description," because they are rooted in a historically and culturally specific practice, and in social interaction, so that it is not possible to think of a form of social organization uncoupled from the speech that "describes" it. Thought, in other words, is never disjoined from action (Austin 1962). Thought and action are but the two faces of the same social process, the same social organization.

According to the overall Pragmatist inspiration that Mills pursued – in the footsteps of Mead – reflection is linked to the problems, obstacles, and barriers that an individual finds in her way in a course of action – problems, obstacles, and barriers that are not necessarily only "material" but can also be of a "moral" or "intellectual" nature. For the natural course of things, Pragmatists tell us, we are driven by habit (Dewey 1922), but when such a natural course of things is interrupted by unforeseen circumstances, we need to reflect. We do this in the midst of forms of relationships and cooperation with others – never really alone (if we think alone, usually it is in the form of a conversation within ourselves). Any type of communication – even that of a thought that seems irrelevant from a practical standpoint – takes place within some form of social organization and, one might add, always imperceptibly transforms reality, even if to the least degree.[9]

All of this is very important from the perspective of "social control." Through the definition of individual motives, and the expectations we have of specific individuals and their actions, we define what we may want to call "a field of possibilities" for them, we point at what we may expect of someone. Such a field of possibilities is therefore likely to become a limitation – in the specific meaning of a drawing of boundaries – not only to the action and behavior of that individual but to her very consciousness, in the sense that her consciousness, her possibilities for action, can never go beyond the barriers, limitations, and boundaries set by her experience and education. This is true even linguistically.[10] Through a discussion of the empirical observation of behavior, Mead had developed a view of the ways in which selves are made and transformed within a process of interaction – a view that became crucial for a whole tradition of sociological studies. In an article written in 1925, Mead held that social control varies with "the degree to which the individuals in society are able to assume the attitudes of the others who are involved with them in common endeavor" (1925: 291). Mead's theory of social control should be understood in the context of the major social problem of the *democratic* integration of conflicting cultures, groups, organizations in what was then called the American "melting pot." The problem was to re-establish a universe of general meanings in a deeply divided and Babel-like society, in which most of the old traditional ties had been lost. The problem of a "generalized other" would have been, maybe, for Freud, the problem of leadership in a group (see above, chapter 2). When this group is a mass society, however, a generalized other is not so much a matter of leader types – as Freud would have claimed, and in regard to which he had found American society wanting – as of the successful construction of a general perspective based on communication, and the creation of "a common object, which will control their common conduct" (Mead 1925: 292). For Mead, in fact, both social control and self-control were construed around "an adequate social object," whose problem

> is not that of becoming acquainted with the indefinite number of acts that are involved in social behavior, but that of so overcoming the distances in space and time, and the barriers of language and convention and social status, that we can converse with ourselves in the role of those who are involved with us in the common undertaking of life . . . Any self is a social self, but it is restricted to the group whose roles it assumes, and it will never abandon this self until it finds itself entering into the larger society and maintaining itself there. (Mead 1925: 292)

In order to enter into the "larger society," in order to grasp the set of "social objects" that make up a person's universe, she must take the role of a "generalized other," in a process mediated by symbols and language (Mead 1934). Social integration is not to be sought, according to Mead, in some "superindividual" entity or in "moral education" or in a "psychic bond." It stems from the mastering of a common language. The process of language learning and language practicing, i.e. the process of communication, is "a principle of social organization" that makes "cooperative activity" possible (1934: 260). "The process of communication is one which is more universal than that of the universal religion or universal economic process in that it is one that serves them both" (1934: 259). This is true because religion and the economy are specific instances of cooperative activity, which, in general, "lie back of the process of discourse" (ibid.). How is such cooperative activity co-ordinated socially? For Mead it was very important to distinguish, in the process of socialization of the child, between the earlier stage of *play*, where the child acts out all possible social roles, and the later stage of *game*, where roles are prescribed by *rules*. Mead comes to the definition of what he calls the "generalized other" by referring to an all-American *game*, baseball:

> The play antedates the game. For in game there is a regulated procedure, and rules. The child must not only take the role of the other, as he [*sic*] does in the play, but he must assume the various roles of all the participants in the game, and govern his action accordingly. If he plays first base, it is as the one to whom the ball will be thrown from the field or from the catcher. Their organized reactions to him he has embedded in his own playing of the different positions, and his organized reaction becomes what I have called the "generalized other" that accompanies and controls his conduct. And it is this generalized other in his experience that provides him with a self. (Mead 1925: 285)

And in his lectures Mead says:

> The organized community or social group that gives to the individual his unity of self may be called "the generalized other." The attitude of the generalized other is the attitude of the whole community . . . It is in the form of the generalized other that the social process influences the behavior of the individuals involved in it and carrying it on, i.e., that the community exercises control over the conduct of its individual members; for it is in this form that the social process or community enters as a determining factor into the individual's thinking. In abstract thought the individual takes the attitude of the generalized other toward himself, without reference to its expression in any particular other individuals; and in concrete thought he takes that attitude in so far as it is expressed in the attitudes toward his behavior of those other individuals with whom he is involved in the given social situation or act. But only by taking the attitude of the generalized other toward himself, in one or another of these ways, can he think at all; for only thus can thinking – or the internalized conversation of gestures which constitutes thinking – occur. (Mead 1934: 154–6)

Insofar as the process of social control allows the self to "rehearse" in front of plural and possibly conflicting "audiences," it is therefore also the process that is at the roots of innovation and individuality. Hans Joas, in a perceptive reconstruction of Meadian ethics (Joas 1980: 121–44), quotes a letter by Mead where he was describing what he was doing as "an attempt to do from my own standpoint what Hegel undertook in his Phenomenology. I hope it won't be as inscrutable" (cited in Joas 1980: 232). This was so because entering larger and larger "audiences" or "universes of discourse" at the same time allowed for a critique of the narrower circles of practice and language in which the self had previously been embedded.

An example taken from literature contemporary to the Chicago School may be useful (on the more general relationship between Chicago sociology and Chicago literature in this period, see Cappetti 1993). In *Native Son*, by Richard Wright (1940), probably the first great novel of the African American tradition, and a text deeply linked, in period, location, environment, and inspiration, to the sociological culture we are referring to, the protagonist, the "bad" Thomas Bigger, a poor young black man, migrates from the South in the 1920s, grows up in the Chicago "Black Belt," and becomes involved, with the inevitability that is typical of the tragic form, in committing two murders. The novel is dominated by what the author, Richard Wright, refers to as a kind of "blindness" – an old device of tragedy, which, however, is now played by Wright no longer as human blindness before the inscrutability of Fate or God, but as the practical impossibility, for Bigger, of gazing through the opaqueness of the social relationships in which his life is embedded. The situations in which Bigger finds himself are determined by the social conditions in which he was thrown. It's a kind of absolute, experiential, blindness; one would almost be tempted to say an "existential" blindness, because Wright's implicit conceptualizations are redolent of existentialism – the European philosophy that at the time was popularized especially in its French version by Jean-Paul Sartre – and this is not accidental because Wright was certainly very much interested in this philosophy (Gilroy 1993: 146–86).[11] It was a kind of blindness produced by poverty and racist discrimination, wherein Bigger can only think of himself as a "colored" person, always inferior to white people – even the sympathetic ones. He therefore loses, or maybe never acquires, the possibility of expressing a "subjectivity" of his own (this aspect would be later questioned by other African American writers, such as James Baldwin; see Gilroy, ibid.). Bigger's "life chances," to use Ralf Dahrendorf's expression (1979), are therefore curtailed by his lack of material resources and by the boundaries of racial discrimination in the sense that these cause his forced "inattention" to alternative ways in which he could escape his destiny.[12] As we have already seen, discussing Beccaria (see above, chapter 1), "free will" seems to be a faculty unequally distributed within the social structure and is related to our capacity, and possibility, of embracing social realities that are broader and maybe even in conflict with those within which we were born.

## Sister Carrie's Less Eligibility

Carla Cappetti, in her work on modernism, ethnography, and the novel in Chicago (Cappetti 1993), mentions *Sister Carrie* at the end of a chapter dedicated to the sociologist W. I. Thomas's work on the "unadjusted girl" (1923), which, Cappetti adds, "foreshadowed some of the urban novels of the thirties and early forties and their stories of delinquent young men and women in the urban jungle," and she mentions, "[a]mong others, James T. Farrell, Nelson Algreen, and Richard Wright," who "would soon create a literature that made room for the subjectivity of the criminal, the delinquent, the prostitute. These novels would transform the prostitute and the delinquent, and by implication the larger class that each symbolizes, from helpless victims of heredity and the environment or passive recipient of social workers' benign intentions to active historical and existential subject" (Cappetti 1993: 106).

One such "active historical and existential subject" was certainly the heroine of Theodore Dreiser (who would later owe his fame to *An American Tragedy* (Dreiser 1925)). In his first novel, *Sister Carrie* (1900), which unfolds at the time when Chicago was taking off, "one day in August 1889 eighteen-year-old Caroline Meeber from Columbia City, Wisconsin – 'Sister Carrie as she was half affectionately termed by her family' – boarded a train for Chicago that was to take her (and the surprisingly but never dependably gifted newspaper reporter from Terre Haute, Indiana, who had just put her into his first novel) into world literature" (as the critic Alfred Kazin retells it in his "Introduction" (1981: vii)). In the narration of the novel, the first shelter Sister Carrie repairs to is her sister's apartment in the city, in both sisters' quite diverse expectation that eventually "Carrie would be rewarded for coming and toiling in the city" (Dreiser 1900: 15). And *toiling* indeed it would have been, even if for a short time. After a few days, she finds work in a shoe factory where – in the fascinating English of the news reporter but still second-generation German, Theodore

Dreiser – "the whole atmosphere was one of hard contract" (Dreiser 1900: 39). The impression of such an atmosphere is not lost on Carrie. Indeed it will stay with her for the rest of the novel, and will bring her, by applying what we could call a sort of personal "less eligibility,"[13] to indeed favoring the opportunity of becoming a "kept" woman – with much scandal to turn-of-the-century readers – rather than set foot again in a place with such an atmosphere.

Once, later in the novel, while Sister Carrie is promenading with her beau, Drouet "the drummer,"

> suddenly a pair of eyes met Carrie's in recognition. They were looking out from a group of poorly dressed girls. Their clothes were faded and loose-hanging, their jackets old, their general make-up shabby. Carrie recognized the glance and the girl. It was one of those who worked at the machines in the shoe-factory. The latter looked, not quite sure, and then turned her head and looked. Carrie felt as if some great tide had rolled between them. The old dress and the old machine came back. She actually started. Drouet never noticed until Carrie bumped into a pedestrian. (Dreiser 1900: 77)

And, toward the end of the novel, after Carrie has found her fortune in New York, making it on Broadway, still the persistent thought of the factory does not abandon her:

> One such as she had only recently been was waiting for her modest salary. It took her back to the few weeks in which she had collected, or rather had received, almost with the air of a donation, four-fifty per week from a lordly foreman in the shoe-factory: a man who in distributing the envelopes had the manner of a prince doling out favors to a servile group of petitioners. She knew that out in Chicago this very day, the same factory chamber was full of poor homely-clad girls working in long lines at clattering machines, that at noon they would eat a miserable lunch in a half-hour, that Saturday they would gather as they had when she was one of them and accept the small pay for work a hundred times harder than she was now doing. Oh, it was so easy now. The world was so rosy and bright. She felt so thrilled, that she must needs walk back to the hotel to think, wondering what she should do. (Dreiser 1900: 457)

Indeed, in a way similar to what happens to the both steel-hard and sweet Sister Carrie, the "delinquents, criminals and prostitutes" that animate the works of art Cappetti (1993: 106) refers to are portrayed as applying a kind of personal less-eligibility calculus to their choices, where the sinister shadows of the factory and the sweatshop loom large in the background, making the "immoral" choice seem so much more benign, so much more "eligible." This may be a point where the literature of the time dared to be more innovative than even the sociology of deviance and crime. Sister Carrie's actions imply the idea of a choice that an understanding but determinist sociological explanation found probably unpalatable, even if it certainly bubbled under the surface especially of ethnographic accounts, with their anthropological detachment and even sympathy. The heart of the matter was that, in periods of impetuous economic development, such as the Chicago of the end of the nineteenth century and the early decades of the twentieth, (potential) workers could afford to apply their own kind of "less eligibility" that was the reciprocal of the official one (could we call it a "more eligibility"?). A "marginal" kind of life was often preferable to "toil in the factories," factories that were nothing more than miserable, life-threatening sweatshops.

## Louis Wirth: Urbanism as a Way of Life

Many of the themes we have seen to be central to the production of the Chicago School would be later encapsulated in Louis Wirth's essay "Urbanism as a Way of Life" (1938). Moving from Georg Simmel's early formulation in his famous essay "The Metropolis and Mental Life" (1903), according to Wirth, urbanism is to be understood as a "way of life" that goes beyond the boundaries of cities. It is first and foremost a cultural attitude that unfolds on the grounds of metropolitan heterogeneity and the impersonality of relationships characteristic of a society dominated by a monetary economy. The social and cultural nexuses of the modern metropolis are the exact opposite of those in the small town. From the furthest corners of the globe, people are attracted to the big city not because they have something in common but, on the contrary, because of their diversity and complementarity. In such a new situation, the old type of solidarity – as Durkheim would have called it – that was typical of traditional society is being increasingly replaced by competition and a formal kind of social control. Secondary relationships replace primary ones. The urban dweller is faced with a trade-off. Whereas she acquires freedom from traditional controls, she loses spontaneity, a shared morality, and feelings of community and belonging. The possibility of "anomie" and "predatory relationships" therefore ensues. Wirth adds:

> The foreign born and their children constitute nearly two-thirds of all the inhabitants of cities of one million and over . . . Never before have such large masses of people of diverse traits as we find in our cities been thrown together into such close physical contact as in the great cities of America. Cities generally, and American cities in particular, comprise a motley of peoples and cultures, of highly differentiated modes of life between which there often is only the faintest communication, the greatest indifference and the broadest tolerance, occasionally bitter strife, but always the sharpest contrast. (Wirth 1938: 19–20)

And he concludes, about social control:

> [S]ocial control in the city should typically proceed through formally organized groups. It follows, too, that the masses of men in the city are subject to manipulation by symbols and stereotypes managed by individuals working from afar or operating invisibly behind the scenes through their control of the instruments of communication. Self-government either in the economic, the political, or the cultural realm is under these circumstances reduced to a mere figure of speech or, at best, is subject to the unstable equilibrium of pressure groups. (Wirth 1938: 23)

If Wirth's description appears to our eyes as particularly up-to-date, in Europe and other parts of the world also, it is because in 1930s America, the essential features of the type of society that would become prevalent after World War II were being created and refined – a type of social model that the American victory over its worldwide Fascist and Communist competitors between the 1940s and the 1980s would then try to export to the remotest corners of the globe.

# 6

# *The 1930s: Between Differential Association and Anomie*

The model of social control elaborated within American society, especially in its "Chicago" version, placed its main emphasis on the transformation of social relationships through the use of "social engineering." As we have seen, the problem was no longer one of *describing* social reality as coherent and cohesive (and, if not, intervening through means of coercion), but of *constructing* social cohesion through social practices. Such an attitude in favor of social engineering and social change had certainly not been uncontested. For many decades, American elites had been closed and hostile toward deep social transformations – with the result of contributing to a history of industrial relations and social strife that was one of the most violent among industrialized societies (see for instance the reconstruction of such history by a Slovenian migrant to the United States, Luis Adamic, in the book *Dynamite* (1934) and his not less intriguing autobiography *Laughing in the Jungle* (1932)). Starting with the "Progressive Era" at the beginning of the twentieth century, such a backward attitude started to unravel. For a long time, however, the social reforms attempted in the most important industrial states – concerning industrial relations, welfare provisions, and forms of control of giant corporations – found a barrier in the traditionalist jurisprudence of the Supreme Court, which would take refuge in a naturalistic concept of rights as part of *laissez-faire* economic institutions, and would therefore strike down every attempt at social regulation of the economy (Mensch 1982). We have already seen in the previous chapter how the "dissenting opinions" of luminaries like Oliver

Wendell Holmes and Louis Brandeis had started to question this conservative leaning of the Supreme Court on the essential issue of "free speech."

Things would change in an even more dramatic manner, though, as a consequence of "Black Friday." On Friday, October 29, 1929, the disastrous "crash" of the New York Stock Exchange set in motion the most serious economic crisis in the history of the United States. Whereas the Chicago "ethos" had been the quintessential expression of Progressivism and later on of the spirit of the 1920s, "the Jazz Age," an era of ruthless capitalist development, optimism, and experimentation, now everything was going to change, or so it seemed. As one of the great cantors of the Jazz Age, Francis Scott Fitzgerald, wrote:

> It ended two years ago, because the utter confidence which was its essential prop received an enormous jolt, and it didn't take long for the flimsy structure to settle earthward. And after two years the Jazz Age seems as far away as the days before the War. It was borrowed time anyhow – the whole upper tenth of a nation living with the insouciance of grand ducs and the casualness of chorus girls . . . Now once more the belt is tight and we summon the proper expression of horror as we look back at our wasted youth. (Fitzgerald 1931: 21–2)

During the following three years, prices and production plunged, whereas unemployment and bankruptcies skyrocketed. In 1932, Franklin Delano Roosevelt was elected president on the basis of a "New Deal" with the American public, whereby Roosevelt launched the idea of a "third way" between *laissez-faire* capitalism and socialism, a third way that constituted also an indirect response to the world-wide competitors of the United States at the time, namely Communism and the Soviet Union on the one hand, National Socialism and Fascism on the other. The main idea behind the New Deal was that government should intervene strongly in the economy, but not through expropriation and nationalization, rather through regulation "for the public good." There had to be "social control" in the sphere of the economy and, for the first time, this very concept moved from the somehow "lesser" areas of urban sociology, deviance, and education toward the "core" social areas of the economy and the law. In the works of economists and legal thinkers such as John M. Clark (1926), Adolf A. Berle and Gardiner C. Means (1932), or Roscoe Pound (1942) – and many others who often worked at

various times and places for the Roosevelt administration – the idea
and concept of "social control" did indeed loom large. All this literature – which had been anticipated in the work of philosopher
John Dewey, for instance in *The Public and Its Problems* (1927) –
emphasized the importance of "control" versus "property." To sum
up the argument of these activists and scholars in one sentence, they
held that the dichotomy between "public" and "private" was quite
irrelevant if "control" – *de facto, real* control – was not brought into
the picture. Real control, however, *if social*, had to be the product of
legal regulation protected by the creation of efficacious *ad-hoc* governmental agencies.[1] In the end, one of the consequences of such
overall political, social, and cultural change was the prevailing of
FDR's reforms also over a conservative, but frightened, Supreme
Court.[2]

## Crime and the New Deal

The period between the 1920s and Roosevelt's New Deal was also
the period when public interest in crime started to develop, and
with it both the implementation of special agencies and legislation devoted to fighting crime, and the study of crime from a
socio-criminological perspective. It was during this period, for
instance, that various attempts were made to establish some kind
of federal police force, every time pushed back by Congress's
reluctance to create what was considered a sort of "secret police"
(Inciardi 1984). What would then become the Federal Bureau of
Investigation was spurred into existence by 1920s "crusades"
against two dangers for American society, or at least so perceived,
both in some way linked to immigration. These were, on the one
hand, the trafficking of women into the United States for prostitution and, on the other, the coming to America of a "wave" of
European radicals, Communists, and/or anarchists after World
War I. In 1919, A. Mitchell Palmer, appointed by Woodrow Wilson
as his attorney general, hired John Edgar Hoover as a special
assistant. Together they launched a campaign against radicals and
left-wing organizations. On November 7, 1919 (the second anni-
versary of the Russian revolution!), they had over 10,000 sus-
pected Communists and anarchists rounded up. Many were then
held without trial for a long time. The vast majority were eventually released but Emma Goldman and many other people were
deported to Russia. On January 2, 1920, another 6,000 were

arrested and held without trial, many of them members of the Industrial Workers of the World (IWW; see above, chapter 5). After these "Palmer raids," which took place in several cities, in 1924 John Edgar Hoover became director of the Bureau of Investigation, which was renamed the FBI in 1935. At this time, after the Depression and in the changed political climate of the "New Deal," his enemies, at least in part, also changed. In the early 1930s, Hoover began a war on "public enemies," who were now high-profile "gangsters" such as John Dillinger or Bonnie Parker and Clyde Barrow. He also contributed to the rationalization and bureaucratization of the Agency, which started collecting data for the Uniform Crime Report from local police forces – the most important source of official crime statistics in the United States. During World War II, Hoover was again in charge of protecting the United States from enemy agents – a task that the ensuing Cold War developed further. He served under eight presidents, until his death in 1972. A highly controversial figure, he secured a tremendous degree of personal power. His obsessive pursuit of left-wing and other allegedly "dangerous" organizations revived during the unrest of the 1960s and continued to the very end, causing many to accuse him of violating civil rights (one of the most notorious among these campaigns being the so-called Counter-Intelligence Program or COINTELPRO against radical activism, especially targeting the Black Panther Party – see next chapter).

During the Depression, the representation of crime and criminals acquired a centrality in public opinion that was going to last. It was a time when, on the one hand, class war first peaked, in the very large sit-down strikes of the 1930s, then increasingly lost centrality, especially thanks to the process of integration of the working class within Franklin Delano Roosevelt's New Deal coalition. On the other hand, instead, the threat coming from criminal individuals and organizations, such as the notorious Al Capone's gang in Chicago, acquired more and more salience, feeding into a collective representation that proceeded together with the increasing importance of the mass media of communication. This was the time in fact when the burgeoning mass cultural industry found that crime was an amazing means of entertainment for large numbers of people, in a situation where radio shows and news were becoming increasingly popular, and movie theaters were spreading in the big cities (see Elizabeth Cohen's 1990 account of the mushrooming of movie houses in 1930s Chicago).

If, later on, in the 1950s, in a new critical mood, C. Wright Mills would be able to state the necessity of turning "private troubles" into "public problems" (Mills 1959), he did that, probably, in order to counter what he felt had happened in the previous decades. Public problems – unemployment, the lack of collective rights, the repression of labor and political opposition – became redefined socially as "private troubles," first of all in the deeds of the great "gangsters." This was only possible, however, because some of those "public problems" could be at least perceived as on their way to solution. In the late 1930s, the fundamental "collective" rights of labor were finally recognized not only by the federal legislation but also by the Supreme Court, the economy was slowly moving again, and the "Fordist" factory was driving a development that would then find in the war economy its seemingly unstoppable flywheel. J. Edgar Hoover and Hollywood could finally entertain the American public with the sordid stories of love, violence, and death that would later on increasingly delight the whole world.

In spite of the rhetoric of the "public enemy" championed by J. Edgar Hoover, the generalized character of economic misfortunes in the Depression kept at least the level of *relative* frustration lower than it might otherwise have been, and the progressive tinge of political solutions kept open the possibility that "public enemies" might not all be chosen from the lower classes (see below on "white-collar criminals"). Imprisonment rates had been increasing during the nineteenth century, in a country that, in many ways, was still taking shape, and then declined in the period between the 1890s and the 1920s (Cahalan 1979; Berk et al. 1981; see figure 4 page 233.). This certainly changed again after 1929, when the unprecedented unemployment of the Depression was accompanied by a sharp rise in imprisonment, but even such a rise was not at all proportional to the extremely sharp upward lift of unemployment, which reached a third of the American labor force (Jankovic 1977). There was, however – as Rusche and Kirchheimer's theory of "less eligibility" would predict – a wholesale decline of living conditions within American prisons and an increase in agitations and riots (interestingly, the earliest contribution we have from Georg Rusche was an article in the daily German newspaper *Frankfurter Zeitung* about prison riots in the United States in 1929–30 (Rusche 1930), where he traced the cause of those riots to the absence of welfare protection for the lower classes in American society, unlike in Weimar Germany).

## The Theory of Differential Association

After receiving his doctorate at Chicago, the young Edwin H. Sutherland went to teach at the University of Illinois, where, among other courses, he was assigned the teaching of a course in criminology. The notes from that course became the basis for the first edition of probably the most important textbook in the history of the discipline, *Criminology* (Sutherland 1924, 1942: 13).[3] In that first edition, among other things, Sutherland wrote:

> Poverty in the modern city generally means segregation in low-rent sections, where people are isolated from many of the cultural influences and forced into contact with many of the degrading influences. Poverty generally means a low status, with little to lose, little to respect, little to be proud of, little to sustain efforts to improve. It generally means bad housing conditions, lack of sanitation in the vicinity, and lack of attractive community institutions. It generally means both parents being away from home for long hours, with the fatigue, lack of control of children, and irritation that go with these. It generally means withdrawal of the child from school at an early age and the beginning of mechanical labor, with weakening of the home control, the development of anti-social grudges, and lack of cultural contacts. Poverty, together with the display of wealth in shop-windows, streets, and picture shows, generally means envy and hatred of the rich and the feeling of missing much in life, because of the lack of satisfaction of the fundamental wishes. Poverty seldom forces people to steal or become prostitutes in order to escape starvation. It produces its effects most frequently on the attitudes, rather than on the organism. But it is surprising how many poor people are not made delinquents, rather than how many are made delinquents. (Sutherland 1924: 169–70)[4]

Sutherland's intellectual debt to the Chicago School (Schuessler 1956: xi) is quite apparent from this early statement. His early interest in criminology was but an application of more general sociological concepts and interests. In a way similar to that of the main Chicago School theorists, he saw a deep connection between the overall socio-economic situation and criminal behavior (according to Schuessler, Sutherland was especially indebted to W. I. Thomas's kind of "interactional sociology"). However, a main intervening variable was a cultural concept of ecology, so much so that, as Sutherland writes, "it is surprising how many poor people are not made delinquents, rather than how many are made delinquents." Later on, in opening up criminological investigation on "white-collar crime," he would show how rich and powerful people too may become engaged in criminal or anyway illicit behavior. The culture of particular environments, groups or social circles – as Georg Simmel (1908) had called them – was what facilitated a criminal choice. Sutherland would, however, tackle the residual ambiguity of the Chicago School about the concept of "social disorganization" and as a consequence the falling apart of primary social controls, shifting to a concept of "differential social organization." In fact, different social groups establish a different relationship with deviant and/or criminal behavior, because the level of acceptance of norms of deviance or of conformity (from the perspective of "official society") vary from one organized group to another. Therefore, beside the concept of "differential social organization" – explaining the rates of crimes within each differential group – the analyst has to consider, from the perspective of the individual, a "differential association" with the various groups. It is this "differential association" that should instead explain the likelihood of individual criminal involvement. A differential individual association with organized groups, each recommending a different relationship with norms of deviance and conformity, will in fact eventually help explain individual criminality. So, for instance, a young person will find himself between the recommendations to conformity of the family, or the school, and those to deviance of the gang to which he belongs.

A concept of "normative conflict" is therefore at the core of the theory of differential association – as Sutherland's theory is commonly referred to – a concept not very far from the idea, developed by legal theorists, of "legal pluralism." Sutherland's notion of "normative conflict" should be kept separate from Thorsten Sellin's contemporaneous notion of "culture conflict" in his famous essay on "Culture Conflict and Crime" (Sellin 1938; see about this an essay by Sutherland's student, and continuer of his theory, Donald R. Cressey (1968)). Sellin, also owing to the Chicago School, had identified three types of conflict, defined in terms of clash between "cultural codes": border conflicts, conflicts that follow the extension of the norms of one code to cover territories previously under a pre-existing code (as in colonial expansions), and conflicts that follow the migration of the members of a cultural group to the territory of another group. Sellin's main problematic definition referred therefore still to the situation of migration, and he was the first to focus on the specific problems of so-called "second generations," that is, the problem of those children, nieces, and nephews of immigrants who find themselves between the cultural code of the parents and the cultural code of the outside world, children "divided between two societies, two societies separated by the door of their home."[5]

Sutherland's concept of conflict centered instead on the idea of "normative conflict" (Sutherland 1942). The conflict was no longer now between norms coming from different cultural, ethnic, or national backgrounds, but between different normative systems (and how the latter related to social and legal norms about deviance and/or crime). This shift, from a cultural to a normative concept of conflict, reflected at least in part the transition of American society from the age of the great migrations – after the more restrictive legislation of the 1920s – to a plurality of normative systems *internal*, so to speak, to American society. It corresponded also to the start of huge internal migratory movements especially by African Americans, from the Southern states (and their "Jim Crow laws") to the big cities of the East, Midwest, and West.

In other words, the standpoint of "normative conflict" – with reference to norms that might be either socially or legally grounded – was based on the awareness of the fact that, in a society characterized by a plurality of normative systems such as the United States, each individual person may find himself or herself in a situation of moral dilemma because of having normative horizons that are not only different but also, sometimes, in conflict; a dilemma that may be at times solved in a direction that is unfavorable to criminal law, i.e. through actions that are sanctioned by criminal law even if socially grounded. The idea of "differential association" therefore consisted in a theory of criminal behavior based on the concept of learning behavior in social interaction:[6] "[a] person becomes delinquent because of an excess of definitions favourable to violation of law over definitions unfavourable to violation of law" (Sutherland and Cressey 1978: 81). Such definitions are learned "in interaction with other persons in a process of communication" (Sutherland and Cressey 1978: 80) but not necessarily with persons or groups labeled as "criminal." The theory's emphasis is rather on "the specific direction of motives, drives, rationalizations, and attitudes" (Sutherland and Cressey 1978: 81). Furthermore, what is learned is also the "techniques of committing the crime, which are sometimes very complicated, sometimes very simple" (ibid.). Criminal behavior is therefore learned like any other behavior and does not presuppose any specific characteristic in the person learning it other than that he or she is placed in the position to learn it (see below for the case of white-collar criminals). Furthermore, "[d]ifferential associations may vary in frequency, duration, priority, and intensity" (ibid.). Learning "within intimate personal groups" (Sutherland and Cressey 1978: 80) and in early childhood is therefore supposed to be pre-eminent compared to later learning. At the time when Sutherland formulated his theory, mass media of communication had not achieved the central social role they have now (one wonders whether Sutherland would have held to this aspect of his theory had he been able to observe such later developments). Also, the prestige and the emotional reactions connected to the source of the definitions are very important for Sutherland.

It is worth pointing out, furthermore, that when Sutherland and Cressey referred to "rationalizations," they did not mean a psycho-analytic concept according to which some of our words or actions may be "rationalizations" of hidden ("unconscious") motives and drives, as at the time "the Freudian School" might have maintained. On the contrary, true to the rather malleable concept of the human being typical of the Pragmatism of the early Chicago School, they conceived of rationalizations as discursive statements, often of a moral nature, that embedded recommendations of this or that course of action. "Rationalization" was for them therefore much more of a cause than a consequence. The idea is closer to what C. Wright Mills (1940) in those very years – and within the same post-Chicagoan intellectual mold – would have called "vocabularies of motives," that is, socially "typical" motives that, by being in fact typical, are more easily accepted either within society at large or within restricted social groupings (see next chapter). As a matter of fact, in his work about embezzlers, *Other People's Money* (1953), which he considered as his most successful sociologically,[7] Donald Cressey employed Mills's idea of "vocabularies of motive" as a sort of logical complement to differential association theory. This was a concept of "rationalization" closer to Weber's and directly opposite to the psychoanalytic one. Rather than as an expression of "inner drives," the Chicagoans conceived of behavior as being imposed (almost) from the outside, as it were. A good example of such oppo-sition may be found in Cressey's answer to criticism according to which the category of "compulsive crimes" would be an obvious exception to differential association theory because "compulsive crimes" would not be "learned from the outside" but "springing from the inside." In a study about "kleptomania," Cressey showed that the type of psychologically pathological behavior defined as "kleptomania" – a sort of compulsive shop-lifting – was diagnosed as such in middle-class offenders, whereas it remained simple shop-lifting, or thieving, among members of the lower class. Cressey derived from such an observation the conclusion that the apparently compulsive behavior that the psychiatrists called "kleptomania" also was a learned behavior, available only to members of the middle class because of their higher educational level, which had exposed them to such a label (indeed, to such rationalization), whereas working-class offenders had no other chance than simply to "steal" (Cressey 1954). It was the idea, of Pragmatist and interactionist origin, that the words we learn in interaction with others become springs for action, rather than disguises of some deep inner instinct.

A later author, Daniel Glaser (1956), contributed to differential association theory further by elaborating what he called "differential identification," a notion intended to correct the discursive emphasis of the original formulation of the theory. Glaser noticed that the power of symbols and images may be extremely strong in promoting identification with certain people or behavior, whether real or imagined. Such symbols or images may fulfill a function of recommending behavior contrary to the law that is at least as strong as "verbal" recommendations. Glaser's elaboration of the theory reflected a time when, especially at the movies, imagery of the struggle between the outlaw and the sheriff, the good and the bad, the gangster and the cop, had become paramount.

## White-Collar Crime

Sutherland's polemic objective in criminology – and, later on, Cressey's, in his re-editions of Sutherland's classic *Criminology* (Sutherland and Cressey 1978) – was what he called "the multiple-factor approach," that is, the idea that "crime is a product of a large number and great variety of factors, and that these factors cannot now, and perhaps cannot ever, be integrated theoretically. That is, . . . no scientific theory of criminal behavior is possible" (ibid. 63, but see, more generally, 63–6). Citing Albert K. Cohen's critique of the multiple-factor approach in criminology (Cohen 1955), Sutherland and Cressey point out that this approach is usually (but not necessarily) connected to the "evil-causes-evil fallacy," the idea, that is,

that "evil" results (crime) must have "evil" precedents (broken home, psychopathic personality, and so on). Thus, when we "explain" crime or almost any other social problem, we tend merely to catalogue a series of sordid and ugly circumstances which any decent citizen would deplore, and attribute causal power to those circumstances. In criminology, this fallacious procedure might stem from a desire to eradicate crime without changing other existing conditions which we cherish and esteem; that is, criminologists tend to identify with the existing social order and seek causes of crime in factors which might be eliminated without changing social conditions that they hold dear, or that may be safely deplored without hurting anyone's feelings. (Sutherland and Cressey 1978: 66)[8]

Sutherland's "discovery" of "white-collar crime" – starting with his address as president of the American Sociological Society in Philadelphia in 1939 (Geis and Goff 1983: ix), then published as an article in the *American Sociological Review* (1940) – is tightly connected to such a programmatic intent in his scientific orientation. Sutherland aimed to elaborate a "general" and unitary theory of crime, able to explain any kind of criminal behavior; a theory, therefore, that should be able to explain also (and especially?) criminal behavior that did not come from "sordid and ugly circumstances" but, on the contrary, from the highest echelons of society, society's most illustrious and shining quarters. The previous decade, the decade of Franklin Delano Roosevelt's "New Deal,"[9] had provided Sutherland with ample opportunity for such a discovery through the copious legislation imposing regulation on many aspects of economic activity. Edwin Sutherland's contribution was probably the best representation of the New Deal's progressive stance within the criminological discipline, exposing the criminal undercurrents present in so much of official society (and connecting that view to his differential association theory). This he did most famously of course in his book *White Collar Crime*, published in 1949. If one considers, however, his earlier *The Professional Thief* (1937), an attitude of benevolent indifference toward thief Chic Conwell goes together with a thinly veiled contempt for the hypocrisy of official society. In his conclusions, discussing "the profession of theft" from the perspective of differential association, Sutherland had written:

[The thief] receives assistance from persons and agencies which are regarded as legitimate or even as the official protectors of legitimate society. In such persons and agencies he frequently finds attitudes of predatory control[10] which are similar to his own. The political machine which dominates the political life of many American cities and rural districts is generally devoted to predatory control. The professional thief and the politician, being sympathetic in this fundamental interest in predatory control, are able to co-operate to mutual advantage. This involves co-operation with the police and the courts to the extent that these agencies are under the control of the political machine or have predatory interests independent of the machine. The thief is not segregated from that portion of society but is in close and intimate communication with it not only in his occupational life but in his search for sociability as well. He finds these sympathizers in the gambling places, cabarets, and houses of prostitution, where he and they spend their leisure time. (Sutherland 1937: 208–9)[11]

The next step, to focus on the very behavior itself of these "sympathizers," was logical enough, even if by "white-collar criminals" Sutherland referred much more to offenders active in the corporate world than to public officers. For Sutherland, white-collar crime was "crime committed by a person of respectability and high social status in the course of his occupation" (Sutherland 1983: 7). As we mentioned, it was the context that to some degree drew attention to this new kind of "crime." The goods protected by the law were no longer only personal safety and property but also public and/or collective goods, such as shareholders' and unions' rights, as well as the public regulation of the physical, economic, and social environments within which corporations found themselves operating. For the first time, "criminals" were not only those inhabiting the bottom end of the social stratification but also those who found themselves at the top. In this sense, Sutherland's "discovery" of white-collar crime is strictly linked to his formulation of "differential association theory." When, in fact, what was publicly meant by "criminal" was the bank robber, the drug addict, or the typical street criminal, it was easy to employ an argument of the evil-causes-evil type, the "evil fallacy" Cressey refers to in the passage quoted above. Once, however, criminals were also powerful people, at the top of their corporate empire as big stakeholders or managers,[12] clearly that type of explanation became senseless and it was necessary to look for a more general theory. In *White Collar Crime*, Sutherland in fact tried to show that there was a relationship between those industries that had the most violations of the law and the diffusion of current, "commonsensical" definitions of behavior favorable to the breaking of the law within their cultural environment, in accordance therefore with the type of prediction one would make based on differential association theory.

One difficulty that haunted Sutherland from the very beginning, however, and that kept haunting his research (and, as a matter of fact, all later research devoted to white-collar crime), was the fact that, often, the unlawful behavior of white-collar criminals was unlawful from the standpoint not of criminal law but of other kinds of law, of a "civil" nature. From a strictly legal point of view, therefore, it was difficult to call white-collar criminals, *criminals*. A scholar contemporary to Sutherland, Paul Tappan, indeed maintained exactly that position (Tappan 1951). This of course opened up a real Pandora's box of problems for Sutherland. There was first of all the theoretical issue of what was the subject-matter of criminology. A strict legal-constructionist position would have consigned the definition of the boundaries of criminology to the hands of those in government, the very ones often implicated in at least protecting, if not practicing, white-collar crime. To leave the definition of the matter of criminology to the criminologist himself or herself, however, would have opened the door to a sort of natural-law "wish list" of criminal behavior based on the very subjective choices of the criminologists (Schwendinger and Schwendinger 1970). Sutherland did not want to drift in this latter direction and discussed the matter from the point of view of the sanctions involved (Sutherland 1983: 45–62). If the sanctions had a "punitive" aspect, such as in the "triple damages" clause inflicted by anti-trust legislation, then the behavior so punished could be defined as "criminal," even if the related suit would be of a "civil" kind brought under tort law.

The problem was, and still is, however, that, if nothing else, there is a very clear distinction between white-collar criminals and other types of criminals, and that resides in the fact that the former have quite a bit of social power both in terms of the resources at their disposal and in terms of connections with the "official" world. This made the publisher of Sutherland's work fearful that naming the corporations analyzed by Sutherland as "criminal" would have meant lengthy and costly legal suits brought by such corporations in defense of their reputation (Geis and Goff 1983). The result was the excision of all references to names of corporations in the original version of *White Collar Crime* and their inclusion only in a "safer," "uncut" publication *33 years* after Sutherland's death, under the protection of statutes of limitation. The matter was not trivial for Sutherland, because one of the main points that he was trying to make was that a major obstacle to public sensitivity on the matter of white-collar crime was the diminished perception of it by the public as in fact a form of crime, with the stigma attached to such a word ("radical criminology" in the 1970s would pick up Sutherland's efforts again by developing the concept of "crimes of the powerful"; Pearce 1976).

The lasting merit of Edwin H. Sutherland's "differential association theory" would in fact be its applicability to any subject, without distinction, as opposed to the hypocritical and self-serving nature of the "multiple-factor approach." Differential association theory's most obvious limitation is its problematic predictive value, because, in order to be able to predict anyone's behavior, we would need to know the most minute details of his or her life-history (in so far as it is always possible that there is a prevalence of definitions favorable to law-breaking over definitions unfavorable by a very slim margin). This may translate therefore in an *a posteriori* explanation: if criminal behavior ensues then there must have been a prevalence of such definitions. It could be objected, however, that this is a more general difficulty with all kinds of social research, not specific to the theory. It was also observed that differential association theory would be a theory of the *transmission* of criminality rather than of the *genesis* of criminality. This is an aspect that has to do, however, with the broader concept of social innovation, a question that was investigated, especially about deviance and crime, by Robert K. Merton.

## Talcott Parsons's "Problem of Order"

The mobilization of all society's forces and energies during the New Deal's economic reconstruction was followed by an even more intense mobilization in the war period. Both efforts furnished American society with a renewed sense of cohesion and unity. This sense was well expressed also by a shift, at the same time geographical and theoretical, away from the fragmented and conflictual but very "open" vision that had characterized a Pragmatist-leaning Chicago School, toward a more structured, unified, and consensual vision that gained a foothold within the great private universities of the Eastern seaboard, such as Harvard, Yale, and Columbia. This crucial answer to 1930s disorientation did not mean going back to ideas of "the State" or of "coercion." It meant instead going further on the path opened up by Chicago, the investigation of the social grounds for communication and

consensus, framed within a more cohesive and unitary concept of civil society.

In particular, the kind of social theory that a young scholar at Harvard, Talcott Parsons, started to articulate in the 1930s and that would find a first but crucial expression in *The Structure of Social Action* (1937) was probably the clearest sign of such a shift taking place. By revisiting and originally synthesizing the great European theorizations of the previous period – from Durkheim to Weber, from Pareto to Freud (this last one in particular in the successive *The Social System* (Parsons 1951)) – Parsons managed to obtain several results at the same time. On the one hand, he managed to create a new sociological canon, orienting to this day the social theory courses of most graduate programs in North America and Europe. On the other, he redefined the central problem of society as Hobbes's "Problem of Order" (Parsons 1937: 89–94; see below). Further, he strengthened sociology's competitive thrust *vis-à-vis* economics and political science. Parsons's proposal meant at the same time continuing with the previous sociological tradition and breaking with it. He emphasized sociology's traditional aversion for the "methodological individualism" of economists, lawyers, and political scientists, constructing at the same time the concept of a social system where normative, moral, and "non-rational" elements played a decisive role. In a manner similar to the way in which Durkheim, in late nineteenth-century France, had addressed the problem of social cohesion in a society run by conflict and a newly rediscovered "anomie," so Parsons was updating and incorporating Durkheim (and other writers) to address the turmoil caused by the worst economic and social crisis in American history. What Durkheim's and Parsons's solutions had in common was the idea that such crises could not be met simply by relying on the "invisible hand" of the market, i.e. by the "providential" coming together of a sum of individual choices, but instead by identifying the sources of common, collective, shared sentiments and institutions.

Sigmund Freud's psychoanalysis contributed powerfully to Parsons's solution to Hobbes's problem of order. By the 1930s, Freud's theory was quite well known in America, albeit in a rather traditionalist version that emphasized the idea of individual socialization through the relationship with the family and particularly with mother and father, in an implicit opposition to Chicago's pluralist concept (it was no accident that Mead had written of a "generalized other" – as we have seen – rather than of a "superego" modeled after the father figure). Parsons thought that the solution to the

Hobbesian problem resulted from reconciling Durkheim with Freud, and lay essentially in the idea of an "introjection" of the social contract mechanism and of its main product, the sovereign, within the individual personality.[13] This was an idea central to the Freudian construction, and spelled out especially in some of Freud's most historical-anthropological works such as *Totem and Taboo* (Freud 1913).[14] In this manner, Parsons internalized Hobbes's voluntarist, rationalist, and contractualist solution, bringing it inside each individual, a non-rational product of a successful socialization process (Lamo de Espinosa 1980).

The turn taken by Parsons in investigating social control carried an affinity for a revival of natural law in philosophy and legal theory that developed especially after World War II as a reaction against both legal realism and legal positivism. Both were in fact seen as having abandoned the ideal of higher values – indirectly contributing, it was claimed, to the moral demise that presided over the tragedy of the war and especially over the National Socialist take-over in Germany, and the subsequent Holocaust. Authors such as Roscoe Pound (1960), Lon L. Fuller (1964), or Philip Selznick (1961) felt the need for anchoring the norms of social life in a *foundation* much more stable than written law or the activities of the judiciary branch. Going back to natural law positions seemed to be the natural response to such a need – a response that carried an affinity for Talcott Parsons's inclination to portray the picture of a systemic social order, monistic and unitary, instead of the chaotic and conflictual pluralism of previous sociological schools, whether of the Chicago or Berlin variety. It is no surprise therefore that, in 1960s Harvard, Talcott Parsons used to teach a seminar with that Lon L. Fuller who had entered into a famous polemical dispute with the most recognized representative, in the English-speaking world, of legal positivism, H. L. A. Hart (Parsons 1970: 67; Fuller 1958, 1964; Hart 1958; Sciulli 1992).

Parsons's revisionism extended to the meaning of the concept of "social control," giving it a new, and lasting, direction. Parsons made in fact a distinction between *socialization* of the young, into the normative structure of the social system, and a concept of "social control" proper, that he limited to *reaction to deviance* – a usage of the term "social control" that is still quite popular today among social scientists. Social control assumed therefore a sort of second-order – or, as it was called, "homeostatic" (Mayhew 1982: 59–60) – status, depending on a concept of deviance that was now conceived in absolute and no longer relative terms, a deviance that was essentially a failure of socialization, for whatever individual or collective reason. The chaotic, conflictual, and plural vision of the world that had been characteristic of Chicago sociology in the period of the great immigration increasingly yielded to a more conservative view, in a society that saw its mission as the integration of different groups within a coherent, cohesive, and unitary social whole (where "integration" was increasingly synonymous with "assimilation" and "Americanization"). "Deviance" was no longer the result of "social disorganization" or, with Sutherland, of a "differential social organization," but of a "deficit" of socialization, so that, when Parsons had to give examples of what he meant by deviance and social control, he used to refer to mental illness and psychotherapy (Parsons 1970). Deviance was not the product of the counterposing of different normative systems, whatever the social weight carried by such systems. The conflict was no longer among different groups, groups that struggled for the definition of what is normal and what is deviant – and, in so doing, in some way supported individual deviance. Now the struggle was between the social whole and the individual who, from some kind of dysfunctionality, did not complete his socialization process. Social control was therefore the job of the police officer, or of the social worker, or of the therapist, who intervened to re-establish a balance endangered by the emerging deviance. In the theory of "anomie" elaborated by Parsons's student and colleague Robert K. Merton, the roots of deviance were to be found in the lack of internalization either of the prescribed shared social goals or of the acceptable means to reach them. For Merton, then, as well as for Parsons, the deviant could hardly escape a choice between opportunism and failure, between "cutting corners" in order to reach the social ends and simply withdrawing from "the rat race."

## Robert K. Merton's Theory of Anomie

A junior colleague of Talcott Parsons at Harvard, in his theory of anomie, or of "structural frustration," Robert K. Merton explored the relationship between the cultural and structural levels of a given social context, aiming at explaining a deviant type of individual "adaptation" as the result of phenomena of attrition, tension, and conflict between these two levels (Merton 1938). Merton distinguished on the one hand the socially defined "culture goals" and on the other the norms pertaining to the legitimate,

Table 1  A typology of modes of individual adaptation (Merton 1938: 676)

| Modes of adaptation | Culture goals | Institutionalized means |
| --- | --- | --- |
| Conformity | + | + |
| Innovation | + | − |
| Ritualism | − | + |
| Retreatism | − | − |
| Rebellion | +/− | +/− |

"institutionalized" means through which such goals ought to be achieved. The acceptance of goals and means by the individual (marked with a "+" sign in table 1), or the rejection of the same (marked with a "−"sign in table 1), produce a series of possible combinations that allow Merton to outline one "conformist" adaptation and four "deviant" ones (innovation, ritualism, retreatism, rebellion).

*Innovation* – understood in a rather different manner from how Durkheim had conceived it (see above, chapter 3) – is the category central to Merton's interest and the one that also comprises a *criminal* type of deviance. Such a form of adaptational behavior results in fact from a dissociation between legitimate, culturally prescribed goals and institutionalized means. The means chosen in order to achieve those goals (violence, fraud, corruption, etc.) are technically effective but are discouraged by social norms. Furthermore, categories of *ritualism* (exemplified by "the bureaucrat"), and especially of *retreatism*, highlight forms of deviant adaptation that would become increasingly central to North American culture and later on to contemporary society more generally (about "retreatism," one has only to think of phenomena such as those of the so-called "counterculture" and especially the "drug culture" of the 1960s and 1970s).

The particular essay by Merton that gave birth to the theory just presented, "Social Structure and Anomie" (1938), became one of the most popular in the history of American sociology. Beyond its criminological interest, in fact, it was soon seen as a sort of commentary on the malaise of American society, on a par with other famous essays of the time, such as *The Neurotic Personality of Our Time*, by Freudian psychoanalyst Karen Horney (1937), who, from a different perspective, made a point very similar to Merton's. Both essays were researching the basic acquisition anxiety that was thought to be characteristic of American culture, and of the "motivational con-stitution" of Americans (Orrù 1987). It is remarkable that the cate-gory where Merton inserts crime, "innovation," even if it has quite a different aspect from Durkheim's usage, is still one of the most fundamental and appreciated facets of "the American character." At that very time, an illustrious colleague of Robert Merton at Harvard, Joseph Schumpeter, saw innovation as a defining feature of capitalist entrepreneurship. He called it "the process of creative destruction" (Schumpeter 1943: 81–6). If this was the process typical of capitalism, however, could not that process of creative destruc-tion extend to the moral domain? Implicitly, and at times explicitly, Merton portrays deviance as a fundamentally "normal" aspect of American culture.

Merton's theory soon acquired a popularity that still holds today. It was criticized and developed by other authors, such as Albert K. Cohen (1955) and Richard A. Cloward and Lloyd E. Ohlin (1960), especially because of its more instrumental and monistic aspects – the culture goals are essentially of a Utilitarian type, and there are no others. These aspects did not seem to fit well with the kind of juvenile behavior that was being observed around the 1950s, espe-cially in relation to the "new" phenomenon of "gang" behavior. This seemed to be better explained by making reference to an "expressive" cultural attitude, alternative to the description emerg-ing from Merton's essay. In their efforts, Merton's critics also tried to have Merton come to terms with Sutherland. In *Delinquency and Opportunity* (1960), for instance, Cloward and Ohlin elaborated a "theory of subcultures" according to which the focus had to be on "collective" rather than "individual" modes of adaptation. Merton's typology should then describe adaptational modes not by individu-als but by social groupings, or "subcultures," that try to adapt to specific social conditions and a given distribution of opportunities. Whereas therefore Cloward and Ohlin make use of Merton's theory in order to explain the *origins* of collective adaptation to the unequal distribution of access to legitimate means, they rely instead on Sutherland's theory in order to explain the *transmission* of such adaptational forms from generation to generation, from social group to social group. Furthermore, in the book Albert K. Cohen pub-lished in 1955, entitled *Delinquent Boys*, he tried to show that gang juvenile behavior seemed to be guided by "expressive" behavioral motivations, as in the case of vandalism, rather than instrumental motivations. It was therefore difficult to insert it within Merton's typology. Cohen also tried to relate Merton's heritage to the by then rising star of symbolic interactionism – which, as we shall see in the next chapter, would take center stage in the decades of the 1960s and 1970s (Cohen 1965).

## Crime, Democracy, and "the American Dream"

Through his theory of anomie, Merton underlined the effects of an egalitarian and democratic ideology as a "normal" source of innovation – whether of a conformist or deviant type – but anyway aiming at the achievement of "the American dream" (Bell 1953). The problem was, and is, of course, the differential availability of "institutionalized means" – essentially cultural and economic resources – to members of different social and ethnic strata. The pressure toward anomic behavior – i.e. toward a purely instrumental approach to the choice of which means to use in order to achieve cultural goals – is therefore much more intense for the members of the lowest socio-economic ranks, who are severely limited in accessing the two most important resources in social competition: money and education.

More recently, Steven F. Messner and Richard Rosenfeld have again retraced the most critical and problematic aspects of the path opened up by Merton, in their *Crime and the American Dream* (1997). It is worth pointing out, however, that the Chicago School tradition had fully anticipated such themes, in the post-Chicagoan contribution by Sutherland, for instance (see above), or – to give an even more poignant example – in Thomas and Znaniecki's closing remarks on the subject of the "sexual immorality" of Polish immigrant "girls" in Chicago:

> Perhaps the girl would settle down unrevoltingly to . . . steady life, however dull, if the apparent possibilities of an entirely different life, full of excitement, pleasure, luxury and showing-off, were not continually displayed before her eyes in an American city. Shop windows, theatres, the press, street life with its display of wealth, beauty and fashion, all this forms too striking a contrast to the monotony of the prospect that awaits her if she remains a "good girl." If she felt definitely and irremediably shut off from this "high life" by practically impassable class barriers, as a peasant girl in Europe feels, she might look at all this show of luxury as upon an interesting spectacle with no dream of playing a role in it herself. *But even aside from the idea of democracy – which though it does not mean much to her politically, teaches her to think that the only social differences between people are differences of*

*wealth* – she feels that some small part at last of this gorgeousness actually is within her reach, and her imagination pictures to her indefinite possibilities of further advance in the future. Sooner or later, of course, she will be forced back into her destined channel by society, by the state, by economic conditions, will be forcibly "reformed" and settled, not into a satisfied, positively moral course of life but to a more or less dissatisfied acceptance of the necessary practical limitations of her desires and of the more or less superficial rules of *decorum*. But before her dreams are dispelled she tries to realize them as far as she can. We have here, of course, only one specification of the unrest which characterizes America and American women. (Thomas and Znaniecki 1918–20: 1820–1, my emphasis)

"The idea of democracy," Thomas and Znaniecki wrote, "teaches her to think that the only social differences between people are differences of wealth." There is, however, another great "equalizer" besides money, in a democratic society, and that is violence, if for just an ephemeral moment (because, as Weber taught us, the "monopoly of violence," of *real* violence, is one of the constitutive elements of the State), or fraud, corruption, prostitution. For those who do not possess money – or that other key to *future* money, education – the temptation is high to try to balance their disadvantage by handling a gun, or using their own body, or swindling and "hustling." At the time when Thomas and Znaniecki, and later Merton, were writing, the attempts of working-class American "girls" and "boys" to realize their "dreams" in the big city were often portrayed in the literary realism of the time – from Theodore Dreiser's *An American Tragedy* (1925) to Richard Wright's *Native Son* (1940)[15] – and reflected the personal moral "freedom" brought about by the revolutionary nature of that great democrat, money, *vis-à-vis* the constraints of a very unequal distribution of opportunities. In a famous 1950s essay, "Crime as an American Way of Life," strangely enough not referenced in Messner and Rosenfeld, Daniel Bell had pointed out that crime has traditionally been a non-secondary aspect in the process of integration and social climbing of all immigrant groups – when Bell was writing, for instance, the Italian one – thanks to the juncture between organized crime and political and economic power (Bell 1953, 1960: 127–50). The "American dream" manifests itself, starting with the immigrant second generation, in a situation of unbalance, frustration, and downright anomie, which has been effectively captured in recent writing by the British "left realist" criminology.

Especially during the 1980s in the United Kingdom, "left realism" was a movement that wished to correct what was defined as the previous "romanticism of crime" within "radical criminology," that is, the 1960s idealization of criminal behavior as an oppositional stance. Left realists claimed instead that the lower classes were the main victims of crime and that therefore a sensible leftist politics should have been fighting crime in all its forms. It was a position that had some connection with the following Labour Party platforms on the issue (Young 1975; Lea and Young 1984). Jock Young, together with other British "left realists," has been among those who most forcefully have revived Merton's hypotheses. Young has concisely summed up Merton's lesson: "Crime occurs where there is cultural inclusion and structural exclusion" (Young 1999: 81). So, for instance, the young "ethnic minority" urban generations in America – no longer Irish or Italian but African Americans or *Latinos* (as they are called) – are perfectly integrated within the world of youth culture (Merton's "culture goals") – as much recent interesting ethnographic research has shown, from Bourgois (1995) to Nightingale (1993) to Anderson (1990) – and yet the obstacles to structural integration, heightened by "race" barriers, are so many that the likelihood of the adoption of the short paths to success of which Merton wrote (the "non-institutionalized means") increases exponentially. More generally, these authors, such as Ian Taylor and the American criminologist Elliot Currie, have pointed to the anomic consequences of "market societies" especially in the neo-liberal phase of capitalism that started in the 1970s (Taylor 1999; Currie 1985, 1997).

# 7

# *From the "Neo-Chicagoans" to Labeling Theory*

Underneath the triumph of Parsons's new orientation within American sociology, a tradition rooted in Chicago still lived, particularly owing to an "interactionist" orientation inspired by Mead's thought. On the one hand, as we have seen, Sutherland's theory of normative conflict meant a further step within such a tradition. On the other, there was the pioneering contribution by Frank Tannenbaum and, especially, the early works of C. Wright Mills and Edwin Lemert. Mills and Lemert further developed the vitality of these conceptions of social control and deviance – emerging as forerunners of that "labeling approach" that, under deeply changed overall conditions, would flourish in the 1960s.

## The Tradition of Chicago: Social Control and the "Power Elite"

Frank Tannenbaum, an Austrian immigrant, was a sort of maverick sociologist-criminologist. He had been a labor activist in the early 1930s, close to the radical positions of the magazine *Mother Jones*, in connection with which he had been arrested, convicted, and sentenced to one year of imprisonment. Later on, he became a prominent historian, an expert on slavery in the Spanish colonies of Latin America. Before this, however, he did research on youth gangs in New York, from which he derived his work *Crime and the Community* (1938), in which he presented that idea of "dramatization of evil" that would be implicit in the labeling (which he called *tagging*) of the young gangster. He would figure prominently in the list of "ancestors" of labeling within the foundational works of the early 1960s, such as Becker's *Outsiders* (1963).

Another pioneering figure, not because of his sociology of deviance but rather in his general sociological perspective, was Charles Wright Mills. First in his PhD dissertation at Madison, Wisconsin (1942) – published later on in 1964 under the title *Sociology and Pragmatism* – then in his early articles, such as "Situated Actions and Vocabularies of Motive" (1940), Mills pushed Mead's ideas on social control in a linguistic and historical-comparative direction influenced by Weber's sociology, with which Mills had become acquainted through the influence of his mentor at Madison, German émigré Hans Gerth. Gerth and Mills would in fact co-author a famous edition of a choice of Weber's writings (Gerth and Mills 1946) and, later on, their own *Character and Social Structure* (Gerth and Mills 1953). According to Mills – and in a manner similar to that of other theoretical proposals of the time, such as Kenneth Burke's (1950) – social control is exercised through the linguistic medium, and more specifically, for Mills, the establishment of "vocabularies of motive" that are "typical" or "normal." Mills claimed that the attribution of motives to human behavior means that, in the context of social interaction, social control is exercised through such "typical" motives:

> Individualistic, sexual, hedonistic, and pecuniary vocabularies of motives are apparently now dominant in many sections of twentieth-century urban America. Under such an ethos, verbalization of alternative conduct in those terms is least likely to be challenged among dominant groups. In this milieu, individuals are skeptical of Rockefeller's avowed religious motives for his business conduct because such motives are not *now* terms of the vocabulary conventionally and prominently accompanying situations of business enterprise. A medieval monk writes that he gave food to a poor but pretty woman because it was "for the glory of God and the eternal salvation of his soul." Why do we tend to question him and impute sexual motives? Because sex is an influential and widespread motive in our society and time. . . . (Mills 1940: 447–8)

In other words, each social grouping, each historical period, each type of society produces motives that are *typical*, belonging in their own context. Using these motivations within the social framework that has produced them means that accounting for given enterprises becomes easier and more acceptable. The attribution of motives, and meaning, takes place within social practices. It is therefore crucial to social control, because people have a tendency to orient themselves toward the expectation that others have of them. If people expect a given type of behavior or action, that behavior or action will be easier to perform. An action that goes instead against current definitions and expectations is much harder to enact. Language itself constitutes therefore a ground for social control. Going back to Mead's concept of "generalized other," Mills states:

> one of the components of a "generalized other," as a mechanism of societal control, is vocabularies of acceptable motives . . . The "control" of others is not usually direct but rather through manipulations of a field of objects. We influence a man by naming his acts or imputing motives to them – or to "him" . . . such lingual behavior is part of the process of social control. (Mills 1940: 444, 445, 451)

We have seen that, according to Mead, the "generalized other" expresses the general attitude of society, or of a specific social group within it (see above, chapter 5). Reflection, however, on the social and political structure of American society throughout the years of the war and then of the so-called "Cold War" would bring Mills to face the fact – which had been still rather unproblematic to Mead – that the field of social interaction, within which processes of social control are located, is increasingly organized in a manner contradictory to the "democratic" principle. The chance of determining the "common sense" of a given society is distributed in an increasingly unequal manner. Together with Mills, we have to face a paradox when we come to consider the relationship between the formal rules of democracy and the actual practice of social control. Whereas the expansion of the democratic form makes the construction of a "consensus" – social control properly speaking – central to the new type of democratic society, the decentered structure of legal and political rights, attributed to each individual, is not at all reproduced in the discursive distribution of society, where the right of speech is actually exercised by the few, and its effective use in order to reach the many is actually practiced by the *very* few. As a matter of fact, the actual use of the right of free speech is distributed in a form that is much more akin to the very unequal and increasingly concentrated manner typical of the distribution of economic power than to the individualist distribution of political and legal rights.

Mills drew out the consequences of such observations in his vision-ary *The Power Elite*, and particularly in the chapter entitled "The Mass Society" (Mills 1956: 298–324). In it he came to the conclusion that the concept of the "public" is fundamentally corrupt and the control of the mass media is increasingly concentrated in the hands of the few who have control of wealth. The control of the mass media, however, is crucial to the control of political power and the latter is in turn crucial to the control of economic power – especially since the time of Roosevelt's "New Deal." The control of economic and political power supports in turn the control of the media. Modern (mass) democratic society is therefore actually controlled by a "power elite" that is not at all a "pathological exception" to the democratic princi-ple, but is on the contrary the normal result of the way in which this type of society works. It is the sum of political, economic, and media power (plus, especially in the United States, military power).

## The Dialectic of Social Control: The Mass Media

One can therefore read the parable of social control, as this can be traced in the United States from E. A. Ross's early proposals, through the Chicago School and G. H. Mead, to the disillusion of John Dewey and C. Wright Mills, within the development of a sort of "dialectic of social control." Such a dialectic is based on Mead's "phenomenology." The individual's standpoint, in transcending the horizon of meaning within which she is initially inscribed and confined – from the family to the school, from the neighborhood to the society, from the State to a cosmopolitan dimension – follows a trajectory that, according to the early Pragmatists, was supposed to be a path to liberation. It meant in fact a transition from the suffocating effects of primary controls in a small community to that *self*-control made possible by an inscription within broader horizons. Such a "phenomenology," or trajectory, developed, however, not only in theory but also in practice, insofar as such a continuous "transcendence" of the given boundaries walked, so to speak, on the legs of millions and millions of individuals who left their birthplace, generally in the countryside, to direct themselves toward farther and farther distant cities. Insofar as such a "multi-tude" – as it has recently been called – was "on the move" (Ander-son 1940), pursuing ever new chances of liberation and at the same time finding ever new chains of servitude, the processes of social control also were becoming more uniform, standardized, centralized, so that the "integration" of a "multitude on the move" could be secured.

As Mead had insightfully argued, the exercise of social control is always the assumption of the perspective of a given group, and so to the movement of broader and broader masses of people, to their insertion within the systems of production and consumption, there had to correspond a broadening of the power of centralizing discourse. In the same way in which market society has been increasingly yielding to the monopolistic developments of capitalism, "the public" also has given way to an increasing standardization of the opinions that circulate in its midst. The unilaterality of the message – whether of information or entertainment does not matter much – tends to prevail. Free debate and dialogue, to early twentieth-century Pragmatists, constituted the very essence of democracy, by allowing the making of a "truth" that could only be the result of a free exchange of opinions (James 1897). They are, however, increasingly replaced by a passive reception of messages coming from a central position, a process that is, in a sense, the generalization of a communicative Panopticon.

What at the beginning was perceived as an opening up of horizons, which, in breaking down the barriers of localism, enriched individual choice, has instead transformed into the passive reception of standardized messages that replace the limited horizon of primary groups by an even more reduced horizon – even if apparently wide and universal (in the same way in which the increasingly universal usage of the English language is slowly replacing and literally destroying languages and dialects). At the same time, and correspondingly, the individual's direct experience is completely devalued in favor of an imaginary sphere recreated by the mass media that certify even what one should be able to know directly. This is a process that is particularly relevant when one talks about crime (in surveys about victimization and personal safety, for instance, one usually obtains more negative results in answer to questions on the situation of "the society" or "the city," and more positive to questions on one's own, or the neighborhood's, personal experience of safety). Mills writes:

> Very little of what we think we know of the social realities of the world have we found out first-hand. Most of "the pictures in our heads" we have gained from these media – even to the point where we often do not really believe what we see before us until we read about it in the paper or hear about it on the radio. (Mills 1956: 311)[1]

And a few pages later:

> [T]he man in the mass does not gain a transcending view from these media; instead he gets his experience stereotyped, and then he gets sunk further by that experience. He cannot detach himself in order to observe, much less to evaluate, what he is experiencing, much less what he is not experiencing. Rather than that internal discussion we call reflection, he is accompanied through his life-experience with a sort of unconscious, echoing monologue. He has no projects of his own: he fulfills the routines that exist. He does not transcend whatever he is at any moment, because he does not, he cannot, transcend his daily milieu. He is not truly aware of his own daily experience and of its actual standards: he drifts, he fulfills habits, his behavior a result of a planless mixture of the confused standards and the uncriticized expectations that he has taken over from others whom he no longer really knows or trusts, if indeed he ever really did. . . . He does not formulate his desires; they are insinuated into him. And, in the mass, he loses the self-confidence of the human being – if indeed he has ever had it. For life in a society of masses implants insecurity and further impotence; it makes men uneasy and vaguely anxious. (Mills 1956: 322–3)

Mills would disappear a few years later, in 1962, when he was only 45, not knowing how much his indictments of the man-in-the-mass and of the power elite would echo in the years to come, in the international "movement" that was to start at around the time of his death. Mills's man-in-the-mass would live again shortly after in central icons of popular culture, from the Beatles' "Nowhere Man" to Bob Dylan's "Mister Jones" in his "Ballad of a Thin Man."

"Life in a society of masses implants insecurity and further impotence; it makes men uneasy and vaguely anxious," Mills wrote in 1956. With the skyrocketing increase in especially property crime that would start soon after, the men and women in the masses would find a definite content for that vague anxiety. The last exit of such a long-term development has been a tried and true "governing through crime," as has been claimed recently (Simon 2007). There is an irony, an ironic inversion, here that it would be a shame to miss, because what is usually considered the very seal of formal social control, penal punishment, seems to be exercising the deepest form of control in the most informal way – in a way that brings Durkheim's view of the "functions of deviance" to its most extreme consequences. It is the *representation* of crime, much more than the *repression* of crime – as we believed in the 1960s! – that plays a central role in social control. This happens in a democracy in which representation is everything, a democracy that has been described thus by one of the foremost American TV icons, Ted Koppel: "We now communicate with everyone and say absolutely nothing. We have reconstructed the Tower of Babel and it is a television antenna. A thousand voices producing a daily parody of democracy, in which everyone's opinion is afforded equal weight, regardless of substance or merit."[2] And of course the commercial basis for the financing of broadcasting, in the United States as well as in most Western European countries now, also tends to concentrate the sources of information and to eliminate the messages that stray too far from a "central tendency."

Certainly, totalitarian regimes were among the first to use mass media of communication. Walter Benjamin, from within the experience of the Nazi regime, had written prophetically:

> The change noted here in the method of exhibition [of the work of art] caused by mechanical reproduction applies to politics as well. The present crisis of the bourgeois democracies comprises a crisis of the conditions that determine the public presentation of the rulers. Democracies exhibit a member of government directly and personally before the nation's representatives. Parliament is his public. Since the innovations of camera and recording equipment make it possible for the orator to become audible and visible to an unlimited number of persons, the presentation of the man of politics before camera and recording equipment becomes paramount. Parliaments, as much as theatres, are deserted. Radio and film not only affect the function of the professional actor but likewise the function of those who also exhibit themselves before this mechanical equipment, those who govern. Though their tasks may be different, the change affects equally the actor and the ruler. The trend is toward establishing controllable and transferable skills under certain social conditions. This results in a new selection, a selection before the equipment from which the star and the dictator emerge victorious. (Benjamin 1936: 247)

It is quite clear why, in 1936, Walter Benjamin could write that, from this new "selection before the equipment . . . the star and the dictator emerge victorious," looking, at the time, at the use of media by European dictators such as Hitler or Mussolini. However, it would be especially under democratic conditions that the power of the new media would develop to the utmost of their possibilities.

It is in fact only under such conditions that the issue of the construction of a consensus becomes a question of life and death for the maintenance of social order. Furthermore, under democratic conditions we have a further paradox. The more the conditions of democratic exchange seem to hold, the stronger and more robust is the kind of social control produced under those conditions.

"[T]hose who govern . . . exhibit themselves before this mechanical equipment," states Benjamin. Sounds familiar? Why therefore could not an actor become president of the United States? Who could do it better? This is what happened in 1980 in the United States. Or why could not a mass media entrepreneur become a State entrepreneur? This is indeed what happened more recently in Italy. What might have seemed like an idiosyncratic fascination with a radical view of the world in Benjamin has become a routine reality of politics in the Western world. The mass media of communication are in fact the ideal solution, from the standpoint of the elites, to the crucial problem of democracy. How is it possible, in fact, to conjugate the reality of a deep inequality of power and the normative prescription of equality in the formation of political will? This had been modern democracy's crucial problem at least since its beginning in the nineteenth century (Marx 1844a). This very question had been framed in the 1920s within the Chicago School as "the problem of social control," that is, the problem of making a "con-sensus," a *common* sense, that may be able to link together the actual inequality of power and the formal prescription of equality. The answer had been found in the construction of a common reference system, a common horizon. What is important is not to agree on everything – otherwise, what kind of democracy would this be? – but to agree on the essentials, on the "rules of the game," on a common "language." The mass media developed, during the course of the twentieth century, together with the making of a response to this "social need," an arena of mediation and management of conflicts. The mass media slowly transformed themselves from being simple mediators to becoming the actual managers of the overall situation – partly through that web of interests linking media ownership to economic wealth and political power, powerfully described by Mills (1956) in *The Power Elite*.

Certainly, the centralization of social control that ends up constituting a "common horizon" of sense and meaning within a given discursive universe does not mean at all that specific political standpoints are going to be presented as the only ones to follow. This in fact would weaken the efficacy of social control, because the legitimation of the whole process rests upon the democratic principle. The situation of fragmentation, heterogeneity, pluralism, and conflict must be and is to be taken for granted. Mead's concept of the "generalized other," however, makes visible how social control is connected to the construction of a common reference framework within which it will then be possible to distinguish specific political options and choices. In other words, in a mass democratic society social control has much more to do with setting boundaries and agendas – defining what may and what may not be a matter of contention – rather than with imposing one point of view, as in a pre-democratic or totalitarian type of society. This is what makes democratic social control much more effective, as a number of commentators had already pointed out, from de Tocqueville to Durkheim to Gramsci.[3] The central issue is the possibility of speaking the same language, whether this be the same *natural* language (hence the emphasis on "Americanization") or the same "cultural" language (i.e. the same general cultural framework of principles and values).

Within such an overall "dialectical" process of social control, the question of crime – meant in the broadest manner – plays a particularly important function. As Durkheim had shown (but also Mead (1917–18)), the criminal is the "public enemy," the one who, by his actions, indeed by his mere presence, helps the system of social control draw the boundaries of that common horizon of sense that will not be possible to overcome but within which it will be possible to have a "frank discussion." It is therefore understandable that the question of crime tends to assume more problematic contours within critical historical situations, when deep social fractures have to be recomposed and the ruling elites attend to the reconstruction of social order, such as after the "New Deal" in the United States. In fact, in situations of deep division and fragmentation, criminal conflicts may become "politicized" more easily – i.e. they can challenge more easily the drawing of the boundaries of the common horizon of sense. It is indeed such boundaries that society is discussing, and crime can very well perform a function of "innovation," as Durkheim argued (Durkheim 1895a; Erikson 1966). In the following period of social pacification and reunification, the setting of boundaries will instead more easily define who is outside as a "criminal" (or something equivalent in the political realm, such as a "terrorist"). In such periods, the criminal is better represented as a kind of moral monstrosity, and a tried and true "economy of fear" sets in (Lefebvre 1932; Corey 2004; Glassner 1999). Social, political, or class enemies become now "public enemies," i.e. enemies of all – in fact the clearest signal that a given position has lost its battle. It is a kind of process much akin to what Mills called the transformation of "public issues" in "private troubles" (Mills 1959). The opposite tends to happen instead during periods of deep reconsideration of the most important moral boundaries, when everything seems to be up for grabs. The latest period when this happened was from the 1960s to the 1970s, and it is no surprise that this was also the period when, in the field of the sociology of deviance and crime, a so-called "labeling theory" made its appearance.

## Labeling Theory

Edwin Lemert was the true pioneer who further developed a Meadian-inspired sociology in the direction of the field of deviance and social control. As early as 1942, in an article entitled "The Folkways and Social Control," Lemert reversed Parsons's "homeostatic" idea of social control. As he later explained, "I proposed that such control [i.e. the control based on folkways, mores, and laws] be termed 'passive,' in contrast to 'active' social control [which] is a process for the implementation of goals and values" (Lemert 1964: 21; in the 1942 article, Lemert (1942: 398) states that the "key" to social control has to be found in "the conditioning process"). This was an important statement because it was only after this reconceptualization of an *active* (or proactive) type of social control that Parsons's passive (or *reactive*) social control could be seen as an instance of a more general social phenomenon that might also produce what, from another point of view, appeared as "deviance" (Lemert 1983: 126–7). It should also be noted that it was only on the ground of this reversal of the Parsonian concept of social control that the future development of an idea of "secondary deviance" – deviance stabilized by interaction with agencies of social reaction – could take place (Lemert 1951, 1967).

The various contributions, in the early 1940s, by C. Wright Mills, the young Ed Lemert, and, as we have seen in the previous chapter, Edwin Sutherland, on the path opened up by the Chicago School and especially by George Herbert Mead, would not fully blossom until the early 1960s. It was then that, in the changed political and cultural climate, sociologists started doing something unusual. As Bill Chambliss was to write in a later reconstruction, "in 1962 a change in the sociological weather was taking place that was affecting us all, and it made us look again at what had often been taken for granted. Sociologists began to look through the windows of police cars and behind the bars of jail cells to discover 'the law in action'" (Chambliss 1978: 14). In other words, sociologists were no longer observing deviants from the standpoint of the agencies of social control – from inside the police cars looking out. Rather, they were looking at the very operation of such agencies, "the law in action," and started studying, and problematizing, "social control" (a few years later, Jason Ditton proposed, half-jokingly, that criminology should by then be called "controlology" (1979)).

It is worth emphasizing that, if the starting point was no longer an "original" deviance but social control – a social control that, as Lemert wrote, was seen as having an "active" function, to the point of "producing" deviation – then we had witnessed a very important change, in scientific and political terms. As we have seen in our discussion of Beccaria, the "power to punish" is among the distinctive characteristics of the sovereign. If such a power is not regulated by law but, in its effective implementation, reflects other types of concerns, political, economic, or cultural, then punishment is no longer an act of justice but is an act of hostility by one "faction" against another, and therefore the victim of such an act of hostility may indeed feel entitled to exercise what the theorists of the social contract called "the right to resist" (according to Locke, for instance, in lectures 5 and 6 of the *Second Treatise*). This makes obviously clear the strong political implications of labeling theory, and helps us understand why it was in the 1960s that such an approach appeared. It also makes abundantly clear why, when the *revanche* against the 1960s and against 1960s criminology started in the mid-1970s, labeling theory became one of the very first culprits to be singled out.

Probably the most representative contribution of this approach was, however, Howard Becker's *Outsiders* (1963). The position of labeling theorists is probably most famously stated in the opening chapter of *Outsiders* where, referring to the prevailing notions of deviance, Becker wrote of:

> . . . the central fact about deviance: it is created by society. I do not mean this in the way it is ordinarily understood, in which the causes

of deviance are located in the social situation of the deviant or in "social factors" that prompt his action. I mean, rather, that *social groups created deviance by making the rules whose infraction constitutes deviance*, and by applying those rules to particular people and labeling them as outsiders. From this point of view, deviance is *not* a quality of the act the person commits, but rather a consequence of the application by others of rules and sanctions to an "offender." The deviant is one to whom that label has successfully been applied; deviant behavior is behavior that people so label.[4] (Becker 1963: 8–9)

This last statement by Becker, "The deviant is one to whom that label has successfully been applied; deviant behavior is behavior that people so label," will be repeated over and over again and will assume mythical status among sociologists of deviance. In *Outsiders*, Becker then goes on to study those who, in 1950s America, had become "marihuana users." One of the most interesting aspects of Becker's reconstruction is where he shows the process of integration and adaptation that takes place, on the one hand, between the individual marihuana user and the "deviant" group of users and, on the other hand, between such a group and society at large. Deviance is seen in the end – as Merton had already pointed out – as problem-solving behavior, even if of the "lesser of two evils" kind. The culture of marihuana users was tied, at the time, to the culture of jazz-club musicians – a culture of which Becker himself had been part as a jazz piano-player. Already quite marginal, the musicians who made use of marihuana constituted a group whose organizing structure was increasingly determined in relation to the reaction of an overall culture that defined marihuana smoking as a criminal action (and a quite serious criminal action, at the time). The group was largely determined also by its general surroundings, where it tried to define its own autonomy and independence. It rejected, certainly, the image of itself that was offered, or better imposed, by the dominant culture, but the necessity of fighting that image, as well as of escaping the heavy legal sanctions connected at the time to marihuana smoking, ended up shaping, in a remarkable way, the identity of the deviant group and of those who were part of it.

In a rather similar way, Edwin Lemert claimed that, "[t]his is a large turn away from older sociology which tended to rest heavily upon the idea that deviance leads to social control. I have come to believe that the reverse idea, i.e., social control leads to deviance, is equally tenable and the potentially richer premise for studying deviance in modern society" (Lemert 1967: v). In fact, as early as his 1951 classic, *Social Pathology*, where he distinguished between a "primary" and a "secondary" type of "deviation," Lemert had noticed that primary deviation develops into a "secondary" form of deviance, deviance proper we could say, only when a primary deviation, a "diversity" in being, action, or behavior, is noted as a "negative" kind of deviation, a stigma – as Erving Goffman was calling it at the time (1963) – that needs to be confronted, remedied, corrected, censored, eliminated, by both informal and formal agencies of social control. This means that the deviant perceives himself or herself indeed as such, a deviant. A primary kind of deviation may be followed therefore by two possible and different outcomes. One is normalization: the diversity is not perceived as substantially negative and is therefore (positively) "normalized" – in this sense we are faced with a version of what Durkheim had termed "innovation." Or, once again, the social reaction warns the deviant that his or her behavior is unacceptable and that therefore it will have to be (negatively) normalized. This may of course happen, especially in the case of a transitory or particularly "light" form of deviance by somebody who is experiencing it for the first time. What may also happen, however – and this is the specific prediction of labeling theory – is that the person, or group, that is so defined finds it in some way easier, or preferable, or anyway better to indulge in the definition of themselves, or their actions or behavior, as deviant, and start a complex process of reconstruction of identity around a deviant identity. The result in this case will be the "fixation," so to speak, of deviance, in a sort of continuous exchange between deviation, social control, and recurring, and more firmly established, forms of deviation. So, for instance, in the example investigated by Becker, the belonging in the group of marihuana users (already within a "fringe" community, such as that of jazz musicians); the moral disvalue attributed by the community at large to marihuana smoking; the risk of revealing such a habit to family, friends, and especially law enforcement officers; the necessity of procuring the drug by means of illegal channels, often controlled by criminal organizations – all these various aspects mean that the community of marihuana users become increasingly self-selected and separated from the rest of society, by which it is stigmatized, and increasingly prone to recognize in such a stigma a not irrelevant aspect of the collective and individual identity of the members of the group.

An aspect that is probably worth emphasizing, and which particularly applies to a field that contributed heavily to the "labeling approach" – that is, the field of "mental illness" – is the idea that, in such a restructuration of the deviant's identity, a not indifferent inducement to this fixation in a role is the "problem solution" aspect of the overall process. Often, this is not a very desirable solution (to the would-be deviant), but it is one nonetheless, and is often better than keeping wallowing in the uncertainty, anxiety, stress, frustration, and conflict of the previous situation. The recognition of a specific situation as an instance of "mental illness," for instance, with the following deresponsibilization and the medical establishment's taking charge, even with specialized hospitals in the most serious cases, may become a way in which the assumption of a deviant and "degraded" role (Garfinkel 1956) is, however, preferable to no role at all (starting, of course, from the experience of deep pain and suffering in which a person who is in the end so defined often finds herself). Often, it is pointed out, the "diagnosis" of the illness and the "certification" of deviance are one and the same thing. Lemert explored the cases of alcoholism, stuttering, and specific forms of mental illness, such as paranoia (Lemert 1962). Building on Norman Cameron's article about the "paranoid pseudo-community" (Cameron 1943) – the fixation the patient develops that the whole world is in some way conspiring against him – Lemert maintains, on the basis of research he did at UCLA on hospitalization, that actually, at least at the beginning of the illness, such a community may not be "pseudo" at all, but may result from difficulties of relationship between the would-be patient and the social environment that surrounds him. Only in the reiteration of deviation, typical of what Lemert termed "secondary deviation," would a true psychotic paranoid delirium then follow. At the early instantiation of his troubles, however, the person who would then be diagnosed as "paranoid" would have good reason, so to speak, to feel that way.

Lemert's basic concept of secondary deviation would be later developed in the United Kingdom by Stanley Cohen in his study of the "moral panic" that swept the country in the early 1960s about the rivalries and clashes between two youth groups, the "Mods" and the "Rockers" (Cohen 1972). Cohen translated the concept of a feedback loop between primary and secondary deviation into that of "amplification" of deviance. Jock Young had already applied this concept to his analysis of drug control in Notting Hill (Young 1971). Apparently, both Cohen and Young had derived the concept of deviancy amplification from Leslie Wilkins (1964; Wilkins would then go on to become the acting dean of the School of Criminology in Berkeley (1966–9), a job he left after his refusal to "name names" and to order the faculty to cross the students' picket lines in the hot days of the student movement; Laub 1983: 74–5[5]). Cohen shows how the agencies of social control, reacting to their perception of primary deviation, end up amplifying the original deviation. The social reaction of the police and the judiciary, in substantial unison with the reaction by the popular press, ended up "constructing" the Mods and the Rockers as "folk devils" (an interesting rendition of these events is the movie *Quadrophenia* (1979), by director Franc Roddam, based on the album of the same title by the Who).

In a nutshell, the attitude of the labeling approach could then be summed up in the idea that *"deviance" (or, more specifically, "crime") is not a quality of the offender (as the Italian positivists would have claimed), nor a quality of his or her actions (as the neo-classical theorists would have claimed), but a quality of the overall situation that is so described.* Clearly, the logic of labeling theory countered the main assumptions of traditional criminal law, of "special" and "general" deterrence. As in the more specific (but very different) case of Freud's "Criminality from a Sense of Guilt" (1916),[6] in the more general case of labeling theory also, the societal reaction to crime becomes an inducement to crime rather than a constraint on it (Alessandro Baratta would draw this consequence most forcefully in his work (1982)). However, George Herbert Mead had already noted, in his devastating critique of a "psychology of punitive justice," that a system of punishment based on retribution or deterrence "not only works very inadequately in repressing crime but also preserves a criminal class" (Mead 1917–18: 219). In a way consistent with what Durkheim had written about 30 years earlier, Mead adds:

> The criminal does not seriously endanger the structure of society by his destructive activities, and on the other hand he is responsible for a sense of solidarity, aroused among those whose attention would be otherwise centered upon interests quite divergent from those of each other. Thus courts of criminal justice may be essential to the preservation of society even when we take account of the impotence of the criminal over against society, and the clumsy failure of criminal law in the repression and suppression of crime. (Mead 1917–18: 227)

The possibly perverse effects of labeling and punishing may be connected with what has been called a "legitimation of violence" or "brutalization" hypothesis. William Bowers and Glenn Pierce (1980) noted that, in the months following capital executions, the rate of homicides tended to increase, not to decrease, as a deterrence effect would predict (analyzing New York State data 1907–63). And Dane Archer and Rosemary Gartner (1984) rigorously developed a study of violence in cross-national perspective, showing that in those countries where the death penalty had been abolished, the homicide rate decreased, not the contrary. Archer and Gartner also showed that homicide rates tend to grow when a country is involved in a war, that this happens especially during and after a war, and that it pertains to all strata of society, not only to "returning veterans." They derived the idea therefore of what they called a "legitimation of violence hypothesis" or, following Bowers and Pierce, a "brutalization hypothesis." "What all wars have in common is the unmistakable lesson that homicide is an acceptable, even praiseworthy, means to certain ends" (Archer and Gartner 1984: 66). A vicious circle would therefore establish itself between crime, especially violent crime, and punitive social reaction, especially severely punitive social reaction. They cite what Justice Louis Brandeis stated in 1928: "Our government is the potent, the omnipresent teacher. For good or ill, it teaches the whole people by its example. Crime is contagious. If the government becomes a lawbreaker, it breeds contempt for the law" (cited in Archer and Gartner 1984: 95).

## David Matza: From "the Subterraneans" to "the Ban"

David Matza was the author who probably best represented the climax of labeling theory and, at the same time, its overcoming – a transition to the next period in the development of the sociology of deviance and social control. The initial and at the same time most famous step in his thinking was an essay published together with Gresham Sykes on so-called "techniques of neutralization" (Sykes and Matza 1957).[7] Sykes and Matza meant by that the "techniques" by which juvenile delinquents "neutralize," in their own eyes and the eyes of the social groups where they belong, the moral and/or legal prohibition to engage in deviant or criminal behavior. In a sense, it is a position not very far from Sutherland and Cressey's differential association, because the techniques of neutralization could be seen simply as "rationalizations" that allow behavior contrary to criminal law (or to "official" morality).

"Techniques of neutralization" do not belong in any "subcultural," "deviant," or "antagonistic" culture. One of Matza's most important premises – probably tied to his programmatic wish of staying close, "naturalistically," to the "subject" studied, the deviant, and his common-sense reality – is to be found in the idea that the moral universe of the deviant is not particularly different from that of common people. Those who are defined as deviant do not challenge a common and shared morality. This is in fact the reason why they need to produce "techniques of neutralization." The young man who cuts school because "today is such a beautiful day" or "that professor is obnoxious" does not take the side of a different moral order. On the contrary, he appeals to shared convictions, views of the world, and values in order to legitimize, as it were, his "deviant" behavior.

This basic orientation connects to another early theme in Matza, that of "subterranean traditions" (1961), an expression that may to some degree echo a famous title of the new literature of the "beat generation" at the time, Jack Kerouac's *The Subterraneans* (1958), and indeed the beats and Kerouac in particular are copiously referred to in Matza's piece.[8] Writing of "subterranean traditions," Matza suggests that these are traditions that are at the margins of society, that are lived in its darker areas, traditions of which we are not proud but of which we are, all in all, tolerant. Going back to Cloward and Ohlin's characterization of deviant subcultures (see previous chapter), Matza refers to the three traditions of youth deviancy: political radicalism, juvenile delinquency and "the gangs," and "bohemian" groups and lifestyles (in relation to which Matza refers to the new, at the time, "beat" culture – what would be called a few years later the "counterculture").

Those who indulge in activities socially defined as "deviant" therefore do it without generally countering hegemonic norms but by "neutralizing" their prohibition. This they do by making recourse to "vocabularies" – as Mills would have called them – that are part of the dominant culture (Sykes and Matza 1957). Such "techniques of neutralization" open up a "field of possibilities," in a Sartreanism-laden language that is quite understandable in an author who, as we have seen, called the counterculturalists "bohemians," and whose exotic idea of deviants was probably at the time that of the black-robed and barefooted "existentialists" who danced in Parisian *caves* to the sound of that African American music, jazz.[9] Within such a field of possibilities, *drift*, or *drifting*, is evoked. For Matza, the condition of "drifting" is the condition of one who wallows between delinquency and non-delinquency; who has commerce with both sides of the law; who is not "committed" to delinquency or conformity, but entertains business with both delinquent and conformist actions and trains of thought. "Drifters" were also at the time those young, and not so young, people who drifted "aimlessly" from town to town, "on the road" (Kerouac 1957), from activity to activity, trying to "make it" in whatever way possible; drifting, also theoretically, between the commitment to freedom of the "classical" school and the commitment to crime of the "positivist" school; between freedom and determinism (which Matza calls "positivism"). Freedom, however, Matza notes, comes in degrees. It is not a discrete condition. It is rather a continuous one. Freedom is essentially self-control, and this is not given to everybody in equal measure (Matza 1964: 27–30). Drifting, crucially, also opens up the possibility of the emergence of *will*:

> The periodic breaking of the moral bind to law arising from neutralization and resulting in drift does not assure the commission of a delinquent act. Drift makes delinquency possible or permissible by temporarily removing the restraints that ordinarily control members of society, but of itself it supplies no irreversible commitment or compulsion that would suffice to thrust the person into the act . . . There is a missing element – an element in the nature of a thrust or an impetus – by which the possibility of delinquency is realized. That element . . . has characteristically been construed in positivist criminology as one or another form of compulsion or commitment. I wish to recommend another construction of that element – a construction that is more consistent with the canons of classical criminology. I wish to suggest that the missing element which provides the thrust or impetus by which the delinquent act is realized is *will*. (Matza 1964: 181)

The sudden appearance, in the last chapter of *Delinquency and Drift*, of the concept of will, with an explicit connection to classical criminology's "free will" – even if Matza was too much of a twentieth-century scholar not to qualify the *amount* of freedom – an emergence that was clearly intended to consign back to "the deviant" that dignity that a century of what Matza calls "positivism" had failed to recognize, was a defining moment in the history of this branch of sociology. If for no other reason, it is so because it shows how the dramatic conservative turn that took place a few years later in the penal field started from positions that had developed from *within* the most radical segments of the sociology of deviance. (One of the few recognitions of this fact can be found in David Greenberg and Drew Humphries's (1980) reconstruction of the way in which the critique of penality in *Struggle for Justice* (AFSC 1971) opened the door to subsequent conservative critiques.) Demands such as determinate sentencing and an end to judicial and parole boards' discretion in the determination of the length of sentences, or the recognition of the delinquent's "free will," were a logical part of the culture of the broader "movement" of which a "critical" kind of criminology was part. These demands were soon increasingly hegemonized, however, by those conservative forces that were to take power in the 1970s and even more in the 1980s (see below, chapter 9). Such "neo-classical" demands were less and less articulated, therefore, within an attitude of respect and "appreciation," as Matza would have it, for the deviant person, and more and more instead within a rhetoric of moral and legal responsibilization of the deviant. They entailed penal severity, broadening of punished behaviors, harshening of convictions, lengthening of prison terms – the kind of situation that would have brought, 20 years later, a true gigantism of the prison system and a sharp positive reappraisal of the death penalty.

The indissoluble coupling by the Classical School of "individual responsibility" on the one hand and "State-administered punishment" on the other went to constitute the centerpiece in the other major work by Matza, a few years later, *Becoming Deviant* (Matza 1969). "Leviathan" literally resurfaced here, as the representative of society's unity and authority. It is Leviathan's responsibility to impose the "ban" that will label the bearer of the deviant stigma. The ban creates the banned (in other languages, the same word as "bandit"). So it had happened to Jean Genet, as he retells in his *The Thief's Journal* (Genet 1949), for instance, when, at a very young age, he had been addressed with the words, "you're a thief!" – a label that would never desert him (Sartre 1952; Matza 1969: 171). This resurfacing of Leviathan is at least as momentous as the (connected) resurfacing of "will" in his previous work. Matza is well aware of that:

> [T]he criminological positivists succeeded in what would seem the impossible. They separated the study of crime from the workings and theory of the state . . . The role of the sovereign, and by extension, instituted authority was hardly considered in the study of deviant

behavior. That lofty subject, unrelated to so seamy a matter as deviation, was to be studied in *political* science. There, as in the curriculum
in government or political sociology, Leviathan had little bearing on
ordinary criminals. And in criminology, the process of becoming an
ordinary criminal was unrelated to the workings of the state. It was,
it must be granted, a pretty neat division ... The main substance
of that state function is the authorized ordaining of activities and
persons as deviant, thus making them suitable objects of surveillance
and control. (Matza 1969: 143–5)

Here Matza introduced a footnote that is understandable only
considering that *Becoming Deviant* was written and published at
the time when the war in Vietnam – and the struggle against it
within the United States – were both reaching an unprecedented
peak:

> In considering the part played by signification in the process of
> becoming deviant, there is little necessity to denounce the state or
> accuse it of unwarranted oppression. All that is required is an appre-
> ciation of uncontested aspects of its rudimentary nature and conse-
> quence – elements of state conceded by conservative and liberal
> political theorists alike. Furthermore, no slight is intended in using
> the term Leviathan; after all, Hobbes was commending, not con-
> demning, the contrivance that would achieve a unity of meaning and
> thus order in society. Finally, connecting the state with the oppressive
> business of signification in no way implies that that is its only work.
> The state organizes welfare, makes wars and does many things in
> between. The important matter here is that we not be unduly misled
> or otherwise confused because state agents and spokesmen some-
> times call internal control and other elements of signification
> "welfare." Recently, our capacity to see through that deception has
> been inadvertently augmented by what is otherwise an ugly and
> brutal affair: other spokesmen for the same state have taken to con-
> ceiving war, too, in the honeyed terms of the welfare and correction
> of far-off peoples who have allegedly wandered from the righteous
> path. To complete the mystification, perhaps, yet other spokesmen of
> the very same state have begun to conceive of their modest welfare
> program in terms of a "war." Instead of rendering us full dizzy, it
> may be hoped that so curious a concatenation of misused terms will
> prove instructive and help restore a closer correspondence of words
> and things. (Matza 1969: 145 note 2)

In *Becoming Deviant*, Matza retraced Becker's work on marihuana
smoking from a perspective inclusive of the role of Leviathan,
coming to the conclusion that,

[b]an hardly makes commitment to a deviant path inevitable; it only assures the compounding of deviation as long as the path is maintained. Such a consequence is neither surprising nor unintended. A main purpose of ban is to unify meaning and thus to minimize the possibility that, morally, the subject can have it both ways. Either he will be deterred or bedevilled. (Matza 1969: 148)

Through the ban, i.e. the official certification of deviance, Matza's "Leviathan" comes to "manage" deviance and crime. In a way not very far from what a few years later Foucault (1975: 257–92) would call the transformation of "illegalities" in "delinquency" – in a move more historically, and less sociologically and psychologically, developed[10] – Matza claims that, by imposing the ban, control and surveillance are made possible. This is done thorough the police, through "zoning," through knowing and filing information on types of activities and people, through informants and agents provocateurs, through imprisonment. A high level of recidivism and the creation of a "dangerous class" – or of an "underclass," as it was later called – is a price that may well be paid for the construction of a "common horizon of meaning." Through the ban, a meaning is attributed to deviance and deviant behavior. An (unequal) fight takes place between Leviathan and the deviant, and Leviathan, through the ban, applies its own brand to what the deviant does and is.

## The Sixties: "Sympathy for the Devil"

In sum, an attitude of appreciation of deviance had re-emerged in the 1960s at the end of one of the most sustained positive trends in economic history and in conjunction with another decade of declining imprisonment rates (Cahalan 1979; Berk et al. 1981; see below, figure 4). Such an attitude went to the point of seeing the deviant as a sort of hero or "saint." Indeed, borrowing from another icon of the 1960s, one can actually speak of "sympathy for the devil" for the kind of attitude shared both by many young people at the time and by the kind of sociology produced by some of these young people.

As I have mentioned, in one of the early classic analytical efforts at studying social control in contemporary Western democracies, Stanley Cohen wrote of a sort of triangulation among "folk devils" (Cohen 1972), i.e. deviant political and cultural individuals and groups, in their interaction with the "myth-makers," the people of the mass media who furnish the public with representations of the folk devils, and the "rule-enforcers" (Becker 1963), the formal agents of control. The "folk devils" were on the one hand the scooter-riding, stylized, modernist Mods and on the other the nostalgic, motor-bike-riding Rockers (Cohen 1972). In the early 1960s, Lambrettas against Harley-Davidsons, they were facing each other on the poor, cold, and windy beaches where the English lower-middle class of the time were spending their "bank holidays." Cohen showed that a reinforcing interaction started, especially between the myth-makers and the rule-enforcers, in which a new type of folk-devil image was created, which, in the end – as Lemert's theory of secondary deviation would have predicted – affected the carriers of the image themselves. The socially constructed folk-devil image was negotiated, especially by the aspiring recruits to the ranks of Mods and Rockers, as a new, valid self-image, certified by the press and television even before it was so within the group itself. The result was an increase in violence, further criminalization, and finally the disappearance of the groups.

In another but similar case, concerning a political movement, Todd Gitlin, today a very well-known sociologist of the media but at that time one of the leaders of the Students for Democratic Society (SDS; in the 1960s the most important US student organization), wrote a book, *The Whole World Is Watching* (Gitlin 1980), where he studied the interaction between the student movement and the mass media (specifically, the TV broadcasting company CBS, at the time host to the most-watched prime-time news, and the *New York Times*). The title was taken from a students' chant in front of the cameras at the high-tension demonstrations for the Democratic Convention in Chicago, in 1968. Gitlin's main thesis is that the SDS's interaction with the media went near causing a true reorganization of the group, effectively replacing, in a sense, its leadership. A main result was the amplification of the most irrational and violent components of the movement. The mass media were in fact interested in what the movement was doing especially when they had the chance of telling stories about conflict, violence, and blood. The movement's leadership, which was actively seeking the media's attention, tended therefore to favor those tactics that "raised the level of conflict" – no doubt also from an autonomous choice that seemed to respond to the "escalation" of the war in Vietnam. In practice, however, this meant traveling farther and farther from the original political platform of the SDS, the 1962 "Port Huron Manifesto," which had espoused a "participatory" form of democracy (Gitlin 1987). It meant also reorienting political action toward political and organizational formulas tinged with Leninism (the myth of the "party of steel") and starting to recruit young people who seemed much more interested in what they had been shown on TV than in the original SDS political platform. A quite typical process of "amplification of deviance"[11] was therefore set in motion. In the end, Gitlin writes, the "movement" was reduced to naught, prey of cannibal factions that were hailing the leadership of distant dictators, leaders of faraway countries that had nothing in common with the social, political, and cultural reality of the United States or of other "late-modern" societies. The "process of social control" had brilliantly succeeded – "planned" by nobody, not the outcome of any conspiracy, and yet the cause of great merriment to what Mills had called the American "power elite." It was a process that had not been preordained but that had certainly been seconded and favored by J. Edgar Hoover's FBI and the other major police forces with their undercover agents and agents provocateurs (Marx 1988), and their destabilization campaigns, such as COINTELPRO,[12] that targeted the likes of Martin Luther King (Inciardi 1984: 210–11).[13]

Violence, and especially the representation of violence, played a most important part in the politics and culture of those years. Indeed, a particularly interesting aspect of Gitlin's reconstruction is the pages he devotes to "the aestheticizing of violence in films." Probably the first and most famous among such films was the 1967 *Bonnie and Clyde*:

> Arthur Penn's *Bonnie and Clyde* was the most skilled, the most pro-vocative, and probably the most popular; it launched not only new fashions but a hero cult; it stylized violence in living color. Though Penn's heroes lived during the Depression and started robbing banks to help out (or make a gesture toward helping out) dispossessed farmers, they were not the creatures of economic ruin. Unlike the characters in 1937 and 1949 movies based on the same real-life Bonnie Parker and Clyde Barrow, Penn's characters were free-standing angels, children of the sixties set three decades back. Their doomed life of crime began as a lark, an escapade of sexualized bravado up against boredom and impotence[14] . . . At the Hollywood premiere, I heard, someone in the audience stood up at the end and yelled, "Fucking cops!" He got the point. The spirit of Bonnie and Clyde was everywhere in the movement – and in the larger youth culture sur-

rounding it – in the summer and fall of 1967 and on into 1968. (Gitlin 1980: 197, 199)

A paranoid symbolic world emerged in which the icons of "the movement" became the likes of Bonnie and Clyde (Cawelti 1973). Probably the most telling sequence in this central piece of the collective imagery of 1968 was the very first in which Bonnie (a very young and naked Faye Dunaway) stares into the void (directly into the camera and at the audience), looking from behind the wooden structure of her cheap, old bed like a caged animal, bored with her petty life and eager for something to happen. After a moment Bonnie sees Clyde (Warren Beatty) intent on stealing her mother's car. He will whisk her away in the just-stolen car to a terrible but fascinating adventure, in which they will rob from the rich to give the poor, shoot the bad cops, and eventually be frightfully punished for their transgressions in an epoch-making, famous, slow-motion final sequence of their death under a storm of bullets – probably the first such sequence in the history of film. The fictional Bonnie and Clyde were no children of the Depression, as the real-life Bonnie Parker and Clyde Barrow had been. Rather, they were radicalized self-images for those who had been the early 1960s teenagers, the children of "boredom and affluence," the children of "sex, drugs, and rock'n'roll" (Goodman 1956; Cohen 1972). According to Gitlin, this rough Freudian-Marxist tale of rebellion against the Father, of ephemeral Liberation in a lull of absolute freedom in which one is the sole arbiter of life and death and is finally frightfully punished, is a good metaphor for the politics of the movement in those years. It was the tale, of course – as Michel Foucault (1976a) was to suggest a few years later with reference to the myth of "sexual liberation" – thanks to which "the movement" was socially reconstructed and controlled within a frame that made its demise possible, mainly by its own hands. In the meanwhile, its deuteragonist, J. Edgar Hoover's FBI, was not much more popular. The fight against gangsters such as Bonnie and Clyde had been the thrust that had catapulted the new-born FBI to notoriety in the 1930s, but when Penn's movie came out 30 years later, Hoover's *G-Men* popularity was at a historical low point, since, as mentioned, they were in fact much better known now for their very questionable activities aimed at fighting oppositional political groups. Therefore, when in the famous final sequence of *Bonnie and Clyde* the two heroes of the movie fall under the bullets of bad and corrupt G-men, the sympathy of the public was not really in doubt, as Gitlin retells.

American sociology of deviance had gone from Howard Becker's "appreciation" of his friends the jazz musicians smoking dope (Becker 1963) to a "Romantic" heroization of the outlaw – or maybe we should say a "sanctification," as in the case of Jean Genet and his *Thief's Journal* (1949): the presence of Jean-Paul Sartre's "Saint Genet" (1952) looms large in Matza's *Becoming Deviant* at the same time that Genet was touring American campuses showing support for the Black Panthers and the Palestinians' cause.[15] It is especially and most powerfully in David Matza's *Becoming Deviant* that this attitude, which was at the same time moral, cultural, and political, emerged most clearly. In this classic work, which could very well be included in a canon of anarchist literature, an old polemical argument that has its roots deep in Enlightenment thought[16] was presented anew. How can Leviathan, whose hands have spilled the blood of thousands or indeed, during the then current century, of millions, dare to judge who is and who is not a criminal? More specifically (at that time), how can the government of the United States, engaged in a war against the civilian population of Vietnam, dare to jail those of its citizens who have engaged in what is officially defined as "crime"? Let's hear it, however, from the sharp and unusual prose of Matza, in his conclusions:

> In its avid concern for public order and safety, implemented through police force and penal policy, Leviathan is vindicated. By pursuing evil and producing the *appearance* of good, the state reveals its abiding method – the perpetuation of its good name in the face of its own propensities for violence, conquest, and destruction. Guarded by a collective representation in which theft and violence reside in a dangerous class, morally elevated by its correctional quest, the state achieves the legitimacy of pacific intention and the appearance of legality – even if it goes to war and massively perpetrates activities it has allegedly banned from the world. But, that, the reader may say, is a different matter altogether. So says Leviathan – and that is the final point of the collective representation. (Matza 1969: 197)

Is there anything to add? Is there anything to add to the very history of criminology itself?[17] Notice the date: 1969. Those were the years not only of a generalized turbulence in North America and Europe, of unprecedented working-class strength (Boddy and Crotty 1975), of a new progressivism and experimentalism in all sectors of social life, but also, consistently, of a generalized, harsh criticism of the traditional ways of penality and especially of the prison. It is no accident that in these years we find concentrated: prison protests and riots in all industrialized countries, continuous calls for penal reform that in some cases came close to asking for the outright abolition of the penitentiary, the emergence of a revisionist history and sociology of punishment that culminated in Michel Foucault's *Discipline and Punish* in 1975, and unsurprisingly a declining trend in imprisonment rates in many Western countries, from the United States (Cahalan 1979) to Italy (Melossi 1998b; see below, figure 4). In the United States, in 1973 the National Advisory Commission on Criminal Justice Standards and the National Council on Crime and Delinquency went as far as recommending a moratorium on prison building and the use of imprisonment as an extremely limited last resort device (Zimring and Hawkins 1991: 65–6, 87). In spite of this (or maybe because of this), the orientation of authoritative recommendations was soon to change very decisively.

# 8

# *From "Labeling" to a "Critical" Kind of Criminology*

David Matza's reintroduction of the concept and term of "the State" within the North American sociology of deviance and crime – from which the concept had been expelled long before, as from political and social sciences more generally (Melossi 1990) – expressed a deep process of change within that society. The "closing up" during the 1950s, the Cold War, the hegemony of a rather stagnant conservatism, corresponded to an increasing role within American society played by central government in all its aspects, not least the military one. It was in fact a Republican president, Dwight Eisenhower, who warned the American public against the danger for democracy represented by the rise of a "military-industrial complex,"[1] a warning not so far from that of the "radical" C. Wright Mills.

It was against such a new constellation of forces in American society that the various 1960s "movements" reacted and claimed they wanted to fight – whether they were the civil rights movement in the South, the "black power" movement in the North, the student movement, or the movement against the war in Vietnam. The years between 1969 and 1971 marked the climax of the social and political conflict in the United States (and indeed, not only there). It was within these conflicts that "the State" resurfaced – "evoked," we might say, by the writings of intellectuals such as Matza – as the image of "the enemy" of these various movements and of any project of democracy and freedom. From here to the next step, an essentially misunderstood encounter with Marxist currents of European origin, was a small move indeed (misunderstood, because the political tradition of the movement was a radical-democratic one, as expressed for instance in the "Port Huron Manifesto"). This was made possible by theoretical orientations among which was central the so-called "Frankfurt School," transplanted from the German city to New York, at Columbia, just before the war, in order to escape the persecution of its mostly Jewish and leftist members (Jay 1973). It was to have an enormous influence on the 1960s movements, from the concept of "the authoritarian state" (Horkheimer 1942), to the popularity of Herbert Marcuse's idea of a "one-dimensional society" (Marcuse 1964), to the specific contribution on the subject of penality by Georg Rusche and Otto Kirchheimer, *Punishment and Social Structure* (1939), the very first work in English published by the newly Columbia-based "Institute for Social Research."[2]

Another author who was particularly relevant at the time was French philosopher Louis Althusser, who, in a famous essay on the "ideological and repressive state apparatuses" (Althusser 1970), importantly contributed to the inauguration of a small but very enterprising industry of works in the "theory of the State" (one of the consequences of this greater attention paid to the "State" was to obscure the second section of Althusser's essay, on "ideology," where he presented ideology as "constituting subjects" through *interpellation* or "hailing," largely anticipating Foucault's later contribution). At the time, such attention had, however, assumed a largely paranoid character. Everything and everybody somehow pertained in the end to an omnipotent and omnipresent "State," from which Gitlin's "free-standing angels, children of the sixties," Bonnie and Clyde look-alikes, as well as their many admirers, had no chance of escape, taken within the thick spider's web of Leviathan from which the only way out seemed to be the slow-motion final sequence of the film, in which their bodies shook like unanimated puppets under a storm of gun fire.

The climax reached at the time in actual confrontations in American society, as well as in statements such as Matza's *Becoming Deviant*, could hardly be negotiated with an eventless flow of the criminological discipline – especially considering that this discipline had essentially emerged about a century earlier as a science ancillary to "Leviathan's" "right to punish" and its criminal law. From the early 1970s, therefore, the whole discursive territory of criminology, sociology of crime, and deviance, not to mention that of the sociology of punishment, was becoming increasingly dispersed, fragmented, factional.

## Zookeepers of Deviance

Labeling theory itself was subjected to criticism, from "the right" by those who called for a decisive return to "positivism" (Gove 1975), from "the center," as it were, in some considerations by Edwin Lemert, who felt the paradigm of "social reaction" had gone too far (Lemert 1974), and, most importantly, at the time, from "the left" by those who, like Alvin W. Gouldner, articulated a critique of "the social reaction perspective" that was destined to be reproduced often in the course of the 1970s:

> Becker's school of deviance is redolent of Romanticism. It expresses the satisfaction of the Great White Hunter who has bravely risked the perils of the urban jungle to bring back an exotic specimen. It expresses the Romanticism of the zoo curator who preeningly displays his rare specimens. And like the zookeeper, he wishes to protect his collection; he does not want spectators to throw rocks at the animals behind the bars. But neither is he eager to tear down the bars and let the animals go. The attitude of these zookeepers of deviance is to create a comfortable and humane Indian Reservation, a protected social space, within which these colorful specimens may be exhibited, unmolested and unchanged. The very empirical sensitivity to fine detail, characterizing this school, is both born of and limited by the connoisseur's fascination with the rare object: its empirical richness is inspired by a collector's aesthetic.
>
> It is in part for this reason that, despite its challenging conception of a partisan sociology and its sympathy with the underdog, Becker's discussion is paradoxically suffused with a surprising air of complacency. Indeed, what it expresses is something quite different from the older, traditional sympathy with the plight of the underdog. Basically, it conceives of the underdog as a *victim*.[3] In some part, this is inherent in the very conception of the processes by means of which deviance is conceived of as being generated. For the emphasis in Becker's theory is on the deviant as the product of society rather than as the rebel against it. If this is a liberal conception of deviance that wins sympathy and tolerance for the deviant, it has the paradoxical consequence of inviting us to view the deviant as a passive nonentity who is responsible neither for his suffering nor its alleviation – who is more "sinned against than sinning." (Gouldner 1968: 106)

Gouldner then goes on, in his devastating *ad hominem* critique, explaining that these "new Turks" of the sociology of deviance are none other than the ideologists of the new welfare society, because

"Overdogs in the welfare state – in Washington bureaucracies and New York foundations – are buyers of underdog research for much the same political reasons that the Johnson regime initiated the 'war on poverty'" (Gouldner 1968: 109). It is quite ironic to see the affinities between such a leftist critique of "welfare liberals" – "liberal" sociology of deviance and criminology included – and the right's burgeoning critique in those very years of both the welfare state and "penal welfarism" (Garland 2001a: 27–51). Gouldner's brilliant but metaphorical imagery of "zookeeping" and "Indian Reservations" for the deviant would resurface, 20 years later, as a way to conceive – now without irony, and without benevolence – of a "custodial state" as "a high-tech and more lavish version of the Indian reservation for some substantial minority of the nation's population" in the notorious *The Bell Curve* (Herrnstein and Murray 1994: 523), a minority that "cannot be expected to function as citizens" (Murray 1990; see next chapter). Certainly, a specific theme of "critical" or "radical" sociology and/or criminology became the criticism of the welfare state – welfare being understood essentially as a form of "social control" – a criticism that extended to penal welfarism, or "correctionalism."

The centers of a critical kind of criminology became, in the United States, most notably the University of California at Berkeley[4] and, in the United Kingdom, an organization called the National Deviancy Conference (NDC). Later on, almost from a rib of the first two, the European Group for the Study of Deviance and Social Control was created. This group called together some of the most representative members of the NDC and a number of young scholars from Continental Europe, mostly from Germany, Belgium, the Netherlands, and the Scandinavian countries, plus a few from Southern and Eastern Europe – reproducing once more a quite precise map of irradiation from centers of cultural influence. The creation of a number of journals went with this diffusion, such as *Crime and Social Justice* (now simply *Social Justice*) at Berkeley, *Kritische Kriminologie* in Germany, *Deviance et société* in France, *La questione criminale* (later on *Dei delitti e delle pene* and now *Studi sulla questione criminale*) in Italy, and many, many others, especially in English and Spanish (mostly in Latin America).

The publication of *The New Criminology*, by English NDC-ers Ian Taylor, Paul Walton, and Jock Young (1973), became the defining moment of this whole development – a book that soon ascended to the status of "bible" for the new kind of criminology and at the same time a very convenient link between faraway California and

Continental Europe. This work was the result of a number of different contributions. They went from labeling theory – especially in David Matza's latest version, with his critique of "positivism," which dovetailed with the analogous and more general critique coming from the Frankfurt School – to a critique of "correctionalism." Furthermore, this new "critical criminology" connected with the emergence, especially in Continental Europe, of a Marxist theory near-hegemonic in social and political sciences.

## A "Critical" Kind of Criminology: The "Criminal Question"

Chambliss's notation about the rise of labeling – the 180-degree turn in the observing gaze, from within the patrol car to outside looking in (see above, chapter 7) – could be applied to critical criminology as well, and this in two main senses. On the one hand, criminology reached maturity, and started considering itself, reflecting on its history and genealogy, and at the same time on the genealogy of "the criminal question." This extravagant phrase, which takes after a late nineteenth-century idiomatic expression (as in "the social question"), derived from the name of an Italian criminology journal, *La questione criminale* in fact, founded in Bologna in 1975. At least in Italy, the term came to embody the meaning and research agenda of what was starting to be called critical criminology. Tamar Pitch has described what the criminal question is thus:

> To study the criminal question is different from studying crime. It means that crime is not considered independently from the procedures by which is it defined, the instruments deployed in its administration and control and the politics and debates around criminal justice and public order. The criminal question can therefore be provisionally defined as an area constituted by actions, institutions, policies and discourses whose boundaries shift. . . . (Pitch 1995: 52)

Pitch went on to claim that we need to "be aware of the fact that the sociologist and the criminologist themselves contribute to the construction of the criminal question through their analyses, discourses, political interventions and debates" and that "what 'the public' think of as crime and what according to the 'public' should be considered crime, or what cultural and symbolic significance is carried by law and criminal justice, is an integral aspect of the criminal question" (1995: 54). In other words, doing a "critical" kind of criminology essentially means doing a sociology of criminal law in its various manifestations, from law-making to policing to sentencing to imprisoning to studying public debate about all of this. A "criminal question" so defined was in a sense, however, but an extension or consequence of labeling theory. A critical criminology was essentially a reflexive criminology and, as I have stated elsewhere (Melossi 1985), its debt to labeling theory could not be more apparent. As we have seen, at the time, some critical criminologists were suspicious of labeling theory and, in a sense, with good cause, because often labeling theorists did not really take their analysis to its logical conclusion, and did not properly take into consideration the structures of power (economic, political, social, cultural) that produced the labeling. However, if one reflects about it now *sine ira nec studio*, it is easy to realize that, as far as criminology was concerned, the boldest, newest, most original step had been taken by labeling theorists. They had been those who had managed to deeply "subvert" the disciplinary field. The rest of the work, for which indeed Marxist theory would be most useful, was, in a sense, a more straightforward job.

In a book that was sort of a sequel to *The New Criminology*, Ian Taylor, Paul Walton, and Jock Young attempted to give a definition of what a "critical criminology" was going to be, indeed a "radical" criminology (Taylor et al. 1975). What they meant by it was a further distanciation from the developments of "labeling theory," which had now gone to feed a "romantic" approach to crime – as Jock Young authoritatively explains in what is probably the centerpiece of the volume, programmatically entitled "Working-Class Criminology" (Young 1975). A "romantic" approach to crime was actually less important in criminology than in politics at the time, and was encapsulated in that "Bonnie-and-Clyde" approach that I tried to describe in the previous chapter. Beyond the "voyeuristic" attitude of the "zookeeping" theorist of deviance, now,

the new deviancy theorists . . . relished the overt attack mounted by the new deviants on the "straight world" – the world of the utilitarian middle class. Whether the deviant in question was a marihuana smoker, a gay, a football hooligan, a sexual deviant, a blackmailer, vandal, greaser or industrial saboteur, the sign was that somebody had sensed that "society" was "wrong" and that, moreover, that somebody had the guts to do something about it . . . now the message of the deviancy theorist to official society was "hands off, you'll only make matters worse" but *at the same time* the implicit ideology was "believe and hope that the new deviant constituencies do represent a genuine threat to the social order." (Young 1975: 69–70)

Also in criminology, or better, sociology of deviance, one of the central shibboleths of 1960s ideology had finally and powerfully emerged. That was that special theme first started in Franz Fanon's *The Wretched of the Earth* (1961), and later expressed especially in Herbert Marcuse's epoch-making *One-Dimensional Man*, published in 1964, the same year when, on the Berkeley campus, Mario Savio, among others, was haranguing the crowd from the top of a besieged police car. This theme centered on a plea for the revolt potential of a "substratum of the outcasts and outsiders, the exploited and persecuted of other races and other colors, the unemployed and the unemployable [who] exist outside the democratic process [and whose] life is the most immediate and the most real need for ending intolerable conditions and institutions" (Marcuse 1964: 256). Radical criminologists were, however, less sanguine than Marcuse about the by then irredeemable one-dimensionality of the traditional working class, and called instead for a process of politicization of deviance that would follow different paths according to the different local situations. In the United Kingdom, this would become the basis for Jock Young's later "left realist" criminology centered on the idea that street crime was a problem especially for the working class, a problem that should be faced and taken seriously (this would bring him to rather heated debates in the 1980s with "Race and Class" group members such as none other than Paul Gilroy (Gilroy 1982; Bridges and Gilroy 1982; Lea and Young 1984)). At the end of *Critical Criminology* one could also find a debate about "radical deviance theory and Marxism" between Paul Q. Hirst on the one hand and Ian Taylor and Paul Walton on the other, which remained one of the very few efforts at conceptually and theoretically discussing the relationship between the new kind of critical criminology and the Marxist intellectual tradition. Whereas Hirst claimed that the concepts belonging in Marxism could not be meshed and diluted with the sociological jargon of the new deviancy theory, the new criminologists of course held otherwise (Hirst 1975; Taylor and Walton 1975; Melossi 1976).

In any case, almost immediately, a true diaspora started, reproducing within the criminological field the habits of factionalism and fragmentation that were typical of the leftist parties and groups to which most critical criminologists were contiguous. Critical criminology followed the path of history (Chambliss 1964; Erikson 1966; Platt 1969; Hay et al. 1975; Thompson 1975), the study and critique of total institutions and policing (see next section), the elaboration of alternative conceptions of social and penal reaction, from abolitionism (Christie 1981; Hulsman 1982) to realism (Young, see above) to reintegrationism (Braithwaite 1989). Very few were the works devoted instead to an "alternative" way of conceiving criminal behavior and criminal theories, and the reason was quite clear. Labeling theorists had in fact already done what it was most important to do, that is, to show that criminal behavior was to a certain extent the product of social control. Furthermore, in order to discuss crime, one had to take seriously the definitions of crime implicit in official definitions, those of a law meant as the expressed will of "the State." The latter was, however, the critical theorists' worst enemy (and with good political cause). Liberal criminologists, starting with Edwin Sutherland, had already had to deal with the issue and had been badly bruised by the impact, as we have seen. So, in the classrooms of the Berkeley School of Criminology, in the early 1970s, one could take classes on such topics as the crimes of imperialism, or of sexism, or of racism, or of classism, in an effort to overturn official definitions, an effort that made it very difficult to avoid the exit of natural law (Schwendinger and Schwendinger 1970; further, consult the wonderfully inspired and truly beautiful collection of the first 20 or so issues of *Crime and Social Justice!*). There were exceptions nevertheless, on both sides of the Atlantic, from Geoffrey Pearson (1983) to Richard Quinney (1970), from Steven Spitzer (1975) to Elliott Currie (1985).

One notable landmark contribution was certainly *Policing the Crisis* (1978, subtitled *Mugging, the State, and Law and Order*), which, under the crucial lead of Stuart Hall, director of the Centre for Contemporary Culture at the University of Birmingham (other authors – Chas Critcher, Tony Jefferson, John Clarke, and Brian Roberts – were all members of the same Centre), managed to do a number of things at the same time. Here too there was an effort at radicalization. What was radicalized, it seems to me, was the labeling theorists' original intuition on the importance of language and social interaction, which Stanley Cohen had brilliantly introduced into British studies of deviance through his *Folk Devils and Moral Panics*, as we have seen. However, with Stuart Hall's theoretical push, the interactionist roots of American sociology of deviance were usefully articulated to a serious engagement with Marxist tradition. Within that tradition, what was emphasized was the centrality of the process of construction of consensus, from Marx's work on ideology to, especially, Gramsci's contribution on the concept of hegemony (Gramsci 1929–35). This meant that it was possible to see the role of "the mugging crisis" as an indicator, a sign, of a much broader crisis in hegemony characteristic of the deep transition that the fundamental social relationships of a Fordist-industrial, capitalist society were going through. Furthermore, the Birmingham group was well equipped to perceive the crucial role played by the whole issue of race and immigration within such a critical transition ("mugging" was in fact seen as a crime committed by African Caribbean immigrants to the United Kingdom). In this, similarly to what had happened with Platt and Takagi's almost contemporary indictment of criminological "realism" in the United States (Platt and Takagi 1977), the analysis by Hall and the others turned out to be quite prophetic of future developments, in the ways also in which the emphasis on crime was central to the criminalization of a diffuse militancy that, all over the Western world, was manifesting itself during the 1970s, from Western Europe to North America, from Eastern Europe to Latin America.

## The Critique of "Total Institutions" from Goffman to Foucault

The critique of so-called "total institutions" in particular was central to the building of a "corpus" of "critical criminology." The influence of studies on psychiatric institutions cannot be overemphasized in this connection. In his pathbreaking study *Asylums* (1961), Erving Goffman had offered a damning list of charges against psychiatric institutions[5] – calling them for the first time "total institutions." This critique was to be welcomed and developed in Italy by psychiatrist Franco Basaglia (1968) and the "anti-institutional" movement of "alternative psychiatry" of which he became the leader, a movement so successful that ten years later, in 1978, Basaglia managed to have a law passed that closed down all Italian (non-criminal) psychiatric institutions (Colucci and Di Vittorio 2001). A further proof that the times were ripe for radical critiques had been the publication in 1961 of the first major work by Michel Foucault, with the title *Folie et déraison*[6] (the work also where Foucault seemed to subscribe to a rhetoric of "repression"). And in 1975, Foucault's epoch-making *Discipline and Punish* was probably the most significant contribution of the literature produced within this cultural movement.[7]

These were all works of remarkable theoretical importance but which, at the same time, proceeded from reflections of a political nature. I have already mentioned the "anti-institutional" movement in Italy. The same, however, was happening within prisons, and, to everyone's great surprise, in the same way in which the fire of revolt seemed to jump from campus to campus all over the Western world – and even beyond that – the same thing was happening from prison to prison. Movements for prison reform and connected "riots" happened between the late 1960s and early 1970s in Western Europe (France, Italy, the United Kingdom, the Scandinavian countries, Germany) and in the United States, where one of the most notorious episodes was the Attica prison riot of 1971. The riot started over a fairly standard set of grievances, escalated into the taking over of the building and of hostages by the inmates, and ended with the New York State National Guard storming the prison. All hostages and about 30 inmates were killed (Welch 2005: 80–2; one year later, during one of his frequent visits to the United States in the 1970s, Michel Foucault visited Attica (Foucault 1974)). Other works contributed, in those years, to deeply question "the right to punish" by the law and "the State" through the investigation into the "materialist historical" bases of the history of punishment and especially of the prison. Besides, as already mentioned, the remarkable republication, in 1968, of Georg Rusche and Otto Kirchheimer's *Punishment and Social Structure*, other later "revisionist" works were Dario Melossi and Massimo Pavarini's *The Prison and the Factory* (1977), Michael Ignatieff's *A Just Measure of Pain* (1978), and, in the 1980s, David Garland's *Punishment and Welfare* (1985) (the first two were discussed above, in chapter 1; for an overview of this literature see Garland (1990) and Melossi (1998a)).

## Michel Foucault Cutting Off the Head of the King

The revisionist milestone of the period was, however, Michel Foucault's *Discipline and Punish* (1975). We have already seen in chapter 1 the main outline of this work. In trying to draw attention to a concept of "power" as "discipline" – and the way in which this concept had been incorporated within the very structure of the prison institution – Foucault was also trying to come to terms with a traditional Marxist vision of power. This was a vision, at the time very influential in Europe, that, as we have seen, placed "the State" at the center of the study of political and social power (Foucault 1976a, 1978). These attempts by Foucault were taking place when European culture was starting to assume a critical posture both toward a "hegemonic" Marxist orientation and toward what at the time was called "realized socialism" (even if the two were by no means seen as synonymous). *Vis-à-vis* a sense of deep disillusionment, Foucault traced a path of "disenchantment" that would appear central to cultural development in the next quarter of a century. Some of the central shibboleths of Marxism, concepts such as those of "repression," "liberation," and, indeed, "the State," were decisively confronted. Foucault's assertion, in the *Introduction* to *The History of Sexuality*, that "[i]n political thought and analysis, we still have not cut off the head of the king"(Foucault 1976a: 88), was going to define a new age.

The concept of social control never actually entered Foucault's toolbox, at least not to the same extent as the concept of "discipline" (see Beaulieu 2005 and Beaulieu and Gabbard 2006). He managed, however, a new way of thinking about it, starting with his implicit – and, as already noted, very Althusserian (Althusser 1970) – indication of a linkage between the world of production and the apparatuses of cultural reproduction in the imagery of the "Panopticon" (to the fame of which Foucault contributed to a much greater degree than its very inventor, Jeremy Bentham). Likewise for Foucault's insistence on "panopticism" (Foucault 1975: 195–308), and then especially his decisive move to free power relations from the State's stifling hold between the *Introduction* to *The History of Sexuality* (Foucault 1976a) and the essay on "Governmentality" (Foucault 1978).

The contributions by Foucault belonged in a time when the disenchantment of the 1960s generation *vis-à-vis* Marxism and socialism was also quickly producing an awareness of the fact that thinking and acting politically were not guided by any "grand narrative" reassuringly external to such thinking and acting – an awareness to which French philosopher Jean-François Lyotard gave at the time the name of "postmodernism" (Lyotard 1979). We have already noted, however, that American Pragmatism's starting point at the beginning of the century had not been all that different, and this in part explains why, in 1983, American neo-Pragmatist philosopher Richard Rorty could write, "James and Dewey . . . are waiting at the end of the road which . . . Foucault and Deleuze are currently travelling" (Rorty 1983: xviii). In other words, Foucault allowed for the introduction, within European social thought, through the elaboration of an apposite new vocabulary, of themes and motifs that, maybe under a different guise, had already been belabored at length within American political and social science. He did that, in fact, exactly at the point when the social model produced in the North American context was readying itself to become hegemonic over Europe and increasingly over the entire globe with the impending fall of realized socialism. In his essay on "Governmentality," Foucault so dismissed the concept of the State:

> The excessive value attributed to the problem of the state is expressed, basically, in two ways: the one form, immediate, affective, and tragic, is the lyricism of the cold monster we see confronting us. But there is a second way of overvaluing the problem of the state, one that is paradoxical because it is apparently reductionist: it is the form of analysis that consists in reducing the state to a certain number of functions, such as the development of productive forces and the reproduction of relations of production, and yet this reductionist vision of the relative importance of the state's role nevertheless invariably renders it absolutely essential as a target needing to be attacked and a privileged position needing to be occupied. But the state, no more probably today than at any other time in its history, does not have this unity, this individuality, this rigorous functionality, nor, to speak frankly, this importance. Maybe, after all, the state is no more than a composite reality and a mythicized abstraction, whose importance is a lot more limited than many of us think. Maybe what is really important for our modernity – that is, for our present – is not so much the statization of society, as the "governmentaliza-tion" of the state. (Foucault 1978: 220)

If the reader thinks she might have recently read something of the kind, it probably was a few chapters above, when we quoted words penned by Arthur Bentley about 80 years earlier (see chapter 5). At the same time, this "governmentalization," of the State but especially of society, had been discussed by American social scientists under the label of "social control." Foucault's emphasis on the intimate connections between "truth," "discourse," and "power," as well as his barely sketched critique of a State-centered model, unfolded within a type of society where social control – as Dewey, Mead, Mills, and many other North American sociologists had cogently predicted – was more and more a matter of constructing a common mind and language rather than of manipulating laws and guns. In a mass democratic system – which only in the 1970s was coming to maturation in much of Europe[8] – it could not be otherwise. The realization that the construction of this common mind and language, this type of "social control at a distance," as Wirth had called it, was taking place within the arena of the mass media of communication was the inevitable corollary of such an overall development.

## Ethnomethodology

A perspective called *ethnomethodology* grew within the same general *Weltanschaung* of symbolic interactionism, but starting from rather different conceptual premises. In spite of the main focus of ethnomethodology being on social analysis in general, rather than on crime, this perspective was very important in orienting a number of studies in the field of deviance and social control also. Originating in a kind of internal critical conversation with Parsons's structural functionalism, ethnomethodology started from Alfred Schutz's phenomenology and was founded by Harold Garfinkel (1967a), who, in a sense, established its canonical version.

Why "ethnomethodology"? The emphasis in the word is on the study of *members'* methods. In other words, ethnomethodologists claimed that their "methodology" did not respond to some abstract scientific canon, but tried to respond to the necessity of studying the methods used by a group's members (the members of the "ethnos") in order to ascertain the reality of, the truth-for-practical-purposes in, our everyday, common interactions. How do we construct our daily reality, how do we do it in practice, in action? How do I make sure that the person I am interacting with is a "reasonable" individual who is not going to assault me or speak a funny language I cannot understand? And so on.

In spite, therefore, of their marginal initial interest in criminological issues, ethnomethodologists have given us highly relevant contributions to exploration of worlds, situations, conditions where the processes of construction of what we call "deviance" and "social control" take place. In interventions such as Aaron Cicourel's on the "organization" of juvenile justice (1968), Lawrence Wieder's on the so-called "convict code" (1974), David Sudnow's on "normal crimes" (1965), Egon Bittner's on police work (1967), Douglas Maynard's on plea bargaining (1984),[9] or Dorothy Smith's on gender and mental illness (1978), a standpoint emerged that emphasized the "methods" used to construct "meanings" and "social reality" among the participants in these various social activities as opposed to the abstract, disembodied categories of "science." It is in fact quite obvious that one of the endeavors in which we are implicated in our ongoing interactions is the construction of "deviance." How do we ascertain, for instance, that somebody may be "suspect" as "being mentally ill," like K. in Dorothy Smith's compelling account (1978)? Long before the doctors' certification, the "methods" used by family, friends, and acquaintances establish the possibility of that diagnosis.[10]

Ethnomethodologists have also made a remarkable contribution both to theoretical innovation and to methodology, since they have originated a new modality of research called "conversational analysis" and have then extended it to the analysis of visual interaction. Thereby, a discipline that had started its career as having a hieratic and hermetic flavor ended up being very much pursued by bureaucratic and corporate enterprises, interested in the analysis of organized interactions, such as emergency call operators or call center companies (Pollner 1991; generally see Heritage 1984).

In close connection with this whole problematic, but particularly influenced by the phenomenological tradition, we should recall also Jack Katz's *Seductions of Crime* (1988) – which would then become a centerpiece also of the new "cultural criminological" approach. Katz's study aims at giving a "thick" description of the behavior and "styles" of inner-city minority ethnic youth (and not only of those) insofar as such lifestyles are connected with "predatory" practices, like street robbery, or "violence," as in the case of the skinheads. This work was certainly among the most innovative in the last quarter of the twentieth century, being able to show the "seductive" and emotional character of criminal lifestyles, and especially of given criminal practices, from the standpoint of those who enact them.

## The Contribution of Feminism: Social Control and the Constitution of a Gendered Subject

It was the question of women and gender, however, that started emerging importantly into the criminological debate in those very years (which does not mean that, in the past, there may not have been several pioneering attempts, the most famous probably being the one by Lombroso and Ferrero; see above, chapter 2). At first, under the pressure of the new "feminist" movement, the question was asked whether women's process of entering the worlds of work and production – worlds that, until then, had been mainly "male" worlds – also meant an increase in women's participation in criminal behavior and criminal justice. This was the hypothesis pursued especially by Rita Simon (1975) and Freda Adler (1975) in the 1970s. It soon appeared, however, that empirical evidence did not really support this hypothesis. On the contrary, in the long term, the opposite seemed to be true. Women's presence within the world of criminal justice seemed to be waning instead of increasing (Feeley and Little 1991). What was also emphasized was the importance of a "patriarchal" type of domination. This was a domination that would cause both a lack of sensitivity toward the victimization of women and an emphasis on pre-penal social control, a system of social control reserved to women and other "minors," therefore more centered in the family and personal relationships and less in criminal justice. Women's presence would therefore be obscured in terms of both victimization and criminalization (Daly and Chesney-Lind 1988).

Adrian Howe (1994) claimed that "revisionist" theories of punishment, from Rusche and Kirchheimer to Foucault, from Melossi and Pavarini to Garland, in their analysis of the "subjectivation" process linked at least in part to the "penitentiary invention," would be missing a "gender" perspective, a "female subject." On the one hand, such forgetfulness, it seems to me, would simply be an amplification of institutional forgetfulness (even if one should remember the work on female prisoners and female incarceration by Pat Carlen in the United Kingdom (1985) and by Nicole H. Rafter in the United States (1985a)). At least in modern times, in fact, male human beings have always been the favored subjects of the penitentiary institutions, the number of women present in prison oscillating between 5 and 7 percent of the daily population of penitentiary institutions (with an increase usually during times of war when the absence of young men – the favored subjects of crime and war – left more room for women). The analyst's forgetfulness would be to some degree justified, therefore, when he or she addressed the most formal type of social control, penal control (the object of the "revisionist" literature mentioned above). On the other hand, however, such forgetfulness would be much less justified if, instead of prisons, we were to analyze "social control" more generally, because from such a perspective we have to ask what social control means as far as women are concerned.

As we have seen above in this chapter, French philosopher Louis Althusser had raised the question of "interpellation" or "hailing" (Althusser 1970). Ideology would constitute the subject, Althusser wrote, by interpellating her, rather in the same way in which, during World War II, the American citizen was hailed by posters portraying

"Uncle Sam" imperiously turning to him with an "I want you!" In that image, the constituted subject was that of the citizen ready to defend his country. Teresa de Lauretis (1996) has seen the analogy between Althusser's concept of ideology and the constitution of gender.[11] Likewise, the construction of gender was investigated from an ethnomethodological perspective by Candace West and Don Zimmerman (1987), who, working on a theme famously forged by Harold Garfinkel (1967b), that of Agnes's "passing" as a female,[12] wrote of the process of "doing gender."

This construction of the female subject would therefore imply the attribution of certain physical and moral qualities, from the construction (literal in the case of Agnes) of female genitalia, to a certain external physical appearance, to the specification of a moral and social attitude that may perhaps be best expressed as that of the "mother," central to the physical and moral reproduction of the species and therefore linked to her role in some kind of family institution. This complex of attributes has been traditionally articulated to an authoritarian and patriarchal order – exemplified in the old Roman concept of *pater familias*. This order centered on the domination and responsibility of the "adult male," domination and responsibility *vis-à-vis* the "minor" members of the family. This condition of "minority" might be ascribed to age or to some other social feature (being female, or of some other "race," a servant, propertyless, etc.). We have seen how, during the Enlightenment, such a condition of minority was argued in terms of "rationality," unsurprisingly for that age (see above, chapter 1). A full and mature rationality, necessary in order to handle the "public sphere," was that of the ("white" and proprietary) man. A different rationality, as useful socially but hierarchically inferior, was that of women, and was typical of the "private." It would therefore follow from this that the kind of social control reserved to the female gender – in a way similar to that exercised on minors and servants – would belong in domesticity and would be delegated, so to speak, to the man head of the family, acting as the representative of society at large within "his" family. Women – as well as servants – would therefore not belong in prisons, if "deviant," because unfit for such institutions. Women's social control is social control in the family. In other words, we would find so few women in prison for reasons very similar to those that, in antebellum United States, would keep African American slaves out of prison (see above, chapter 4).

Women who end up in prison are therefore those who somehow withdraw themselves from "being women," who have in a sense given up on "doing gender" (in a way similar to Lombroso's idea that criminal women represented a "more masculine" type of woman, a misconceived woman). In her historical work on women in prison in the United States, for instance, Nicole H. Rafter (1985a) shows how African American women have always been treated more "like men." When convicted, they would be assigned, in the Southern states, to chain gangs, which would never happen to "white ladies," no matter their crime:

> Women were supposed to be delicate, shrinking, dependent, child-like, men to be strong, assertive, independent, and adult. But the formulas involved race as well as gender: it was easier for white than black women to be "womanly." In addition, criminal justice authorities found it harder to believe that white women would act out of role. These authorities perceived white women as unfit for incarceration in custodial prisons,[13] except in extreme cases where offense type indicated the contrary. (For instance, during a prison investigation of 1870 in Georgia, a convict was asked whether "white and colored women mixed together" on a railroad work gang, to which he replied, "There were no white women there. One started there and I heard Mr. Alexander [the lessee] say he turned her loose ... He said his wife was a white woman, and he could not stand it to see a white woman work in such places" ...). For white women, then, gender interacted with race to keep their numbers in custodial prisons low. Black women, in contrast, were put at a disadvantage by both race and gender. Perceived as more masculine ..., they were more readily sent to custodial prisons, institutions that were masculine in character. (Rafter 1985b: 241–2)

During the recent period of "mass incarceration" in the United States (see next chapter), the growth rate of its female component has certainly been higher than the male one, and this has happened in a period when the same kind of process took place also in the labor market. However, women's entry into the labor market has been going on now for much longer than a century. If, then, the increased participation of women in the criminal justice system were owed to a corresponding increased "publicization" of their social role, we would still have to understand why, in the very long run, the percentage of women in prison has remained more or less stable, with the exception of war periods, or has even declined. In fact, as we have seen, according to Malcolm Feeley and Deborah Little's historical research (1991), between the eighteenth and the twentieth centuries, women's presence within correctional institutions, especially in Northern Europe, has been declining, not increasing. A possible hypothesis Feeley and Little mention in order to explain this fact is that the transition from the extended family of rural society to the small nuclear family of bourgeois and urban-industrial society may have greatly emphasized the division of labor based on gender, increasingly relegating women to within family boundaries. In an interesting passage from his 1936 theoretical introduction to the Frankfurt School's series of studies on authority and the family, Herbert Marcuse noted, with special reference to the Protestant Reformation:

> As is well known, a programmatic reorganization of the family and a notable strengthening of the authority of the *pater familias* took place in the context of the bourgeois-Protestant teachings of the Reformation. It was firstly a necessary consequence of the toppling of the Catholic hierarchy; with the collapse of the (personal and instrumental) mediations it had set up between the individual and God, the responsibility for the salvation of the souls of those not yet responsible for themselves, and for their preparation for the Christian life, fell back on the family and on its head, who was given an almost priestly consecration. On the other hand, since the authority of the temporal rulers was tied directly to the authority of the *pater familias* (all temporal rulers, all "lords" became "fathers"), their authority was consolidated in a very particular direction. The subordination of the individual to the temporal ruler appears just as "natural," obvious, and "eternal" as subordination to the authority of the father is meant to be, both derived from the same divinely ordained source. Max Weber emphasizes the entry of "calculation into traditional organizations brotherhood" as a decisive feature of the transformation of the family through the penetration of the "capitalist spirit": the old relationships of piety decay as soon as things are no longer shared communally within the family but "settled" along business lines. But the obverse side of this development is that the primitive, "naïve" authority of the *pater familias* becomes more and more a planned authority, which is artificially generated and maintained. (Marcuse 1936: 74)

Such a fundamental historical process would not be offset by women's increasing entry into the workforce starting with the industrial revolution (and happening at different times in different countries). The belonging of women within the family, such a deeply rooted feature of our culture, cannot disappear simply because women "exit" families to go to work. In the same way in which women keep doing both "outside" waged work and "inside" unpaid domestic work, so they keep negotiating two images, with all the conflicts involved in such a negotiation: the image of a wage earner and that of the guardian of domesticity. The female role of "guardian of domesticity" makes of women at the same time the objects of patriarchal social control and the active representatives of the perspective that Mead called "the generalized other," especially in relation to children. An aspect of this socially attributed women's role is that of being the representatives of moral values within the family. That is the case toward the female children – in the sense of the reproduction of the female gender role – but also toward the husband and the male children, in the sense of a "civilizing" effect on what are socially considered to be the least pleasant aspects of the male gender role.

The political role played by middle-class, "enlightened" women in the course of the twentieth century was to some degree connected to this aspect. These were women often active in "progressive" causes such as temperance leagues (Valverde 1991) or the "child saving" movement (Platt 1969). This distinctive tradition is certainly still present in current feminist positions, especially in the English-speaking world, and is often associated with requests for an intensified criminalization of those men who orient their violence against women and minors. Similarly, an old wisdom of studies in juvenile delinquency is that there is nothing better than a "good girl" to "cure" the worst juvenile delinquent. Once again the family is seen as the nucleus of social order and, within the family, the woman is the very representative of a stance of decency and social correctness.

Within criminal justice systems, instead, we largely find those types of women who have in some way expressed a rejection of their submissive role in a patriarchal order. These women range from those involved in sex work – given that "prostitution," as Lombroso noted (see above, chapter 2), is the female deviance *par excellence* – to those, more recently, involved in the world of "drugs," from women defined by their ethnicity and nationality before their gender, to *political* or *social* rebels (in a precarious balance with that contiguous sphere of deviance that is mental illness, a specific "construction" of women's deviance that has indeed played a large role (Chesler 1972; Smith 1978)).

Finally, the emergence of the question of gender together with that of male violence toward women (not only sexual violence but also domestic violence; Stanko 1985) has helped also in focusing on the connection between concepts of "masculinity," violence, and crime for the pathbreaking role of studies such as R. W. Connell's

(1995) and James Messerschmidt's (1993). They emphasize the plurality of masculine styles, or of "masculinities," detailed by age, class, and "racial" positions. "Doing gender" applies to males as well, and forms of criminal behavior, especially behavior implying vandalism and violence, represent unconventional but very traditional ways of "doing gender," especially for lower-class males. The different class styles of "doing" male gender had been researched in a pioneering study by William Chambliss (1973), describing the deeds of the middle-class "Saints" and of the working-class "Roughnecks," and then by British sociologist Paul Willis in *Learning to Labour* (1977). Willis very convincingly showed how the "oppositional" male style of working-class "lads" in the classroom, within the strict British class structure, ended up reproducing their membership within the ranks of the working class (the growing male disadvantage in educational attainments, linked also to the pressure of male role conformity, has been increasingly noted in many countries).

# Part III

## *The "Crisis Decades":*
## *"State," Social Control, and*
## *Deviance Today*

# 9

# The End of "the Short Century" between Inequality and Fear

During the 1960s, social inequalities had diminished farther and farther (for the United States, see Boddy and Crotty 1975). However, right after that, a 20-year-long period of rising unemployment, harshening of social hierarchies, deep changes in the economy, and harsh "disciplining" of the working class began to unfold. This period was dubbed a "silent depression" (Peterson 1994), marked by the fact that, between the early 1970s and early 1990s, the average hourly wages of Americans *declined* by almost 20 percent and, even after the prosperity of the Bill Clinton years, they were still lower than when Reagan took office at the White House (Friedman 2004). The reason why the average *income* of families stayed more or less the same was to be found in the massive increase of working time, especially of women's working time, given that they entered the market of waged labor by the millions during the same period (Schor 1991). The strongest sectors of the working class were at the same time either expelled from the labor market or lost the centrality they used to hold.

## The Social Crisis of the 1970s and Mass Imprisonment in the United States

It is conventionally agreed that this new era started in the year of the oil and energy crisis, 1973 – the year when, according to historian Eric Hobsbawm, the "crisis decades" began (Hobsbawm 1994). The tide of penality (as well as of many other social processes) turned also around this same year. *Before* 1973, *recorded* "crime" had been on the increase especially in aspects – so-called "street crime" – that were particularly worrisome for the middle class (*before*, because the US victimization survey, which started in 1973, has shown no definite trend toward an increase, contrary to common credence, as Katherine Beckett explains in her review of Garland's *The Culture of Control* (Garland 2001a; Beckett 2001)[1]). Crime's ascendance in the 1960s was taken to represent the general crisis in authority and conformist values and traditions. The archetype of such representational work was to be found in 1960s speeches by radical conservatives in their at first unsuccessful attempts to "stem the tide" of "liberalism." They elaborated the kind of political vision that would then become successful with the Reagan presidency and that would shape the new American national consensus until our day. One of the most creative speakers was Barry Goldwater, who, in his 1964 San Francisco acceptance speech of the Republican candidacy for president, said:

> The growing menace in our country tonight, to personal safety, to life, to limb and property, in homes, in churches, on the playgrounds and places of business, particularly in our great cities, is the mounting concern – or should be – of every thoughtful citizen in the United States. Security from domestic violence, no less than from foreign aggression, is the most elementary and fundamental purpose of any government, and a government that cannot fulfill this purpose is one that cannot long command the loyalty of its citizens. History shows us, demonstrates that nothing, nothing prepares the way for tyranny more than the failure of public officials to keep the streets safe from bullies and marauders. Now, we Republicans see this as more – much more – than the result of mere political differences or mere political mistakes. We see this as the result of a fundamentally and absolutely wrong view of man, his nature, and his destiny.[2]

A few years later it was Robert Nixon's vice-president Spiro Agnew who became famous for speeches like this: "When I talk about troublemakers, I'm talking about muggers and criminals in the streets, assassins of political leaders, draft evaders and flag burners, campus militants, hecklers and demonstrators against candidates for public office and looters and burners of cities" (quoted in Braithwaite 1980: 198).

The rhetorical move is clear enough: the question of crime is not simply the question of crime. Crime is what links political opposition on one side to the worst kind of terror on the other, burning cities, assassinating political leaders. Crime was basically portrayed as the tip of the iceberg of rebelliousness and signaled a complete breakdown in control – or so it was claimed – that had been developing during the apparently sleepy years of the 1950s and at an increasingly faster pace during the 1960s. It could be seen in the civil rights movement and in the more confrontational ethnic minority organizations in the big cities. It could be seen on university campuses, especially when these revolted against the escalation of the Vietnam War in 1969. It could be seen in the disaffection of young workers toward factory jobs that were increasingly considered as a way to make money for the weekend rather than as an opportunity for the expression of one's work ethic. It could be seen in the breakdown of "traditional family values" and the emergence of women's and gays' movements. It could be seen in the burgeoning rise of a "counterculture" of "drugs, sex, and rock'n'roll." It could be seen in the turmoil that permeated all kinds of social institutions and especially "total institutions" such as prisons.

Not all of these manifestations of crisis, malaise, and struggle had the same subversive potential. Some could be co-opted, others could be listened to, others could be ignored, some others could be safely repressed. Each one of them, however, had to be dealt with somehow. A conservative front coalesced that was to bring its *revanche* against the danger of subversion. This subversion, however, was to be portrayed as, essentially, "crime" (later on, increasingly joined by the label "terrorism"). Through the discourse of "crime," American cultural conservatives discovered and popularized also a "traditional" cultural nexus between racism, crime, and fear – a nexus that only some of the greatest African American writers, such as Richard Wright (1940) and Ralph Ellison (1952), had been able to explore, with an awareness that, on the liberal side, was later lost.[3]

In the same way in which American Progressivism had found its apostle in Roosevelt and his "New Deal," so Ronald Reagan, at the beginning of his presidency in 1981, marked the rhetorical – but equally meaningful – goal of going back to "before the New Deal."[4] These early positions of the new president – immediately emphasized by his clash with the powerful air controllers' union – gave the signal of a conservative *revanche* that has yet to subside, except for the more "moderate" parenthesis of Bill Clinton's presidency. The reader may usefully compare the increase in inequality with the curve representing

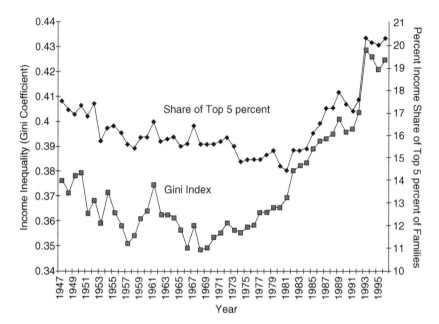

Figure 2   Inequality in the distribution of family income, by year, United States, 1947–96 (Kovandzic et al. 1998: 573). (The Gini index is an index elaborated by demographers in order to measure inequality.)

the growth of imprisonment rates in the United States (see figures 2 and 4).

It is hard to avoid at least formulating the hypothesis – based on a tradition of studies that, as we have seen, started with the work of Georg Rusche and Otto Kirchheimer (1939) – that the deep restructuring of the economy (a transition to a new "post-Fordist" phase) connected with an extended process of social disciplining that was emphasized particularly within the realm of "less eligible" institutions – prisons. The most massive process of incarceration that ever happened in the West, from the days of "the great internment" in seventeenth-century Europe, started taking place in the United States. The total numbers of those in prisons or under some kind of correctional control came quite close to a sizeable portion of the demographic groups at the bottom of the social stratification, such as the African Americans and the unemployed (Melossi 1993; Beckett 1997; Western and Beckett 1999; Tonry 1995; Miller 1997; Western 2006). Bruce Western and Katherine Beckett were able to show in fact that if one were to add the number of inmates to that of the "official" unemployed in the United States, the total result would not be very far from the average one of the European Union. In the United States, the year 1972 had marked the trough of imprisonment rates,[5] but right after that a seemingly unstoppable process of harshening penality took the number of people in state and federal prisons in the year 2000 over the threshold of two million. On December 31, 2005, the total number of inmates in prison or jail custody was 2,193,798, with an incarceration rate of 743 per 100,000 – seven times higher than some of the highest rates of Western Europe. Another five million people were under the control of other "correctional" authorities, on probation or on parole. If we consider males between 25 and 29 years of age – the demographic group most "at risk" of being incarcerated – we come to the extraordinary total of 1 percent of whites and 8 percent of African Americans incarcerated, a number that in inner cities gets easily close to half of the resident population of that sex and age. Furthermore, there were 107,518 women incarcerated, only 7 percent of the total, but because of the extremely high total number, they were more than all of the inmates of Italy in the same year (one should consider that the number of women incarcerated, in all penal systems, hovers around 5–7 percent, no matter the total, and that the general Italian population is about one fifth of the American one; in any case the rising pace of women's imprisonment in the United States has been higher than men's at least since the early 1990s).[6]

Such a dramatic increase in imprisonment rates in the 1970s–1990s gave the lie to all the main explanatory mechanisms identified by the 1970s sociology of punishment, explanations that by and large based themselves on the previous behavior of American imprisonment rates, whether these could be defined as oscillating around a "stable" level if one looked at the medium range period (Blumstein et al. 1977), or even on a "decarceration" course if one looked at the immediately previous period (Scull 1977), or, finally, and quite problematically, if one tried to link the pace of incarceration to rates of unemployment (Jankovic 1977; Greenberg 1977).[7]

## "Realist" Criminologies

Such a new tune in practice was accompanied by a change in criminologists' theoretical mood. On the one hand, we should not forget the pathbreaking role played by a thinker as original as David Matza, who, as we have seen, had rediscovered the two milestones of neo-classicism, "free will" (Matza 1964) and "Leviathan" (Matza 1969). One may suggest that Matza's work was critical of his own times as well as foretelling the future. This was the case not only because, as has often been remarked, Matza's veering toward an anti-determinist position opened the way to a future rhetoric of responsibility and retribution, but especially because the coupling of Leviathan and penal policies was to become tighter and tighter in the years to follow. Penal policies are implemented by the State, Matza wrote, in order to achieve one of the main features of the State and "its" not least accomplishment: the representation of society as a unified (and hierarchically ordained) structure (Matza 1969; Melossi 1990: 155–68). A few years after the publication of *Becoming Deviant*, in the United States at least, the ethos that more and more prevailed was one of forceful unification of society after years and years during which everything had been questioned and, it seemed, broken into pieces.

A similar fate would befall another furious 1970s struggle, the fight against "indeterminate sentencing" in a text like *Struggle for Justice* (AFSC 1971). However, once models for determinate sentencing were enacted, at the federal and state levels, what they meant in practice was longer actual sentences served. Even, many years later, aberrations such as the "three strikes and you're out" rules might be seen as having some connection with the request for fixed, pre-determined sentences (Greenberg and Humphries 1980). Rehabilitation was seen as an "instrument of social control" also. Robert Martinson's famous "What Works?" piece – where he systematically tried to show that the record of rehabilitation was an abysmal failure (Martinson 1974) – would be the basis for a crucial right-wing fight (Cullen 2005).

The social transformations at work between the 1970s and the 1990s produced at the same time a historically rooted criminal phenomenology and an account of it that was reflected in criminologists' work. Both the types of crime and the criminological accounts were different from those characteristics of the previous period. The attitudes of "distance/proximity" or "sympathy/antipathy" are not simply, after all, solipsistic, idealist, constructionist products of more or less ideologically inclined criminologists, but are socially produced attitudes, rooted in solid circumstances such as, in the 1970s–1990s period, a higher unemployment rate, racism, a consumerist culture, a society fostering violence. Criminologists powerfully contributed to the validation of the overall redirection of social relationships in the United States and other societies in the period considered. The representation of crime became a way in fact of talking about society and society's ills that went far beyond phenomena and types of behavior legitimately identified as criminal by penal law. Rather, this representation addressed the moral value of society as a whole.

Criminologists could not afford to ignore the changed *Zeitgeist*. In a 1977 article endowed with remarkable foresight, Anthony Platt and Paul Takagi identified a new *realist* criminology. This was the kind of criminology that – as if taking its revenge on yesteryear's *enfant prodige*, labeling theory – was to rediscover that the harm inflicted by criminals on individuals and communities was *real*; that criminals were often mean and/or inferior types of human individuals; that penality did indeed serve the positive function of protecting society from "predators" of all kinds, people who are not deserving of our sympathy. This criminology, in other words, took upon itself the task of restoring and shoring up – contributing to the solidification, legitimation, and complacency of – a community of well-behaved people who needed guidance and orientation after a period of deep, tumultuous change.

## Control Theory

An early contribution to the creation of such a climate may be considered the theory of "control" or of "social bonds," first introduced by Travis Hirschi in a pioneering work in 1969 and then more recently revised, as a "theory of *self*-control," with Michael R. Gottfredson (Gottfredson and Hirschi 1990). This theory considers the motivation to commit crimes as dependent on the interaction between a "natural" tendency to break the law (in a world imagined, in a way very close to Parsons's (see above, chapter 6), as an association of Hobbesian actors), and the degree of control that society is able to exert on these actors through fundamental social institutions such as the family and the school. Hirschi believes in fact that what we need to explain is not so much criminal behavior as what detains us from engaging in criminal behavior. This he sees in that net of "social bonds" within which our socialization unfolds. More specifically, in *Causes of Delinquency* (1969), Hirschi identified four dimensions of social bonds: *attachment* to significant others, *commitment* to and *involvement* in pursuing society's traditional goals, and the *belief* that conventional social norms ought to be observed. According to Hirschi, in order to produce criminal behavior, it would not be necessary to have a belief favorable to the violation of criminal law – as Sutherland and Cressey and also, to a certain extent, Matza would have claimed – but simply a falling apart, for whatever reason, of conformist ties to society.

Especially the original version of Hirschi's theory, based on the concept of "social bonds," had certainly the merit of helping the researcher focus on what goes on in the very first years of the individual's life, and in his or her relationships with "significant others." It holds also – similarly to differential association theory – an interesting universalistic approach to the issue of deviance. One of the most characteristic results of Hirschi's original work, using the method of self-reported delinquency – which he helped to pioneer – was that deviance is distributed quite equally across different social groups. The criminal overrepresentation of minorities and males is therefore largely due, it is implied, to the much higher likelihood of their encounters with the police and with the criminal justice system, rather than to a self-reported delinquency that is only slightly higher than that of other groups (this stands in curious contrast with Hirschi's criticism of the "official reaction hypothesis" approach throughout his 1969 work). In fact, on the specifics of "race" and social class, Hirschi wrote, "[i]n the case of Negroes, the official reaction hypothesis as an explanation of differential official rates is particularly persuasive" (1969: 78) and, further, "[i]t is of the essence of social class that it can create differences in reward where none exists in talent, that it can impose differences in punishment where none exists in obedience to rules" (1969: 82).

Hirschi therefore invited readers to turn their attention to the importance of early education and the child's relationships with figures of importance in the family and in school – an importance that had only slight connections with class or "race." In the more recent *General Theory of Crime*, Hirschi, together with Gottfredson (Gottfredson and Hirschi 1990), developed the same general idea in the direction of the importance of "self-control," by emphasizing now the process of internalization of social norms rather than the processes of creation of social bonds. According to this work, those who are able to exert self-control are also those who will exhibit a lower level of criminal behavior. It is, however, obvious that in order to explain self-control, the analyst has once again to turn to the institutions that are able to create social bonds, therefore first of all to the family. Hirschi believes that the new version of the theory is able to account for a particular (and controversial[8]) result of empirical investigations, namely that deviant behavior emerges at a very early age and tends to be stable in time – something that Gottfredson and Hirschi try to explain on the grounds of the processes of socialization in the very early years of life (and once more the relationship of Hirschi's theory to Parsons's "Freudian" theory of deviance and social control could not be more apparent). Let's hear it directly from Gottfredson and Hirschi in a central passage of their *General Theory of Crime*:

> Criminal acts provide *immediate* gratification of desires. A major characteristic of people with low self-control is therefore a tendency to respond to tangible stimuli in the immediate environment, to have a concrete "here and now" orientation. People with high self-control, in contrast, tend to defer gratification.
>
> Criminal acts provide *easy or simple* gratification of desires. They provide money without work, sex without courtship, revenge without court delays. People lacking self-control also tend to lack diligence, tenacity, or persistence in a course of action.
>
> Criminal acts are *exciting, risky, or thrilling*. They involve stealth, danger, speed, agility, deception, or power. People lacking self-control therefore tend to be adventuresome, active, and physical. Those with high levels of self-control tend to be cautious, cognitive, and verbal.
>
> Crimes provide *few or meagre long-term benefits*. They are not equivalent to a job or a career. On the contrary, crimes interfere with long-term commitments to jobs, marriages, family, or friends. People with low self-control thus tend to have unstable marriages, friendships, and job profiles. They tend to be little interested in and unprepared for long-term occupational pursuits.
>
> Crimes require *little skill or planning*. The cognitive requirements for most crimes are minimal. It follows that people lacking self-control need not possess or value cognitive or academic skills. The manual skills required for most crimes are minimal. It follows that people lacking self-control need not possess manual skills that require training or apprenticeship. Crimes often result in *pain or discomfort for the victim*. Property is lost, bodies are injured, privacy is violated, trust is broken. It follows that people with low self-control tend to be self-centered, indifferent, or insensitive to the suffering and needs of others. It does not follow, however, that people with low self-control are routinely unkind or antisocial. On the contrary, they may discover the immediate and easy rewards of charm and generosity. Recall that

crime involves the pursuit of immediate pleasure. It follows that
people lacking self-control will also tend to pursue immediate plea-
sures that are *not* criminal: they will tend to smoke, drink, use drugs,
gamble, have children out of wedlock, and engage in illicit sex.
(Gottfredson and Hirschi 1990: 89–90)

The reader, increasingly worried by such a crescendo, is happy to
find out, in the end, that smoking, drinking, and engaging in illicit
sex are, after all, *non*-criminal activities! Notice that Gottfredson and
Hirschi make ample use of "therefore" and "it follows," but it is
hard to escape the impression of a substantially tautological procedure. People with low self-control are criminal, and criminals with
low self-control have a lot of other negative traits, which seem to
have in common the fact of contravening the usual, middle-class,
work-ethic, "American" way of doing things. Gottfredson and
Hirschi's attention seems therefore to be focused on the kind of
crimes that only lower-class criminals commit. It is a criminology
of "street crime" at best, in that tradition of "realism" excoriated by
Platt and Takagi, the realism that has as one of its focuses the criminality of the working class and tends to forget white-collar crime or
even organized crime, whose protagonists are business-like people
very much capable of self-control (cf. Edwin H. Sutherland's (1937)
and William Chambliss's (1972) book-length works on "professional
criminals").

## Criminologies of the Self and the Other

The criminology of the period between the 1970s and the 1990s
took certainly many forms, differing among themselves in theoretical inspiration, politics, criminal policy recommendations. David
Garland has usefully made a distinction, however, between a *criminology of the self*, which "characterizes offenders as rational con-
sumers," and a *criminology of the other*, "of the threatening outcast,
the fearsome stranger, the excluded and the embittered" (Garland
1996: 461). Apart from the differences between such different orientations, which we will see below, almost as important is what
they have decisively in common, i.e., in Garland's words, "an official criminology . . . in which amorality, generalized insecurity and
enforced exclusion are coming to prevail over the traditions of
welfarism and social citizenship" (Garland 1996: 462; for his more
general argument, see Garland 2001a). They express an attitude of

distance, antipathy, even contempt, for their object of analysis. The general emphasis on "predatory street crime" is particularly revealing, as Platt and Takagi had noticed. For instance, the routine activity approach (Cohen and Felson 1979; Felson 1998) started from the assumption that the "predatory" nature of criminals was a given, not to be explained. Only criminals' opportunity to commit crimes was to be explained. From here it would be a short step indeed to the idea that criminals' genetic inferiorities should not be excluded and would often correlate with race (Wilson and Herrnstein 1985; Herrnstein and Murray 1994). Furthermore, an "actuarial" penology rediscovered the value of the positivists' concept of "dangerousness" (Blumstein and Cohen 1979; Blumstein 1983; Greenwood 1982 – for a critique see Feeley and Simon 1992, 1994).

## Criminologies of the Self

Even in those criminologies that Garland has defined as "criminologies of the self" (or of "everyday life"), the starting point seems to be a Hobbesian image of society as a pre-contractual condition where human life is "nasty, brutish and short" and where the honest and respectable individual – usually very akin to the criminologist – must continuously be on the alert to respond to possible attacks by "predators" whose only preoccupation is to suddenly jump on such an individual or on his or her property. The animalistic imagery of the predator, which can hardly be presented as a term expressing detached scientific description, fits nicely with the "evolutionary ecological" theoretical assumptions of this approach, which harks back to Spenserian motifs and Hobbesian suggestions. Theoretical premises, when they are offered, incline toward social Darwinism and socio-biology (Felson 1998; Cohen and Machalek 1988). As Gottfredson and Hirschi explained very well above, these predators are not similar to the criminologists who are writing. Rather, they are male, young, poor, uneducated, and usually exhibit a skin whose hue is some tonality of "dark" (Cohen and Felson 1979; Felson 1998). What is, however, different from the "criminologies of the other," as we will see, is the fact that there is here a complete lack of interest in "the criminal," who is rather seen as some kind of *natural* presence, almost as an "act of God." The analyst's interest is instead completely directed toward understanding (and avoiding!) the process of *victimization*. These criminologies –

whatever the label they go under, from "everyday life" to "common sense," from "routine activity approach" to "opportunities" – are inclined to examine the various stages of the "victimization process." They study the characteristics and lifestyle of the potential victim, the availability and protection of the goods that are the "target" of the aggressor, and finally the possibility that through criminal policies based on deterrence or incapacitation the likelihood of the risk of victimization may be reduced (Felson 1998; Becker 1968; Cohen and Felson 1979; Newman 1972; Greenwood 1982).

Some of the analytical consequences of this outlook are not without interest from a sociological perspective. For instance, they postulate a relationship between economic prosperity and an increase in crime opportunities, rather than the more traditional idea that motivation to crime may be linked to a deterioration of economic conditions. In an enhanced economic situation, there will be a greater availability of particular goods and also a greater ex-position to lifestyle risks (night-life, absence from home of both working parents and children, etc.). At the same time, those goods will be less protected especially because of women's recruitment into the ranks of waged work. The routine activity approach tries therefore to make sense of a common result in research on relationships between crime and economic conditions. In fact, measures of the two phenomena are often *positively* correlated instead of *negatively* – as traditionally one would expect. Even more often, there seems to be no correlation whatsoever between them. Probably the analysis would have to distinguish between a negative correlation, between motivation for crime and economic decline, and a positive correlation, between opportunity for crime and economic prosperity. When both are present at the same time, they seem to cancel each other out and there appears to be no connection at all between crime and changing economic conditions (Cohen and Felson 1979; Chiricos 1987; Field 1990). A few historical puzzles in the last half-century would therefore be amenable to this kind of explanation. In the decades of economic development between the 1950s and the 1970s, in many Western countries, and especially in the United States (in Italy, however, this happened almost ten years later), a situation of strong economic development and low unemployment went with a strong increase in crime, rather than the decrease one would have expected. It is certainly more difficult to understand what happened later, in the 1990s, when economic prosperity went with a marked decline in crime (especially violent crime).

## Victimization and Self-Report Studies

Between the 1960s and 1970s, two new methodological instruments helped revamp the field of criminology, especially in its "positivist" variant. These were the study of victimization, especially by means of victimization surveys, and the self-report inquiry, which had been pioneered, as we have seen, by Travis Hirschi. Both were directed at trying to come to terms with the traditional limit of criminological research, i.e. the necessity of making use of "official" records and therefore the issue of the so-called "dark number" of crime, those crimes that are "committed," but not recorded by any official agency. (Of course, to talk of "crimes" that are not "recorded" is problematic, almost a contradiction in terms, because it is a "naturalistic" manner of looking at crime, which is typical of what David Matza called a "positivistic" criminology. The claim of victimization studies lies in fact in making assertions about a concept of "crime." This is in fact a juridical concept, however. It is not by chance that there are very complex procedural rules to come to determine whether a given natural event is indeed, in the end, a crime, and what kind of crime it is. If the issue were as simple as it seems to be in victimization studies, there would not be millions of people around the world making a living – sometimes a very good living – working as police officers, judges, and attorneys. At the most, we could say that the events unearthed by victimization surveys are natural events that one could suppose would be defined as crimes if observed by an agent qualified by the legal order to define what is a crime and what is not. In any case, to compare "recorded crime" with the results of "victimization surveys" is a very problematic operation not only practically but also conceptually.)

In short, since the early 1970s in several countries (the United States, the United Kingdom, the Netherlands), "victimization surveys" have been launched in order to have measures of this "dark number." A sample of the population was interviewed and its members were asked whether they had been "victimized" in a given period of time, usually the previous year, and also many other questions pertaining to crime and social reaction to it. These surveys have produced interesting results. We have learned, for instance, that, in the United States, the "victimization rate" has been remarkably stable – even if oscillating – from the beginning of these surveys, 1973, to the early 1990s, and remarkably downward afterwards (this National Crime Victimization Survey (NCVS), ongoing from 1973 but redesigned in 1992, is the United States' main source of information on criminal victimization, based on a nationally representative sample of 77,200 households yearly surveyed). More generally, these results are useful in order to plan a kind of "situational" prevention – i.e. a prevention based on preparing means of defense and protection grounded in the environment, in the "situation" (Felson 1998). Beside the problem with the judgment and memory of the interviewees, the strongest limit of these surveys has been that of reproducing the traditional bias of criminology, i.e. the emphasis placed on the most "visible" crimes and criminals and therefore, once more, on "street crime." Those kind of crimes where the victim is a participant or, even more, where the victim may not be fully aware of being in fact a victim (financial and environmental crimes, incriminations generally geared to defending "the public") are in fact seriously underestimated in these surveys. Furthermore, these are usually, computer-assisted telephone interviews (CATI), and therefore tend to exclude populations that are either very poor, or homeless, or institutionalized, or very mobile – and it is hard to claim that these types of populations are not prone to victimization. It is indeed more likely the opposite.

Another instrument that was devised to collect more information about the "dark number" and the world of crime generally is the so-called self-report survey. In this kind of research, a small group of people – usually people of whom it is reasonable to expect a higher incidence of criminal and/or deviant activities, such as a group of established offenders or of young people – are asked questions about their own deviance and/or criminality. In this case, the research goals are both the discovery of the distribution of these activities and – not less interesting – the relationship between deviant behavior and a number of standard social variables, such as gender, age, socio-economic status, national, cultural, and religious origins, etc. At least two interesting outcomes resulted from this kind of research. On the one hand, it was generally found that deviance is a very widespread and common occurrence. Almost all respondents have broken some social and/or legal rule (the questions usually concern minor crimes for the young groups and more substantial ones for the established offenders). However, as commonly happens with statistical distributions, two "outlying" groups are also usually identified, one of hyper-conformists on the one hand and another one of "high rate offenders" on the other. These latter were the so-called HROs, and the symbol "lambda" [$\lambda$] was selected to express the number of crimes committed by a given individual in a temporal interval. HROs have, by definition, a high lambda [λ] number (Blumstein et al. 1988; Horney and Marshall 1991). Furthermore, the distribution of people who report deviant behavior is much broader than those usually involved in *officially recorded* criminal behavior, comprising especially more women and more middle-class people. If this is to be expected because a criminality that comes to be officially recorded is probably a more serious criminality, at the same time it is also quite likely that the control exercised by criminal justice agencies is more often directed at males, and especially at males of low social status (where "low" status may be because of class, ethnicity, national or cultural origins, etc.).[9] These are the "predestined targets," so to speak, of criminal justice systems.

## Actuarialism

In the conservative mood of the 1980s backlash, the implication that criminologists derived from this type of research was aimed especially toward the identification of these so-called HROs. Researchers from an important Santa Monica private think tank, the Rand Corporation, hypothesized that, if it were possible to predict which young offenders would later evolve into HROs, it would also be possible to selectively incapacitate them, reaching two virtuous goals at the same time: to decrease crime and invest prison resources more wisely. Soon, a policy of "selective incapacitation," as it was called, was tried and tested. The novelty here – compared for instance to the old positivistic emphasis on "dangerousness" (see above, chapter 2) – was essentially in the instrument, which substituted a statistical concept of danger based on risk for the old one that was based on clinical observation (Castel 1991). Bernard Harcourt has recently shown how this was the umpteenth "penal technocratic Utopia" in the history of prediction, a history that had started at Chicago with none other than Ernest W. Burgess, and that had then spread to many aspects of the criminal justice process, from the determination of parole to sentencing to even the death penalty (Harcourt 2007). It was a family of predictive schemes that had replaced the clinical emphasis of old-style positivism with an actuarial concept of "risk" (Harcourt 2007: 106–7; Castel 1991). "Actuarial practices" would be, according to critic Jonathan Simon, those that rely on "techniques that use statistics to represent the distribution of variables in a population" (Simon 1988: 771). Harcourt is quick to point out, however, that this has not meant at all an abandonment of individualization.

In the hopes of the prediction technocrats, this was instead to bring about a better, i.e. more efficient kind of individualization. In any case, in what was to the most visible application of such an actuarial stance, in the 1980s, Peter Greenwood, Joan Petersilia, and others applied an "actuarial" concept of "risk" to a very old activity indeed, the identification of "dangerous subjects," an identification that was to happen at a very early age, when the early encounters with the criminal justice system occurred, and that would be based on those personal traits of the subject whose correlation with future criminal behavior seemed to be high, such as having had juvenile precedents or a drug history, or being unemployed (Greenwood 1982). One of the very unfortunate consequences of this way of thinking, and of acting, is, however, "racial profiling," as Bernard Harcourt shows very effectively. The assumption that, within a certain population, the likelihood of catching offenders will be higher will lead to increasing sections of that population being arrested, convicted, and detained. It is what Harcourt calls a "ratchet effect."

The theory of "selective incapacitation" became very popular at the beginning of the 1980s, first among its proponents, later on among its critics and detractors, who made it a centerpiece of the new label of "actuarial" justice or penology (Feeley and Simon 1992, 1994). However, those who had first advanced the ideas linked with "selective incapacitation" soon recognized that the number of "false positives" was remarkably high. There was therefore the risk of punishing on the ground of very elusive evidence, and they came to the conclusion that the theory should be abandoned. The language of selective incapacitation did not disappear, however, and probably produced an effect of legitimation of policies that were not "selective" in any conceivable sense, but if anything "general" in their incapacitative effects. A massive, "general" kind of incapacitation was in fact developing in those years in the United States but was driven by the more traditional goals of "retribution" and "general deterrence" rather than by "selective incapacitation." Theories that linked punishment to the emergence of a "moral indignation" and a feeling of "resentment" among the middle class, according to a perspective of social psychology, responded certainly much better to what was happening at the time (Ranulf 1938).

## Broken Windows and Zero Tolerance

In 1982, a political scientist, James Q. Wilson, who had published the best-selling conservative tract *Thinking about Crime* (Wilson

1975), wrote a popular article for the journal *Atlantic Monthly* together with George L. Kelling (Wilson and Kelling 1982). There, they maintained that disorder and urban incivilities – represented in their narration by the example of "broken windows" – are related to lack of formal and informal controls in certain urban areas and therefore also to crime. "Broken windows" and other such phenomena, like graffiti, vandalism, prostitution, unclean streets, etc., would in other words trigger a vicious circle of social disorganization, decline of real-estate value, transformation in the social composition of the neighborhood, criminality. It was the kind of thesis that would develop into so-called "zero tolerance" policies because – as the reasoning went – the lack of tolerance toward apparently "minor" forms of deviance and crime might be able to stop the escalation toward more serious forms of crime. In the 1990s, the rhetoric of "zero tolerance" was linked to the policies of Mayor Rudolph Giuliani in New York City – policies that were presented as one of the results of that type of analysis. This position was reinforced by Wesley G. Skogan's *Disorder and Decline* (1990), which also claimed that disorganization, disorder, and rowdy behavior in a neighborhood contributed to making it less safe.

It would later appear, however, that this was more rhetoric than substance because, if it is true that New York experienced in those years a dramatic decline in crime rates, the same happened also in many other American cities and it started even before the enactment of Giuliani's policies – implying therefore a much more "systemic" explanation for the fall in crime rates in the 1990s. The question nevertheless remains about the more general validity of "broken window theory." An evaluation based on the city of Baltimore (Taylor 2001) came to the conclusion that Wilson and Kelling's hypothesis is just one factor among many that influence criminal phenomena in a given area, and certainly not the most relevant. Therefore to consider it as a sort of magic wand and concentrate all resources on police repression is certainly wrong.

Bernard Harcourt's *Illusion of Order* (2001) added to criticism by pointing out how the notion of order underlying Wilson and Kelling's hypothesis, as well as those of other proponents of the centrality of orderliness, is basically a socially constructed idea, within a process very similar to the one described by David Garland in *The Culture of Control* (2001a). Robert Sampson's theoretical proposal represents an interesting alternative to Wilson and Kelling's point of view. Sampson has been working from the heritage of the Chicago School, linking it with current sociological debate about "social capital," the idea, that is, that beyond "financial" and "human" types of capital there is also a *social* capital, that is, the amount and quality of social relationships that are characteristic of an individual or a group (Putnam 1993; Coleman 1990; Bourdieu 1986). It has been easy for Sampson to connect this perspective to Chicago's traditional emphasis on "informal" or "primary" social controls. He has furthermore introduced the concept of "collective efficacy." In an important study of Chicago neighborhoods, Sampson and Raudenbush (1999) have shown that the relationship between incivilities and crime is mediated through "collective efficacy," that is, the capacity for mobilization of a neighborhood on questions of collective, common interest. It is only where the level of collective efficacy is low that the transition from incivility to crime – predicted by "broken window theory" – actually unfolds. Chicago's traditional preventive recommendation is therefore once more confirmed, a recommendation according to which it is important to strengthen the social structure and organization of the community, a recommendation that sees social control as a property of the community – essentially *primary* social control – and not as something that is *brought* to the community from the outside – *secondary* social control. A successful level of social control in the community cannot be separated therefore from a policy of *self-empowerment* of the community.

## The Criminology of "the Other" and the "Underclass"

Two good examples of "criminologies of the other" are certainly two texts – actually not written by criminologists – that have become enormously popular within the overall conservative climate that took hold of the United States with the first Reagan presidency in the early 1980s: *Crime and Human Nature* by that very James Q. Wilson and Richard J. Herrnstein (1985) and then, later on, *The Bell Curve* by Herrnstein and Charles Murray (1994). Whereas the former accepted the derivation of inferiorities from genetic constitution as a hypothesis,[10] it was especially the second, *The Bell Curve*, that offered the most openly racist type of statement. Building on the established "bell curve" distribution of most social variables, Herrnstein and Murray claimed that, within the lowest section of such a distribution, one could find the traits characteristic of a true "underclass," i.e. a low average IQ and a high crime rate (besides other social pathologies). These, however, overlapped with certain sections of the American population, i.e. minorities and especially African Americans. The consequences in social and political terms would be obvious: the implication of Herrnstein and Murray's analysis was that the reason for the high number of "social patholo-gies" amidst certain American minorities would be their genuine constitutional inferiority and not some socio-historical cause. There-fore investing social funds in that direction would be a mere waste of money, and the only possible course of action would be – in a way not very dissimilar from what was recommended by Italian positivists *vis-à-vis* "the born delinquent" – surveillance, control, and incapacitation. It is not surprising therefore that the "political" conclusions drawn by Herrnstein and Murray are true political Dystopias of the worst kind, a kind scarcely heard since the years of Fascist State racism in the 1930s:

> Over the next decades, it will become broadly accepted by the cogni-tive elite that the people we now refer to as the underclass are in that condition through no fault of their own but because of inherent shortcomings about which little can be done . . . In short, by custodial state, we have in mind a high-tech and more lavish version of the Indian reservation for some substantial minority of the nation's population, while the rest of America tries to go about its business. In its less benign forms, the solutions will become more and more totalitarian . . . One possibility is that a variety of old police practices – especially the stop and frisk – will quietly come back into use in new guises. New prisons will continue to be built, and the cells already available will be used more efficiently to incarcerate danger-ous offenders . . . Technology will provide new options for segregat-ing and containing criminals, as the electronic bracelets are being used to enforce house arrest (or maybe "neighborhood arrest") . . . The underclass will become even more concentrated spatially than it is today. (Herrnstein and Murray 1994: 523–4)

Earlier, Murray had written of a "custodial democracy, which takes as its premise that a substantial portion of the population cannot be expected to function as citizens" (Murray 1990). In sum, in only 20 years, the metaphor of "the Indian reservation" had gone from being a left-wing critique of the most benign forms of sociology of deviance, such as in Gouldner's scolding comments on Becker (see above, chapter 8), to a "serious" political proposal on how to deal with a relevant section of American minorities.

The specifics of Herrnstein and Murray's argument centered on the concept of IQ and on this crucial aspect they have been sharply criticized (Gould 1994, repeating some of the arguments that he had already advanced in Gould 1981). There is in fact ample evidence that the results of IQ testing may be much less genetically determined than Herrnstein and Murray seem to think, and dependent instead on social and historical factors. In other words, IQ performances may be responsive to the environment and learning, therefore the pessimistic conclusions of Herrnstein and Murray about the effects of social programs and education are not warranted.

At the same time, it is also important to notice that a crucial premise of this kind of analysis was the fact of ignoring the process of criminalization altogether – i.e. the process on the study of which the 1960s sociology of deviance had most impinged. It is not by accident therefore, one should say, that some of the authors who became the protagonists of the debate in these very years were not sociologists of deviance or even "criminologists," but came from other disciplines, such as economics, demography, political science, philosophy, etc. Their deep ignorance of sociological criminology was undoubtedly very useful, because it allowed them to skip the issue of criminalization altogether, as if it had never been discussed, and to take seriously the traditional "goals" of the criminal justice system – from deterrence to retribution to incapacitation to, even, rehabilitation! – without confronting the deep critique that the 1960s sociology of deviance had elaborated, as we have seen, of such goals. Furthermore, whereas many of these analyses developed neo-positivist types of explanation of criminal behavior, going back to "constitutional" factors, the main legal framework remained essentially neo-classical, in order not to compromise the deterrent and retributionist rhetoric of penal policies. Proper social behavior should in fact be demanded even of those who are described as unable to deliver it. To recognize otherwise would have meant raising doubts about a system of repression that was developing faster and faster and that was becoming the so-called "correctional-industrial complex" (Christie 1994).

Once uprooted from its embeddedness in the complexity of social relationships, the question of crime became then a question for moral edification. The main issue was one of combating the "bad" morality of the 1960s by means of a new, "good" morality. In this tried and true *revanche*, the appreciative or agnostic stances of the previous criminology were often expressly evoked as having contributed to the fall – Charles Murray and his colleagues at the Manhattan Institute being as much concerned with the treasons and perversities of the intellectuals themselves as with the predations of the underclass (Wacquant 1999). In ways similar to what had happened in the late 1920s and 1930s, when the rise to power of Fascist regimes in Europe had been accompanied by their also then successful polemic against the "softness" of liberal regimes on crime (the 1930s Nazi *leitmotiv* of the "Weimar prison paradise"; Rusche and Kirchheimer 1939: 179), the criminal was represented as a *monstruum* – a being whose features are inherently different from ours and shocking to the well-behaved. For instance, in their *Body Count* (1996), William Bennett, John DiIulio, and John Walters wrote of a "new generation of street criminals," "superpredators," "the youngest, biggest, and baddest generation any society has ever known" (this was on the eve of the big drop in violent crime, and actually afterwards DiIulio called for a stop to the mindless construction of new prisons). The criminal was once again portrayed as an incarnation of the ultimate sin of breaking the fabric of society apart, somebody who had to be contained through incapacitation or death in order to restore the unity and order of society, i.e., in the colorful language of Matza, the power of Leviathan. These monstrosities were paraded around in the media on occasions too numerous to be all recorded here. Suffice it to recall perhaps the most infamous, or maybe the most politically useful: the case of "Willie" Horton. Horton was a black Massachusetts convict who had committed the rape of a white woman while on a furlough program when Michael Dukakis was governor of the state. The Horton case became a favorite card in George Bush's 1988 presidential campaign against the same Dukakis (whose vice-presidential candidate was the African American leader Jesse Jackson). In the words of one of the producers of the political advertisement about Horton in the Bush campaign, this was "a wonderful mix of liberalism and big black rapist" (Karst 1993: 73–4).

The devaluation of the criminal, from official statistics often an African American person, went together with the collective devaluation of the social group in which criminals were seen as belonging, namely that underclass, racially defined, that was demonized in the American media. The devaluation of the *underclass*, however, went hand in hand with the devaluation of the *class* as such, that is, of the *working class* as a whole. Bruce Western in *Punishment and Inequality in America* (2006) shows the social consequences of "mass imprisonment" in the United States. Western convincingly outlines the social structure involved in the imprisonment binge, which has targeted especially lower-class ethnic minorities (measured by their educational achievement). These have been hit by the reach of "correctional authorities" to the point that certain sections of this group, such as young black males who live in the inner city, see imprisonment as one of the most likely events in their life, a state of affairs that was simply unthinkable in the period before mass imprisonment. Western explains also that they may be the ones committing most crimes that are noticed by social control agencies, but the striking fact is that, in the last 30 years, they have been engaging in criminal behavior less and less while they have been going to prison more and more. In other words, they have been increasingly crowding prisons because criminal justice polices have become much tougher and, in Western's felicitous phrase, "crime has become the context rather than the cause" of imprisonment (2006: 48–9). As the labeling theorists would have said, these people's crimes are enormously *amplified* by the functioning of American society and its social control mechanisms. Western emphasizes the role of "law and order" campaigns and Republican national and especially local administrations in this connection. We have already seen how, in an article of a few years ago, Western and Beckett (1999) had claimed that if one were to add the great mass of imprisoned people to the official American rate of unemployment, the American economic advantage over Europe, advertised as evidence of the superiority of American neo-liberal policies over slow-moving, inefficient European "corporatism," would basically disappear, and the rate of joblessness in the United States would appear to be much closer to the European one. The same would happen, Western shows now, with wage levels. Because a whole low-wage sector of American labor was taken off the market, and hidden within prisons, the 1990s "prosperity," for instance, could be apologetically extended to ethnic minorities and particularly to African Americans. However, Western shows that if one were to consider the social strata hidden away in correctional institutions, African Americans' gains in wages in the 1990s would be much more contained. In fact, Western maintains, those strata did not take any advantage of 1990s prosperity, and President Kennedy's maxim that "a rising tide lifts all boats" (Western 2006: 94) actually was not true for poor African Americans even in the prosperous 1990s. They were basically locked away, and uncounted. In short, imprisonment is a sort of "pathway to the secondary labor market" and in this sense seems to represent a crucial socio-economic institution, quite central to the make-up of American society.

Once again, the articulation of structural and cultural effects could not be tighter. As we have seen, in the 1960s, crime had often been seen as innovative, sometimes as a challenge to unjust institutions, whether these were political or economic institutions. It was possible to identify with the lowest stratum of society because such a stratum was not described as sordid and shameful. Starting in the early 1970s, all of this changed. Crime was built up to be a synonym for everything that was wrong in American culture. It was necessary to "say no" to illicit behavior, whether the consumption of illegal substances or the committing of crimes. There was nothing glamorous in crime and drugs, whether illicit or licit (the very successful campaign to vilify tobacco smoke is a good example of such strategies). Drugs were consumed by inferior, not glamorous, people, of lower-class, often ethnic minority, extraction (Reinerman 1979).

In short, the criminal was no longer a human being similar to us, as Sutherland had written, or whose destiny we could even appreciate, as Becker and Matza had proposed, or, god forbid really, an innovator and a hero. Again in the 1970s, 1980s, 1990s, the spotlight of the criminologist, very much like the spotlight of police helicopters in the Dystopian LA portrayed in Mike Davis's *City of Quartz* (1990), has been focusing on people who are not at all nice or charming. On the contrary, they are dangerous. They are either bad or saddled with some kind of personal deficit that makes them act as bad people. Even the self-image of criminals was not immune to such deterioration. After all, the 1980 New Mexico State prison riot, probably the most bloodthirsty uprising in the rich history of North American prison riots, took place exactly at the beginning of the new Reagan "law and order" era (Morris 1983; Colvin 1992; Rolland 1997).

## The Turn of the 1990s

At the beginning of the 1990s, the protracted horse cure administered to American society by neo-liberal policies – policies that were anti-union, anti-working-class, racist, illiberal, and intentionally pursuing increasing inequality – had produced a social landscape well represented in the classic book by Mike Davis, *City of Quartz* (1990), a sociological, historical, and literary tribute to the most intensely postmodern city in America, Los Angeles. It was, however, also a prophetic text, because soon after, the absolution of those police officers who, in 1992, had pummeled an African American man, Rodney King, under the, for them, unfortunate eye of a video

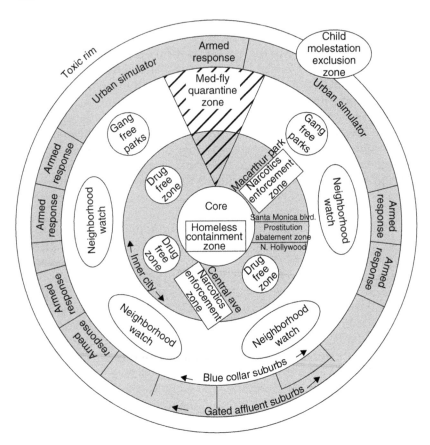

Figure 3   The ecology of fear according to Mike Davis (Davis 1998: 365)

camera triggered a violent urban riot, such as America had not seen in decades. That riot was also an implicit revolt against the type of control of urban space described by Davis in that book and in a series of later works (Davis 1992a, 1992b, 1998). Such Dystopian imagery was well captured in Davis's revisiting of Park and Burgess's famous 1920s Chicago map (shown above, figure 1, and see figure 3), a revisiting expressed in the concept of an "ecology of fear," as Davis calls it – as if somebody had redrawn Park and Burgess's map under the influence of some kind of potent drug, during a definitely bad "trip."

Davis had the insight of capturing the huge importance an accumulated fear had come to have in American society – a fear that had accompanied that society at least since the 1960s – a kind of fear, or paranoia, well summed up in a famous 1960s bumper sticker, "Just because you're paranoid it doesn't mean they aren't out to get you" (ironically reaffirming, in a sense, Ed Lemert's argument in his famous 1962 piece, as we have seen). Sociologist Barry Glassner, in his *The Culture of Fear* (1999), put it this way:[11]

> Why are so many fears in the air, and so many of them unfounded? Why, as crime rates plunged throughout the 1990s, did two-thirds of Americans believe they were soaring? How did it come about that by mid-decade 62 percent of us described ourselves as "truly desperate" about crime – almost twice as many as in the late 1980s, when crime rates were higher? Why, on a survey in 1997, when the crime rate had already fallen for a half dozen consecutive years, did more than half of us disagree with the statement "This country is finally beginning to make some progress in solving the crime problem"? In the late 1990s the number of drug users had decreased by half compared to a decade earlier; almost two-thirds of high school seniors had never used any illegal drugs, even marijuana. So why did a majority of adults rank drug abuse as the greatest danger to America's youth? Why did nine out of ten believe the drug problem is out of control, and only one in six believe the country was making progress? Give us a happy ending and we write a new disaster story. (Glassner 1999: xi)

Year after year, fear of crime had run Americans' lives, with people fearful of crossing certain streets or going into certain areas, walking after a certain hour, or riding public transport. This had happened during a period when crime had basically been oscillating around a mean and then, in the 1990s, had dramatically declined. And about events the probability of which was in any case quite remote. And that would tend in any case to happen mostly to people who knew each other. It was becoming increasingly difficult for people then to distinguish what in this pervasive fear was "real" and what was "constructed," what was based on direct or at least hearsay experience and what was based on words amplified by the media, and by politicians who believed they were giving "the people" what the people wanted.

What David Garland has called "the reality of a high crime society" (2001a: 139–65), and the fact that people got used to such a reality, should then be confronted with Beckett's argument that, as we have seen, since the first 1973 victimization survey, such surveys portrayed quite a different reality, where crime was not really rising (Beckett 2001). Certainly, crime rates had gone up in the 1960s – even if in that decade we did not have victimization data and there is some indication of a tendency toward increased reporting at all levels, as Beckett points out. Against such a backdrop, I think it difficult to overstate the importance, in recent American history, of the 1992 Los Angeles riots. In fact, on the one hand they contributed to starting the critique of the most brutal aspects of the neo-liberal project – opening the way to Bill Clinton's middle-of-the-road presidency – and on the other hand they were situated at a time when the deep restructuring of the economy that had gone on for a good 20 years finally got its payback and the "prosperity years" of the 1990s could start.

After Rodney King went on TV to say, "We all have to live together," there were also attempts at pacification and social cohesion that I believe cannot be discounted. Also as a response to Rodney King's statement, in April 1993 hundreds of representatives of "gangs" from all over the United States met together with community activists in Kansas City for a "National Urban Peace and Justice Summit" that had among its goals that of ending the devastation of violence within American ethnic minority communities (cf. the *Progressive*, July 1993; Childs 1997) – a type of violence that had climaxed in those years because of the wars about the control of the "crack" market (Blumstein 2000). In New York, David C. Brotherton and Luis Barrios (2004) have studied and documented the transformation of the "Latin Kings" "gang" into what they call a "street organization" in this very period. It was about at that time when crime rates, and especially violent crime rates, started declining in American cities, a puzzle for American criminologists over which many are still scratching their heads (Blumstein and Wallman 2000; Rosenfeld 2002; Zimring 2006).

## Automated Control

It may be that the most accurate account of contemporary forms of control can be found not in social scientists' stories but in fiction. First, there is the fiction of an adopted Californian maverick writer, Philip Kindred Dick, who died prematurely in 1982, when the most famous film inspired by one of his novels, *Blade Runner*, was being shot.[12] Especially in another short story by Dick, "The Minority Report" (1956), we find all the control styles of the brave new world we live in, some of which we have already seen. We find in fact the idea of predicting crime before it happens, as in the Utopia of selective incapacitation. We find also, however, a foreboding of the style of control that has been emerging, according to Gary Marx, as the central contemporary one, i.e. technologically supported situational prevention, which we may want to call, for brevity, *automated control*. The reader who has seen the 2002 film inspired by Dick's story, *Minority Report*, may recall the scene in which the protagonist, having donned, for camouflage purposes, the pupils of somebody else, is greeted at the entrance of a department store by a welcoming message addressing him by the name of the original owner of the pupils. I thought this to be science fiction – as the saying goes – until recently I went through an airport in London and I saw "customers" go through passport control without any passport to show, or any officers to show it to, but only looking firmly "eye-to-eye" into a machine. According to Gary Marx, "situational prevention" may be the first step toward a completely new Utopia of control:

> With the trend toward ubiquitous computing, surveillance and sensors in one sense disappear into ordinary activities and objects – cars, cell phones, toilets, buildings, clothes and even bodies. The relatively labor-intensive bar code on consumer goods that requires manually scanning may soon be replaced with inexpensive embedded RFID (Radio Frequency Identification) computer chips that can be automatically read from short distances. The remote sensing of preferences and behavior offers many advantages such as controlling temperature and lighting in a room or reducing shipping and merchandising costs, while also generating records that can be used for surveillance. There may be only a short interval between the discovery of the information and the automatic taking of action. The individual as a subject of data collection and analysis may also almost simultaneously become the object of an intervention, whether this involves the triggering of an alarm or the granting (or denial) of some form of access e.g., to enter a door, use a computer or make a purchase. (Marx 2005: 818)

The idea of access control as a new form of control had been presented by Gilles Deleuze in his "Postscript on the Societies of Control" (Deleuze 1990; for a development of this idea in connection with post-Fordism see De Giorgi 2002: 67–89). There Deleuze referred to an intuition by another great American writer, William Burroughs, who, in a short essay in *semiotext(e)*, presented a very simple, but brilliant, idea. The idea is that control, to be called properly control, presupposes a will that has to be controlled (Burroughs 1978). In an extraordinarily sharp sociological insight – one not unexpected from an outstanding writer, and that the reader of this volume will, by now, be ready to accept! – Burroughs maintains that control presupposes words, words to persuade, words to counsel, words to tell one's rights, words to threaten, words to manipulate, but still words in order to orient a will. That is not the case any longer with situational prevention. Situational prevention may mean, for instance, Crime Prevention Through Environmental Design (CPTED). As Mike Davis comments on the 1992 Los Angeles riots, in a chapter appropriately entitled "Beyond *Blade Runner*":

> The 1992 riots vindicated the foresight of Fortress Downtown's designers. While windows were being smashed throughout the old business district, Bunker Hill lived up to its name. By flicking a few switches on their command consoles, the security staffs of the great bank towers were able to cut off all access to their expensive real estate. Bullet-proof steel doors rolled down over street-level entrances, escalators instantly froze, and electronic locks sealed off pedestrian passageways. As the *Los Angeles Business Journal* pointed out, the riot-tested success of corporate downtown's defenses has only stimulated demand for new and higher levels of physical security. (Davis 1998: 366)

Or, situational prevention may mean the recognition of the iris in *Minority Report* or at an airport, or Gary Marx's RFID computer chip implanted in a piece of merchandise, or in the brain of a human being. In all of these cases, there is no will to control left. Especially in the last case, the human being is not a human being anymore, or at least he or she is not treated as such, but is treated instead as a thing, "a tape recorder, a camera, a robot" (Burroughs 1978: 38). This is a case of what I would call an "automated" kind of control. This is different from *social* control. The history of social control, as we have seen it, has been a history tightly connected to that of democracy, insofar as "words," to tell it with Burroughs, have been the very substance of both. Words are the materials with which a consensus is created, persuasion is achieved, counsel is offered. Even in the starkest penitentiaries, the words of the priest and the words of the warden are there to redeem the soul of the sinner. After all, the "penitentiary" was invented, as we have seen, in the land of "friendly persuasion," William Penn's land. Not so anymore in the case of automated control. In this case, I do not tell you what to do, I do not persuade you, I do not even threaten you with a gun (which was after all the very naive form of control that a more sophisticated "Republican" form had replaced). No, in the case of situational prevention what I do is to make it impossible for you to do otherwise, rather in the same way in which crowd control is organized in Disney World (Shearing and Stenning 1985). There is no alternative possible, whether you will it or not, the only way is to follow the path. Once again, this end may be reached through architecture, or it may be reached by giving you access through some kind of automatic means. Or this can be reached by implanting an RFID computer chip in your brain or under your skin. Different degrees of automated control, different degrees of treating human beings like robots, but the same basic idea: I do not bother with orienting your will, by persuasion or coercion, I just make it impossible for you to do otherwise (or at least so I hope – resistance is, as always, wholly unpredictable).

Why, however, do I do that? Why do I do that, right at the end of a period in which human rights and human will were celebrated as the most crucial values of society, in the 1960s–1970s? Why do I do that at a time when the very source of capitalism's "destructive creativity" – as a response in fact to that flourishing of human will – is to be found in people's ideas and imagination, as de Giorgi (2002) shows very effectively happens in what he calls "post-Fordism"? Could it have something to do exactly with these very aspects? Could it have something to do with the *irreducibility* of will, or at least with a representation, by the ruling class, of an irreducibility of will of the (no-longer) subordinate classes, and the loss of any hope therefore that such a will could be "controlled," if not through "automated" means? And could it have something to do also with that long-term decline of democracy that we have seen again and again decried especially in the United States throughout the twentieth century? The lack of faith that the construction of a consensus would still be possible? This is a movement that would be consistent with a general decline in the notion of consensus and therefore of democracy. We may hypothesize that "automatic control" would be a more appropriate form of control for the era of the Empire (Hardt and Negri 1990) or for Giorgio Agamben's "State of exception" (Agamben 2003).

*Incapacitation* would then be the logical answer even if, as has always been the case in the history of penality, that irreducibility that would call for incapacitation would be argued in terms of "unfitness" – an unfitness, by certain individuals or social strata, from which it would only be possible to defend "ourselves." (One has only to think of the connection between "the Southern Question," the idea of dangerousness, and the principle of "social defense" in the Italian Positive School.) That is why, then, many have seen in the "actuarial" turn a "post-disciplinary" mark (Castel 1991: 293–6; Simon 1993; De Giorgi 2002: 77–80). After all, what is the point of teaching discipline to somebody that we judge basically unfit? We are not interested in including him, even if in a subordinate position, we only wish to exclude him, marginalize him, and "defend our society" (Foucault 1976b) from the danger that he brings with him. However, there is also a third possibility. It is that irreducibility and unfitness may have been associated by the ruling elites with the generation of the crisis and transformation between the 1970s and the 1990s, but that, with the re-establishment of their full hegemony in the 1990s, the new generations might become again the objects of a program of *subordinate inclusion* into the social pact, albeit under the new terms and conditions of the society emerging in the 1990s. It is to that possibility that we now turn in the tenth and last chapter.

# 10

# *The Cycle of the Canaille*

The promenader who, a few months before September 11, 2001, strolled down the streets of the "world cities," the cities at the center of the "Empire" (Hardt and Negri 2000), from New York to London, from Los Angeles to Tokyo, would have seen in many shop windows, among the imperial goods proudly shown, many signs for "help wanted." That was the case partly because, at the end of the 1990s, the unemployment rate had declined to a historical minimum and had been there for some time, so much so that economic historians are now uncertain whether the 1990s may actually have been more prosperous than even the "fabulous" 1960s. And those signs for "help wanted" fitted a pattern of employment that is well captured in George Ritzer's metaphor of "McDonaldization" (see below). At the same time, criminologists Alfred Blumstein and Richard Rosenfeld pointed out that the economic upturn might have had something to do with the 1990s decline in crime rates, given that the children or the younger brothers of those who years before seemed to be mired in nothing else but gang life and the struggle for the control of the crack market now seemed to have an alternative to being killed or spending the rest of their lives in jail – even if the alternative of working in a "McDonald's job" was not all that attractive (Blumstein and Rosenfeld 1998; Rosenfeld 2002).

## A Theory of Long Cycles

What happened in the United States between the 1970s and the 1990s may well be seen as a phase in the latest among many "cycles" that we have considered up to this point, especially in their impact on penal practices and criminology's theorizations. It was, in particular, the declining phase in a "long" cycle that had started after World War II, a cycle of which we have already considered the cultural aspects in its "upswing" period in chapter 7, the deeply subversive élan that characterized the 1960s and early 1970s together with their skepticism about definitions of normality and deviance. The successive phase instead, a declining phase, as usually happens, was related to deep transformations in the economy. These implied changes in the driving sectors and in the prevailing type of technology, changes that were directed at the same time to respond to the demands that had emerged during the previous phase, and to re-establish control over society.

According to this "long cycle" or "long wave" perspective, what is most significant in international socio-economic development, considered in terms of technological innovation and/or class conflicts, happens in long cycles of roughly 50 years, where the peak and the trough of the cycle are separated by periods of about 25 years (very close to the span of a generation). This would be a historical-economic concept more readily connected and employed in order to understand phenomena of an essentially cultural nature, like those of penality, which tend to be characterized by slow and viscous movements, than more straightforward "economic" movements, which are instead better captured by the more common concept of "short" business cycles (Schumpeter, Pareto, Sorokin, Kondratieff, and Kalecki are the names most commonly linked to some kind of long-cyclical theory of socio-economic development; see Rennstich 2002).

The long-cyclical view sees the movements in the cycle as induced by the efforts of the actors in the economic and political arena – essentially entrepreneurs and workers, with "the State" as a third party increasingly important in the adjudication of the results of conflict between the first two. Each one of these actors tries to overcome the limitations imposed on its development and "freedom," so to speak, by the adverse activities of the other. Innovation – Schumpeter's "process of creative destruction" – would therefore constitute a crucial tool by which entrepreneurs undercut and "destroy" the power of labor in situations where a prolonged spell of prosperity has placed workers in a privileged position. The result of such innovation – usually backed by political-legal power – is to destructure and disorganize the type of economy in which the former type of working class achieved its dangerous (for the entrepreneurs) power. Likewise, adapting to the innovations implemented, the "new" type of working class recruited under the new conditions – often from "lowly" "immigrant" quarters – would eventually find the way to reorganize and to bring increasingly effective action (at least as effective as the "old" type of working class was able to bring) to the new setting of social relationships and power. At this point, the cycle starts anew, similar to the preceding one in pattern, completely different instead in detail.

It may be useful at this point to reconnect to Georg Rusche's insights. Rusche's concept of a connection between punishment – and especially imprisonment – and the labor market can be framed as one of the slowly moving aspects of this larger picture. Imprisonment rises, and conditions within prisons become harsher, in periods when the entrepreneurial elite is on the attack in order to respond to the "intolerable" levels of power reached by the working class. Later on, after the re-establishment of entrepreneurial hegemony, when the working class is slowly reconstructing its power and organization, imprisonment will again be on the decline and conditions of penality will tend to become more prone to "reform." All such connections should not be thought of as an "understructure" determining a "superstructure" but rather – as Max Weber did – as a network of relations of affinity, where the long-cyclical movements are caused by the autonomous but interactive contributions, economic, political, cultural, of all the actors involved.

In the one effort today to develop such a line of analysis, Charlotte Vanneste has identified, on the grounds of the existing literature, the location of the "peaks" and "troughs" of such long cycles for the period for which we have information, approximately the last century and a half (Vanneste 2001: 56). The "peaks" are of paramount importance in order to understand the logic of the "long cycle" argument in relation to change in imprisonment. It is around the peak that a long spell of prosperity ends and turns into an "economic crisis." Prosperity means, in fact, from the standpoint of the working class, increasing extension and power, stronger organization, and a robust capacity for wage demands. On the opposite side, that of the entrepreneurs, the strength of the working class translates into fast-reducing profit margins and the necessity for change and innovation. Innovation is often the technological result of a socially widespread feeling that the boundaries of the "old" social system are too rigid and suffocating for the development that the long period of prosperity has made possible (this may be a way also to express what de Giorgi calls "surplus" (2002: 41–65)). The most enterprising sectors of the elite are thereby able to sidestep at the same time both their long-established competitors and the type of working class that has grown together with prosperity – not to mention what is most important in terms of class conflict, i.e. to smash the given organizational forms of the "old" working class.

During the prosperity period leading to the "peak" years, the years when the "showdown" between labor and capital takes place, punishment has become less of a "necessity" for the social system as a whole. When most people who look for work can find it, the general social attitude is one of good disposition even toward the lowest members of the working class. There is the expectation that even if left to himself in a condition of freedom, the first-time offender will be able to reinsert himself into society and find some source of income. Someone who has already committed a crime can still be rehabilitated through a short prison stint or through some "alternatives to imprisonment," and only the most callous criminals will be thought of as deserving long spells of detention. Furthermore, prison conditions will be decent, and it will be possible to work within prisons, both because this is deemed to be a good tool for "rehabilitation" and because the high wages outside make it worth producing at least certain goods at "controlled" prices (something that often the unions outside object to). Furthermore, the basic stability of periods of prosperity means that no "strangers" have to be called in to work, and anyway, even if they are, the general climate of tolerance and the good disposition of society extend also to them.

The opposite happens in the following period. The defeat of the "old" working class as well as of the least competitive economic sectors translates into a progressive devaluation of human beings, an increasing recourse, especially around the "peak," to a "new" kind of working class – youth, women, immigrants – that do not share in the values and general "ethos" of the old one, with strong resentments, conflicts, and, what is most important, divisions being created within the working class. The number of the unemployed increases, "crime" becomes more and more associated with the "newcomers," tolerance disappears, prison work and "alternative programs" are also shelved, and a general mean feeling of envy and *revanche* takes hold in a society increasingly structured around lines of hierarchy, authoritarianism, and exclusion.

If we accept a "measurement" all of this by means of the indicator of imprisonment rates – an unsatisfactory one maybe, but for the time being the only one we have available – it may represent a useful exercise to compare, if only in a merely suggestive way, the "slope" prediction of the "long cycle" model, according to Vanneste – an "ideal type" that applies to the generality of capitalist development in the most advanced countries – with the actual behavior of imprisonment rates in two countries, Italy and the United States, for which we were able to collect the necessary information (see figure 4). According to Vanneste's reconstruction, the peaks would be located *grosso modo* around 1870, 1920, and 1970, and the troughs around 1845, 1895, 1945, and 1995. Because, according to the hypothesis, the imprisonment rate should "behave" in countercyclical fashion, we would derive the prediction of an increase in imprisonment rates in the three cyclical "downswings," 1870–95, 1920–45, and 1970–95, and a decrease instead in the three "upswings," 1845–70, 1895–1920, and 1945–70. Today we would find ourselves in the middle of a new decrease (1995–2020).

When we look at figure 4, the vertical axes correspond to the above-mentioned "peaks" and "troughs", around which the theo-

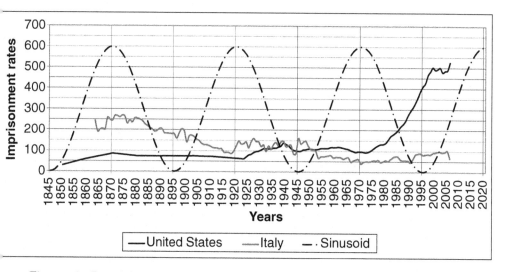

Figure 4  Imprisonment rates per 100,000, United States and Italy, 1850–2006[1]

retical sinusoid line representing the long cycles is drawn. The behavior of imprisonment rates seems to – roughly – correspond to the predicted one only for the twentieth century, i.e. the last two "long cycles" (1895–1945 and 1945–95) but not for the previous one in the nineteenth century (1845–95). Furthermore, whereas we may be able to predict the general direction of the slope, the specificity of the size of incremental change year by year may vary greatly in different countries and under different circumstances. If we compare for instance the US and Italian rates in the period 1895–1920, we can observe a strong decline in the Italian case and a slight one in the US one. The years of the ensuing Depression, on the other hand, see a moderate increase in the United States and simply an interruption of the previous downward trend in Italy. After World War II, we have again a definite declining trend in Italy and a substantially stable situation in the United States. Finally, after 1970, Italian rates edge up a little, amidst oscillations, while in the United States we witness the well-known "mass incarceration" of the last quarter of the twentieth century. At the very least, one should note that the "long cycles" should here be taken together with Schumpeter's notion of a "secular trend" (Schumpeter 1939, 1: 193–219) that is strongly declining in the case of Italy and strongly increasing in the case of the United States (Melossi 2003a; Melossi et al. forthcoming).

## The Perennial Reproduction of the Canaille

A few years ago, during the celebrations for the centenary of the union movement in the town of Reggio Emilia, near Bologna, historians narrated that the workers of Reggio Emilia, at the end of the nineteenth century, used to chant, "united we are everything, divided we are *la canaille*" (*uniti siamo tutto, divisi siam canaglia*). *Canaille* is an old word of the Romance languages, coming from the Latin *canis* "dog," which is usually translated in English as "rabble, riffraff." What those workers from Reggio Emilia meant, however, was something more than that, and it is that richer meaning that I wish to capture by using it in this context. The concept of the canaille contains both an objective/descriptive and a moral/evaluative component. What is meant by "canaille" is first of all the new contribution to the working class from sections of the population coming from the countryside, be this countryside at close range, as it used to be in the past, or very distant, as it is usually nowadays, made up of former peasants or peasants-turned-vagrants, not yet understanding themselves as working-class and therefore deprived of that possibility for a feeling of mutual "solidarity" that will be the hallmark of their *becoming* working-class. As such, exactly like Foucault's *délinquance* (1975), *la canaille* constitutes a *masse de manoeuvre* of capital, so to speak. As Foucault writes:

> No doubt delinquency is a form of illegality; certainly it has its roots in illegality; but it is an illegality that the "carceral system," with all its ramifications, has invested, segmented, isolated, penetrated, organized, enclosed in a definite milieu, and to which it has given an instrumental role in relation to the other illegalities. In short, although the juridical opposition is between illegality and illegal practice, the strategic opposition is between illegalities and delinquency. (Foucault 1975: 277)

*Délinquance, la canaille,* is often linked to "scabs," "rats," and those who lend themselves to capital forgetting their worth as working-*class*. The old (and losing) sections of the working class often characterize *la canaille* in racist terms.[2] Someone who is part of *la canaille* pursues his or her own interests, forgetful of the broader picture of the class of which he or she does not yet know himself or herself to be part, as well as of that set of attributes that others in society would describe as indicating some degree of "dignity." Members of the canaille would rather pursue their own individual interest in all possible ways. Work may be one of these, but it is quite interchangeable with crime, prostitution, membership of a racket, violence, fraud, mendicancy, etc. That is why the workers of Reggio Emilia were all too aware that, "united we are everything, divided we are *la canaille.*"

History has offered plenty of examples of ever-new incarnations of *la canaille*. Think of the "vagrants" that constituted Marx's "original" proletariat in the process of so-called "primitive" accumulation (Marx 1867; Melossi and Pavarini 1977), or of the *classes dangereuses,* the *canaille sans phrase* of the nineteenth century (Chevalier 1958), the period of pioneering industrialization when even women and children were employed in "Satan's mills." Later on, at the end of the nineteenth century, in an economy dominated by the production of heavy mechanical goods (such as railways and everything that went with them), the central working role was that of the skilled worker, the craftsman. Decades of transition would soon follow from this age to that of the assembly line and the automobile (Baran and Sweezy 1966), a process fed by the huge mass migration of (industrially) unskilled former Southern and Eastern European peasants to America, which made "Fordism" (the "scientific" management of work ("Taylorism") plus the rationalization of factory work ("Fordism" proper)) possible. There was a great panic also about their "criminality" (Teti 1993; Salvatore and Aguirre 1996), as well as about that of the internal migrants, the "hoboes" (Anderson 1923). And when the American legislators introduced a "quota" system to contain such "undesirable" populations, a mass migration of African American rural workers from the South to the North started, workers who were escaping the Jim Crow laws and the blatant racism of the post-bellum era, as narrated most famously by Richard Wright (see above, chapter 5), but whose descendents eventually went to feed what would come to be called the "American underclass" in more recent years (Wilson 1987; Davis 2003).

After World War II, in Europe, there would be a mass movement of Southern Europeans toward Central and Northern Europe, also marked by a panic about their criminality (Ferracuti 1968). Finally, after 1970, the mass migration would now be of Northern African, Asian, and Eastern European workers, toward the countries of the European Union, this time also Southern European countries, and here too the unmistakable outcry about the "criminal" invasion followed (Tonry 1997; Marshall 1997). This latest economic cycle – apparently centered in the "immaterial" economy of the network society (Castells 1996) – is the one within which so-called "post-Fordism" made its entry onto the scene (De Giorgi 2002). Kitty Calavita has cogently shown the nexus between the paradoxes of current migration, especially to Southern Europe, and the requirements of a "post-Fordist" economy (Calavita 2005). In all of these very different examples, we witness a bifurcation in the "moral economy" of the working class (Thompson 1971) between a respectable "old" working class, expressing moral indignation at the mores of the newcomers, and a "new" working class, subject to extensive processes of criminalization. This whole social process is the phenomenon I call the "cycle of production (and re-production) of *la canaille*," of the rabble (in the fall of 2005, in the midst of the revolts in the French *banlieues*, another all-French word was added to this list, thanks to the then French minister of the interior Nicolas Sarkozy: *racaille*).

## Post-Fordist Corrections

In the same way in which the season of labeling theory and stable or declining imprisonment rates belonged in the upswing cycle – and mood! – of Fordism, so the criminologies of *revanche* and the extraordinary process of "mass imprisonment" (Garland 2001b) that took place in the United States in the "crisis decades" after 1972 belonged in the downswing cycle of post-Fordism. I have mentioned more than once the historical linkage of "the prison" and "the factory" (Melossi and Pavarini 1977). However, if the factory was, in these post-Fordist times, on its way out, why should a practice of penality shaped after the factory/prison survive? At first, it was reasoned, if the prisons had no function left, because "those members of the underclass committed to state prisons no longer provided a coherent target for strategies of integration and normalization" (Simon 1993: 255), and yet prisons were still there, and growing, then the only residual function should be one of "warehousing" inmates (Cohen 1985). Later on, as we have seen, Jonathan Simon – first by himself, then with Malcolm Feeley – refined the critique of such a situation by formulating the theoretical understanding that became quite well known as "actuarial penology" (Feeley and Simon 1994).

Certainly, two views seemed to cohabit among conservative social and political commentators in the 1990s, one supporting a deterrent and neutralizing tendency and another that we could call authoritarian and correctional. If in fact, on the one hand, as we have seen, Richard J. Herrnstein and Charles Murray had advanced their cynical concept of a "custodial state" or "custodial democracy" just before the 1990s economic boom, on the other hand, Lawrence Mead expressed a more activist "new paternalism" a few years later:

> Political discussions of freedom in America tend to define it as the absence of restraint. But people who live without limits soon sacrifice their own interests to immediate gratifications. To live effectively, people need personal restraint to achieve their own long-run goals. In this sense, obligation is the precondition of freedom. Those who would be free must first be bound. And if people have not been effectively bound by functioning families and neighborhoods in their formative years, government must attempt to provide limits later, imperfect though they must be. (Mead 1997: 23)

The moniker "neo-paternalism" seems to be very apt indeed. It may well be, also, that the latter, promoting a kind of "subordinate inclusion," could emerge only when, in the late 1990s, economic development had laid the ground for such a possibility, which had not existed until then. It seems to me that, analyzing what has happened in the United States in the last 30 years, we should at least consider the possibility that the enormous expansion of the prison system starting during the 1970s, the "Reagan revolution," and lasting at least until the second reign of Bush the second, instead of responding to an "obsolescence" of the penitentiary institution responded to its revitalization. This revitalization may have at first followed logics of "warehousing" or of "actuarial penology." Later, however, it pursued a goal of mass imprisonment of the marginal ethnic strata of the population. Mass imprisonment had a disciplining effect, it seems to me, not so much on the most outcast and downtrodden sectors of the "young inner-city ethnic minority male" population – given that these barely entered the labor market even during the 1990s, as Bruce Western shows. It probably had an impact instead on the social strata that were contiguous to them, their children, women, or younger brothers and sisters maybe, or simply those who were slightly better off. These would then be the protagonists of the labor market expansion of the 1990s, those young people, largely female, who finally had the option of going to work in a McDonalds instead of dealing crack in the streets, or living with somebody dealing crack in the streets (Rosenfeld 2002). So, for instance, when in 2002 Philip Bourgois went back to the site of his enthralling ethnography of the crack market in New York East Harlem, in which he had been engaged between the late 1980s and early 1990s, he found that several of the protagonists in his research now held "legit" jobs, and that "heroin and crack continued to be spurned by Latino and African American youth who had witnessed as children the ravages that those drugs committed on the older generations in their community" (Bourgois 2003: xvii). Both aspects were to some degree linked to the fact that "the dramatic improvement in the US economy in the late 1990s forced employers and unions to integrate increasing numbers of marginalized Puerto Ricans and African Americans into the labor market" (Bourgois 2003: xix; Bourgois also adds that a "large sector of street youth" were, however, still excluded; in any case, starting with the economic crisis of 2001–2, things again took a turn for the worse and crime rates were to stabilize or increase in many American cities).

The point is, however, that not only the stick but also the carrot was needed. They both helped steer the marginalized strata of American society toward their role as subordinate members of society. Something quite similar has been happening in Europe with recent immigration (Melossi 2003b; Calavita 2005). One should not be distracted by the fact that the central "productive" labor of the new post-Fordist times is what de Giorgi (2002) calls "immaterial labor." That may certainly be the case, but for every few workers able to engage in immaterial labor and therefore *ipso facto* becoming part of a new skilled labor aristocracy there are many more who are destined to prepare their food, clean their house, wash their clothes, arouse their sexual pleasure, furnish them with their drugs of choice, etc.

Starting from Niels Christie's classic *Crime Control as Industry* (1994), the imagery of the gulag has been increasingly applied to the American situation, whether in Mark Dow's *American Gulag* (2004), about the US immigration prisons, or Ruth Gilmore's *Golden Gulag* (2007), about the burgeoning California prison system. What should give everybody pause, it seems to me, is especially the consideration of the kind of policies that were followed in the expansion of the "American gulag." A "Malthusian" policy, implicit at least in the "warehousing" theme, would have implied the crowding of inmates into old buildings functioning much beyond "capacity." This has certainly not been the case. California, for instance, which has the largest prison system in the world, had only 12 prisons and incarcerated 24,000 people in the late 1970s. There are now 34 prisons, and over 160,000 people are held prisoners. In other words, two thirds of the California prison system – a system already quite large – was built in about 20 years, one prison a year. Is it realistic to think that this was done simply to the end of "warehousing" inmates? Is not this a sign that the trust in the *disciplining* of the population prevailed over any other "warehousing" or "actuarial" end? And is not this a sign of an incredible trust in the "civilizing mission" of the prison – probably even greater than admitted? This would seem a kind of trust not very dissimilar from that with which "civilization" has been and is currently being brought to "far-off peoples," in Matza's words (Matza 1969: 145), and often with very similar instruments. What seems to reappear here is that peculiar ambivalence of the criminological – and criminalizing – enterprise, which "exports" outside of its borders ideas and attitudes first developed when faced with its own domestic "savages."

It seems to me that a possible answer to these questions depends on the way one reads the social function of imprisonment in post-Fordist society. On the one hand, I do not think we should forget too easily the "Durkheimian" effect of social cohesiveness through scapegoating that politicians have been pursuing in the United States, an end hardly distinguishable from traditional retributionism. On the other hand, what we also tend to forget is the *permanent* "correctionalism" of the penal system and of the prison institution, even if, of course, it is a correctionalism that lends itself to many uses and to many situations – a correctionalism "for all seasons," so to speak. It is a correctionalism, however, that is deeply tied to the coming into life of what I have called *la canaille*. Prisons are inextricably linked to *délinquance* and *la canaille*, in a way that was surmised by Foucault in *Discipline and Punish*: "The penitentiary technique and the delinquent are in a sense twin brothers . . . They appeared together, the one extending from the other, as a technological ensemble that forms and fragments the object to which it applies its instruments . . . Delinquency is the vengeance of the prison on justice" (Foucault 1975: 255). On the one hand, the historical appearance of *la canaille* immediately evokes the vitality of prisons. On the other hand, all histories of the working class are marked by the aspiration by the workers' "vanguard" toward transforming *la canaille* into the working class, a project that capitalists as such usually do not particularly like. All in all, it is much better to take the chance of being robbed once in a while by a solitary gunman than that of having to face a determined class of organized employees. In the latter case, the loss, in terms of power and money, is much greater. And in fact it is rather typical of the ruling class (in its various components) to be divided over the issue. (See for instance what is happening today in Europe about immigration. Many members of the elites, backed up in various countries by racist and Fascist-like political groupings, would rather go on feeding – by means of the current prohibitionist immigration policy – that "clandestine" immigration that is the best producer of *la canaille*, and that, together with cheap drugs and prostitution, gives Europeans also a lot of very cheap labor (actually it is the same thing: cheap labor in both legitimate and illegitimate goods and services). Obviously a policy of actual *im-migration* would still give cheaper labor than the indigenous one, but not *as* cheap, and it might favor the integration of this emerging section of immigrant labor into the working class – therefore emancipating it from its *canaille* role (Calavita 2005).)

The prison, as a sort of "training ground for waged work," is suddenly brought back to life every time it has to deal with its "eternal" guests, so to speak – i.e. former peasants who had to leave the countryside and were pushed to the margins of the city. Internal or external migrants – whether they are citizens or not, whether they are "legal" or not – constitute therefore the subjects "of choice" of the prison system, together with their offspring, and those involved in the "traditions of crime" set up in order to try and "make it" in the city. It is no surprise therefore that at the height of Fordist times, in the early 1970s, prisons were deemed to be "obsolete." There was nothing for them to do, no appropriate guests or very few. How fast things changed under the blows of historical development on Fordism, and with the construction of the whole new reality of post-Fordism! What a true "Renaissance" did the penal system of Italy, for instance, know when migrants, especially young migrants, started to crowd at its gates! Or that of the United States, when the inner-city minority males started to be considered "unfit" for productive employment in a post-industrial world!

## What Does "Rehabilitation" Mean?

One should not be misled, in fact, by what is meant by "correction" or "rehabilitation" or "re-education" or "resocialization." We should distinguish between *criminologists' rehabilitation* – so carefully defended for instance by Francis Cullen (2005) and others like him, the kind of rehabilitation that was the butt of Robert Martinson's famous 1974 essay on its "failure" – and *the social system's rehabilitation*, i.e. teaching the lesson of subordination. This latter, basic, foundational core of the prison system is not to be confused with future lack of recidivism, does not mean "learning the ropes of waged work," is not about understanding what went wrong, is not about behaving well in prison (even if the latter gets behavioristically closer to the "system's meaning" of rehabilitation). The argument of *The Prison and the Factory* (Melossi and Pavarini 1977) has been misunderstood more than once to mean that prisons originated within some kind of "vocational" school. This is not the point we were trying to make. On the basis of the historical material, our claim was – and is, as far as I am concerned – that prisons were first devised as places in which to teach the attitude of obedience and disciplined behavior that would seem proper to the outside world

– a behavior the first model for which was and is that of the disciplined laborer. The permanent meaning of rehabilitation within prison systems is about learning to lower one's head and execute orders, understanding that one is on the receiving hand of the deal. It is about the attitude of "the laborer" described by Marx at the end of the chapter in *Capital* that deals with the buying and selling of labor power. There, Marx moves from discussing circulation and the market, that "very Eden of the innate rights of man," where "alone rule Freedom, Equality, Property and Bentham," into the closed abode of production, the factory:

> On leaving this sphere of simple circulation or of exchange of commodities, which furnishes the "Free-trader Vulgaris" with his views and ideas, and with the standard by which he judges a society based on capital and wages, we think we can perceive a change in the physiognomy of our *dramatis personae*. He, who before was the money-owner, now strides in front as capitalist; the possessor of labor-power follows as his laborer. The one with an air of importance, smirking, intent on business; the other, timid and holding back, like one who is bringing his own hide to market and has nothing to expect but – a hiding. (Marx 1867: 176)

This attitude, of "the one who has nothing to expect but a hiding," is indeed the *permanent* lesson that penitentiary institutions have been teaching, especially in those times when they are seen as giant entrance gates to the niceties of the social contract and their function resides – it is commonly assumed – in literally "breaking in" the newcomers. This is not a function that should be underemphasized, or go unnoticed. It is a powerful instrument of government, which teaches discipline. This has nothing to do with the kind of "labor" that goes on inside prisons, or with "rehabilitation" as commonly intended. Or, if it is a kind of "rehabilitation," it is a peculiar type. It has much more to do with *maintaining* a social stratum of the canaille – in much the same way in which Durkheim (1895a), Mead (1917–18), and especially Foucault (1975) had all made this same point – than with *transforming* it. The point of discipline seems to be to submit yourself to what the bearers of social power want you to do. No more, no less. From this perspective, American post-Fordist leadership seems to have had a confidence in the prison as a tool of government certainly much stronger than that of many of their critics. In this sense, goals of collective incapacitation, so-called "actuarialism," discipline, and general deterrence are not really in contradiction with each other.

Such a concept of correction, of what has to be done, is profoundly akin to the existence of *la canaille* in society and, with it, to a pervasive feeling of *fear*. It is a fear of crime that, as Corey (2004) pointed out, in a sense is the result of transferring – as psychoanalysts would say – an unsaid fear of the elites, and of their prisons, on to fear of powerless people. Self-empowerment, the repudiation of fear, the disappearance of the canaille (and of a racist concept of it), and the possibility of actual prison reform are all of a piece. Georg Rusche was the first to note that, according to the principle of "less eligibility," the given conditions of class relationships would set an unsurpassable limit to the possibilities for penal reform (Rusche 1933: 4). It will only be by bridging the gap with *la canaille* ("united, we are everything . . . !") that, almost by magic, prisons will again become dusty monuments to an uncivilized past rather than harbingers of civilization.

## Penality and Government of Populations

Expanding a bit on such reflections, we may want to reconsider the Marxist tradition of studies about penality. Within this tradition, penal institutions have often been considered "ancillary" to what is called "the economy" (see above, chapter 1), a view also received by critics of Marxism, such as David Garland in *Punishment and Modern Society* – where the Marxist tradition is opposed to Foucault's on the grounds of the supposedly "economist" and "statalist" character of the former (Garland 1990: 130–3). It is instead my opinion that the notion of discipline – central to Foucault's work, and to Marx's, as we have seen – is still today a more useful concept in order to tackle this whole set of issues. It is a notion that allows us to reconsider Marx on the issue of penality, freed from the weight of teleology and more open to "cultural" aspects. Furthermore, such a reconsideration allows us to see penality as a set of practices that have often *pioneered*, instead of *followed*, "the government of populations" – turning on its head, therefore, the "superstructural metaphor" – the idea, that is, that "cultural" and "legal" phenomena would have to follow from something "economic." Instead, once Marxist theory is properly understood, as it should be, as a theory of class struggle, as a "critique of political economy," such a *steering* role of penality makes better sense and can be historically reconstructed within crucial passages in the history of the institution. Penality becomes, in this sense, the standard-bearer of the ruling class. It gives moral direction and orientation to class struggle from the perspective of ruling elites. It is, in a sense, a Utopia – or, if you would prefer, a Dystopia – of an ideal social order (this would also explain, by the way, why all leading "progressive" and "reformist" thinkers seem to have had a try at "penal reform").

As we have seen in the first chapter, in the origins of the prison institution, for instance, in the seventeenth century, Amsterdam merchants literally "invented" what would then become the future "form" of the prison (but also, at the same time, of the manufacture, the proto-factory) in the "workhouse," to the end of punishing and teaching to labor at the same time (Sellin 1944). "Penality," in the English bridewells as in Dutch seventeenth-century institutions, was at the very core of the constitution of a "capitalist" mode of production. It was no detail, no occasional "help." Rather, it was at the center of the "making" of the working class, because only a "disciplined" "working class" could become "labor power," i.e. a section of capital, ready to produce profit. At the same time, however, this overall project was at the service of a certain *vision* of man, woman, and society, of a certain kind of *rationality*, that was to reform and transform all aspects of social life, morality as well as work. In this sense, a certain way of thinking of imprisonment is an indicator of the historical change that was taking place in those centuries, as coherent and as telling as the introduction of the factory, the market, and all the other accoutrements of capitalism.[3]

Another exemplary transition in this usage of penality in order to govern populations took place in the American post-bellum period. Suddenly, in fact, the end of the regime of legal slavery and the acquisition of at least formal rights of citizenship by the African American minority meant the end of the "domestic" punishments that had dominated up to that moment – by which the slave master, true *pater familias*, exercised on the slaves the same kind of power that he could exercise on the other "minors," i.e. children and women. Instead there started that "disproportion" in the experience of (public) penality that stayed on thereafter in the African American experience. Also the Southern states saw, after the civil war, a sudden and massive increase in the African American presence within prisons, similar to what had already happened in the North, where a small free section of the black population was already filling the public prisons. There appeared at this point quite clearly what Thorsten Sellin (1976), developing an intuition by Gustav Radbruch (1938), called *penal slavery*. As Angela Davis explains (2003), missing slave labor was therefore replaced by forced prison labor – with the introduction of the lease system and the chain gangs, for instance – bringing blacks back to the plantation but this time as convicts, submitting them to the same "domestic" punishments, but this time as disciplinary punishments within the penal realm. First as "chattel," then as forced labor under contract, they were exposed to the danger of full fungibility. Whether they came closer to being an example of what Giorgio Agamben has called "naked or bare life" (1995) as one or the other is hard to tell. The mind turns to German concentration camps during World War II or Stalin's gulags – a concept of full fungibility of labor power that is hard to detach from what Foucault has called "State racism" (1976b).

Angela Davis, and Loïc Wacquant (Wacquant 2001) as well, point out the continuity in the African American experience of penality with its most recent period, when, as we have seen, mass imprisonment accompanied and supported the "flexibilization" of labor essential to post-Fordist transformations. What happened in Europe at the same time was that the same marginal strata – largely immigrants – became likewise the object of interest of the European penal systems, but not under a regime of *mass* imprisonment. The result was a huge disproportion in the representation of immigrants and minorities within those systems, even higher than in the United States (Calavita 2005; Melossi 2003b, 2005; Young 2003; De Giorgi 2002). In the same way in which the neo-liberal and neo-Utilitarian turn was in the United States much more radical than anywhere else – carrying also the burden of "showing the way" – so the process of extensive penalization in the United States was much more pervasive than in Europe, especially Continental Europe.[4] I would maintain, however, that the "mass imprisonment" in the United States between the early 1970s and the early 1990s was as preparatory to the economic boom of the 1990s as was the massive introduction of computers and the obsolescence of a "Fordist" style of production. For vast sectors of the American working class, or would-be working class, imprisonment was the other face of "McDonaldization" (Ritzer 1993). So, on the one hand, under the new conditions of post-Fordism, a kind of "immaterial labor" unwittingly went to form a "labor aristocracy" nineteenth-century style. On the other hand, "the process of colonization of the life-world" (Habermas 1981b: 301–403) implied the "marketization" of those goods and services that had not been on the market until very recently – goods and services that largely concerned youth's and women's work, from the management of eating to the care of children and elderly people. These latter types of work have actually become the most numerous and typical post-Fordist jobs, in conjunction with the decline of Fordist wages and the increased participation of women in the waged work market. Only a working class defeated, humiliated, demoralized, and beaten, after the insurgent times of the 1960s–1970s, could succumb to working in the kitchens of Mr McDonald. This was a specific course of action that American capitalism took. American "neo-liberal" elites reacted to that period of insurgency by following two different, but not alternative, paths. On the one hand, they pursued the high course of robotization, automation, the information economy, and that peculiar kind of "post-Fordism" that has been called "Toyotism." All of this gave a strong boost to productivity. On the other hand, the penal *revanche* that took off between the Nixon and Reagan presidencies obliged millions of young men and women from minority ghettoes or from poor white working-class suburbs to feed an economic recovery largely built on cheap labor (and therefore scarcely productive). In this very specific sense, once again it is wrong to read penality, through nineteenth-century lenses, as a "superstructure" of the economy. Rather, penality – as a form of "government" of human conduct – is part and parcel of the overall *project* of a "political economy." There is a strict articulation that links the kind of "workplace discipline" that makes profit, hence capitalism, possible to the more general "social discipline." If, therefore, the realm of penality is particularly effective in marking the rules of social discipline, penality could very well be seen as symbolically *driving* (a certain kind of) social and economic development.

It is indeed a consistent type of rationality, a *Weltanschauung* maybe, that is constructed by the converging action of such different actors in different domains. We do not have to think of such two- or three-pronged attacks through the obsolete language of "superstructure." Rather, we are faced with a complex and consistent project, a true moral vision of the world – of which crime and punishment are the standard-bearers. Penality in this view, rather than being the product or outcome of economic choices, is on the contrary truly *constitutive* of such choices. We might be able to see the American "mass incarceration" of the last quarter of the twentieth century, in this perspective, not as a *result* of class conflict, but rather as an integral *aspect* of class conflict. This is true first of all symbolically and culturally, as I have tried to show here. It is true, however, at the same time also as a crucial socio-economic institution, in the sense made clear by Bruce Western. Imprisonment has been in fact a sort of "pathway to the secondary labor market" (Western 2006: 120) and in this sense has performed a very important function in the make-up of American society in the last 30 years.

## Post-Fordism, Globalization, and Social Control

Penality has also been increasingly evolving into an aspect of international relationships, insofar as the increasing hegemony of a discursive punishment within the borders of the United States would then fulfill a pedagogic function also in terms of international relationships. Americans' way of thinking about the world would tend to be structured more and more according to a basic narrative of crime and punishment. The American public and American elites have in fact been educated by their incessant familiarity with concepts of "crime" and "punishment" to see the roots of "crime," as well as of "terrorism," in the "evil choice" of given individuals rather than in the overall situation within which those choices are made. This kind of view, which started to become hegemonic in American culture in the 1970s, goes a long way toward explaining both the frightening increase in punishment and the kind of action taken in "the war on terror" (Welch 2006; we have already seen the way in which Archer and Gartner's empirical research had called attention to the relationships between official acts of government, such as wars and the death penalty, criminal violence, and punishment in a process of "brutalization" of the populace).

The sense of separateness between internal and external borders became, especially after September 11, 2001, extremely tenuous. The description of enemy states in terms of the internal enemy, the criminal – as in the expression "the rogue states" – echoes the use instead of war metaphors to win internal "wars" against criminality. The reach of the domestic power of some countries, *in primis* the United States in such documents as the so-called "Patriot Act" (Dworkin 2002, 2003; Steinert and Pilgram 2003), is decreed to extend to the entire globe – as it was graphically illustrated by the practice of "extraordinary rendition," which extended a *de facto* American police/prosecutorial power to all the countries that tolerated it. In some more specific and different instances, such as in Europe, the process of a European constitution – but something similar has already been announced for Mercosur – means that the tangle among "international," "communitarian," and "domestic" law has become almost inextricable.

We may think of such developments as an "Empire" that has come into being as the new environment within which we operate (Hardt and Negri 2000), or as the intentional world-wide extension, by a radical group of "Neocons" in the United States (Drew 2003; Baker 2003, reviewing Krugman 2003), of the Weberian principle of the "monopoly of violence" to become the seedling of a new global State. In any case, often the same think tanks, and even the same authors, have pushed a connected agenda in the fields of the economy (Bockman and Eyal 2002), international relations (Drew 2003), and penality (Wacquant 1999; Garland 2001a), an agenda that has come to define a certain kind of rationality as the new creed to be spread to the furthest-flung corners of the globe. This is nothing new in kind. After all, anyone who has studied the diffusion of economic rationality, penality, and "the white man's burden" in the modern era has witnessed the extension of a certain kind of rationality, a certain way of thinking about man and society. The diffusion of the neo-liberal creed found a very helpful and apt summary in what Loïc Wacquant (1999) has called a new "penal common sense" because the basic principles of this common sense seemed to be crucial to the neo-liberal project – the central values of punishments, rewards, and individual responsibility. So it is no surprise if we find that some of the very same think tanks and right-wing intellectuals are behind all of these ventures, in a renewed instance of penality as the standard-bearer of elites' beliefs. All of which was seasoned, I should add, with a helpful dose of *machismo*, because the values of economic and military entrepreneurship are of course the privilege of valiant and self-reliant males – even when they are personified by females.

Increasingly, in the last few years, the language of war and the language of punishment have tended to approximate one another. In the same way in which, according to the social contractualists from Hobbes to Beccaria, punishment constituted the signpost of the common repository of sovereignty in a social contract, ready to impart the lesson of *pacta sunt servanda* to transgressors, so in the new world order, the seed of a new global State is ready to punish those "rogue states" that behave as the "usurpers of the common good," in Beccaria's words (1764: 9). The power of war and the power of punishment have therefore become less and less distinguishable, whether one thinks of "punishing" the evil-doing of wayward states, or of bringing war to domestic enemies, terrorists, *narcotraficantes*, and common criminals. As Ronald Dworkin writes:

> Conservatives have for many years wanted government to have the powers that administration officials now claim are legitimate: September 11 may have served them only as an excuse. John Ashcroft's Justice Department has been using its new powers under the Patriot Act, which were defended as emergency provisions against terrorists, to investigate and prosecute a wide variety of more ordinary crimes, including theft and swindling. (Dworkin 2003: 38; cf. Eric Lichtblau 2003)

## Conclusions: Crime, Punishment, and Social Structure

Let us try to summarize finally the argument presented in this volume. I have identified two "typical" scenarios between which modern societies have found themselves. One scenario sees a fractured, quickly changing society expressing a concept of itself as a plural and conflictual entity, within which deviance, or indeed crime, is relative to the standpoint of the one who is doing the defining, and the representation of the criminal is an essentially contested representation: *some* criminals, at least, play more the role of innovators and heroes than that of villains. We have found these kinds of societies in turn-of-the-century Europe, the 1920s in the United States, the 1960s and early 1970s world-wide. As we have seen, these periods were also characterized by declining imprisonment rates and by a public rhetoric of discourse centered on inclusiveness, social innovation, experimentation, and change. Furthermore, in these periods, the discourses of sociology and criminology reflected such a climate, as in the most progressive aspects of the Italian Positive School, the debate on anomie in France, the Chicago School's and Sutherland's crucial contributions, and finally the so-called "neo-Chicagoans" and labeling theory in the United States.

Such "open" types of society have followed or preceded societal periods when, at least from the standpoint of elites, the fracturing and disorganization reached "unthinkable excesses," and the requirement for re-instituting a unity of authority, purpose, and hierarchy (even if under a somewhat changed balance of power) asserted itself as a matter of social life and death. During these periods, predominant ("monist") theories of social order were oriented toward unity and cohesion, the normative order was consensually shared, and views about criminals were centered on the label of "the public enemy." Wrongdoers were now seen as morally repugnant individuals, in the eyes of criminologists and the public alike, especially because offenders were considered to bring a deadly threat to society's moral order (different definitions of this threat could be found, for instance, in Beccaria, Lombroso, the structural functionalists, Gottfredson, and Hirschi). The causes of such a threat, if at all relevant, were now to be found within the criminal himself or herself, and not in any societal cause. The periods when nation-states were first established in the nineteenth century, the reaction in the 1930s against the "revolutionary" 1920s, and "the crisis decades" after 1973 are all good examples of such situations. As we have seen, these were also times when imprisonment rates tended to increase, and the public rhetoric was one re-emphasizing the value of the collectivity around concepts of "State," "Nation," or "Community."

It is worth stressing that, in orienting the activities of the many social institutions that frame the question of "crime" and "punishment," representations of crime and punishment perform an essential work in connecting the main articulations of "the social structure." Publicly produced and shared representations link the ways in which human agents perceive of and give accounts to themselves and others of phenomena of crime and punishment, with regularly changing "structural" variables indicating specific aspects of the economy, the polity, and society. The socially shared activity of "labeling" does not therefore represent some idiosyncratic, solipsistic ideological choice – a kind of "breakfast theory of society"[5] – but is in itself understandable according to basic social structural elements. It is in fact "grounded" in society and history (Melossi 1985). Not only therefore are the representations of crime and criminals produced and used by society's members to the end of dealing with the issues of crime and criminals in constructing public images, drafting penal policies, asking for specific public policies, etc. They are also produced and used in order to represent, as in a modern mystery play, the trajectories and fate of sinners and culprits, their value for the whole of society, as well as what should be done with them and why (a "what should be done" that, as we have seen, may acquire a much larger resonance than the one confined to criminal and penal matters). It may indeed become a way to express the very center of social drama.

This was certainly the case for Beccaria's contribution to the Enlightenment, or, almost as important, the elaborations of Italian positivism in the second half of the nineteenth century. It acquired a crucial political impetus in the social conflicts of the 1920s and 1930s both in Europe and in the United States, and then again in the 1960s, when would-be revolutionaries and men of order would gladly often take on the personas of cops and robbers (after 1973, only the cop-personas managed to survive). All of this, furthermore, is amplified in an age when the mass media of communication increasingly occupy center stage. This overall reconstruction of the oscillating, cyclical nature of these images intends therefore to bring a contribution to the idea that such social imagery constitutes in a sense the glue that sticks the parts of the social structure together, as well as the oil that makes the whole creaking machine twist and turn.

Is therefore the overall project of a criminological "science" completely purposeless, given that the main breaking points and scientific commitments that we have reconstructed may be so smoothly brought back to social and cultural features that have nothing to do with the professed scientific orientations of their proponents, probably more greatly influenced by the *Zeitgeist* whirling around their lives than by the methodologies adopted to conduct their research? To recognize the importance or the specific constellations of values and interests under which we conduct our studies does not imply in the least a doubt of their interest and validity. To this kind of question, which, I am afraid, will stay with us to haunt researchers for a long time to come, I know no better answer than the one Max Weber gave more than a century ago writing about "objectivity" in social science:

> We have designated as "cultural sciences" those disciplines that analyze the phenomena of life in terms of their cultural significance. The significance of a configuration of cultural phenomena and the basis of this significance cannot however be derived and rendered intelligible by a system of analytical laws, however perfect it may be, since the significance of cultural events presupposes a value-orientation toward these events. The concept of culture is a value-concept. Empirical reality becomes "culture" to us because and insofar as we relate it to value ideas. It includes those segments and only those segments of reality that have become significant to us because of this value-relevance. Only a small portion of existing concrete reality is colored by our value-conditoned interest and it alone is significant to us. It is significant because it reveals relationships that are important to us due to their connection with our values. (Weber 1904: 76)

And so it happened for Beccaria's idea of liberty, or Lombroso's of human evolution, or the Chicagoans' orientation toward a cultural ecology, or Merton's toward his concept of anomie, or the idea of "labeling," or that of actuarial prediction, and so forth, and so on. All of them are in a sense "scientific" concepts, but all of them are also deeply rooted in the values, interests, conflicts, and struggles of their times (in a specific way that I have tried in turn to link to a long-cyclical or oscillating structure). Nothing different is happening today, and this does not detract in the least from the efforts of those who are currently engaged in doing "criminology." It should help, however, in my opinion, to be aware of not being the first, or the last, and to ask ourselves the question, "What is the connection between the sociological discourse I am producing about social control and deviance, and the society in which I live today?" This work has the ambition of helping in formulating this question and at least beginning to propose a possible answer.

# Notes

## Chapter 1   Leviathan's Subjects: From the Social Contract to Cesare Beccaria

1   This was one of the very first examples of the use of the term "socialism."
2   On the influence of the Scottish "Science of Man" on Beccaria and the whole group of Milanese Enlightenment thinkers, see Beirne (1993: 24–9), who specifically refers to the influence of Francis Hutcheson, David Hume, John Millar, Adam Ferguson, and Adam Smith.
3   See Joseph Schumpeter's glowing appreciation of Beccaria, the economist, preferred even to Adam Smith (Schumpeter 1954: 179–81).
4   For a relatively recent variation on such theme, cf. *Salò* (1975), the last film of Italian writer, poet, and film-maker Pier Paolo Pasolini, which is an adaptation of Marquis de Sade's *The 120 Days of Sodom* (1785), set in Salò, the small town on Lake Garda that became the capital of Mussolini's Nazi-supported puppet government in Northern Italy between 1943 and 1945.

## Chapter 2   The "Positive School," Urban Crowds, and the Social Question

1   The realist or positivist criticism ignored, however, the specific "pedagogic" intent of such an "abstract" attitude: the individual is held responsible for reasons of political opportunity. The one who is expected to be responsible for his or her own actions – it is hoped – will end up in fact learning such basic responsibility. This may be a reason why the ideology of "classic criminology" has always been the

dominant ideology of criminal law, even if tempered here and there with contributions from "realist" schools. However, in both common law and civil law systems, the fundamental corpus of criminal law has always been consistent with the basic tenets of classic criminology, in spite of the recurring denunciations of the "failure" of criminal law (one of the latest being Foucault's in *Discipline and Punish* (1975: 257–92)).

2   An Italian author and follower of Lombroso, Scipio Sighele, disputed with Le Bon the primacy of the study of the crowd, having published in 1891 his *La folla delinquente* (*The Criminal Crowd*), where, applying Lombroso's notion of "atavism" (see below in the text), he claimed that the infamous deeds committed by crowds are due to a temporary regression to atavistic states, induced by a state of collective exaltation.

3   The deafening street was screaming all around me.
Tall, slender, in deep mourning – majestic grief –
A woman made her way, with fastidious hand
Raising and swaying festoon and hem;

Agile and noble, with her statue's limbs.
And there was I, who drank, contorted like a madman,
Within her eyes – that livid sky where hurricane is born –
Gentleness that fascinates, pleasure that kills.

A lightning-flash . . . then night! – O fleeting beauty
Whose glance all of a sudden gave me new birth,
Shall I see you again only in eternity?

Far, far from here! Too late! or maybe, *never?*
For I know not where you flee, you know not where I go,
O you I would have loved (o you who knew it too!)
                              (Beaudelaire, cited in Benjamin 1939: 169)

4   However, a similar discussion would take place also within the "natural" sciences, for instance in the discussion of the so-called "Heisenberg principle." About this whole discussion, at least as far as social sciences are concerned, today it is still hard to go much beyond Max Weber's statements in his "methodological writings" (Weber 1904, 1917).

5   See two very recent presentations in English of Cesare Lombroso's work, both edited by Mary Gibson and Nicole Hahn Rafter, *Criminal Man* (2006; Lombroso 1876–97), a condensation of the five original editions in Italian of the book, and *Criminal Woman, the Prostitute, and the Normal Woman* (2004), a translation of the original work by Cesare Lombroso and Guglielmo Ferrero that appeared in Italian in 1893. See also Beirne (1993: 147–55), Gibson (2002), Horn (2003), Becker and Wetzell (2006), and the Italian biography by Delia Frigessi (2003).

6 Foucault would frame the issue thus: "The penitentiary technique and the delinquent are in a sense twin brothers. It is not true that it was the discovery of the delinquent through a scientific rationality that introduced into our old prisons the refinement of penitentiary techniques. Nor is it true that the internal elaboration of the penitentiary methods has finally brought to light the 'objective' existence of a delinquency that the abstraction and rigidity of the law were unable to perceive. They appeared together, the one extending from the other, as a technological ensemble that forms and fragments the object to which it applies its instruments. And it is this delinquency, formed in the foundations of the judicial apparatus, among the *'basses oeuvres'*, the servile tasks, from which justice averts its gaze, out of the shame it feels in punishing those it condemns; it is this delinquency that now comes to haunt the untroubled courts and the majesty of the laws; it is this delinquency that must be known, assessed, measured, diagnosed, treated when sentences are passed. It is now this delinquency, this anomaly, this deviation, this potential danger, this illness, this form of existence, that must be taken into account when the codes are rewritten. Delinquency is the vengeance of the prison on justice. It is revenge formidable enough to leave the judge speechless. It is at this point that the criminologists raise their voices" (Foucault 1975: 255).

7 Revealed, however, in that close of the passage at the end of *The Born Delinquent* quoted above in this chapter, "a relative concept of divinity and morality."

8 Notice also that the concept of "Western," or even "European," is far from being an intelligible, homogeneous one. English-speaking authors (such as Connell) usually refer to English-speaking societies, and more rarely German- or French-speaking ones, as representative of "Western" or "European" cultures: how should the quite different Catholic/ Southern European traditions be characterized? I refer by this to the Italian and, especially important on a world-wide scale, the Spanish. See Salvatore and Aguirre (1996) for similar themes about Latin America and, more generally, Melossi, Sparks and Sozzo (forthcoming). Rosa del Olmo had pioneeringly fashioned some of the views here presented connecting the Italian "Southern Question" and the history of Latin American criminology in *América Latina y su Criminología* (Del Olmo 1981).

9 Ferri's positions could be usefully compared to the almost contemporary ones of Dutch criminologist William Bonger (Taylor et al. 1973: 222–36).

10 According to Dane Archer and Rosemary Gartner (1984), for instance, a society like the United States – which encourages violence as an important resource to solve conflicts – will very probably end up fostering a higher violent crime rate. The opposite will happen in a society in which violence is shunned but cunning and fraud are more

benignly considered, such as, for instance, Italian society (Melossi 1994).

11 One should not forget, furthermore, Enrico Morselli's work on suicide (1879), where he anticipated Durkheim's later idea (see next chapter) of a connection between suicide and egoism in modern society.

## Chapter 3　Emile Durkheim's Sociology of Deviance

1 In the concept of "solidarity," Durkheim refers to the bond that unites the members of a society. His inspiration in this may indeed have been a classic one, going back at least to ancient Rome and the famous apologue of Menenius Agrippa, who had been sent by the patrician government of Rome to convince the plebs, who had defected from the city, to come back. In an inspired speech to the plebs, Agrippa compared the various social classes to the different organs of the body, each fulfilling a different function but all equally necessary. The plebeians were fooled and agreed to go back to the city.

2 In one of the very first instances of the use of the term, de Tocqueville had written that "Individualism is a mature and calm feeling, which disposes each member of the community to sever himself from the mass of his fellows and to draw apart with his family and his friends, so that after he has thus formed a little circle of his own, he willingly leaves society at large to itself" (1840: 98).

3 It was of course also crucial in facilitating the success of Gutenberg's invention, the printing press – consider the "Gutenberg Bible."

4 As often, but not always voluntarily, happens to us, non-mother-language speakers!

5 See Tarde's criticism and Durkheim's answer (Tarde 1895; Durkheim 1895b; cf. Beirne 1993: 165–70).

6 See the paper by George Sorel (1895) where Sorel took a position on the debate among the positivists, Tarde, and Durkheim.

7 From Nelson Mandela's Inaugural Address, May 10, 1994.

8 About this see Melossi (1990: 52–7).

9 In order to understand Durkheim's point, it should be kept in mind that he compared detentive punishments to the previous penal forms of corporal and capital punishments.

10 Cf. e.g. the beginning scene in Michel Foucault's *Discipline and Punish* (1975: 3–7) with the description of Damiens's torturous execution.

11 "Leniency" is in the English translation (Beccaria 1764: 63). Actually Beccaria entitles chapter xxvii of *On Crimes and Punishments*, "*dolcezza delle pene*," literally "the sweetness of punishments."

12  Therefore Durkheim's position is not that far from Foucault's in *Discipline and Punish*, according to which the discovery of the modern system of disciplinary punishment is to be found in the "producing" character of power, instead of a mere "negative, censorial" attitude – which makes Foucault's silence about Durkheim's contributions even more surprising. See, in the next chapters, how this "active" concept will be at the roots of the very idea of "social control" in the American experience.

## Chapter 4  Social Control and Deviance in the New Republic

1  From the US "Declaration of Independence" (1776).
2  On Freud's more general position, see above, chapter 2.
3  Gramsci (1929–35: 1240–7) was of the opinion that "Fordist" America was characterized by a "rational demographic composition," i.e. a class composition where only bourgeoisie and labor were present. This would make for a kind of society where the element of consent was to prevail over that of coercion.
4  See Marshall Berman's book on modernity, which takes its title from this passage by Marx (Berman 1988).
5  Hardt and Negri's ambiguity about the "American" or "global" character of their "Empire" (2000) derives, it seems to me, from a lack of appreciation for this deeply Utopian aspect of the American project. True to its roots, the American "mission" is a historical mission, the fate of the world. It therefore finds in American power its vehicle, but is not at all bounded by such power; it is truly global, *and yet*, because it is only in America that such a mission has become fully hegemonic, it is only there that it had found its "promised land," the historical form in which it seems to have actualized itself is the global expansion of the American social formation, capitalistic *and* democratic (the form that – and this is a crucial point – has been until now the legitimating force of this whole expansion; were America instead to take seriously the talk of those who, whether "left" or "right," describe it as an "empire," this would certainly be the beginning of the end).
6  Guenther Roth has pointed out that Georg Jellinek's *The Declaration of the Rights of Man and Citizens* (1895), in which the author had affirmed the importance of the Protestant world-view for the establishment of the declarations of rights of man in the new American states, "was the immediate precursor of [Weber's] *The Protestant Ethic*" (Roth and Schluchter 1979: 133). Weber referred to Jellinek's work on the declarations of rights in *Economy and Society* (Weber 1956: 1209).
7  Marcuse's reference is to Luther, *Selected Writings of Martin Luther*, vol. III, Philadelphia, 1967, p. 466.

8   Horkheimer and Adorno's interest in this matter may also be gathered from the fact that a few years before, as we have seen, Horkheimer, head of the Frankfurt Institute, had given to the young Georg Rusche the task of writing an account of punishment according to the perspective of the Frankfurt School. The result was Georg Rusche and Otto Kirchheimer's *Punishment and Social Structure*, published in 1939 in the United States, the first American publication of the transplanted Institute. For a reconstruction of the intricate vicissitudes of that book, see my introduction to the new edition (Melossi 2003a).

9   Similar points would be made by Durkheim and Gramsci (see above, chapter 3, and note 3 in this chapter).

10  On the positions of the various religious orders – particularly the Dominicans – on the theological grounds for the *Conquista*, see Skinner (1978, vol. 2: 135–73).

## Chapter 5   Social Control and Deviance in Chicago

1   It is important to note the contribution to the rise of American sociology of two protagonists of those years often unjustly ignored: not only Jane Addams, but the African American sociologist W. E. B. DuBois, who wrote a pathbreaking account of "the Negro community" in Philadelphia at the end of the nineteenth-century (DuBois 1899; see Gilroy 1993: 111–45).

2   For a reconstruction of the very interesting sociological and political details of the scandal, see the volume by Carla Cappetti, *Writing Chicago* (1993: 87–92).

3   The "Pinkertons" were the members of the Pinkerton National Detective Agency, founded in 1850 in Chicago by Allan Pinkerton. They became famous for hunting and bringing to justice – when not assassinating – some of the most famous bandits of the "Wild West." Later on they specialized in fighting against the unions and protecting strikebreakers, here also often without much respect for "legal niceties" (Inciardi 1984: 200–1).

4   Later on, and about New York, see Marshall Berman's reconstruction of the urban planner Robert Moses's "destructive" impact on the city, as well as of Jane Jacobs's 1960s critique (Berman 1988: 287–348; Jacobs 1961).

5   An interesting study would consist in showing how the basic innovations in "popular" culture are usually at first created and experienced within the most marginal sectors of the working class.

6   One should also mention, however, the contribution by Charles Horton Cooley, who was not from Chicago but from the University of Michigan, Ann Arbor, and who was perhaps the keenest observer of the relationship between communication and democracy in this period (Cooley 1909).

7 According to Paul Rock's *The Making of Symbolic Interactionism* (1979), formalism complemented Pragmatism in the interactionst perspective.

8 Starting in 1900, and then into the 1930s, Mead taught a very influential course on "Social Psychology." He never published his thoughts in a systematic manner, but some of "his" most important books are taken from the notes of his courses (Mead 1934).

9 Marx's very distinction between a "structure" and a "superstructure" (Marx 1859) belongs in the classical, Cartesian mode of thinking, the idea of a dualism of matter and mind, of forms of social organization and forms of description. The latter, however, are absolutely essential to the very possibility of being of the former. We cannot think of forms of social organization in a way separate from the ways in which they can be described, understood, and expressed linguistically. Max Weber criticized Marxism in *The Protestant Ethic and the Spirit of Capitalism* (1904–5) for this very reason, among others, and used a language of "elective affinity" to express the relationship between the organizational level of "capitalism" and the intellectual and cultural level of "Protestantism" (Howe 1978). Through his collaboration with Hans Gerth, Mills would meet Weber's thought, and connect it with his Pragmatist background.

10 A famous Italian "activist" priest of the 1960s, Don Milani, used to say that "masters know one thousand words, workers three hundred, this is why they are the masters."

11 It is quite interesting to see Paul Takagi's view on a critical criminological usage of Sartre's thought (Takagi 1982).

12 At the time, in a move quite close to Mead's, the psychiatrist Harry Stack Sullivan was writing of a "selective inattention" (Sullivan 1940). According to Sullivan, as a person interacts with the environment, a whole array of data is available to her conscious attention. When, however, aspects of that data threaten to increase the person's anxiety, those aspects will be treated to a "selective inattention," in order to maintain emotional stability. Differently from Freud, who assumed unconscious motivations, Sullivan believed that this work of exclusion was fundamentally conscious.

13 According to which the worst, i.e. lowest-paid, "free" work outside ought to be more "eligible" than life in prison, to the end of safeguarding deterrence (Rusche 1933; Rusche and Kirchheimer 1939).

## Chapter 6   The 1930s: Between Differential Association and Anomie

1 Of course, the authors of the New Deal would all concur with George Herbert Mead's dictum (see previous chapter) that "human rights are

never in such danger as when their only defenders are political institutions and their officers" (1915: 169). The delegitimation of capitalism, the social and economic crisis that followed, and the perceived danger that what had happened "in Russia" might happen also in the United States, helped create a generation of politicians and intellectuals for whom social control was the true gospel.

2  Frightened because Roosevelt had threatened to "pack the Court" by changing the number of its members, something that, with his large popular support, he felt probably confident of being able to obtain. In any case, the threat was enough and in 1937 the Supreme Court finally accepted the labor reforms of the Roosevelt administration. Such a change of mind among the members of the Supreme Court became history as "the switch in time that saved the nine."

3  Ten other editions followed, the fifth to the tenth written also by his last student, Donald R. Cressey, after Sutherland's death in 1950. A former student of Cressey, David F. Luckenbill, co-wrote the eleventh (Sutherland et al. 1992).

4  I owe this passage to Wayne Morrison's *Theoretical Criminology* (1995: 248).

5  From a sentence in an interview I collected with a North African immigrant to Italy (Melossi 2000b: 37).

6  Ronald Akers (1996, 1998) has recently revived and reshaped the theory, calling it a theory of "social learning."

7  Personal communication.

8  The tendency to connect the question of crime with that of "race" in the United States or of "immigration" in Europe is an expression of a similar attitude.

9  A rather large bronze bust of Franklin Delano Roosevelt adorned Don Cressey's office in the University of California, Santa Barbara when I met him there, his last PhD student (1979–86).

10  Note the changing fortunes of the term "predator" that the *revanche* criminology of the 1970s–1990s would of course reserve to the lumpen element ("the underclass"). Sutherland (1937: 208) has a footnote thanking A. B. Hollingshead for suggesting the term "predatory control."

11  In the late 1970s Cressey (1978) would still define white-collar criminals as "subversives."

12  In 1932, in their classic book *The Modern Corporation and Private Property*, Adolf Berle, a lawyer who later became a New Deal brainstruster, and economist Gardiner Means were the first to discuss the chasm in twentieth-century capitalism between property rights and managers' control in large corporations.

13  See the chapter of *The Structure of Social Action* entitled "Emile Durkheim, III: The Development of the Theory of Social Control" (Parsons 1937: 376–408).

14   See above, chapter 2.
15   See the previous chapter.


## Chapter 7   From the "Neo-Chicagoans" to Labeling Theory

1   Mills refers here to Walter Lippmann's *Public Opinion* (1922). Certainly neither Lippmann nor Mills had a full knowledge of what this whole process would become with the appearance of television (cf. Spigel 1992).
2   As reported by Barbara Matusow for the *Washingtonian Magazine* and reprinted in the *Sacramento Bee*, October 27, 1987.
3   See above, chapters 3 and 4.
4   Here Becker inserts a note where he credits earlier statements by Frank Tannenbaum (see above) and Ed Lemert (1951), and refers to John Kitsuse's almost contemporary piece (1962).
5   The School of Criminology would then be closed after five years of turmoil in 1974 by an act of authority by the University of California administration. On this, see the first few issues of the journal *Crime and Social Justice*, which in a sense continued the "struggle" of the radicals from the School, thereby also founding, together with the British Taylor, Walton, and Young (1973), a "radical" or "critical" criminology (see next chapter).
6   See above, chapter 2.
7   In 1958 Gresham Sykes published *The Society of Captives: A Study of a Maximum Security Prison*, a classic sociological study of prison life.
8   See *a contrario* Paul Goodman's quite vitriolic view of Jack Kerouac in his *Growing Up Absurd* (1956).
9   The early "beats" and the "existentialists" belong in the same period, even if on different sides of the Atlantic, and one wonders about the reciprocal influence. That France had been a haven to expatriated black American artists, jazz musicians, and writers, is, however, a fact (see among others, Paul Gilroy's reconstruction of "the Black Atlantic" (1993: 146–86)). Sartre appears in Matza's later *Becoming Deviant* in association with his "presentation" of Jean Genet in "Saint-Genet" (Sartre 1952; Matza 1969: 13, 171, 179).
10   I attended Matza's lectures in Berkeley at a time, the end of the 1970s, when Foucault's fame was peaking in the United States. Particularly on the Berkeley campus, Foucault was the rage, in conversations and often in person, to great acclaim. Matza could not hide his irritation at this, since Foucault had nowhere shown, in his work, appreciation for those sociological theories of deviance, such as Matza's – and, I would add, for sociological theories of many other things too – that had predated *Discipline and Punish* and said things not very different. Very probably Foucault had no notion whatsoever of their existence.

11  With keen attention to an area of studies far from his own, Gitlin refers to Stanley Cohen's work in this respect (Gitlin 1980: 142, 246).
12  See above, chapter 6.
13  Against the most radical organizations this meant also the use of lethal violence, as in Chicago, on December 4, 1969, when the 21-year-old leader of the Chicago Black Panther Party, Fred Hampton, was shot and killed by police working under the Cook County State's Attorney, when they conducted a raid on the BPP headquarters. Another member of the BPP, Mark Clark, age 22, was killed, and six others were wounded during the raid.
14  On the issue of "youth problems" during the pre-1960s years, cf. Albert K. Cohen (1955) and Paul Goodman (1956).
15  The term "saint" to indicate a condition of moral "deviance" that, instead of being a sign of moral inferiority, points to an exceptional, truth-seeking human being – after the image of the Christ or of the Buddha – circulates widely in the literature of these years. Probably the best-known example is the Dean Moriarty/Neal Cassady of Jack Kerouac's *On the Road* (1957).
16  Most eloquently, as we have seen (above, chapter 1), in a short tract by none other than the Marquis de Sade within *Philosophy in the Bedroom* (1795), entitled *Yet Another Effort, Frenchmen, If You Would Become Republicans*.
17  It is no great surprise that David Matza would scarcely add any other work in the field of criminology to his career.

## Chapter 8   From "Labeling" to a "Critical" Kind of Criminology

1  This was in Eisenhower's farewell speech from the presidency (January 17, 1961): "The potential for the disastrous rise of misplaced power exists and will persist. We must never let the weight of this combination endanger our liberties or democratic processes. We should take nothing for granted. Only an alert and knowledgeable citizenry can compel the proper meshing of the huge industrial and military machinery of defense with our peaceful methods and goals, so that security and liberty may prosper together."
2  On the very intricate vicissitudes of this work, see my "Introduction" to the 2003 edition (Melossi 2003a).
3  A victim, and author of "victimless" crimes (Schur 1965), one might add.
4  See previous chapter.
5  Another pathbreaking contribution by Goffman is *Stigma* (1963), but the foundations of his analysis are to be found in *The Presentation of Self in Everyday Life* (1959). See also the work by Thomas Scheff (1966) and by Dorothy Smith (1978).

6  Published in English in 1965 in a shortened version under the title *Madness and Civilization*.

7  In the North American context, see also the important historical works by David Rothman, *The Discovery of the Asylum* (1971) and *Conscience and Convenience* (1980).

8  Partly because, in the situation of the "Cold War," all European societies, East and West, basically shared a status of "limited democracies" in which the type of socio-economic regime and the membership in one international field could not be changed.

9  On plea bargaining see also, from an interactionist perspective, Rosett and Cressey (1976).

10  Dorothy Smith connected in her work, in a very stimulating way, ethnomethodology with Marxist and feminist analyses (Smith 1976, 1981).

11  I owe this observation to Teresa Degenhardt. On ideology, see also Dorothy Smith's contribution (1976).

12  "Agnes," born a boy, had become a female during puberty.

13  I.e. prisons for women established adjacent to men's prisons, reserved only to women felons. Reformatories were instead devoted to the punishment of minor offenses.

## Chapter 9   The End of "the Short Century" between Inequality and Fear

1  See *Criminal Victimization*, 2003, at p. 5 (Bureau of Justice Statistics).

2  From "Goldwater's Acceptance Speech to GOP Convention," *New York Times*, July 17, 1964.

3  Until recently: see for instance the book by sociologist Barry Glassner (1999), cited by Michael Moore as one of the topical references for his landmark 2002 film *Bowling for Columbine*.

4  See the first Inaugural Address of his presidency, speech of January 20, 1981.

5  And not only in the United States: in Italy and many other countries also, the period around the early 1970s marked a trough in imprisonment rates (see next chapter).

6  For all these data see the publication *Prisoners in 2005* (Bureau of Justice Statistics).

7  On the possible applicability of Rusche and Kirchheimer's model to the United States in the period 1970–92, see Melossi (1993).

8  See *contra* Sampson and Laub (2005).

9  Cf. William Chambliss's classic study on the "Saints" and the "Roughnecks" (1973).

10  Together with previous works that had emphasized the importance of the excess Y chromosome in relation to violent behavior (Jacobs et al. 1971), these texts have again underlined the importance of

constitutional and genetic factors in the insurgence of criminal behavior, together with selected social factors, such as the falling apart of the family institution among the poor and minorities.

11    Barry Glassner would then be consultant to Michael Moore's enormously popular documentary *Bowling for Columbine*; it is hard to think of anybody more effective than Michael Moore to make the American (and not only American) public aware of some of the themes here proposed.

12    I thank Olivia Guaraldo for pointing out to me the importance of Dick's work.

## Chapter 10    The Cycle of the Canaille

1    Italian data are my elaboration of data assembled by the official governmental institute of statistics in Rome (ISTAT). They go from 1863 to 2006 and are equal to the sum of inmates in all adult prison institutions. US data go from 1850 to 2006 and are equal to the sum of inmates in state and federal prisons. They are based on my update of the data originally collected and elaborated by Margaret Cahalan (1979; the line between 1850 and 1925 is a linear interpolation based on the years for which we have data, that is 1850, 1860, 1870, 1880, 1890, 1904, 1910, and 1923). They do not include jail data. A theoretical sinusoid line represents long cycles. I would like to thank Tommaso Gennari and Ester Massa for their help with the drawing of figure 4.

2    The Italian word for "scabs," *crumiri*, derives from the name that was given to a Northern African people at the turn of the nineteenth century and that was increasingly used with racist overtones in France. From there it came to Italy and it assumed the specific contemptuous meaning of strikebreakers (it helped to popularize the name in Italy that a popular brand of Piedmontese cookies carried the stereotyped image of this people on its label, *crumiri* being also the name of the cookies). In the United States, in the same period, Italians were often characterized in a similar manner.

3    In this connection, I should recall a *boutade* by my main dissertation adviser in Santa Barbara, Don Cressey, the style of which his many former students will not have any difficulty in recognizing. Once, in his office, we were struggling with trying to identify an "indicator" for the situation of class relationships, to relate to changing punishment levels (the "obvious" indicator for which was the imprisonment rate). Suddenly Don snapped, "the imprisonment rate!" Don was not a Ruschean, but he had an uncanny ability for reading his students' minds.

4    Given the current huge disproportion in imprisonment rates between the United States and Europe, the temptation is always very high to

explain it on the basis of some kind of long historical process. For instance, James Q. Whitman, in his very suggestive *Harsh Justice: Criminal Punishment and the Widening Divide between America and Europe* (2003), tries to explain this disproportion on the basis of a long historical process of the expansion of "low-status" punishments in America and "high-status" punishments in Europe, as if in a spreading of democratic egalitarianism in one case and of aristocratic spirit in the other. Another possibility is to point at the Catholic/Protestant divide, as I was tempted to do concerning the comparison between the United States and Italy (Melossi 2001). However, if one looks at long-term developments in imprisonment rates (see above, figure 4), one immediately realizes that what we really have to explain is mainly what has happened in the United States since the early 1970s (and, to a lesser extent, what has happened in Europe since 1945).

5  In the same way in which legal realists were scolded for putting forward what their critics ridiculed as a "breakfast theory of law," i.e. a theory of law based, the critics said, on what the judge had eaten in the morning.

# References

Please note: the date after the name of the author (and in the text) is that of the original edition of the work. The date at the end of the reference, *if different*, pertains to the edition used.

ADAMIC, Louis 1932 *Laughing in the Jungle*. New York: Harpers.
ADAMIC, Louis 1934 *Dynamite: The Story of Class Violence in America*. New York: Chelsea House.
ADDAMS, Jane 1910 *Twenty Years at Hull-House*. New York: Penguin, 1998.
ADLER, Freda 1975 *Sisters in Crime*. New York: McGraw-Hill.
ADORNI, Daniela 1997 "Il brigantaggio." Pp. 283–319 in Violante (1997).
AFSC (American Friends Service Committee) Working Party 1971 *Struggle for Justice*. New York: Hill and Wang.
AGAMBEN, Giorgio 1995 *Homo Sacer: Sovereign Power and Bare Life*. Stanford: Stanford University Press, 1998.
AGAMBEN, Giorgio 2003 *State of Exception*. Chicago: University of Chicago Press, 2005.
AKERS, Ronald L. 1996 "Is Differential Association/Social Learning Cultural Deviance Theory?" *Criminology* 34: 229–47.
AKERS, Ronald L. 1998 *Social Learning and Social Structure: A General Theory of Crime and Deviance*. Boston: Northeastern University Press.
ALEXANDER, Franz and Hugo Staub 1931 *The Criminal, the Judge and the Public*. New York: Macmillan.
ALTHUSSER, Louis 1970 "Ideology and Ideological State Apparatuses." Pp. 121–73 in L. Althusser, *Lenin and Philosophy and Other Essays*. London: New Left Books, 1971.
ANDERSON, Elijah 1990 *Streetwise*. Chicago: University of Chicago Press.

ANDERSON, Nels 1923 *The Hobo*. Chicago: University of Chicago Press.

ANDERSON, Nels 1940 *Men on the Move*. Chicago: University of Chicago Press.

ARCHER, Dane and Rosemary Gartner 1984 *Violence and Crime in Cross-National Perspective*. New Haven, CT: Yale University Press.

AUSTIN, John L. 1962 *How to Do Things with Words*. Cambridge, MA: Harvard University Press, 1975.

BAIMA BOLLONE, Pier Luigi 1992 *Cesare Lombroso ovvero il principio dell'irresponsabilità*. Torino: Società Editrice Internazionale.

BAKER, Russell 2003 "The Awful Truth." *New York Review of Books* November 6: 6–12.

BARAN, Paul A. and Paul M. Sweezy 1966 *Monopoly Capital: An Essay on the American Economy and Social Order*. New York: Monthly Review Press.

BARATTA, Alessandro 1982 *Criminologia critica e critica del diritto penale*. Bologna: Il mulino.

BARNES, Harry Elmer 1930 *The Story of Punishment*. Boston: Stratford.

BASAGLIA, Franco (ed.) 1968 *L'istituzione negata*. Torino: Einaudi.

BEAULIEU, Alain 2005 *Michel Foucault et le contrôle social*. Montreal: Les presses de l'Université Laval.

BEAULIEU, Alain and D. Gabbard (eds) 2006 *Michel Foucault and Power Today: International Multidisciplinary Studies in the History of the Present*. Lanham, MD: Lexington Books.

BEAUMONT, Gustave de and Alexis de Tocqueville 1833 *On the Penitentiary System in the United States and Its Application in France*. Carbondale and Edwardsville: Southern Illinois University Press, 1964.

BECCARIA, Cesare 1764 *On Crimes and Punishments and Other Writings*. Cambridge: Cambridge University Press, 1995.

BECKER, Gary S. 1968 "Crime and Punishment: An Economic Approach." *Journal of Political Economy* 76: 169–217.

BECKER, Howard S. 1963 *Outsiders: Studies in the Sociology of Deviance*. New York: Free Press.

BECKER, Peter and Richard F. Wetzell (eds) 2006 *Criminals and Their Scientists: The History of Criminology in International Perspective*. Cambridge: Cambridge University Press.

BECKETT, Katherine 1997 *Making Crime Pay*. New York: Oxford University Press.

BECKETT, Katherine 2001 "Crime and Control in the Culture of Late Modernity." *Law and Society Review* 35: 899–930.

BEIRNE, Piers 1993 *Inventing Criminology: Essays on the Rise of "Homo Criminalis."* Albany: State University of New York Press.

BELL, Daniel 1953 "Crime as an American Way of Life." *Antioch Review* 13: 131–54.

BELL, Daniel 1960 *The End of Ideology: On the Exhaustion of Political Ideas in the Fifties*. Cambridge, MA: Harvard University Press, 2000.

BENJAMIN, Walter 1936 "The Work of Art in the Age of Mechanical Reproduction." Pp. 217–52 in Walter Benjamin, *Illuminations*. New York: Schocken, 1969.

BENJAMIN, Walter 1939 "On Some Motifs in Baudelaire." Pp. 155–200 in Walter Benjamin, *Illuminations*. New York: Schocken, 1969.

BENNETT, William J., John B. DiIulio, Jr., and John P. Walters 1996 *Body Count: Moral Poverty . . . and How to Win America's War Against Crime and Drugs*. New York: Simon and Schuster.

BENTHAM, Jeremy 1787 "Panopticon." Pp. 37–66 in *The Works of Jeremy Bentham*. New York: Russell and Russell, 1971.

BENTHAM, Jeremy 1789 *An Introduction to the Principles of Morals and Legislation: Works of Jeremy Bentham*. New York: Oxford University Press, 1996.

BENTLEY, Arthur F. 1908 *The Process of Government*. Cambridge, MA: Harvard University Press.

BERK, Richard A., David Rauma, Sheldon L. Messinger, and Thomas F. Cooley 1981 "A Test of the Stability of Punishment Hypothesis: The Case of California, 1851–1970." *American Sociological Review* 46: 805–29.

BERLE, Adolf A. and Gardiner C. Means 1932 *The Modern Corporation and Private Property*. New York: Macmillan.

BERMAN, Marshall 1988 *All That Is Solid Melts Into Air*. New York: Penguin.

BITTNER, Egon 1967 "The Police on Skid-Row: A Study of Peace Keeping." *American Sociological Review* 32: 699–715.

BLACK, Donald (ed.) 1984 *Toward a General Theory of Social Control*. 2 vols. New York: Academic Press.

BLUMER, Herbert 1969 *Symbolic Interactionism*. Berkeley: University of California Press.

BLUMSTEIN, Alfred 1983 "Selective Incapacitation as a Means of Crime Control." *American Behavioral Scientist* 27: 87–108.

BLUMSTEIN, Alfred 2000 "Disaggregating the Violence Trends." Pp. 13–44 in Blumstein and Wallman (2000).

BLUMSTEIN, Alfred and Jacqueline Cohen 1979 "Estimation of Individual Crime Rates from Arrest Records." *Journal of Criminal Law and Criminology* 70: 561–85.

BLUMSTEIN, Alfred and Richard Rosenfeld 1998 "Explaining Recent Trends in U.S. Homicide Rates." *Journal of Criminal Law and Criminology* 88: 1175–1216.

BLUMSTEIN, Alfred and Joel Wallman (eds) 2000 *The Crime Drop in America*. Cambridge: Cambridge University Press.

BLUMSTEIN, Alfred, Jacqueline Cohen, and Daniel Nagin 1977 "The Dynamics of a Homeostatic Punishment Process." *Journal of Criminal Law and Criminology* 67: 317–34.

BLUMSTEIN, Alfred, Jacqueline Cohen, and David P. Farrington 1988 "Longitudinal and Criminal Career Research: Further Clarifications." *Criminology* 26: 57–74.

BOCCACCIO, Giovanni 1348–53 *The Decameron*. Oxford: Oxford University Press, 1998.

BOCKMAN, Johanna and Gil Eyal 2002 "Eastern Europe as a Laboratory for Economic Knowledge: The Transnational Roots of Neoliberalism." *American Journal of Sociology* 108: 310–52.

BODDY, Raford and James Crotty 1975 "Class Conflict and Macro-Policy: The Political Business Cycle." *Review of Radical Political Economics* 7: 1–19.

BOURDIEU, Pierre 1986 "The Forms of Capital." Pp. 241–58 in J.G. Richardson (ed.), *The Handbook of Theory and Research for the Sociology of Education*. New York: Greenwood.

BOURGOIS, Philippe 1995 *In Search of Respect: Selling Crack in El Barrio*. Cambridge: Cambridge University Press.

BOURGOIS, Philippe 2003 "Preface to the 2003 Second Edition." Pp. xvii–xxiii in P. Bourgois, *In Search of Respect: Selling Crack in El Barrio. Second Edition*. Cambridge: Cambridge University Press.

BOWERS, William J. and Glenn L. Pierce 1980 "Deterrence or Brutalization: What is the Effect of Executions?" *Crime and Delinquency* 26: 453–84.

BRAITHWAITE, John 1980 "The Political Economy of Punishment." Pp. 192–208 in E. L. Wheelwright and K. Buckley (eds), *Essays in the Political Economy of Australian Capitalism*. Sydney: Australia and New Zealand Book Company, 1975–83.

BRAITHWAITE, John 1989 *Crime, Shame and Reintegration*. Cambridge: Cambridge University Press.

BRECHER, Jeremy 1972 *Strike!* Boston: South End Press.

BRIDGES, L. and Paul Gilroy 1982 "Striking Back." *Marxism Today* 26: 34–5.

BROTHERTON, David C. and Luis Barrios 2004 *The Almighty Latin King and Queen Nation: Street Politics and the Transformation of a New York City Gang*. New York: Columbia University Press.

BULMER, Martin 1984 *The Chicago School of Sociology*. Chicago: University of Chicago Press.

BURCKHARDT, Jacob 1860 *The Civilization of the Renaissance in Italy*. Oxford: Phaidon, 1945.

BURKE, Kenneth 1950 *A Rhetoric of Motives*. Berkeley: University of California Press, 1969.

BURROUGHS, William 1978 "The Limits of Control." *semiotext(e)* III (2): 38–42.

CAHALAN, Margaret 1979 "Trends in Incarceration in the United States since 1880." *Crime and Delinquency* 25: 9–41.

CALAVITA, Kitty 2005 *Immigrants at the Margins: Law, Race, and Exclusion in Southern Europe*. New York: Cambridge University Press.

CAMERON, Norman 1943 "The Paranoid Pseudo-Community." *American Journal of Sociology* 49: 32–8.

CAPPETTI, Carla 1993 *Writing Chicago*. New York: Columbia University Press.

CARLEN, Pat 1985 *Criminal Women*. Cambridge: Polity.

CASTEL, Robert 1991 "From Dangerousness to Risk." Pp. 281–98 in G. Burchell and C. Gordon (eds), *The Foucault Effect: Studies in Governmentality*. Chicago: University of Chicago Press.

CASTELLS, Manuel 1996 *The Rise of the Network Society*. Oxford: Blackwell.

CAVADINO, Michael and James Dignan 2006 *Penal Systems: A Comparative Approach*. London: Sage.

CAVAN, Ruth 1928 *Suicide*. Chicago: University of Chicago Press.

CAWELTI, John (ed.) 1973 *Focus on Bonnie and Clyde*. Englewood Cliffs, NJ: Prentice Hall.

CAYLEY, David 1998 The *Expanding Prison: The Crisis in Crime and Punishment and the Search for Alternatives*. Cleveland, OH: Pilgrim Press.

CHAMBLISS, William J. 1964 "A Sociological Analysis of the Law of Vagrancy." *Social Problems* 12: 67–77.

CHAMBLISS, William J. (ed.) 1972 *Box Man: A Professional Thief's Journey*. New York: Harper and Row.

CHAMBLISS, William J. 1973 "The Roughnecks and the Saints." *Society* November/December: 24–31.

CHAMBLISS, William J. 1978 On *the Take: From Petty Crooks to Presidents*. Bloomington: Indiana University Press.

CHAUCER, Geoffrey 1386–1400 *The Canterbury Tales*. New York: W. W. Norton, 2005.

CHESLER, Phyllis 1972 *Women and Madness*. New York: Avon Books.

CHEVALIER, Louis 1958 *Labouring Classes and Dangerous Classes in Paris During the First Half of the Nineteenth Century*. New York: Howard Fertig, 2000.

CHILDS, John B. 1997 "The New Youth Peace Movement: Creating Broad Strategies for Community Renaissance in the United States." *Social Justice* 24 (4): 247–57.

CHIRICOS, Theodore G. 1987 "Rates of Crime and Unemployment: An Analysis of Aggregate Research Evidence." *Social Problems* 34: 187–212.

CHIRICOS, Theodore G. and Miriam A. DeLone 1992 "Labour Surplus and Punishment: A Review and Assessment of Theory and Evidence." *Social Problems* 39: 421–46.

CHRISTIE, Nils 1968 "Changes in Penal Values." *Scandinavian Studies in Criminology* 2: 161–72.

CHRISTIE, Nils 1981 *Limits to Pain*. Oslo: Universitetsforlaget.

CHRISTIE, Nils 1994 *Crime Control as Industry: Towards GULAGs, Western Style*. London and New York: Routledge.

CICOUREL, Aaron 1968 *Social Organization of Juvenile Justice*. New York: Wiley.

CLARK, John M. 1926 *Social Control of Business*. New York: Whittlesey House.

CLOWARD, Richard and Lloyd Ohlin 1960 *Delinquency and Opportunity: A Theory of Delinquent Gangs*. Glencoe, IL: Free Press.

COHEN, Albert K. 1955 *Delinquent Boys: The Culture of the Gang*. New York: Free Press.

COHEN, Albert K. 1965 "The Sociology of the Deviant Act: Anomie Theory and Beyond." *American Sociological Review* 30: 5–14.

COHEN, Elizabeth 1990 *Making a New Deal*. Cambridge: Cambridge University Press.

COHEN, Lawrence E. and Marcus Felson 1979 "Social Change and Crime Rate Trends: A Routine Activity Approach." *American Sociological Review* 44: 588–608.

COHEN, Lawrence E. and Richard Machalek 1988 "A General Theory of Expropriative Crime: An Evolutionary Ecological Approach." *American Journal of Sociology* 94: 465–501.

COHEN, Stanley 1972 *Folk Devils and Moral Panics: The Creation of the Mods and Rockers*. New York: St Martin's Press, 1980.

COHEN, Stanley 1985 *Visions of Social Control*. Cambridge: Polity.

COHN-BENDIT, Daniel and Thomas Schmid, 1992 *Heimat Babylon. Das Wagnis der multikulturellen Demokratie*. Hamburg: Hoffman und Campe.

COLAJANNI, Napoleone 1903 *Latini e Anglo-Sassoni: Razze inferiori e razze superiori*. Rome and Naples: Rivista popolare.

COLEMAN, James S. 1990 *Foundations of Social Theory*. Cambridge, MA: Harvard University Press.

COLUCCI, Mario and Pierangelo Di Vittorio 2001 *Franco Basaglia*. Milan: Bruno Mondadori Editore.

COLVIN, Mark 1992 *The Penitentiary in Crisis: From Accommodation to Riot in New Mexico*. Albany: State University of New York Press.

CONNELL, R. W. 1995 *Masculinities*. Cambridge: Polity; Berkeley: University of California Press.

CONNELL, R. W. 1997 "Why Is Classical Theory Classical?" *American Journal of Sociology* 102: 1511–57.

COOLEY, Charles H. 1909 *Social Organization: A Study of the Larger Mind*. New Brunswick, NJ: Transaction, 1983.

COREY, Robin 2004 *Fear: The History of a Political Idea*. New York: Oxford University Press.

COSTA, Pietro 1974 *Il progetto giuridico*. Milan: Giuffre.

CRESSEY, Donald R. 1953 *Other People's Money*. Glencoe, IL: Free Press.

CRESSEY, Donald R. 1954 "The Differential Association Theory and Compulsive Crimes." *Journal of Criminal Law, Criminology and Police Science* 45: 29–40.

CRESSEY, Donald R. 1968 "Culture Conflict, Differential Association, and Normative Conflict." Pp. 43–54 in M. E. Wolfgang (ed.), *Crime and Culture*. New York: Wiley.

CRESSEY, Donald R. 1978 "White Collar Subversives." *Center Magazine* 11: 44–9.

CRESSEY, Paul 1932 *The Taxi-Dance Hall*. Chicago: University of Chicago Press.

CULLEN, Francis T. 2005 "The Twelve People Who Saved Rehabilitation: How the Science of Criminology Made a Difference." *Criminology* 43: 1–42.

CURRIE, Elliott 1985 *Confronting Crime: An American Challenge.* New York: Pantheon.

CURRIE, Elliott 1997 "Market, Crime and Community: Toward a Mid-Range Theory of Post-Industrial Violence." *Theoretical Criminology* 1: 147–72.

DAHRENDORF, Ralf 1979 *Life Chances: Approaches to Social and Political Theory.* Chicago: University of Chicago Press.

DALY, Kathleen and Meda Chesney-Lind 1988 "Feminism and Criminology." *Justice Quarterly* 5: 497–535.

DARWIN, Charles 1871 *Descent of Man.* London: John Murray.

DAVIS, Angela 2003 *Are Prisons Obsolete?* New York: Seven Stories Press.

DAVIS, Mike 1990 *City of Quartz: Excavating the Future in Los Angeles.* London: Verso.

DAVIS, Mike 1992a *L.A. Was Just the Beginning.* Westfield, NJ: Open Magazine Pamphlet Series.

DAVIS, Mike 1992b *Beyond Blade Runner: Urban Control/The Ecology of Fear.* Westfield, NJ: Open Magazine Pamphlet Series.

DAVIS, Mike 1998 *Ecology of Fear: Los Angeles and the Imagination of Disaster.* New York: Metropolitan Books.

DE GIORGI, Alessandro 2002 *Re-Thinking the Political Economy of Punishment: Perspectives on Post-Fordism and Penal Politics.* Aldershot and Burlington, VT: Ashgate, 2006.

DE LAURETIS, Teresa 1996 *Sui generis.* Milan: Feltrinelli.

DEEGAN, Mary Jo 1988 *Jane Addams and the Men of the Chicago School, 1892–1918.* New Brunswick, NJ: Transaction.

DEL OLMO, Rosa 1981 *América Latina y su criminologia.* Mexico City: Siglo Veintiuno Editores.

DELEUZE, Gilles 1990 "Postscript on the Societies of Control." *October* 59 (1992): 3–7.

DEWEY, John 1922 *Human Nature and Conduct.* New York: Random House, 1957.

DEWEY, John 1927 *The Public and Its Problems.* Denver: Alan Swallow.

DEWEY, John 1931 "Social Science and Social Control." *New Republic* 67: 276–7.

DICK, Philip K. 1956 "The Minority Report." In Philip K. Dick, *Minority Report.* London: Gollancz, 2002.

DIGGINS, John P. 1981 "The Three Faces of Authority in American History." Pp. 17–31 in J. P. Diggins and M. E. Kann (eds), *The Problem of Authority in America.* Philadelphia: Temple University Press.

DITTON, Jason 1979 *Controlology: Beyond the New Criminology.* London: Macmillan.

DOW, Mark 2004 *American Gulag: Inside U.S. Immigration Prisons.* Berkeley: University of California Press.

DREISER, Theodore 1900 *Sister Carrie.* New York: Penguin, 1981.

DREISER, Theodore 1925 *An American Tragedy.* New York: Boni and Liveright.

DREW, Elizabeth 2003 "The Enforcer." *New York Review of Books* May 1: 14–17.

DUBOIS, William E. B. 1899 *The Philadelphia Negro: A Social Study.* Philadelphia: University of Pennsylvania Press, 1996.

DUMM, Thomas L. 1987 *Democracy and Punishment: Disciplinary Origins of the United States.* Madison: University of Wisconsin Press.

DURKHEIM, Emile 1887 "Guyau. *L'irréligion de l'avenir: Etude de sociologie."* *Revue philosophique* 23: 299–311.

DURKHEIM, Emile 1893 *The Division of Labor in Society.* New York: Free Press, 1984.

DURKHEIM, Emile 1895a *The Rules of Sociological Method.* New York: Free Press, 1982.

DURKHEIM, Emile 1895b "Crime and Social Health." Pp. 92–101 in S. Lukes and A. Scull (eds), *Durkheim and the Law.* New York: St Martin's Press, 1983.

DURKHEIM, Emile 1897 *Suicide.* Glencoe, IL: Free Press, 1951.

DURKHEIM, Emile 1898–1900 *Professional Ethics and Civic Morals.* Glencoe, IL: Free Press, 1958.

DURKHEIM, Emile 1900 "Two Laws of Penal Evolution." *Cincinnati Law Review* 38 (1969): 32–60.

DURKHEIM, Emile 1902 "Preface" to the Second Edition of Durkheim (1893).

DWORKIN, Ronald 2002 "The Threat to Patriotism." *New York Review of Books* February 28: 44–9.

DWORKIN, Ronald 2003 "Terror and the Attack on Civil Liberties." *New York Review of Books* November 6: 37–41.

ELIAS, Norbert 1939 *The Civilizing Process: The History of Manners.* New York: Urizen Books, 1978.

ELLISON, Ralph 1952 *Invisible Man.* New York: Random House.

ENGELS, Frederick 1845 *The Condition of the Working Class in England in 1844.* New York: International, 1975.

ENGELS, Frederick 1850 *The Peasant War in Germany.* New York: International, 2000.

ENGELS, Frederick 1884 *The Origin of the Family, Private Property and the State.* New York: International, 1972.

ERIKSON, Kai 1966 *Wayward Puritans.* New York: Wiley.

FANON, Franz 1961 *The Wretched of the Earth.* New York: Grove Press, 1968.

FARRIS, Robert E. L. and H. Warren Dunham 1934 *Mental Disorders in Urban Areas.* Chicago: University of Chicago Press.

FEDERN, Paul 1919 "Zuer Psychologie der Revolution: Die vaterlose Gesellschaft." *Der Oesterreichische Volkswirt* 11: 571–4, 595–8.

FEELEY, Malcolm M. and Deborah L. Little 1991 "The Vanishing Female: The Decline of Women in the Criminal Process, 1687–1912." *Law and Society Review* 25: 719–57.

FEELEY, Malcolm M. and Jonathan Simon 1992 "The New Penology: Notes on the Emerging Strategy of Corrections and Its Implications." *Criminology* 30: 449–74.

FEELEY, Malcolm M. and Jonathan Simon 1994 "Actuarial Justice: The Emerging New Criminal Law." Pp. 173–201 in Nelken (1994).

FELSON, Marcus 1998 *Crime and Everyday Life*. Thousand Oaks, CA: Pine Forge Press.

FERRACUTI, Franco 1968 "European Migration and Crime." Pp. 189–219 in M. E. Wolfgang (ed.), *Crime and Culture: Essays in Honor of Thorsten Sellin*. New York: Wiley.

FERRAJOLI, Luigi 1990 *Diritto e ragione*. Bari: Laterza.

FERRI, Enrico 1884 *Sociologia criminale*. Turin: Bocca.

FERRI, Enrico 1886 "I contadini mantovani all'Assise di Venezia." Pp. 1–62 in Enrico Ferri, *Difese penali e studi di giurisprudenza*. Turin: Bocca, 1899.

FERRI, Enrico 1921 *Relazione sul Progetto preliminare di Codice Penale Italiano*. Milan: Vallardi.

FIELD, Simon 1990 *Trends in Crime and their Interpretation: A Study of Recorded Crime in Post-War England and Wales*. Home Office Research Study 119. London: HMSO.

FITZGERALD, F. Scott 1931 "Echoes of the Jazz Age." Pp. 13–22 in *The Crack-Up*. New York: New Directions, 1956.

FITZPATRICK, Peter 1995 "The Constitution of the Excluded: Indians and Others." Pp. 191–212 in I. Loveland (ed.), *A Special Relationship? American Influences on Public Law in the United Kingdom*. Oxford: Clarendon Press.

FOUCAULT, Michel 1965 *Madness and Civilization*. New York: Random House.

FOUCAULT, Michel 1974 "Michel Foucault on Attica: An Interview." *Telos* 19: 154–61.

FOUCAULT, Michel 1975 *Discipline and Punish*. New York: Pantheon, 1977.

FOUCAULT, Michel 1976a *The History of Sexuality. Vol. 1: An Introduction*. New York: Random House, 1978.

FOUCAULT, Michel 1976b *Society Must Be Defended*. New York: Picador, 2003.

FOUCAULT, Michel, 1978 "Governmentality." *Ideology and Consciousness* (1979) 6: 5–21.

FRANKLIN, Benjamin 1751 "Observations Concerning the Increase of Mankind." In *The Papers of Benjamin Franklin*, vol. 4. New Haven, CT: Yale University Press.

FREUD, Sigmund 1913 *Totem and Taboo*. Pp. 1–161 in *The Standard Edition*, vol. 13. London: Hogarth, 1955.

FREUD, Sigmund 1916 "Criminality from a Sense of Guilt." Pp. 332–33 in *The Standard Edition*, vol. 14. London: Hogarth Press.

FREUD, Sigmund 1917 *Introductory Lectures on Psychoanalysis*. Pp. 1–240 in *The Standard Edition*, vol. 15. London: Hogarth, 1963.

FREUD, Sigmund 1921 *Group Psychology and the Analysis of the Ego*. Pp. 65–141 in *The Standard Edition*, vol. 18. London: Hogarth, 1955.

FREUD, Sigmund 1930 *Civilization and Its Discontents*. Pp. 57–146 in *The Standard Edition*, vol. 21. London: Hogarth, 1961.

FREUD, Sigmund 1933 *New Introductory Lectures on Psychoanalysis*. Pp. 1–182 in *The Standard Edition*, vol. 22. London: Hogarth, 1964.

FREUD, Sigmund 1939 *Moses and Monotheism*. Pp. 7–137 in *The Standard Edition*, vol. 23. London: Hogarth, 1964.

FRIEDMAN, Benjamin M. 2004 "Bush and Kerry: A Big Divide." *New York Review of Books* 51 (16): 27–9.

FRIES, Sylvia D. 1973 "*Staatstheorie* and the New American Science of Politics." *Journal of the History of Ideas* 34: 391–404.

FRIGESSI, Delia 2003 *Cesare Lombroso*. Turin: Einaudi.

FRITZSCHE, Peter 1998 "Talk of the Town: The Murder of Lucie Berlin." Pp. 377–400 in Becker and Wetzell (2006).

FULLER, Lon L. 1958 "Positivism and Fidelity to Law: A Reply to Professor Hart." *Harvard Law Review* 71: 630–72.

FULLER, Lon L. 1964 *The Morality of Law*. New Haven, CT: Yale University Press.

GARFINKEL, Harold 1956 "Conditions of Successful Degradation Ceremonies." *American Journal of Sociology* 61: 240–4.

GARFINKEL, Harold 1967a *Studies in Ethnomethodology*. Englewood Cliffs, NJ: Prentice Hall.

GARFINKEL, Harold 1967b "Passing and the Managed Achievement of Sex Status in an 'Intersexed' Person." Pp. 116–85 in Garfinkel (1967a).

GARLAND, David 1985 *Punishment and Welfare*. Aldershot: Gower.

GARLAND, David 1990 *Punishment and Modern Society: A Study in Social Theory*. Chicago: University of Chicago Press.

GARLAND, David 1996 "The Limits of the Sovereign State." *British Journal of Criminology* 36: 445–71.

GARLAND, David 2001a *The Culture of Control: Crime and Social Order in Contemporary Society*. Oxford: Oxford University Press.

GARLAND, David (ed.) 2001b *Mass Imprisonment*. London: Sage.

GAROFALO, Raffaele 1891 *Criminologia*. Turin: Bocca.

GEIS, Gilbert 1964 "Sociology and Sociological Jurisprudence: Admixture of Lore and Law." *Kentucky Law Journal* 52: 267–93.

GEIS, Gilbert and Colin Goff 1983 "Introduction." Pp. ix–xxxiii in Sutherland (1983).

GENET, Jean 1949 *The Thief's Journal*. New York: Grove Press, 1964.

GERBI, Antonello 1955 *La disputa del Nuovo Mondo: Storia di una polemica, 1750–1900*. Milan: R. Ricciardi.

GERTH, Hans H. and C. Wright Mills 1946 "Introduction: The Man and His Work." Pp. 3–74 in Hans H. Gerth and C. Wright Mills (eds), *From Max Weber: Essays in Sociology*. New York: Oxford University Press.

GERTH, Hans H. and C. Wright Mills 1953 *Character and Social Structure: The Psychology of Social Institutions*. New York: Harcourt, Brace.

GIBSON, Mary 2002 *Born to Crime: Cesare Lombroso and the Origins of Biological Criminology*. Westport, CT: Greenwood.

GIBSON, Mary and Nicole H. Rafter 2004 "Editors' Introduction." Pp. 3–38 in Lombroso and Ferrero (1893).

GIBSON, Mary and Nicole H. Rafter 2006 "Editors' Introduction." Pp. 1–36 in Lombroso (1876–97).

GIDDENS, Anthony 1971 *Capitalism and Modern Social Theory*. Cambridge: Cambridge University Press.

GIDDENS, Anthony 1976 *New Rules of Sociological Method*. New York: Basic Books.

GIDDENS, Anthony 1984 *The Constitution of Society*. Berkeley: University of California Press.

GILMORE, Ruth W. 2007 *Golden Gulag: Prisons, Surplus, Crisis, and Opposition in Globalizing California (American Crossroads)*. Berkeley: University of California Press.

GILROY, Paul 1982 "The Myth of Black Criminality." Pp. 47–56 in *Socialist Register*. London: Merlin Press.

GILROY, Paul 1993 *The Black Atlantic: Modernity and Double Consciousness*. Cambridge, MA: Harvard University Press; London and New York: Verso.

GINSBERG, Benjamin 1986 *The Captive Public: How Mass Opinion Promoted State Power*. New York: Basic Books.

GITLIN, Todd 1980 *The Whole World Is Watching*. Berkeley: University of California Press.

GITLIN, Todd 1987 *The Sixties: Years of Hope, Days of Rage*. Toronto: Bantam Books.

GLASER, Daniel 1956 "Criminality Theory and Behavioral Images." *American Journal of Sociology* 61: 433–44.

GLASSNER, Barry 1999 *The Culture of Fear: Why Americans are Afraid of the Wrong Things*. New York: Basic Books.

GLOWACKI, Peggy and Julia Hendry 2004 *Hull-House (Images of America)*. Charleston, SC: Arcadia.

GOFFMAN, Erving 1959 *The Presentation of Self in Everyday Life*. Garden City, NY: Doubleday Anchor Books.

GOFFMAN, Erving 1961 *Asylums: Essays on the Social Situation of Mental Patients and Other Inmates*. Garden City, NY: Anchor Books.

GOFFMAN, Erving 1963 *Stigma*. Englewood Cliffs, NJ: Prentice Hall.

GOODMAN, Paul 1956 *Growing Up Absurd*. New York: Random House.

GORING, Charles 1913 *The English Convict: A Statistical Study*. London: HMSO.

GOTTFREDSON, Michael R. and Travis Hirschi 1990 *A General Theory of Crime*. Stanford: Stanford University Press.

GOULD, Stephen J. 1977 *Ontogeny and Phylogeny*. Cambridge, MA: Harvard University Press.

GOULD, Stephen J. 1981 *The Mismeasure of Man*. New York: W. W. Norton.

GOULD, Stephen J. 1994 "Curveball." *New Yorker* November 28: 139–49.

GOULDNER, Alvin W. 1968 "The Sociologist as Partisan: Sociology and the Welfare State." *American Sociologist* 3 (2): 103–16.

GOVE, Walter R. (ed.) 1975 *The Labelling of Deviance: Evaluating a Perspective*. New York: Halsted Press.

GRAEBNER, William 1987 *The Engineering of Consent: Democracy and Authority in Twentieth-Century America*. Madison: University of Wisconsin Press.

GRAMSCI, Antonio 1926 "Some Aspects of the Southern Question." Pp. 441–62 in Antonio Gramsci, *Selections from Political Writings (1921–1926)*. London: Lawrence and Wishart, 1978.

GRAMSCI, Antonio 1929–35 *Prison Notebooks*. 3 vols. New York: Columbia University Press, 1991–2007.

GREENBERG, David F. 1977 "The Dynamics of Oscillatory Punishment Processes." *Journal of Criminal Law and Criminology* 68: 643–51.

GREENBERG, David F. and Drew Humphries 1980. "The Cooptation of Fixed Sentencing Reform." *Crime and Delinquency* 26: 206–25.

GREENWOOD, Peter 1982 *Selective Incapacitation*. Santa Monica: Rand.

GUERRY, André-Michel 1833 *Essai sur la statistique morale de la France*. Paris: Crochard.

GUYAU, Jean M. 1887 *L'irréligion de l'avenir: Etude de sociologie*. Paris: Alcan.

HABERMAS, Jürgen 1981a *The Theory of Communicative Action. Vol. One: Reason and the Rationalization of Society*. Boston: Beacon, 1984.

HABERMAS, Jürgen 1981b *The Theory of Communicative Action. Vol. Two: Lifeworld and System: A Critique of Functionalist Reason*. Boston: Beacon, 1988.

HACKING, Ian 1986 "Making Up People." Pp. 222–36 in T. Heller, M. Sosna, and D. E. Wellbery (eds), *Reconstructing Individualism*. Stanford: Stanford University Press.

HALL, Stuart, Chas Critcher, Tony Jefferson, John Clarke, and Brian Roberts 1978 *Policing the Crisis: Mugging, the State, and Law and Order*. London: Macmillan.

HALLEMA, A. 1936 *In en om de Gevangenis: Van vroeger Dagen in Nederland en Nederlandsch-Indie*. The Hague: Belinfante.

HALLEMA, A. 1958 *Geshiedenis van het gevangenizwesen*. The Hague: Staatsdrukkerij.

HAMILTON, Gary and John Sutton 1989 "The Problem of Control in the Weak State. Domination in the United States, 1880–1920." *Theory and Society* 18: 1–46.

HANUSHEK, Eric A. and John E. Jackson 1977 *Statistical Methods for Social Scientists*. New York: Academic Press.

HARCOURT, Bernard E. 2001 *Illusion of Order: The False Promise of Broken Windows Policing*. Cambridge, MA: Harvard University Press.

HARCOURT, Bernard E. 2007 *Against Prediction: Profiling, Policing, and Punishing in an Actuarial Age*. Chicago: University of Chicago Press.

HARDT, Michael and Antonio Negri 2000 *Empire*. Cambridge, MA: Harvard University Press.

HART, H. L. A. 1958 "Positivism and the Separation of Law and Morals." *Harvard Law Review* 71: 593–629.

HAY, Douglas, Peter Linebaugh, John G. Rule, E. P. Thompson, and Cal Winslow 1975 *Albion's Fatal Tree: Crime and Society in Eighteenth-Century England*. New York: Pantheon.

HAYNER, Norman S. 1923 "The Hotel: The Sociology of Hotel Life." PhD thesis, University of Chicago.

HEGEL, Georg W. F. 1821 *Philosophy of Right*. London: Oxford University Press, 1967.

HERITAGE, John 1984 *Garfinkel and Ethnomethodology*. Cambridge: Polity.

HERRNSTEIN, Richard J. and Charles Murray 1994 *The Bell Curve*. New York: Free Press.

HIRSCHI, Travis 1969 *Causes of Delinquency*. Berkeley: University of California Press.

HIRST, Paul Q. 1975 "Marx and Engels on Law, Crime and Morality." Pp. 203–32 in Taylor et al. (1975).

HOBBES, Thomas 1651 *Leviathan*. New York: Collier, 1962.

HOBSBAWM, Eric J. 1959 *Primitive Rebels*. New York: W. W. Norton.

HOBSBAWM, Eric J. 1969 *Bandits*. London: Weidenfeld and Nicolson.

HOBSBAWM, Eric J. 1994 *The Short Twentieth Century 1914–1991*. London: Abacus.

HOPE, Tim 1995 "Building a Safer Society." Pp. 21–89 in M. Tonry and D. P. Farrington (eds), *Crime and Justice: Vol. 19*. Chicago: University of Chicago Press.

HORKHEIMER, Max 1942 "The Authoritarian State." *Telos* 15 (1973): 3–20.

HORKHEIMER, Max and Theodor W. Adorno 1944 *Dialectic of Enlightenment*. New York: Continuum, 1989.

HORN, David G. 2003 *The Criminal Body: Lombroso and the Anatomy of Deviance*. New York: Routledge.

HORNEY, Julie and Ineke H. Marshall 1991 "Measuring Lambda Through Self-Reports." *Criminology* 29: 471–95.

HORNEY, Karen 1937 *The Neurotic Personality of Our Time*. New York: W. W. Norton.

HOWE, Adrian 1994 *Punish and Critique*. London: Routledge.

HOWE, Richard H. 1978 "Max Weber's Elective Affinities: Sociology Within the Bounds of Pure Reason." *American Journal of Sociology* 84: 366–85.

HULSMAN, L. 1982 *Peines perdues: Le système pénal en question*. Paris: Centurion.

IGNATIEFF, Michael 1978 *A Just Measure of Pain*. London: Macmillan.

INCIARDI, James A. 1984 *Criminal Justice*. Orlando, FL: Academic Press.

JACOBS, Jane 1961 *The Death and Life of Great American Cities*. New York: Random House.

JACOBS, P. A., W. Price, S. Richmond, and R. Ratcliff 1971 "Chromosome Surveys in Penal Institutions and Approved Schools." *Journal of Medical Genetics* 8: 49–58.

JAMES, William 1897 *The Will to Believe and Other Essays in Popular Psychology*. New York: Dover, 1956.

JANKOVIC, Ivan 1977 "Labor Market and Imprisonment." *Crime and Social Justice* 8: 17–31.

JAY, Martin 1973 *The Dialectical Imagination*. Boston: Little, Brown.

JELLINEK, Georg 1895 *The Declaration of the Rights of Men and Citizens*. New York: Holt, 1901.

JOAS, Hans 1980 *G. H. Mead: A Contemporary Re-Examination of His Thought*. Cambridge: Polity, 1985.

JOAS, Hans 1983 "System Integration and Social Integration from the Perspective of Symbolic Interactionism." Paper presented at the International Conference of Social Action and Social Systems, Varna, Bulgaria.

KAIRYS, David (ed.) 1982a *The Politics of Law: A Progressive Critique*. New York: Pantheon.

KAIRYS, David 1982b "Freedom of Speech." Pp. 140–71 in Kairys (1982a).

KANT, Immanuel 1784 "An Answer to the Question: 'What is Enlightenment?'" In Immanuel Kant, *Practical Philosophy*. Cambridge: Cambridge University Press, 1996.

KARST, Kenneth L. 1993 *Law's Promise, Law's Expression: Visions of Power in the Politics of Race, Gender and Religion*. New Haven, CT: Yale University Press.

KATZ, Jack 1988 *Seductions of Crime*. New York: Basic Books.

KAZIN, Alfred 1981 "Introduction: Theodore Dreiser and *Sister Carrie* Restored." Pp. vii–xvi in Dreiser (1900).

KELSEN, Hans 1922 "The Conception of the State and Social Psychology." *International Journal of Psychoanalysis* 5 (1924): 1–38 (German original in "Der Begriff des Staates und die Sozialpsychologie." *Imago* (1922) 8: 97–141).

KEROUAC, Jack 1957 *On the Road*. London: Penguin, 1972.

KEROUAC, Jack 1958 *The Subterraneans*. New York: Grove Press.

KITSUSE, John 1962 "Societal Reactions to Deviant Behavior: Problems of Theory and Method." *Social Problems* 9: 247–56.

KNIGHT, Louise W. 2005 *Citizen: Jane Addams and the Struggle for Democracy*. Chicago: University of Chicago Press.

KOVANDZIC, Tomislav V., Linne M. Vieraitis, and Mark R. Yeisley 1998 "The Structural Covariates of Urban Homicide: Reassessing the Impact of Income Inequality and Poverty in the Post-Reagan Era." *Criminology* 36: 569–600.

KROEBER, Alfred L. 1920 "Totem and Taboo: An Ethnologic Psychoanalysis." *American Anthropologist* 22: 48–55.

KROEBER, Alfred L. 1939 "Totem and Taboo in Retrospect." *American Journal of Sociology* 45: 446–51.

KRUGMAN, Paul 2003 *The Great Unraveling: Losing Our Way in the New Century*. New York: W. W. Norton.

LACAN, Jacques 1956 "The Freudian Thing, or the Meaning of the Return to Freud in Psychoanalysis." Pp. 114–45 in Jacques Lacan, *Ecrits: A Selection*. New York: W. W. Norton, 1977.

LAMO DE ESPINOSA, Emilio 1980 "Social and Legal Order in Sociological Functionalism." *Contemporary Crises* 4: 43–76.

LASCH, Christopher 1965 *The New Radicalism in America 1889–1963*. New York: W. W. Norton.

LASCHI, Rodolfo 1899 *La delinquenza bancaria*. Turin: Bocca.

LAUB, John H. 1983 *Criminology in the Making: An Oral History*. Boston: Northeastern University Press.

LE BON, Gustave 1892 *The Crowd: A Study of the Popular Mind*. New York: Viking Press, 1960.

LE BRUN, Annie 1986 *Sade: A Sudden Abyss*. San Francisco: City Lights Books, 1990.

LEA, John and Jock Young 1984 *What Is to Be Done About Law and Order?* Harmondsworth: Penguin.

LEFEBVRE, Georges 1932 *The Great Fear of 1789: Rural Panic in Revolutionary France*. London: New Left Books, 1973.

LEMERT, Edwin M. 1942 "The Folkways and Social Control." *American Sociological Review*, 7: 394–9.

LEMERT, Edwin M. 1951 *Social Pathology: A Systematic Approach to the Theory of Sociopathic Behavior*. New York: McGraw-Hill.

LEMERT, Edwin M. 1962 "Paranoia and the Dynamics of Exclusion." Pp. 197–211 in Lemert (1967).

LEMERT, Edwin M. 1964 "Social Structure, Social Control, and Deviation." Pp. 3–30 in Lemert (1967).

LEMERT, Edwin M. 1967 *Human Deviance, Social Problems, and Social Control*. Englewood Cliffs, NJ: Prentice Hall.

LEMERT, Edwin M. 1974 "Beyond Mead: The Societal Reaction to Deviance." *Social Problems* 21: 457–68.

LEMERT, Edwin M. 1983 "Interview with Edwin Lemert". Pp. 118–30 in Laub (1983).

LEOPARDI, Giacomo 1845 "La ginestra o il fiore del deserto." Pp. 243–56 in Giacomo Leopardi, *Canti XXXIV*. Turin: Loescher, 1966.

LEPS, Marie-Christine 1992 *Apprehending the Criminal: The Production of Deviance in Nineteenth-Century Discourse*. Durham, NC, and London: Duke University Press.

LICHTBLAU, Eric 2003 "US Uses Terror Law to Pursue Crimes from Drugs to Swindling." *New York Times* September 28.

LINDNER, Rolf 1990 *The Reportage of Urban Culture: Robert Park and the Chicago School*. Cambridge: Cambridge University Press, 1996.

LIPPMANN, Walter 1922 *Public Opinion*. New York: Macmillan.

LOMBROSO, Cesare 1862 *In Calabria*. Reggio Calabria: Casa del libro, 1973.

LOMBROSO, Cesare 1876–97 *Criminal Man*. Trans. and intro. Mary Gibson and Nicole Hahn Rafter. Durham, NC: Duke University Press, 2006.

LOMBROSO, Cesare 1878 *L'uomo delinquente*. Turin: Bocca.

LOMBROSO, Cesare 1894 *Gli anarchici*. Turin: Bocca.

LOMBROSO, Cesare 1911 "Introduction." In Gina Lombroso Ferrero, *Criminal Man According to the Classification of Cesare Lombroso*. New York: Putnam.

LOMBROSO, Cesare and Guglielmo Ferrero 1893 *Criminal Woman, the Prostitute, and the Normal Woman*. Trans. and intro. Mary Gibson and Nicole Hahn Rafter. Durham, NC: Duke University Press, 2004.

LOMBROSO, Cesare and Rodolfo Laschi 1890 *Il delitto politico e le rivoluzioni in rapporto al diritto, all'antropologia criminale ed alla scienza di governo*. Turin: Bocca.

LYOTARD, Jean François 1979 *The Postmodern Condition*. Manchester: Manchester University Press, 1984.

MACAULEY, Stewart 1963 "Non-Contractual Relations in Business: A Preliminary Study." *American Sociological Review* 28: 55–67.

MACHIAVELLI, Niccolò 1513 *The Prince*. New York: W. W. Norton, 1977.

MACHIAVELLI, Niccolò 1519 *The Mandrake*. In *The Comedies of Machiavelli*. Dartmouth: Dartmouth University Press, 1985.

MALINOWSKI, Bronislaw 1926 *Sex Repression in Savage Society*. London: Routledge and Kegan Paul.

MARAT, Jean Paul 1780 *Plan de législation criminelle*. Paris: Rochette, 1790.

MARCUSE, Herbert 1936 "A Study on Authority." Pp. 49–155 in H. Marcuse, *Studies in Critical Philosophy*. London: New Left Books, 1972.

MARCUSE, Herbert 1964 *One-Dimensional Man*. Boston: Beacon.

MARQUES, Tiago Pires 2007 "Mussolini's Nose: A Transnational History of the Penal Code of Fascism." PhD thesis, Florence, European University Institute.

MARSHALL, Ineke H. (ed.) 1997 *Minorities, Migrants, and Crime*. London: Sage.

MARTINSON, R. 1974 "What Works? Questions and Answers About Prison Reform." *Public Interest* 35: 22–54.

MARTUCCI, Pierpaolo 2002 *Le piaghe d'Italia*. Milan: FrancoAngeli.

MARX, Gary 1988 *Undercover: Police Surveillance in America*. Berkeley: University of California Press.

MARX, Gary 2005 "Surveillance and Society." Pp. 816–21 in George Ritzer (ed.), *Encyclopedia of Social Theory*. Thousand Oaks, CA: Sage.

MARX, Karl 1844a "On the Jewish Question." Pp. 26–52 in Tucker (1978).

MARX, Karl 1844b "Contribution to the Critique of Hegel's Philosophy of Right: Introduction." Pp. 175–87 in *Karl Marx – Frederick Engels: Collected Works*, vol. 3. London: Lawrence and Wishart, 1975.

MARX, Karl 1853 "Capital Punishment." *New-York Daily Tribune* February 17–18.

MARX, Karl 1859 "Preface to *A Contribution to the Critique of Political Economy*." Pp. 3–6 in Tucker (1978).

MARX, Karl 1867 *Capital: Vol. I*. New York: International, 1967.

MARX, Karl 1871 "The Civil War in France." Pp. 618–52 in Tucker (1978).

MARX, Karl and Frederick Engels 1845–6 *The German Ideology*. New York: International, 1970.

MARX, Karl and Frederick Engels 1848 *The Communist Manifesto*. London: Penguin, 1985.

MATZA, David 1961 "Subterranean Traditions of Youth." *Annals of the American Academy of Political and Social Science* 338: 102–18.

MATZA, David 1964 *Delinquency and Drift*. New York: Wiley.

MATZA, David 1969 *Becoming Deviant*. Englewood Cliffs, NJ: Prentice Hall.

MAYHEW, Leon H. 1982 "Introduction." Pp. 1–62 in T. Parsons (1982).

MAYNARD, Douglas W. 1984 *Inside Plea-Bargaining*. New York: Plenum.

McDOUGALL, William 1920 *The Group Mind*. Cambridge: Cambridge University Press.

McKELVEY, Blake 1977 *American Prisons: A History of Good Intentions*. Montclair, NJ: Patterson Smith.

McMAHON, S. H. 1999 *The Legacy of Edward A. Ross*. New Brunswick, NJ: Transaction.

McPHAIL, Clark 1991 *The Myth of the Madding Crowd*. New York: Aldine de Gruyter.

MEAD, George H. 1915 "Natural Rights and the Theory of the Political Institution." Pp. 150–70 in George H. Mead, *Selected Writings*. Indianapolis: Bobbs-Merrill, 1964.

MEAD, George H. 1917–18 "The Psychology of Punitive Justice." Pp. 212–39 in George H. Mead, *Selected Writings*. Indianapolis: Bobbs-Merrill, 1964.

MEAD, George H. 1925 "The Genesis of the Self and Social Control." Pp. 267–93 in George H. Mead, *Selected Writings*. Indianapolis: Bobbs-Merrill, 1964.

MEAD, George H. 1934 *Mind, Self, and Society*. Chicago: University of Chicago Press.

MEAD, Lawrence 1997 *The New Paternalism*. Washington, DC: Brookings Institution.

MELOSSI, Dario 1976 "The Penal Question in *Capital.*" *Crime and Social Justice* 5: 26–33.

MELOSSI, Dario 1977 "Prison and Labour in Europe and Italy during the Formation of the Capitalist Mode of Production." Pp. 9–95 in Melossi and Pavarini (1977).

MELOSSI, Dario 1985 "Overcoming the Crisis in Critical Criminology: Toward a Grounded Labelling Theory." *Criminology* 23: 193–208.

MELOSSI, Dario 1990 *The State of Social Control: A Sociological Study of Concepts of State and Social Control in the Making of Democracy.* Cambridge: Polity; New York: St Martin's Press.

MELOSSI, Dario 1993 "Gazette of Morality and Social Whip: Punishment, Hegemony, and the Case of the USA, 1970–92." *Social and Legal Studies* 2: 259–79.

MELOSSI, Dario 1994 "The 'Economy' of Illegalities: Normal Crimes, Elites, and Social Control in Comparative Analysis." Pp. 202–19 in Nelken (1994).

MELOSSI, Dario (ed.) 1998a *The Sociology of Punishment.* International Library of Criminology, Criminal Justice and Penology. Aldershot: Dartmouth.

MELOSSI, Dario 1998b "Omicidi, economia e tassi di incarcerazione in Italia dall'Unità ad oggi." *Polis* 12: 415–35.

MELOSSI, Dario 2000a "Changing Representations of the Criminal." *British Journal of Criminology* 40: 296–320.

MELOSSI, Dario 2000b "Alla ricerca di una 'vita tranquilla': immigrazione, criminalità e *Italian way of life.*" Pp. 17–69 in Dario Melossi (ed.), *Multiculturalismo e sicurezza in Emilia-Romagna: Seconda parte.* Quaderno 21 del Progetto Città sicure. Bologna: Regione Emilia-Romagna.

MELOSSI, Dario 2001 "The Cultural Embeddedness of Social Control: Reflections on the Comparison of Italian and North-American Cultures Concerning Punishment." *Theoretical Criminology* 5: 403–24.

MELOSSI, Dario 2003a "The Simple 'Heuristic Maxim' of an 'Unusual Human Being.'" Pp. 9–46 in Rusche and Kirchheimer (1939, 2003 edn).

MELOSSI, Dario 2003b "'In a Peaceful Life': Migration and the Crime of Modernity in Europe/Italy." Pp. 371–97 in Symposium Issue of *Punishment and Society* (5/4) on "Migration, Punishment and Social Control in Europe."

MELOSSI, Dario 2005 "Security, Social Control, Democracy and Migration within the 'Constitution' of the EU." *European Law Journal* 11: 5–21.

MELOSSI, Dario (forthcoming) "Neoliberalism's 'Elective Affinities': Penality, Political Economy and International Relations." In Melossi et al. (forthcoming).

MELOSSI, Dario and Massimo Pavarini 1977 *The Prison and the Factory.* London: Macmillan, 1981.

MELOSSI, Dario, Richard Sparks, and Maximo Sozzo (eds) (forthcoming) *Travels of the Criminal Question: Cultural Embeddedness and Diffusion.* Oxford: Hart.

MENSCH, Elizabeth 1982 "The History of Mainstream Legal Thought." Pp. 18–39 in Kairys (1982a).

MERTON, Robert K. 1938 "Social Structure and Anomie." *American Sociological Review* 3: 672–82.

MESSERSCHMIDT, James W. 1993 *Masculinities and Crime*. Lanham, MD: Rowman and Littlefield.

MESSNER, Steven F. and Richard Rosenfeld 1997 *Crime and the American Dream*. Belmont, CA: Wadsworth.

MILLER, Jerome 1997 *Search and Destroy: African-American Males in the Criminal Justice System*. Cambridge: Cambridge University Press.

MILLS, C. Wright 1940 "Situated Actions and Vocabularies of Motive." Pp. 439–52 in C. Wright Mills, *Power Politics and People*. New York: Oxford University, 1963.

MILLS, C. Wright 1942 *Sociology and Pragmatism*. New York: Oxford University Press, 1966.

MILLS, C. Wright 1943 "The Professional Ideology of Social Pathologists." Pp. 525–52 in C. Wright Mills, *Power Politics and People*. New York: Oxford University Press, 1963.

MILLS, C. Wright 1956 *The Power Elite*. New York: Oxford University Press.

MILLS, C. Wright 1959 *The Sociological Imagination*. New York: Oxford University Press.

MOEDE, W. 1915 "Die Massen- und Sozialpsychologie in kritischen Überblick." *Zeitschrift für pädagogische Psychologie* 16: 385.

MOLFESE, Franco 1964 *Storia del brigantaggio dopo l'Unità*. Milan: Feltrinelli.

MONTESQUIEU, Charles de Secondat, Baron de 1748 *The Spirit of Laws: A Compendium of the First English Edition*. Berkeley: University of California Press, 1977.

MOORE, Barrington, Jr. 1966 *Social Origins of Dictatorship and Democracy: Lord and Peasant in the Making of the Modern World*. Boston: Beacon.

MORE, Thomas 1516 *Utopia*. Arlington Heights, IL: AHM, 1949.

MORRIS, Robert 1983 *The Devil's Butcher Shop: The New Mexico Prison Uprisings*. New York: Franklin Watts.

MORRISON, Wayne 1995 *Theoretical Criminology: From Modernity to Post-Modernism*. London: Cavendish.

MORSELLI, Enrico 1879 *Suicide: An Essay on Comparative Moral Statistics*. London: C. Kegan Paul, 1881.

MURRAY, C. 1990 *The Underclass Revisited*. AEI Papers and Studies. January 1, available at http://www.aei.org/publications/pubID.14891,filter.all/pub_detail.asp.

NELKEN, David (ed.) 1994 *The Futures of Criminology*. London: Sage.

NEWMAN, Oscar 1972 *Defensible Space*. New York: Macmillan.

NIETZSCHE, Friedrich 1887 *On the Genealogy of Morals*. New York: Vintage Books, 1967.

NIGHTINGALE, Carl 1993 *On the Edge*. New York: Basic Books.

O'CONNOR, James 1987 *The Meaning of Crisis: A Theoretical Introduction.* Oxford: Blackwell.

ORRÙ, Marco 1987 *Anomie: History and Meanings.* London: Allen and Unwin.

PARK, Robert E. 1904 *The Crowd and the Public.* Chicago: University of Chicago Press, 1972.

PARK, Robert E. 1922 *The Immigrant Press and Its Control.* Westport, CT: Greenwood, 1970.

PARK, Robert E. and Ernest W. Burgess 1921 *Introduction to the Science of Sociology.* Chicago: University of Chicago Press, 1969.

PARK, Robert E., Ernest W. Burgess, and Roderick D. McKenzie 1925 *The City.* Chicago: University of Chicago Press, 1967.

PARSONS, Talcott 1937 *The Structure of Social Action.* New York: McGraw-Hill.

PARSONS, Talcott 1951 *The Social System.* New York: Free Press.

PARSONS, Talcott 1970 "On Building Social System Theory: A Personal History." Pp. 22–76 in *Social Systems and the Evolution of Action Theory.* New York: Free Press, 1977.

PARSONS, Talcott 1982 *On Institutions and Social Evolution: Selected Writings.* Chicago: University of Chicago Press.

PASSERIN D'ENTRÈVES, Alessandro 1967 *The Notion of the State.* Oxford: Clarendon Press.

PATEMAN, Carole 1988 *The Sexual Contract.* Cambridge: Polity.

PAVARINI, Massimo 1997 "La criminalità punita: Processi di carcerizzazione nell'Italia del xx secolo." Pp. 981–1031 in Violante (1997).

PAZ, Octavio 1979 "Mexico and the United States." Pp. 355–76 in Ocatvio Paz, *The Labyrinth of Solitude.* London: Penguin, 1985.

PEARCE, Frank 1976 *Crimes of the Powerful.* London: Pluto Press.

PEARSON, Geoffrey 1983 *Hooligan: A History of Respectable Fears.* London: Macmillan.

PERROT, Michelle (ed.) 1976 *L'impossible prison.* Paris: Seuil.

PERROT, Michelle and Philippe Robert (eds) 1989 *Compte général de l'administration de la justice criminelle en France pendant l'année 1880 et rapport relatif aux années 1826 à 1880.* Geneva and Paris: Slatkine Reprints.

PETERSON, Wallace G. 1994 *Silent Depression: The Fate of the American Dream.* New York: W. W. Norton.

PITCH, Tamar 1995 *Limited Responsibilities.* London: Routledge.

PIZZORNO, Alessandro 1963 "Lecture actuelle de Durkheim." *Archives Européennes de Sociologie* 4: 1–36.

PLATT, Anthony M. 1969 *The Child Savers: The Invention of Delinquency.* Chicago: University of Chicago Press, 1977.

PLATT, Anthony and Paul Takagi 1977 "Intellectuals for Law and Order: A Critique of the New 'Realists.'" *Crime and Social Justice* 8: 1–16.

POE, Edgar Allan 1840 "The Man of the Crowd." Pp. 49–63 in *The Works of Edgar Allan Poe,* vol. 5. New York: P. F. Collier, 1903.

POLLNER, Melvin 1991 "Left of Ethnomethodology: The Rise and Decline of Radical Reflexivity." *American Sociological Review* 56: 370–80.

POPPER, Karl 1959 *The Logic of Scientific Discovery.* London: Hutchinson.

POUND, Roscoe 1908 "Mechanical Jurisprudence." *Columbia Law Review* 8: 605–23.

POUND, Roscoe 1922 *An Introduction to the Philosophy of Law.* New Haven, CT: Yale University Press.

POUND, Roscoe 1942 *Social Control Through Law.* New Haven, CT: Yale University Press.

POUND, Roscoe 1960 "Natural Natural Law and Positive Natural Law." *Natural Law Forum* 5: 70–82.

PUTNAM, Robert D. 1993 *Making Democracy Work: Civic Traditions in Modern Italy.* Princeton, NJ: Princeton University Press.

QUETELET, Adolphe 1835 *Sur l'homme et sur les développements de ses facultés, ou Essai de physique sociale.* Paris: Bachelier.

QUINNEY, Richard 1970 *The Social Reality of Crime.* Boston: Little, Brown.

RADBRUCH, Gustav 1938 "Der Ursprung des Strafrechts aus dem Stande der Unfreien." Pp. 1–11 in Gustav Radbruch, *Elegantiae Juris Criminalis.* Basel: Verlag für Recht und Gesellschaft.

RADZINOWICZ, Sir Leon 1999 *Adventures in Criminology.* London: Routledge.

RAFTER, Nicole H. 1985a *Partial Justice: Women in State Prisons 1800–1935.* Boston: Northeastern University Press.

RAFTER, Nicole H. 1985b "Gender, Prisons, and Prison History." *Social Science History* 9: 233–47.

RAFTER, Nicole H. 1997 *Creating Born Criminals.* Urbana and Chicago: University of Illinois Press.

RANULF, Svend 1938 *Moral Indignation and Middle Class Psychology: A Sociological Study.* Copenhagen: Levin and Munksgaard.

RAWLS, John 1971 *A Theory of Justice.* Cambridge, MA: Harvard University Press.

RECKLESS, Walter C. 1933 *Vice in Chicago.* Chicago: University of Chicago Press.

REIK, Theodor 1925 *The Compulsion to Confess: On the Psychoanalysis of Crime and Punishment.* New York: Farrar, Straus and Cudahy, 1959.

REINERMAN, Craig 1979 "Moral Entrepreneurs and Political Economy: Historical and Ethnographic Notes on the Construction of the Cocaine Menace." *Contemporary Crises* 3: 225–54.

RENNSTICH, Joachim K. 2002 "The New Economy, the Leadership Long Cycle and the Nineteenth K-Wave." *Review of International Political Economy* 9: 150–82.

RITZER, George 1993 *The McDonaldization of Society: An Investigation into the Changing Character of Contemporary Social Life.* Newbury Park, CA: Pine Forge Press.

ROCK, Paul 1979 *The Making of Symbolic Interactionism*. London: Macmillan.

ROLLAND, Mike 1997 *Descent into Madness: An Inmate's Experience of the New Mexico State Prison Riot*. Cincinnati: Anderson.

RORTY, Richard 1983 *Consequences of Pragmatism*. Minneapolis: University of Minnesota Press.

ROSENFELD, Richard 2002 "Crime Decline in Context." *Contexts* 1 (1): 25–34.

ROSETT, Arthur and Donald R. Cressey 1976 *Justice by Consent: Plea Bargains in the American Courthouse*. New York: Lippincott.

ROSS, Edward A. 1901 *Social Control*. Pp. 1–127 in Edward A. Ross, *Social Control and the Foundations of Society*. Boston: Beacon, 1959.

ROTH, Guenther and Wolfgang Schluchter 1979 *Max Weber's Visions of History*. Berkeley: University of California Press.

ROTHMAN, David J. 1971 *The Discovery of the Asylum*. Boston: Little, Brown.

ROTHMAN, David J. 1980 *Conscience and Convenience*. Boston: Little, Brown.

RUGGIERO, Vincenzo 2006 *Understanding Political Violence: Crime and Justice*. Buckingham: Open University Press.

RUSCHE, Georg 1930 "Prison Revolts or Social Policy: Lessons from America." *Crime and Social Justice* 13 (1980): 41–4.

RUSCHE, Georg 1933 "Labor Market and Penal Sanction." *Crime and Social Justice* 10: 2–8.

RUSCHE, Georg and Otto Kirchheimer 1939 *Punishment and Social Structure*. New Brunswick, NJ: Transaction, 2003.

SABOL, William J. 1989 "Racially Disproportionate Prison Population in the United States." *Contemporary Crises* 13: 405–32.

SADE, Donatien-Alphonse-François, Marquis de 1785 *Les 120 Journées de Sodome*. Pp. 31–7 in *Selected Writings of De Sade*. New York: British Book Centre, 1954.

SADE, Donatien-Alphonse-François, Marquis de 1795 *Yet Another Effort, Frenchmen, If You Would Become Republicans*. In Donatien-Alphonse-François, Marquis de Sade, *Philosophy in the Bedroom*, pp. 177–367 in *The Complete Justine, Philosophy in the Bedroom, and Other Writings*. New York: Grove Press, 1965.

SADE, Donatien-Alphonse-François, Marquis de 1797 *Juliette*. New York: Grove Press, 1968.

SALVATORE, Ricardo D. and Carlos Aguirre (eds) 1996 *The Birth of the Penitentiary in Latin America: Essays on Criminology, Prison Reform, and Social Control, 1830–1940*. Austin: University of Texas Press.

SAMPSON, Robert 2006 "Open Doors Don't Invite Criminals." *New York Times* March 11.

SAMPSON, Robert J. and J. H. Laub 2005 "A Life-Course View of the Development of Crime." *Annals of the American Academy of Political and Social Science* 602: 12–45.

SAMPSON, Robert J. and Stephen W. Raudenbush 1999 "Systematic Social Observation of Public Spaces: A New Look at Disorder in Urban Neighborhoods." *American Journal of Sociology* 105: 603–51.

SARTRE, Jean-Paul 1952 *Saint Genet: Actor and Martyr*. New York: George Braziller, 1963.

SAVELSBERG, Joachim 1994 "Knowledge, Domination, and Criminal Punishment." *American Journal of Sociology* 99: 911–43.

SCHEFF, Thomas 1966 *Being Mentally Ill: A Sociological Theory*. New York: Aldine.

SCHOR, Juliet B. 1991 *The Overworked American*. New York: Basic Books.

SCHUESSLER, Karl 1956 "Introduction." Pp. ix–xxxvi in Edwin H. Sutherland, *On Analyzing Crime*. Chicago: University of Chicago Press, 1973.

SCHUMPETER, Joseph A. 1939 *Business Cycle*. 2 vols. New York: McGraw-Hill.

SCHUMPETER, Joseph A. 1943 *Capitalism, Socialism and Democracy*. London: Unwin.

SCHUMPETER, Joseph A. 1954 *History of Economic Analysis*. New York: Oxford University Press.

SCHUR, Edwin M. 1965 *Crimes Without Victims*. Englewood Cliffs, NJ: Prentice Hall.

SCHUTZ, Alfred 1944 "The Stranger: An Essay in Social Psychology." *American Journal of Sociology* 49: 499–507.

SCHWENDINGER, Herman and Julia Schwendinger 1970 "Defenders of Order or Guardians of Human Rights?" Pp. 113–46 in Taylor et al. (1975).

SCIULLI, David 1992 *Theory of Societal Constitutionalism*. New York: Cambridge University Press.

SCULL, Andrew T. 1977 *Decarceration: Community Treatment and the Deviant – A Radical View*. Englewood Cliffs, NJ: Prentice Hall.

SELLIN, Thorsten 1938 *Culture Conflict and Crime*. New York: Social Science Research Council.

SELLIN, Thorsten 1944 *Pioneering in Penology*. Philadelphia: University of Pennsylvania Press.

SELLIN, Thorsten 1951 "The Significance of Records of Crime." *Law Quarterly Review* 67: 489–504.

SELLIN, Thorsten 1953 "Philadelphia Prisons of the Eighteenth Century." *Transactions of the American Philosophical Society* 43 (I): 326–30.

SELLIN, Thorsten 1964 "Tocqueville and Beaumont and Prison Reform in France: Introduction." Pp. xv–xl in de Beaumont and de Tocqueville (1833, 1964 edn).

SELLIN, Thorsten 1976 *Slavery and the Penal System*. New York: Elsevier.

SELZNICK, Philip 1961 "Sociology and Natural Law." *Natural Law Forum* 6: 84–108.

SERENI, Emilio 1948 *Il capitalismo nelle campagne (1860–1900)*. Turin: Einaudi.

SHAW, Clifford R. 1930 *The Jack-Roller: A Delinquent Boy's Own Story*. Chicago: University of Chicago Press.

SHAW, Clifford and Henry D. McKay 1942 *Juvenile Delinquency and Urban Areas*. Chicago: University of Chicago Press.

SHEARING, Clifford D. and Philip C. Stenning 1985 "From the Panopticon to Disney World: The Development of Discipline." Pp. 335–49 in Anthony N. Doob and Edward L. Greenspan (eds), *Perspectives in Criminal Law: Essays in Honour of John Ll. J. Edwards*. Toronto: Canada Law Book.

SHIBUTANI, Tamotsu 1962 "Reference Groups and Social Control." Pp. 128–47 in A. M. Rose (ed.), *Human Behavior and Social Processes*. Boston: Houghton Mifflin.

SIGHELE, Scipio 1891 *La folla delinquente*. Venice: Marsilio, 1985.

SIMMEL, Georg 1903 "The Metropolis and Mental Life." Pp. 409–24 in G. Simmel, *The Sociology of Georg Simmel*. Glencoe, IL: Free Press, 1950.

SIMMEL, Georg 1908 "The Web of Group Affiliations." Pp. 125–95 in G. Simmel, *Conflict and the Web of Group Affiliations*. Glencoe, IL: Free Press, 1955.

SIMON, Jonathan 1988 "The Ideological Effects of Actuarial Practices." *Law and Society Review* 22: 771–800.

SIMON, Jonathan 1993 *Poor Discipline: Parole and the Social Control of the Underclass, 1890–1990*. Chicago: University of Chicago Press.

SIMON, Jonathan 2007 *Governing Through Crime: How the War on Crime Transformed American Democracy and Created a Culture of Fear*. New York: Oxford University Press.

SIMON, Rita 1975 *Women and Crime*. Lexington: D. C. Heath.

SKINNER, Quentin 1978 *The Foundations of Modern Political Thought*. 2 vols. Cambridge: Cambridge University Press.

SKINNER, Quentin 1979 "The Idea of a Cultural Lexicon." *Essays in Criticism* 29: 205–24.

SKOGAN, Wesley G. 1990 *Disorder and Decline: Crime and the Spiral of Decay in American Neighborhoods*. Berkeley: University of California Press.

SMITH, Dorothy E. 1976 "The Ideological Practice of Sociology." *Catalyst* 8: 39–54.

SMITH, Dorothy E. 1978 "'K is Mentally Ill': The Anatomy of a Factual Account." *Sociology* 12: 23–53.

SMITH, Dorothy E. 1981 "On Sociological Description: A Method from Marx." *Human Studies* 4: 313–37.

SOREL, George 1895 "Théories pénales de MM. Durkheim et Tarde." *Archivio di Psichiatria, Scienze Penali ed Antropologia Criminale* 16: 219–28.

SPARKS, Richard 1992 *Television and the Drama of Crime: Moral Tales and the Place of Crime in Public Life*. Buckingham: Open University Press.

SPENCER, Herbert 1879 *The Principles of Sociology*, vol. II. New York: Appleton, 1904.

SPIGEL, Lynn 1992 *Make Room for TV: Television and the Family Ideal in Postwar America*. Chicago: University of Chicago Press.

SPITZER, Steven 1975 "Toward a Marxian Theory of Deviance." *Social Problems* 22: 638–51.

STANKO, Elizabeth 1985 *Intimate Intrusions: Women's Experience of Male Violence.* London: Routledge.

STEINERT, Heinz and Arno Pilgram (eds) 2003 *Welfare Policy from Below: Struggles Against Social Exclusion in Europe.* Aldershot: Ashgate.

STONEQUIST, E. V. 1937 *The Marginal Man.* New York: Russell and Russell, 1961.

SUDNOW, David 1965 "Normal Crimes." *Social Problems* 12: 255–76.

SULLIVAN, Harry S. 1940 *Conceptions of Modern Psychiatry.* Washington, DC: W. A. White Psychiatric Foundation.

SUMNER, Colin 1994 *The Sociology of Deviance: An Obituary.* Buckingham: Open University Press.

SUTHERLAND, Edwin H. 1924 *Criminology.* Philadelphia: Lippincott.

SUTHERLAND, Edwin H. 1934 "The Decreasing Prison Population of England." Pp. 200–26 in A. Cohen, A. Lindesmith, and K. Schuessler (eds), *The Sutherland Papers.* Bloomington: Indiana University Press, 1956.

SUTHERLAND, Edwin H. 1937 *The Professional Thief.* Chicago: University of Chicago Press.

SUTHERLAND, Edwin H. 1940 "White-Collar Criminality." *American Sociological Review* 5: 1–12.

SUTHERLAND, Edwin H. 1942 "Development of the Theory." Pp. 13–29 in Edwin H. Sutherland, *On Analyzing Crime.* Chicago: University of Chicago Press, 1973.

SUTHERLAND, Edwin H. 1983 *White Collar Crime: The Uncut Version.* New Haven, CT: Yale University Press.

SUTHERLAND, Edwin H. and Donald R. Cressey 1978 *Criminology.* Philadelphia: Lippincott.

SUTHERLAND, Edwin H., Donald R. Cressey, and David F. Luckenbill 1992 *Principles of Criminology.* New York: General Hall.

SYKES, Gresham M. 1958 *The Society of Captives: A Study of a Maximum Security Prison.* Princeton, NJ: Princeton University Press.

SYKES, Gresham and David Matza 1957 "Techniques of Neutralization: A Theory of Delinquency." *American Sociological Review* 22: 664–70.

TAKAGI, Paul 1975 "The Walnut Street Jail: A Penal Reform to Centralize the Powers of the State." *Federal Probation* December. Reprinted as pp. 48–56 in Tony Platt and Paul Takagi (eds), *Punishment and Penal Discipline.* Berkeley: Crime and Social Justice Associates, 1980.

TAKAGI, Paul 1982 "Delinquency in School and Society: The Quest for a Theory and Method." *Crime and Social Justice* 17: 37–49.

TAKAKI, Ronald 1979 *Iron Cages: Race and Culture in 19th-Century America.* New York: Knopf.

TANNENBAUM, Frank 1938 *Crime and the Community.* New York: Ginn.

TAPPAN, Paul W. 1951 *Contemporary Correction.* New York: McGraw-Hill.

TARDE, Gabriel 1890 *Les lois de l'imitation*. Paris: Alcan.

TARDE, Gabriel 1895 "Criminalité et santé sociale." *Revue Philosophique* 39: 148–62.

TAYLOR, Ian 1999 *Crime in Context: A Critical Criminology of Market Societies*. Cambridge: Polity.

TAYLOR, Ian and Paul Walton 1975 "Radical Deviancy Theory and Marxism: a Reply to Paul Q. Hirst's 'Marx and Engels on Law, Crime and Morality.'" Pp. 233–7 in Taylor et al. (1975).

TAYLOR, Ian, Paul Walton, and Jock Young 1973 *The New Criminology: For a Social Theory of Deviance*. London: Routledge.

TAYLOR, Ian, Paul Walton, and Jock Young (eds) 1975 *Critical Criminology*. London: Routledge.

TAYLOR, Ralph B. 2001 *Breaking Away from Broken Windows: Baltimore Neighborhoods and the Nationwide Fight Against Crime, Grime, Fear, and Decline*. Boulder, CO: Westview Press.

TETI, Vito 1993 *La razza maledetta: Origini del pregiudizio antimeridionale*. Rome: manifestolibri.

THAYER, Horace S. 1982 *Pragmatism: The Classic Writings*. Indianapolis: Hackett.

THOMAS, William I. 1923 *The Unadjusted Girl*. Boston: Little, Brown.

THOMAS, William I. and Florian Znaniecki 1918–20 *The Polish Peasant in Europe and America*. Chicago: University of Chicago Press, 1958.

THOMPSON, Edward P. 1971 "The Moral Economy of the English Crowd in the Eighteenth Century." *Past and Present* 50: 76–136.

THOMPSON, Edward P. 1975 *Whigs and Hunters: The Origin of the Black Act*. London: Penguin.

THRASHER, Frederic M. 1927 *The Gang*. Chicago: University of Chicago Press.

TINLAND, Franck 1985 "Hobbes, Spinoza, Rousseau et la formation de l'idée de démocratie comme mesure de la légitimité du poivoir politique." *Revue philosophique* 2: 195–222.

TOCQUEVILLE, Alexis de 1835 *Democracy in America*, vol. 1. New York: Schocken, 1961.

TOCQUEVILLE, Alexis de 1840 *Democracy in America*, vol. 2. New York: Schocken, 1961.

TÖNNIES, Ferdinand 1887 *Community and Society: Gemeinschaft und Gesellschaft*. East Lansing: Michigan State University Press, 1957.

TONRY, Michael 1995 *Malign Neglect: Race, Crime and Punishment*. New York: Oxford University Press.

TONRY, Michael (ed.) 1997 *Ethnicity, Crime, and Immigration: Comparative and Cross-National Perspectives*. Chicago: University of Chicago Press.

TREIBER, Heinz and Heinz Steinert 1980 *Die Fabrikation des zuverlaessigen Menschen*. Munich: Moos.

TROTTER, Wilfred 1916 *Instincts of the Herd in Peace and War*. London: Ernest Benn.

TUCKER, Robert C. (ed.) 1978 *The Marx–Engels Reader*. New York: W. W. Norton.

ULLMANN, Walter 1961 *Principles of Government and Politics in the Middle Ages*. London: Methuen.

VALVERDE, Mariana 1991 *The Age of Light, Soap and Water*. Toronto: McClelland and Stewart.

VANNESTE, Charlotte 2001 *Les chiffres des prisons*. Paris: L'Harmattan.

VIOLANTE, Luciano (ed.) 1997 *La criminalità: Annali 12, Storia d'Italia*. Turin: Einaudi.

WACQUANT, Loïc 1999 "How Penal Common Sense Comes to Europeans: Notes on the Transatlantic Diffusion of Neo-Liberal Doxa." *European Societies* 1–3: 319–52.

WACQUANT, Loïc 2001 "Deadly Symbiosis: When Ghetto and Prison Meet and Mesh". Pp. 82–120 in Garland (2001b).

WEBER, Max 1904 "'Objectivity' in Social Science and Social Policy." Pp. 49–112 in Max Weber, *Methodology of the Social Sciences*. Glencoe, IL: Free Press, 1949.

WEBER, Max 1904–5 *The Protestant Ethic and the Spirit of Capitalism*. New York: Scribner's, 1958.

WEBER, Max 1906 "The Protestant Sects and the Spirit of Capitalism." Pp. 302–22 in Hans H. Gerth and C. Wright Mills (eds), *From Max Weber: Essays in Sociology*. New York: Oxford University Press, 1946.

WEBER, Max 1917 "The Meaning of 'Ethical Neutrality' in Sociology and Economics." Pp. 1–47 in Max Weber, *Methodology of the Social Sciences*. Glencoe, IL: Free Press, 1949.

WEBER, Max 1956 *Economy and Society*. New York: Bedminster, 1968.

WELCH, Michael 2005 *Ironies of Imprisonment*. Thousand Oaks, CA: Sage.

WELCH, Michael 2006 *Scapegoats of September 11th*. Piscataway, NJ: Rutgers University Press.

WEST, Candace and Don H. Zimmerman 1987 "Doing Gender." *Gender and Society* 1: 125–51.

WESTERN, Bruce 2006 *Punishment and Inequality in America*. New York: Russell Sage Foundation.

WESTERN, Bruce and Katherine Beckett 1999 "How Unregulated is the U.S. Labor Market? The Penal System as a Labor Market Institution." *American Journal of Sociology* 104: 1030–60.

WHITMAN, James Q. 2003 *Harsh Justice: Criminal Punishment and the Widening Divide between America and Europe*. New York: Oxford University Press.

WIEBE, Robert H. 1967 *The Search for Order 1877–1920*. New York: Hill and Wang.

WIEDER, D. Lawrence 1974 *Language and Social Reality: The Case of Telling the Convict Code*. The Hague: Mouton.

WILKINS, Leslie 1964 *Social Deviance: Social Policy, Action and Research*. London: Tavistock.

WILLIS, Paul 1977 *Learning to Labour*. London: Saxon House.

WILSON, James Q. 1975 *Thinking About Crime*. New York: Basic Books.

WILSON, James Q. and Richard J. Herrnstein 1985 *Crime and Human Nature*. New York: Simon and Schuster.

WILSON, James Q. and George L. Kelling 1982 "The Police and Neighborhood Safety." *Atlantic Monthly* March: 29–38.

WILSON, William Julius 1987 *The Truly Disadvantaged: The Inner City, the Underclass and Public Policy*. Chicago: University of Chicago Press.

WIRTH, Louis 1938 "Urbanism as a Way of Life." *American Journal of Sociology* 44: 1–24.

WOLIN, Sheldon S. 1981 "The Idea of the State in America." Pp. 41–58 in J. P. Diggins and M. E. Kann (eds), *The Problem of Authority in America*. Philadelphia: Temple University Press.

WRIGHT, Richard 1940 *Native Son*. New York: Harper and Row.

YAGO, Glenn 1984 *The Decline of Transit*. New York: Cambridge University Press.

YOUNG, Jock 1971 "The Role of the Police as Amplifiers of Deviancy, Negotiators of Reality and Translators of Fantasy: Some Consequences of Our Present System of Drug Control as Seen in Notting Hill." Pp. 27–61 in S. Cohen (ed.), *Images of Deviance*. Harmondsworth: Penguin.

YOUNG, Jock 1975 "Working-Class Criminology." Pp. 63–94 in Ian Taylor, Paul Walton, and Jock Young (eds), *Critical Criminology*. London: Routledge.

YOUNG, Jock 1999 *The Exclusive Society*. London: Sage.

YOUNG, Jock 2003 "To These Wet and Windy Shores: Recent Immigration Policy in the UK." *Punishment and Society* 5: 449–62.

YOUNG, Jock 2004 "Voodoo Criminology and the Numbers Game." Pp. 13–28 in J. Ferrell, K. Hayward, W. Morrison, and M. Presdee (eds), *Cultural Criminology Unleashed*. London: Glasshouse Press.

ZIMRING, Franklin E. 2006 *The Crime Drop in America*. New York: Oxford University Press.

ZIMRING, Franklin E. and Gordon Hawkins 1991 *The Scale of Imprisonment*. Chicago: University of Chicago Press.

ZORBAUGH, Harvey W. 1929 *The Gold Coast and the Slum*. Chicago: University of Chicago Press.

# Index

*A Just Measure of Pain* 185
"A une passante" 41, 42
abolitionism, penal 182
actuarialism and actuarial
    prediction 209, 213–14, 228,
    237–8, 242, 252
Adamic, Louis 128
Addams, Jane 104
Adler, Freda 190
Adorno, Theodor 35, 92, 93
adult white male European
    proprietor protestant 19, 102
affinity, elective 6, 7, 10
African Americans
    (black) slaves 23, 95, 97, 244
    (blacks) 51–2, 98, 112, 166, 202,
        203, 217, 219–221, 238, 244–5
    migrating from the south to the
        north 236
Agamben, Giorgio 227, 245
Agnew, Spiro 200
Alexander and Staub 76
Althusser, Louis 177, 190–1
America
    south and north 96
American
    dream 147–9
    *Gulag* 239

    post-bellum period 244
audiences 122, 123
Austin, John 120
Austria 33
*American Sociological Review* 138
American Sociological Society 138
*American Tragedy, An* 124, 148
ancillary institutions 26, 27, 243
Anderson, Nels 105, 108, 115
Anderson Elijah 149
anomie 18, 67–71, 128, 144–9, 249,
    252
anonymity 111, 126
antipathy toward the criminals 6
anxiety 155
appreciation 103–5, 170, 174
Archer, Dane 165
Archer and Gartner 247
Argentina 103
asceticism 19
associationism 31, 32
*Asylums* 184
atavism 47, 48, 53, 60, 61
atonement 90
Attica 185
Austria 33
authoritarianism 94, 95
average man 46

Baldwin, James 123
Baltimore 215
ban 168
Banlieues 236
Baratta, Alessandro 164
Barrios, Luis 224
Barrow, Clyde 131, 172
Basaglia, Franco 184
Beaumont, Gustave de 96
Beatles 155
Beatty, Warren 173
Beaudelaire, Charles 41, 42
Beccaria, Cesare 15, 21, 25, 27, 30,
    31, 32, 33, 35, 75, 89, 95, 123,
    160, 248, 250, 252
Becker, Howard 151, 160, 161, 169,
    174, 178, 221
Beckett, Katherine 200, 223–4
*Becoming Deviant* 168, 169, 174,
    177, 204
Beirne, Piers 30, 31, 32
*Bell Curve, The* 179, 216
Bell, Daniel 148
Benjamin, Walter 41, 42, 65, 156
Bentham, Jeremy 18, 25, 26, 30
Bentham, Samuel 25
Bentley, Arthur F. 1, 100, 101, 187
Berkeley, George 72, 73, 182
Berle, Adolf A 129
Berlin 43, 106, 143
*Beyond Blade Runner* 226
Bittner, Egon 188
*Black Panther Party* 131, 174
*Blade Runner* 224
Blumer, Herbert 117
Blumstein, Alfred 229
Boccaccio, Giovanni 16
*Body Count* 219
Bohemian groups 166
Bologna 24
*Bonnie and Clyde* 172, 173, 177
boredom and affluence 173
born criminal 48, 52, 53, 55, 58, 59,
    61, 217
Boswell, James 72, 73
bourgeoisie 28

Bourgois, Philippe 149, 238
Bowers, William 165
Brandeis, Louis 101, 107, 109, 110,
    129
bridewells 21
brigandage 25, 53, 56, 104
broken windows 214–16
Brotherton, David C. 224
brutalization 247
Buenos Aires 104
Burgess, Ernest W. 106, 108, 213
Burke, Kenneth 151
Burroughs, William 225, 226
Bush, George Sr 219
Bush, George Jr 238
business district 114

Cabrini project 111, 112
Calabria 53
Calavita, Kitty 236
California 239
Calvin and Calvinism 90
*canaille* 41
    cycle of 7, 229–52
    the word 234
cannibalism 63
capital punishment 22, 165
*Capital, The* 27, 43, 242
    *laissez-faire* 128, 129
capitalism 18, 20, 23, 24, 26, 68
capitalism, *laissez-faire* 128, 129
Capone, Al 131
Cappetti, Carla 124–5
Carlen, Pat 190
Cartesian philosophy 18, 116, 119
Catholicism 88, 90, 91, 92, 94, 95,
    97
Computer Assisted Telephone
    Interview (CATI) 212
Cattaneo, Carlo 25
causal fallacy 49–50
*Causes of Delinquency* 205–6
Cayley, David 90
CBS 171
cell in a monastery 21
censorship 110

Centre for Contemporary
Culture 183, 184
ceremonial institutions 102
chain gangs 245
Chambliss, William J. 160, 195, 208
*Character and Social Structure* 151
chattel 245
Chaucer, Geoffrey 16
Chicago
and Chicago school 3, 43, 99–
128, 131–4, 141, 143, 144, 147,
150–9, 215–16, 249, 252
Area Project (CAP) 114, 115
Democratic Convention of
1968 171
map 113, 222
children 62
Christie, Niels 239
Cicourel, Aaron 188
city 24, 25, 41, 43, 126–7
*City of Quartz* 221
Clark, John M. 129
*classes dangereuses* 235
class struggle 27, 232, 246
Clinton (Bill) presidency 199, 201,
224
Cloward and Ohlin 146, 166
*code civil* 43
Cold War 131, 176
conformism 145
Connell, Robert W. 54, 194
consensus 93, 116, 152
construction of 9, 157
Continental Europe 39, 43, 103
coercion 93, 141
Cohen, Albert K. 137, 146
Cohen, Elizabeth 131
Cohen, Stanley 163, 164, 170–1,
183
COINTELPRO 131, 172
Colajanni, Napoleone 55
Cold War 131, 176
collective consciousness 74
collective efficacy 216
colonization 54
colonization of life worlds 19, 245

Columbia University 141, 177
Commons, John R. 101
communication, process of 121
Communism 87, 127, 129
community, the 9
*Compte général de l'administration de
la justice criminelle* 45
*Compulsion to Confess, The* 64
compulsive crimes 136
conflicts 3, 252
conformism 145
Connell, R. W. 54, 194
consensus 93, 116, 152
construction of 9, 157
Continental Europe 39, 43, 103
contracts, non-contractual elements
of 66
control by the public 130
control group 50
control, automated 224–8
controlology 160
convict code 188
convict lease system 97, 245
corporal punishments 22
corporations and corporatism 68
corrections and
rehabilitation 237–43
counterculture 145, 166
Cressey, Donald R. 23, 134, 136,
137, 139
Cressey, Paul 116
crime
and criminals, representation
of 6–10, 155–6, 200–1, 205,
249–51
and inequality 46
as the equalizer 148
in the streets 200
natural and artificial 58
normal 188
objective notion of 31, 35
of the powerful 141
predatory 209
prevention of 33
rate 223, 224
rates and economic change 210

recorded 200
romanticism of 149, 178, 181
social cartography of 46
social causes of 58
statistics 52
Crime Prevention Through
    Environmental Design
    (CPTED) 226
*Crime and Human Nature* 216
*Crime and Social Justice* (later *Social
    Justice*) 179
*Crime and the American Dream*
    147
*Crime and the Community* 150
*Crime as an American Way of
    Life* 148
*Crime Control as Industry* 239
criminal
    anthropology 48
    as *homo oeconomicus* 28
    epileptic 53, 59
    mad 53, 59
    occasional 53, 59
    question, the 13, 180–184
    radical 149
*Criminal Sociology* 59
criminalization process 51, 52
criminality
    and sense of guilt 64, 164
    by women 60
    financial 59
    political 59
*Criminality From a Sense of
    Guilt* 164
criminals, professional 208
criminal
    anthropology 48
    as *homo oeconomicus* 28
    epileptic 53, 59
    question, the 13, 180–184
criminology 6, 8, 133, 140, 252
    as a science 251–2
    classical school 33, 39, 48, 75,
        168, 204
    control theory 205–8
    critical 168, 176–95

cultural 189
left-realist 148, 149, 182,
    184
of the other 208–9, 216–21
of the revanche 201
of the self 208–16
radical 149
realist 203–5
*Criminology* 133, 137
crisis 5, 10, 39
    and depression 234
    between the 1970s and the
        1990s 199–204, 228, 245
    decades, the 8, 197–252
    of 1929 and 1930s Depression 8,
        129–32, 172–3
*Critical Criminology* 182
crowd 103
    behavior 61
    in the city 39–42
*Crowd, The* 41
Cullen, Francis 241
cultural
    conflict 134, 135
    consistency theory of
        punishment 23
    /normative conflict 3
    specificities 9
culture
    goals 144–9
    of control 3
*Culture Conflict and Crime* 134
*Culture of Control, The* 200, 215
*Culture of Fear, The* 223
Currie, Elliot 149, 183
custodial democracy 217, 237

Dahrendorf, Ralf 123
dangerous classes 19, 40
dangerousness 48, 59, 103, 209,
    213, 214, 221, 227–8
dark number of crimes 46, 52, 211,
    212
Darwin, Charles 47, 62
Davis, Angela 244, 245
Davis, Mike 221–2, 226

de Beaumont and de
    Tocqueville 4, 98
de Giorgi, Alessandro 227, 231,
    239
de Lauretis Teresa 191
decarceration 203
Deleuze, Gilles 225
*Delinquency and Drift* 167
*Delinquency and Opportunity* 146
*Delinquent Boys* 146
democracy 2, 20, 87, 92, 93, 94, 95,
    99, 110, 116, 120, 147–9, 152,
    156, 157, 227
    as rationalization of collective
    consciousness according to
    Durkheim 78, 79
*Democracy in America* 78, 92, 93, 95
democracy
    custodial 217, 237
    participatory 172
democratic participation 4
democratization 19
deportations 130, 131
determinate and indeterminate
    sentencing 168, 204
deterrence 23, 28, 214
deviance
    amplification of 163, 164, 171,
    172
    pervasiveness of 212
    primary and secondary (devia-
    tion) 159, 162, 163
    sociology of 73
    zookeepers of 178–82
*Deviance et société* 179
Dewey, John 18, 104, 116–19, 130,
    153, 187
*Dialectic of Enlightenment* 35, 92, 93
dialectic of life and form 42
Dick, Philip K. 224, 225
dictator, the 156
differential
    association 128, 133–41
    identification 137
    social organization 134, 144
Dillinger, John 131

discipline and disciplining 8, 19,
    23, 25, 27, 239, 242, 244, 246
*Discipline and Punish* 25, 26, 92,
    175, 184, 240
discourse 11
disenchantment 186
Disney World 227
*Disorder and Decline* 215
disproportionality rate in
    imprisonment between north
    and south of the US 97
Ditton, Jason 160
*Division of Labor in Society, The* 65–
    7, 73–5, 81
    1902 Preface to 68
division of labor, forced or
    anomic 68
Dostoyevsky, Fjodor 41
Dow, Mark 239
Dr Johnson 72, 73
draft (military) 43
dramatization of evil 150
Dreiser, Theodore 124–6, 148
drift and drifters 167
drugs and tobacco 194, 221
Dukakis, Michael 219
Dumm, Thomas 93
Dunaway, Fay 173
Durkheim, Emile 3, 5, 6, 9, 10, 18,
    23, 35, 44, 60, 65–82, 92, 102,
    106, 126, 142, 143, 146, 158,
    164, 240, 242
Dworkin, Ronald 249
Dylan, Bob 116, 155
*Dynamite* 128

Eastern Europeans 104
ecological theory 110, 115, 252
economy 248
ego 62
ego (knowing) 18
Eisenhower, Dwight 176
Elias, Norbert 81
elites 7, 249
elitism 103
Ellis Island 104

Ellison, Ralph 201
embezzlement 136
empire 227, 229, 248
Engels, Frederick 40
England 39, 43
*English Convict, The* 49
English, the 94
Enlightenment 15, 29, 30, 31, 33–7, 191, 250
  abstractness of 39, 44
entrepreneurship 231–2
environmental criminology 3
epistemology 44
Erikson, Kai 9, 77
ethic of capitalism 20
ethnic enclaves 114
ethnic minorities 149
ethnography 115
ethnomethdologists and ethnomethodology 66, 188–9
*European Group for the Study of Deviance and Social Control* 1
European Union 203, 247
evil-causes-evil fallacy 137, 138, 139
evolution of punishment according to Durkheim 81
evolutionary theory 47, 252
exclusion 4, 5, 6, 20, 94, 96
existentialism 123
extraordinary renditions 247

Facchinei, Ferdinando 30
fact 44
factories 25
falsification of a theory 50
families, income distribution of 202
family, bourgeois 193
Fanon, Franz 182
fascism 59, 68, 103, 127, 129, 217–19
father figure 63
fatherless societies 86, 87
FBI 8, 130, 131, 172, 173
fear 39, 40, 42, 159, 199–228, 243

ecology of 222
Federn, Paul 85, 86
Feeley, Malcolm M. 237
Feely, Malcolm M. and Little, Deborah L. 192, 193
*Female Offender, The* 60, 61
feminism 189
Ferrero, Guglielmo 60
Ferri, Enrico 47, 53, 55, 56, 59, 64
  defenses 57
  Project of Criminal Code 59
Fitzgerald Francis Scott 129
*Folie et Déraison* 184
folk devils 164, 170, 171
*Folk Devils and Moral Panics* 183
*Folkways and Social Control* 159
Fordism 132, 184, 236–245
Foucault, Michel 1, 9, 10, 19, 23, 22, 25, 26, 27, 93, 94, 170, 173, 175, 177, 184–8, 190, 235, 240–5
France 21, 43, 61, 65, 67, 97, 98, 142, 236
Frankfurt School 91, 177–81
*Frankfurter Zeitung* 132
Franklin, Benjamin 96
free cities 16, 43
free speech 78, 79, 93, 107, 129, 152
  and First Amendment 109
free will 27, 30, 32, 34, 48, 124–6, 167–8, 204, 226
freedom 23, 25, 31, 35, 167, 252
French revolution 36
Freud, Sigmund 1, 26, 35, 38, 48, 62, 63, 64, 76, 85, 86, 121, 142, 143, 164, 173
*Freudian Thing, The* 86
friendly persuasion 89, 93, 226
Fuller, Lon L. 143

gangs and gangsters 116, 131–132, 146, 150, 151, 166, 224
Garfinkel, Harold 188
Garland, David 3, 27, 185, 190, 200, 208–9, 215, 223, 243
Garofalo, Raffaele 58
Gartner, Rosemary 165

gazette of morality 6
gender and doing gender 189–95
Genealogy of Morals 37
general equality of conditions, in
    America 88
General Theory of Crime, The 206
generalized other, the 116, 119–22,
    142, 152, 154
Genet, Jean 168, 174
Geneva 21
genocide 95, 96
Gerbi, Antonello 86
German concentration camps 245
    and Germany 21, 24, 91, 96, 104,
    143
    Staatswissenschaft 100
Germany, Weimar 132
Gerth, Hans H. 151
Ghent 89
Gibson and Rafter 60
Giddens, Anthony 11
Gilmore, Ruth 239
Gilroy, Paul 182
Ginsberg, Benjamin 110
Gitlin, Todd 171, 172, 177
Giuliani, Rudolph 215
Glaser, Daniel 137
Glassner, Barry 223
globalization 247–9
G-men 173
Goffman, Erving 162, 184–5
Golden Gulag 239
Goldman, Emma 130
Goldwater, Barry 200
Goring, Charles 49
Gorringe, Timothy 90
Gottfredson and Hirschi 209, 250
Gottfredson, Michael 54, 205–8
Gould, Stephen J. 218
Gouldner, Alvin W 178
governing through crime 155
government of populations 243–7
governmentality 186, 187
gradient, theory of 112
Gramsci, Antonio 54, 55, 87, 102,
    158, 183

Great Fear of 1789 39
Greenberg and Humphries 168
Greenwood, Peter 214
grounded theory 250
group or mass psychology 62, 63,
    106
Group Psychology and the Analysis of
    the Ego 63
Guerry, André-Michel 3, 45, 46, 47
guilt 64
Guthrie, Woody 116
Guyau, Jean-Marie 67

Habermas, Jürgen 19
habit 120
Haeckel, Ernst 47
Hall, Stuart 183, 184
Hallema, A. 21
Hamburg 21
Hanseatic League 21
Harcourt, Bernard 213, 215
Harley-Davidsons 171
Harvard 141, 143, 146
Hegel, Georg W. F. 19, 35, 37, 79,
    123
hegemony 7, 183, 184
    global 20
Herrnstein, Richard J. 216, 217,
    218, 237
heterogeneity 102, 111, 126
high-rate offender (HRO) 212, 213
Hirschi, Travis 54, 205–8, 211
Hirst, Paul Q. 182
Hitler, Adolf 156
Hobbes, Thomas 15, 17, 18, 35,
    142, 143, 169, 205, 209, 248
Hobo, The 105, 108, 115
hoboes 105, 236
Hobsbawm, Eric 8, 199
Hollywood 132
Holmes, Oliver Wendell 101, 107,
    109, 129
Holocaust 143
holy experiment 90
homeostatic
    concept of social control 143

mechanism 10
honest people 76
Hoover, John Edgar 130–2, 172–3
Horkheimer, Max 35, 92, 93
Horney, Karen 145
Horton, Willie 219
hotel life 116
House of Correction in Milan 21, 34,
houses of correction 21
Howe, Adrian 190
high-rate offender (HRO) 212, 213
Hugo, Victor 41
Hull House 104, 105
hypnosis 61

I 117, 119, 142
id 62
identity 94
ideology 177, 190, 191
Ignatieff, Michael 185
*Il caffè* 30, 32
illegalities and delinquency 170, 235, 240
*Illusion of Order* 215
immigrant press 107
*Immigrant Press and Its Control, The* 108
immigrants and immigration 51, 99, 105, 111, 114, 127, 130, 231
   African-Caribbean to the UK 184
   first generation 111, 112
   in Europe today 112, 235, 240, 245
   second generation 111, 112, 134
imperialism 20
incapacitation 227
incivilities 215
inclusion 4, 5, 20, 94, 96
   subordinate 228, 238
income of the families 199
Indian reservations 178, 179, 217
indicator, social 66
individual 3, 18, 44, 117

responsibility 168
*blasé* 43
individualism, morality of 66, 67
indulgence 91, 97
industrial conflict 128
Industrial Revolution 43
Industrial Workers of the World (IWW) (Wobblies) 107–10, 115, 131
industrialization 99
inequality 199–228
   measures of 202
innovation 5, 7, 8, 77, 78, 145, 146, 158, 230, 231
Institute for Social Research 177
integration 108
interaction and interactionism 3, 11, 135
interactionism, symbolic 117, 188
international relations 248
*Introduction to the History of Sexuality* 186
*Introduction to the Principles of Morals and Legislation, An* 28
*Introduction to the Science of Sociology* 106, 108
IQ 216–18
Irish-Americans 104
Italian
   Fascist Penal Code of 1930 (Rocco code) 59
   imprisonment and unemployment rates 56
   migration to the Americas 56
   positive school of criminal law and criminology 9, 39, 47, 49, 52, 53, 55, 59, 62, 75, 217, 227–8, 249, 251
Italy 21, 24, 47, 157, 175
   law closing down all psychiatric institutions 184
   north and south 53, 54, 56, 57
   socialism in 56
   southern question 52, 54, 55
   unification of 1861 53
   unions in 56

Jackson Jesse 219
jazz 161, 166
jazz age, the 129
Jews 103, 104
Joas, Hans 122
juvenile delinquency and juvenile
    justice 105, 116, 146, 166, 188

Kalecki, Michal 230
kamikaze in WW2 70, 71
Kansas City 224
Kant, Immanuel 35
Katz, Jack 37, 189
Kazin, Alfred 124
Kelling, George l 215
Kelsen, Hans 1, 17, 87
Kennedy, President 220
Kerouac, Jack 166
King, Martin Luther 172
King, Rodney 221, 224
Kirchheimer, Otto 7, 22, 23, 27
kleptomania 136, 137
Kondratieff, Nikolai 230
Koppel, Ted 156
*Kritische Kriminologie* 179
Kroeber, Alfred L. 63
Kuliscioff, Anna 61

*L'irreligion de l'avenir* 67
la boje 56
*La folla delinquente* 61
*La questione criminale* (*then Dei
    delitti e delle pene* then *Studi
    sulla questione criminale*) 179,
    180
labeling and labeling theory 3,
    117, 150–95, 237, 249, 252
labor 4, 5, 7, 21,
    contract 19, 23, 24
    market 22, 24, 199
    market in the US 220, 247
    power 22, 27
Labour Party 149
Lacan, Jacques 86
Lamarck, Jean-Baptiste 47, 61, 62
lambda 212, 213

Lambrettas 171
Lang, Fritz 40
language 72, 105, 108, 119–24,
    248
Laschi, Rodolfo 59, 60
"Latin Kings" 224
*Laughing in the Jungle* 128
law 18, 101, 102
    criminal 140
    in action 160
    living 101
    natural 140, 143
Le Bon, Gustave 41, 61, 63, 103
Le Brun, Annie 36
learning theory 136, 137
*Learning to Labour* 195
Lefebvre, George 39
legal constructionism 140
legal pluralism 134
Leghorn 21
legitimate institutionalized
    means 145–149
legitimation of violence or
    brutalization hypothesis 165
Lemert, Ed 150, 159–163, 178, 223
Leopardi, Giacomo 28
Leps, Marie-Christine 10
less eligibility 125–6, 132, 202,
    243
Leviathan 5, 15, 16, 17, 18, 168–70,
    174, 177, 204, 219
liberals 179
liberation 173
life chances 123
life, liberty, and the pursuit of
    happiness 85
life, liberty, and property 19
Locke, John 15, 160
Lombroso, Cesare 33, 45, 47–55,
    58, 59, 64, 250, 252
    and Ferrero 60, 189, 194
    daughters 61
London 21, 229
long cycle or long wave
    perspective 7, 229–34
Loop, the 111, 114

Los Angeles 221, 229
  map according to Davis 222
  riot in 1992 222–4, 226
Luther, Martin 21, 90, 91

Machiavelli, Niccolò 15, 16, 17, 18
Madison, Wisconsin 151
*Magnifiche sorti e progressive* 28
Maison de force 89
Malinowsky, Bronislaw 63
man in the mass 155
*Man of the Crowd, The* 42
Manchester 40
Mandela, Nelson 78
Manhattan Institute 218
Mantua 56
manufactories 25
Marat, Jean-Paul 36
Marcuse, Herbert 91, 177, 182, 193
marginal human behavior 116
Maria Teresa of Austria 21, 34
marihuana 161, 174
Market societies 149
Marquis de Sade 35, 36, 37
Martinson, Robert 204, 241
Marx, Gary 3, 225, 226
Marx, Karl 11, 21, 24, 26, 27, 29,
  40, 43, 46, 65, 91, 173, 235, 242
Marx and Engels' *Manifesto* 41, 88
Marxism 27, 176, 181–3, 186, 243
masculinities 194
mass
  democracy 158
  education 44
  imprisonment 8, 9, 192, 199–20,
    237–8, 245
  media of communication 117,
    136, 153–9, 171, 251
  migrations 236
  society 103, 121, 153
*Masse und Publikum (The Crowd and
  the Public)* 106
Matza, David 5, 11, 105, 165–70,
  176–7, 180, 204, 206, 211, 219,
  221, 239
Maynard, Douglas 188

McCarthyism 77
Mcdonaldization of society 8, 229,
  238, 245–6
McKay, Henry D. 111, 112, 114, 115
Mead, George Herbert 10, 104,
  116–23, 142, 150–4, 158, 164,
  187, 242
Mead's phenomenology 123, 153
Mead, Lawrence 237
Means, Gardiner C. 129
mechanical jurisprudence 101
Mediterranean 53
Melossi, Dario 1, 6, 22, 23, 26, 27,
  102
Melossi and Pavarini 185, 190
mental illness 163, 184–5
mental illness and gender 188, 189
Mercosur 247
Merton, Robert K. 3, 46, 141, 144–
  9, 161, 252
Messerschmidt, James 195
Messner, Steven F 147, 148
metapsychological studies 1
methodological individualism 71,
  142
*Metropolis* 40
*Metropolis and Mental Life, The* 126
Mexico 94
Middle Ages 15, 18, 20, 22
migrants and migrations 24, 51,
  52, 97, 98, 103
migration
  and crime 112
  of Africans Americans from the
    South 135
Milan 21, 32–34
military–industrial complex 176
Mills, C. W. 61, 102, 117–20, 132,
  136, 150–9, 166, 172, 176, 187
  public issues and private
    troubles 153, 159
*Minority Report* 224, 225, 226
mnemotechnics 37
mobility 111
modernization 54
Mods 163, 171

monasteries 21
monetary nexus 126
monist theories of the State 8
monistic concept of social
   control 3, 249
monopoly of violence 248
*monstruum* 6
Montesquieu, Baron de 34
moral
   disorganization 16
   economy of the
      working-class 236
   indignation 214
   panic 5, 163
morality 44
   of individualism 66, 67
More, Thomas 40
*Moses and Monotheism* 63
*Mother Jones* 150
movie theaters 131
mugging 183
multiple-factor approach 137,
   141
multitude 15, 35
   on the move 153, 154
Müntzer, Thomas 87, 90
murder 112
Murray, Charles 216–18, 237
Mussolini, Benito 156

Napoleonic period 43, 45
National Crime Victimization
   Survey (NCVS) 211, 212
National Deviancy Conference
   (NDC) 179
national socialism 129, 143
National Urban Peace and Justice
   Summit 224
native Americans 95, 96, 97
*Native Son* 123, 148
neo-Chicagoans 150–75, 249
neo-conservatives 248
neo-liberalism 149, 221, 245, 246,
   248
Netherlands 21
neurosis 62

*Neurotic Personality of Our Time,
   The* 145
*New Criminology, The* 179, 181
New Deal 129–32, 138, 141, 153,
   201
New England 94, 97
New York 104, 150, 215, 224,
   229
   East Harlem 238
*New York Daily Tribune* 46
*New York Times, The* 171
Nietzsche, Friedrich 3, 37, 63
Nightingale, Carl 149
nineteenth-century 8, 22, 65, 142,
   250
Nixon Robert 200, 246
normality of crime 76
normalization 162
normative conflict 134, 135
North America 95
novel in Chicago 124

objectivity in social science 251
obscurantism 29, 44, 47
Oedipus complex 62, 63, 64
Ohlin, Lloyd 146, 166
*On Crimes and Punishments* 21, 28,
   30–2, 33, 35
*One-Dimensional Man* 182
one-dimensional society 177
ontogeny 47
ontology 44
order, problem of 141–4
Orrù Marco 67
*Other People's Money* 136
Other, the 119
*Outsiders* 151, 160, 161

pain threshold 50, 51
Palestinians 174
Palmer, A. Mitchell, Attorney
   General 107, 130
Palmer raids 107, 130, 131
panopticon and panopticism 18,
   25, 26, 89, 186
paranoia 163, 223

parental relationships, structure
    of 72
Paris 25, 41, 65, 166
Paris commune 41
Park, Robert 105–10
Parker, Bonnie 131, 172
parole 203
Parsons, Talcott 3, 35, 66, 141–4,
    150, 159, 205
Passerin d'Entrèves, Alessandro 2,
    101
Pateman, Carole 62
*pater familias* 191
paternalism, new 237, 238
patriarchy 190
Patriot Act 247
Pavarini, Massimo 22, 23, 27
Paz, Octavio 94, 95
Pearson, Geoffrey 183
peasants' war in Germany 91
pecuniary punishment 24
penal
    reform 175
    sanctions, functions of 4
    servitude 23, 97, 244
penality 6, 7, 243–8
    and international
        relationships 247–9
penitentiaries 17, 23, 91, 93–7
penitentiary invention 20, 22, 23,
    34, 190
Penn, Arthur 172
Penn, William 21, 89, 90
Pennsylvania 21, 96, 97
Pertini, Sandro 77
Petersilia, Joan 214
phenomenology 188
Philadelphia 89, 92
phylogeny 47
Pierce, Glenn 165
Pitch, Tamar 180
*Plan de législation criminelle* 36
Platt and Takagi 205, 208–9
play and game, according to
    Mead 121, 122
plea-bargaining 188

Poe, Edgar Allan 41, 42
police work 43, 188
*Policing the Crisis* 183–4
*Polish Peasant, The* 105, 107
political and electoral systems 44
political legitimation 11
political science 100
politicians 139
*Port Huron Manifesto* 172, 177
positivism 11, 44, 45, 167, 180, 211
positivism, sociological 45
post-disciplinary 228
post-Fordism 8, 202, 227, 236–49
post-Fordism in Europe 9
postmodernism 186
Pound, Roscoe 101, 129, 143
power elite 150–9
*Power Elite, The* 117, 118
power to punish in Beccaria 5, 160
pragmatism 100, 103, 105, 116,
    119–20, 141, 186
pragmatism, truth according
    to 154
predatory relationships 127
prevention, situational 212
primeval horde of brothers 62
primitive or original accumulation
    of capital 24, 40
primitive peoples 48
Prince Potemkin 25
*Prince, The* 16
principle of irretroactivity 30
principle of legality 30
*Principles of Sociology* 102
*Prison and the Factory, The* 26, 185,
    237, 241
prison
    as warehousing 5
    birth of 23
    building moratorium on 175
    conditions 232
    reform 185
    riot in New Mexico State Prison
        in 1980 221
    riots 174, 175, 185
    riots in the US in the 1930s 132

prison (cont.).
  system 43
  system in California 239
probabilism 31, 32
probation 203
*Process of Government, The* 1, 100
*Professional Ethics and Civic Morals* 78, 106
*Professional Thief, The* 138
progressive era 2, 99, 103, 108, 201
prostitution 60, 105, 116, 194
psychiatry, alternative 184
psychoanalysis 62, 136, 142
*Public and its Problem, The* 118, 130
public enemies 8, 131–2, 158, 159, 250
public, the 105–10, 153–4
Puerto Ricans 238
punishment 20, 22
  as deprivation of freedom 23
*Punishment and Inequality in America* 219
*Punishment and Social Structure* 22, 177, 185
*Punishment and Welfare* 185

*Quadrophenia* 164
Quakers 89, 90, 91, 94
Quételet, Adolphe 3, 45, 46, 47, 52
Quinney, Richard 183

*Race and Class* 182
race and racism 49, 51, 53, 54, 217
racial and national profiling 206, 214
racialization 53, 54
Radbruch, Gustav 23, 244
radical criminology 149
radicalism, political 166
radicals from Europe 130
Rafter, Nicky 60, 190, 192
Rand Corporation 213
Rates of imprisonment 5, 7, 8, 9, 10, 51, 132, 175, 203, 231–3
rates of imprisonment in Italy 233

and rates of unemployment 203, 220, 231–2
  by gender 192
  in the US 233
  of African Americans 97
rationality 17, 18, 19, 28, 191, 244, 246
rationalization 19, 25, 136, 166
Reagan, Ronald 199, 238, 246
rebellion 145
recapitulation (repetition) 47, 61
redemption 90
reduced form description 10
reference groups 111, 117
reflexivity 11
Reformation (Protestant) 18, 21, 23, 24, 87–98, 193
refusal to work 21
Reggio, Emilia 234
regularities of deviance and crime 73
rehabilitation and corrections 22, 204, 232, 237–43
Reik, Theodor 64
reintegrationism 183
relative deprivation 46
relativity of a concept of deviance 3
religion 67
religion civile 36
Renaissance 18
  of the prison systems in Post-fordism 241
Republic of South Africa 78
Republican machines 4, 94
resentment 214
Restoration 39, 43
retreatism 145
revanche criminology 201, 218, 232, 246
Revolution of 1848 37
Radio Frequency Identification Device (RFID) 225–7
Ribot, Theodore 61
right to resist 160
risk 213–14

ritualism 145
Ritzer, George 229
Robertson, Smith 62
Robespierre, Maximilien 36
Rocco, Alfredo 59
*Rockers* 163, 171
Roddam, Franc 164
Roosevelt, Franklin Delano, and
    his administration 129, 130,
    131, 138, 153, 201
Rorty, Richard 186
Rosenfeld, Richard 147, 148, 229
Ross, Edward A. 102, 103, 106, 153
Rousseau, Jean Jacques 36
routine activity approach 209, 210
*Rules of Sociological Method,
    The* 71–8
Rusche and Kirchheimer 4, 10,
    132, 177, 185, 190, 202, 219
Rusche, Georg 7, 22, 23, 27, 132,
    231, 243
Rush, Benjamin 4, 94
Russia 25

saint 170, 174
Sampson and Raudenbush 216
Sampson, Robert 112, 215
sanctions
    repressive 66, 74, 75
    restitutory 66
    social 72, 73
Sarkozy, Nicolas 236
Sartre, Jean-Paul 123, 166, 168
savage peoples 48, 62
Savio, Mario 182
scabs 235
scandal 105
scenarios, typical 249–51
School of Criminology, University
    of California at Berkeley 1,
    164, 173, 179
Schumpeter, Joseph A. 146, 230
Schumpeter's process of creative
    destruction 230
Schutz, Alfred 188
Seattle general strike 107

security 31
*Seductions of Crime* 37, 189
selective incapacitation 213, 214,
    225
self, the 121
self-control 23, 27, 29
    and delinquency 207–8
self-government 4, 27, 29, 93
self-report studies 206, 211–13
Sellin principle 51, 52
Sellin, Thorsten 21, 52, 105, 134,
    244
Selznick, Philip 143
sensationalism 31, 32
September 11, 2001 71, 229, 247
serfdom, abolition of 24
settlement movement 105
seventeenth century 21, 22, 23
sex, drugs, and rock'n'roll 173, 201
*Sexual Contract, The* 62
sexual immorality of Polish
    immigrant girls in
    Chicago 147–8
sexual liberation 173
Shaw, Clifford 111, 112, 114, 115
Shibutani, Tamotsu 111, 117
Sicilian-Americans 112
Sighele, Scipio 61–3, 103
silent depression 199
Simmel, Georg 3, 25, 42, 106, 126,
    134
Simon, Jonathan 155, 213, 237
Simon, Rita 190
*Sister Carrie* 124–6
*Situated Actions and Vocabularies of
    Motive* 151
situational prevention 225
sixteenth century 21
Skinner, Quentin 15
Slogan, Wesley g 215
slum, the 116
Smith, Dorothy 188
social
    capital 216
    circles 106, 134
    cohesion 128

social (cont.).
    contract 2, 4, 15, 17, 18, 19, 20,
        23, 28, 94
    contract, introjection of 143
    defense 59
    disorganization 108–15, 134, 215
    elites 5
    engineering 101, 128
    experiment 105
    fact 3, 44, 71, 72
    facts, as things 72
    facts, constraint 72
    facts, exteriority 72
    facts, pathological or normal
        character of 73
    interaction 116
    laboratory 105
    process, the 104
    question 39, 40
    reform 128
    structure, reproduction of 44
social control
    according to Durkheim 76
    according to Parsons 143
    and gender 189–95
    and language 119–24
    and the self 117
    as reaction to deviance 143
    as "the central problem of
        society" 106, 107
    at a distance 127
    homeostatic 159
    negative and positive concepts
        of 110
    passive vs. active 159
    primary and secondary 43, 111,
        115, 126, 153, 216
    relative and plural 105
*Social Pathology* 162
*Social Structure and Anomie* 145
socialism 30, 55, 68
    realized 186
society of saints, according to
        Durkheim 76, 77
sociological theory 54
sociology 142

of crime 218
of punishment 203
*Sociology and Pragmatism* 117, 151
solidarity
    mechanical 66, 74
    organic 66, 74
Sorokin, Pitirim 230
Southern Europeans 103
Southern Italy 103, 104
sovereignty 2, 5
Spanish conquest of America 94,
        95
*Spectator* 30
Spencer, Herbert 23, 66, 67, 68, 102
sphere of circulation 26, 242
sphere of production 26, 27, 242
*Spirit of Laws, The* 34
Spitzer, Steven 183
stability of punishment
        hypothesis 203
"Stadluft macht frei" 24, 43
Stalin's gulags 245
state
    apparatuses, ideological and
        repressive 177
    as Makroanthropos 1
    as civil society 15
    as Leviathan 15
    concept, its dissolution 2, 101,
        187
    of exception 227
    racism 245
    right to punish 30
    theories of 177
    weak 93
    welfare 179
statistic 45
stigma 162
stratification of the soul 61
strongly held states of the
        collective consciousness 74
structural frustration 144
structure 7, 11, 231, 250
structure and superstructure 243–7
*Structure of Social Action, The* 142
*Struggle for Justice* 168, 204

Students for a Democratic Society (SDS) 171, 172
stuttering 163
subculture, deviant 166
subject legal 18
*Subjection of Women, The* 61
subjectivation 20, 25, 26, 190
subjective and objective spirit 42
subjective right 37
subjects, constituting, making up, interpellating or hailing the 4, 17, 19, 25, 177, 190
subterranean traditions 166
*Subterraneans, The* 166
suburbs 114
Sudnow, David 188
suicide 116
suicide and education 69, 70
suicide
  and family institution 69, 70
  and religion 69, 70
  altruistic 70
  anomic 70
  egoistic 69, 70
*Suicide* 67–71
Sumner, Colin 3
superego 62, 142
superpredators 219
superstructure 7, 11, 231
Supreme Court 107, 128–32
surplus value 27
Sutherland, Edwin H. 23, 60, 133, 134, 137–40, 144, 150, 159, 183, 208, 221, 249
Sutherland and Cressey 51, 137, 138, 165, 206
sweatshops 126
Sykes, Gresham 165
sympathy
  for the devil 170–5
  toward the criminals 7
structural functionalism 250

tagging 150
Takaki, Ronald 96
Tannenbaum, Frank 150

Tappan, Paul 140
taxation 43
taxi dancers 105, 116
Taylor, Ian 149
Taylor, Ian; Walton, Paul; Young, Jock 11, 47, 179, 181, 182
techniques of neutralization 165, 166
terrorism 201, 247
theft 34, 136, 138
*Thief's Journal, The* 168, 174
*Thinking about Crime* 214
Thomas and Znaniecki 147, 148
Thomas, William I 104–7, 124, 133
Thrasher, Frederic 116
three strikes and you're out 204
Tokyo 229
Tönnies, Ferdinand 23, 67, 68
total institutions 182, 184–5
*Totem and Taboo* 62, 64
Toyotism 246
transitional area 111
triple damages 140
Turati Filippo 61
twentieth century 25, 199–228
*Two Laws of Penal Evolution* 80–2
typology of modes of individual adaptation 145
tyranny of the majority 78, 93

*Unadjusted Girl, The* 105, 124
unconscious 61, 62
underclass 216–21, 236
unemployed in the US 203
Uniform Crime Report 131
United Kingdom 163
United States
  unity of the state 8
University of Birmingham 183–4
University of Illinois 133
urbanism 126–7
*Urbanism as a Way of Life* 126–7
urbanization 99
utilitarianism 26, 28, 31, 33
Utopia 18, 85
*Utopia* 40

vagrancy 21, 25, 39, 235
Vanneste, Charlotte 231, 232
*Verdrängung* 36
Verri brothers 30
Verri, Pietro 32
victimization studies 210–13
victimization surveys 211, 223
   in the US 200
Vietnam (War) 169, 171, 174, 201
Villella, the brigand 48, 50, 57, 64, 103
violence 172, 173
   in cross-national perspective 165
vocabularies 15, 108
vocabularies of motive 136, 151, 152, 166

Wacquant, Loïc 245, 248
wages, average hourly 199
Walnut Street Jail 89
warehousing 237–9
wars 165
*Wayward Puritans* 77
Weber, Max 7, 19, 65, 80, 136, 151, 251
Weimar prison paradise 219
*Wergeld* 22
West and Zimmerman 191
Western and Beckett 202, 203, 220
Western, Bruce 219, 238, 246
*What is Enlightenment?* 35
*What Works?* 204
*White Collar Crime* 138, 139, 140
white-collar crime and criminals 59, 60, 134, 137–41, 208

*Who, The* 164
*Whole World Is Watching, The* 171
Wieder, Lawrence 188
Wilkins, Leslie 164
Willis, Paul 195
Wilson, James Q. 214, 216
Wilson, Woodrow 130
Windelband, Wilhelm 106
Wirth, Louis 25, 43, 126–7
women in prison 190, 192, 203
women in the South 192
women rebels 194
women trafficked 130
women's criminality 60
women's inferiority 60
words 119
workhouses 18, 20, 23, 25, 89, 90, 244
working class 7, 199, 219, 231, 235, 240, 244
   its defeat in the 1970s–1990s 246
*Working Class Criminology* 181
World War I 85
World War II 22, 127, 131, 236
*Wretched of the Earth, The* 182
Wright, Richard 123, 124, 148, 201, 236
Wundt, Wilhelm M. 119

Yale 141
*Yet Another Effort, Frenchmen if You Would Become Republicans* 36, 37
Young, Jock 46, 149, 163, 181–2

zero tolerance 214–16
Znaniecki, Florian 107